Project Management for Modern Information Systems

Dan Brandon, PhD, PMP
Christian Brothers University, USA

D1501983

IRM Press

**Publisher of innovative scholarly and professional
information technology titles in the cyberage**

Hershey • London • Melbourne • Singapore

Acquisitions Editor:	Michelle Potter
Development Editor:	Kristin Roth
Senior Managing Editor:	Amanda Appicello
Managing Editor:	Jennifer Neidig
Copy Editor:	Becky Shore
Typesetter:	Diane Huskinson
Cover Design:	Lisa Tosheff
Printed at:	Integrated Book Technology

Published in the United States of America by
　　　　IRM Press (an imprint of Idea Group Inc.)
　　　　701 E. Chocolate Avenue, Suite 200
　　　　Hershey PA 17033-1240
　　　　Tel: 717-533-8845
　　　　Fax: 717-533-8661
　　　　E-mail: cust@idea-group.com
　　　　Web site: http://www.irm-press.com

and in the United Kingdom by
　　　　IRM Press (an imprint of Idea Group Inc.)
　　　　3 Henrietta Street
　　　　Covent Garden
　　　　London WC2E 8LU
　　　　Tel: 44 20 7240 0856
　　　　Fax: 44 20 7379 0609
　　　　Web site: http://www.eurospanonline.com

Library of Congress Cataloging-in-Publication Data

Brandon, Dan, 1946-
　Project management for modern information systems / Dan Brandon.
　　　p. cm.
　Summary: "This book describes and illustrates practices, procedures, methods, and tools for IT project management that address project success for modern times"--Provided by publisher.
　Includes bibliographical references and index.
　ISBN 1-59140-694-3 (softcover : alk. paper) -- ISBN 1-59140-695-1 (ebook : alk. paper)
　1. Project management. 2. Management information systems. I. Title.
　HD69.P75.B733 2005
　004'.068'4--dc22
　　　　　　　　　　　　　　　2005022459

ISBN (hardcover) 1-59140-693-5

British Cataloguing in Publication Data
A Cataloguing in Publication record for this book is available from the British Library.

Dedication

This book is dedicated to my family, who had to settle for less of my attention during the writing of this book, but who, nonetheless, enthusiastically supported me; specifically to my father and mother, Dan and Shirley, who instilled in me the principles and ethics that have guided my life, and to my children, Madison and Victoria, whose presence are my greatest blessing.

Project Management for Modern Information Systems

Table of Contents

Preface

In the past, the formal discipline of project management was applied primarily to very large projects lasting several years and costing millions of dollars; this was as true for information technology (IT) projects as it was for other industries. Furthermore in the 20th century, project management methods were largely based upon "command and control" techniques. These techniques evolved from ancient military regimes and dictatorial governments, where relatively few educated people directed large numbers of uneducated people. Some industries are still that way, but many companies and most IT organizations are evolving into team- and project-based environments using knowledge workers, independent contractors, and, perhaps, various forms of outsourcing. Competitive advantage today is increasingly based upon knowledge assets instead of upon the traditional assets of land, labor, and capital. In addition there is now a separation of "work" from "workplace," and operations may be performed on a global scale.

To be successful in our IT projects (and most IT projects are still not successful), it is imperative that we apply formal project management methods and tools to all IT project-based work. Also the formal methods and tools of project management need to evolve to address the changes in modern software engineering and our high-tech global workplaces. In the past, project success was defined too narrowly as simply meeting time and cost constraints for a given scope of work. However, in order for an IT project to be completely successful, that basic definition of success needs to be extended. This extension is particular with regard to product quality, stakeholder satisfaction, security, organizational human capital, and long-term factors such as maintainability and adaptability. With that extended definition of success, management techniques and tools can be extended or otherwise modified to be more effective.

This book describes and illustrates practices, methods, and tools for IT project management that address this extended definition of project success for modern times. As such, this book is directed to IT project managers, those IT personnel aspiring to become project managers, and also to experienced IT personnel who wish to learn of new project management concepts, methods, and tools. This book is also designed for use as a textbook or reference in graduate or upper-level undergraduate university programs in IT or project management. Throughout the book, a number of IT project management "standard forms" are presented and a number of spreadsheet models are also developed. An open source general Web-based project management software system (FiveAndDime) is used to illustrate many of the methods and applications discussed in the book. An appendix of the book contains a glossary of the IT project management and software engineering terms and acronyms used.

Chapter I introduces and defines a project, project management, the project manager, and project stakeholders. These management concepts are discussed relative to our modern IT dominated world and in context with today's "information revolution" and to the business and technical forces that drive this revolution. The distinctions of IT project management as compared to general project management are also identified here.

Chapter II introduces the concept of project "critical success factors." A key factor leading to the continued failure in IT projects is the lack of identification and appreciation for all the major components of project success. Critical success factors are those things that must be done or handled properly for a project to be successful. A comprehensive model of critical success factors for IT projects permits the development of better management plans, processes, and metrics particularly for risk, quality, and performance control. In this chapter, general critical IT success factors are identified and techniques for the management of those factors are introduced. The notion of a "dual stage gate process" for the comprehensive and effective management of these success factors is also introduced in this chapter; later chapters define metrics and control methods for these success factors using dual stage gating.

Chapter III discusses project initiation and selection. The careful selection of which projects to initiate is vital to the success of an organization. Project initiation represents a future commitment of both human and financial resources as well as of management attention. In this chapter, methods for the proper selection and initiation of projects are discussed with regard to overall organizational goals and business justification. In this chapter, project initiation and the processes and documents involved with project evaluation from a business perspective are discussed and illustrated. Standard forms for the "project proposal" and "project business plan" are presented. (Later, Chapter VI continues with the life of a project after an organization has committed to perform said project.)

Chapters IV and V discuss project management and software engineering from a disciplinary perspective, as these concepts and terms are used throughout the remainder of this book. A number of worldwide professional organizations have been developed to foster the project management discipline, and these organizations and their bodies of knowledge are presented in Chapter V.

Although software engineering is not a formal part of project management, it is vital for the proper planning of IT projects. Even for IT projects that primarily involve software acquisition and integration instead of software development, the software engineering embedded in the products that are acquired will significantly affect long-term project success factors. In Chapter V, modern software engineering and its relation to IT project management is discussed. Key challenges to software engineering in the 21st century are presented as well as how software engineering together with project management can address those challenges.

Chapter VI formalizes overall project planning and requirements analysis. Getting off to a fast start in the right direction is important in any endeavor, and overall planning and requirements are two of the most important aspects of IT project management. Standard forms are presented for the project charter, overall project plan, software management plan, and requirements document. The process of IT requirements' discovery and documentation is formalized and illustrated. Once a complete and clear set of requirements has been documented and approved by all relevant stakeholders, detail project planning can begin; such detail planning is covered in the following chapters.

Chapter VII is concerned with detail project planning, particularly the schedule and cost plan. In this chapter, the formulation of a detail schedule and cost plan is discussed and illustrated. WBS formulation, task sequencing, task estimation, scheduling, and costing methods are all covered. The detail scope, time, and cost planning of this chapter forms the basis for other detail plans—including the risk plan, procurement plan, HR plan, quality plan, control plan, and change plan—described in subsequent chapters.

Success in the modern business world involves taking some risk. All the systems that are really changing the world today are very risky systems, but one needs to know how to manage risk, including how to identify risk sources, quantify risk parameters, and develop plans to handle risks; these are the topics covered in Chapter VIII. The total project risk-management process is described and illustrated and standard forms are developed for an IT risk-management plan. A framework based upon critical success factors for analyzing project risk threats and hazards is also presented.

Once a project is planned and underway, the project manager cannot simply walk away and assume that everything will go according to plan. In Chapter IX, project performance control metrics and techniques are defined and discussed. Performance metrics for each critical success factor are identified and illustrated. Standard forms for status reports and stage gate reviews are presented. Corrective actions to bring a project back in compliance with the plan are also identified and discussed.

As a project proceeds, quality is often the most difficult area to keep on track. Chapter X discusses the many quality aspects of project management, and project success factors are used as the basis for key quality metrics. A quality management plan for IT projects includes both verification and validation, and such a plan is presented here. Other important quality topics are also discussed in this chapter, including the many types and methods of software testing, software development standards, and quality organizations and programs. Standard forms for quality standards and quality stage gates are included here.

Change is a fact of life for most projects, particularly IT projects. A major cause of IT project overruns is changes in scope. Change can be good or bad, but change is expected, and change has to be managed. Chapter XI is concerned with the overall IT change management process, including version control and configuration control. Project closeout and related topics such as lessons learned are also included and illustrated. Standard forms for change control plans, change orders, and project closeout are presented in this chapter.

Many IT projects involve the purchasing of goods or services, and some IT projects are mostly procurement activities, at least from a cost perspective. With the increase in IT outsourcing and outsourcing offshore, there is an increasing need for very formal procurement management, and that overall management process is the subject of Chapter XII. This chapter covers general project procurement and the formal procedures and documents used in procurements such as the statement of work, request for proposal, and contracts. The different types of procurement documents are discussed and which types are used in which situations and with what types of contracts. In particular for IT projects the subject of outsourcing is also covered in detail.

The identification and management of a project's stakeholders is vital to the complete success of a project. Often, well-planned and properly executed projects can still fail due to a lack of relationships or inappropriate relationships between the project manager and various stakeholders. Chapter XIII discusses matters related to the human side of project management including stakeholder relations, communications, team management, and security. Standard forms are presented for the project communications plan, human resources plan, and security plan.

Traditional methods of progress performance reporting are often inaccurate and misleading. Earned value analysis (EVA) has proven to be an extremely effective tool for project time and cost management, providing good estimates of actual project completion cost and date. EVA is also is a good early indicator of project problem areas, so that appropriate corrective action can be initiated. In Chapter XIV, EVA is defined, discussed, and illustrated in detail. EVA is one of the key metrics in the management-for-success philosophy that is developed in this book via critical success factors and dual stage gates. EVA is often difficult to implement effectively and can have a number of problem areas. However, this chapter identifies the EVA problem areas and their practical solutions.

There is a vast amount of project management software available today in a wide variety of capabilities, applicability, platform requirements, and prices. These software products significantly enhance a PM's job of managing a project in almost all aspects including selection, planning, scheduling, execution, control, risk, communications, and so forth. Therefore, PMs should be aware of the types of tools available and the features and applicability of those tools. In Chapter XV, types of software products and some specific products are identified and discussed, including spreadsheet models and open source software.

Management of IT projects and being on an IT project team used to be simpler. PMs typically had one project to manage and team members were only on one team. All the team members were located in close geographic proximity, and the work was all done at the workplace. Today, however, the project landscape has become much more complex, where everyone is concerned, with multiple projects and teams spread out all over the world. The business needs of cutting costs to the bone and being quicker to market have increased the pressures on project teams and their managers. Chapter XVI discusses modern ways that organizations can effectively deal with these complexities, including the use of project management offices (PMOs), project portfolio optimization, knowledge management, project dashboards, and PMO portals. Chapter XVI also discusses project management from a strategic perspective.

Acknowledgment

My sincere thanks and appreciation goes out to the many individuals both in the academic world and in the commercial sector who discussed various book topics with me. My particular appreciation goes to those who helped review the content and style of the book: Jonathan Pierce at Computer Science Corporation; Richard Flaig at the NASA Stennis Space Center; Professors Frank Marion, James Aflaki, and Larry Schmitt, all at Christian Brothers University; and communication specialist Diane Brandon.

Chapter I

Today's
IT Environment

A competitive advantage comes only with superior IT.

(Aetna Healthcare Chairman/CEO Richard Huber)

In the last few years, information technology (IT) has significantly impacted the operation of most businesses, and even though most corporations still spend only 3% to 8% of their revenue on IT, businesses depend upon IT for their day-to-day operations. For many businesses, IT is a, if not the, key factor in their competitive strategy. Due to IT, we have all experienced many changes, some good some bad, in our personal lives. In fact, probably not since the industrial revolution have people all over the world experienced such dramatic life-style changes. One is reminded of the opening sentence from *A Tale of Two Cities,* by Charles Dickens: "It was the best of times, it was the worst of times." Dickens was referring to the French Revolution, but in the 21st century we are well into the "IT Revolution." In regard to project management, there are two IT related matters: the utilization of IT in managing all types of projects and the management of IT projects. Before we further discuss these project management matters in this modern IT dominated world, we need to consider the technical and business forces that are shaping this new environment.

The Information Revolution

According to the RAND organization (Hundley, 2004),

Advances in information technology are affecting most segments of business, society, and governments today in many if not most regions of the world. The changes that IT is bringing about in various aspects of life are often collectively called the "information revolution."

The current IT revolution is not the first of its kind. Historians and nations may debate the exact time and place of previous information revolutions, but they are as follows:

- Invention of writing, first in Mesopotamia or China, around 3000 BC
- Invention of the written book in China or Greece, around 1000 BC
- Gutenberg's printing press and engraving, around AD 1450

Major revolutions help some people and some organizations, and, therefore, for them it is the "best of times;" but revolutions also hurt some people and organizations, and for them it is the "worst of times." With big revolutions, there always will be big winners and big losers. As an example, when the printing press was invented, the largest occupation in Europe was the hand copying of books in thousands of monasteries, each of which was home to hundreds of monks; 50 years later, the monks had been completely displaced. The impact to society was enormous, not because of the displacement of monks by other craftsmen and machines, but because the price of books dropped so drastically that common men could now afford to educate themselves.

For many, this new IT revolution is bringing great things with unprecedented improvements in the quality and efficiency of all we do as organizations and as individuals. For others, however, IT is a two-edged sword, bringing about many problems, disturbances, and unresolved issues. A great digital divide is being created, and this divide has three dimensions: income, age, and education. This divide will further separate the *haves* from the *have-nots* as manufacturing operations move to lesser developed countries, where over 1 billion low-paid workers will be available in a few years. In the future, for developed countries, workers may be divided into InfoWorkers and McWorkers. In addition IT security and privacy problems are getting out of control, as evidenced by computer viruses, worms, e-mail fraud and spam, compromise of personal and private digital information, spyware, piracy of intellectual property, ID theft, hacking, and other computer crimes. Today, there are major and numerous security "holes" in most software that corporations and individuals use every day.

The most important technology of this information revolution has to be the Internet, which is the combination of several underlying technologies. Consider the penetration rate (in the time to reach 50 million users) of recent milestone information technologies compared to the Internet:

- It took the telephone 40 years to reach 50 million users.
- It took radio 38 years to reach 50 million users.
- It took cable TV 10 years to reach 50 million users.
- It only took the Internet only 5 years to reach 50 million users!

The Internet and related technologies are, however, beginning to cause significant industrial disruptions:

- Internet shopping is disrupting traditional sales channels for hard goods.
- Internet sharing and distribution is disrupting traditional intellectual property rights and sales of soft goods (print, audio, video, multimedia).
- Voice Over IP combined with ultra-high-speed optical and wireless media will start to disrupt traditional telecommunications.
- Open source software with community online support will start to disrupt the traditional software marketplace.
- Separation of work from workplace will disrupt corporate and personal real estate and related business sectors.
- As national barriers (political, physical, economic, and temporal) are removed, massive globalization will allow the free flow of both work and product.
- The need for retraining and lifetime learning, coupled with distance education, is transforming the traditional higher education landscape.

The process and results of these disruptions has been called "creative destruction" by the RAND corporation, and this results in the "economic eclipse" of organizations not embracing the new IT world. Traditional mechanisms of government (i.e., jurisdiction, taxation, regulation, permits, and licenses, etc.) will also significantly be disrupted in response to these other disruptions, as will the insurance and finance industries. Likewise this process of creative disruption will result in the career destruction of managers (including project managers) not embracing modern IT.

In his essay on this modern information revolution, business guru Peter Drucker (2004) noted, "This revolution will surely engulf all major institutions of modern society," and "[t]his revolution will force us to redefine what the business enterprise actually is—the creation of value and wealth."

Furthermore, he questioned whether management is prepared for the full impact of this revolution, and he saw no sign of it at that time.

Better, Cheaper, Faster

The battle cry of the 1990s, what with the advent of client-server technology to replace mainframes, was

> Better!
> Cheaper!
> Faster!

These themes are still dominant in the 21st century. That battle cry continues from the board room down through the management chain, because these themes are the crux of market positioning (quality, cost, and time to market), as illustrated in Figure 1.1.

To produce better and cheaper products or services and get them to market quicker requires better, cheaper, faster processes, as is illustrated in Figure 1.2. In today's world, information systems play a key role and an ever-increasing role in the overall process of producing and delivering products or providing services. Today, almost every aspect in the design, creation, delivery, and support of products or services depends strongly on IT.

As Tom Cruise said in the movie *Top Gun* (Paramount Pictures, 1986), "I feel a need, a need for speed." Upper management emphasizes that need for speed to IT project managers and software development teams. Many managers and technologists see speed as a solution to the problem illustrated in Figure 1.3. The world is changing so fast that, by the time we develop an IT solution for a business problem, the shape of that problem has changed.

Newer and faster project management and software engineering methods can address a portion of this problem. Speed, however, is not the only way to address the problem shown in Figure 1.3 (as this book will show). Compounding the problem is the fact that too many in IT and general management have though that better-cheaper-faster processes are obtained primarily by better-cheaper-faster people. Thus management methods as exporting work to cheaper locations, importing cheaper workers, or dismissing (or buying out) older workers have become common. Another management misconception is that better and faster is obtained by using better and faster tools; but better-faster tools without better practices and methods simply allow one to build the wrong product even faster.

A basic premise of this book is that the best long-term solution to better-cheaper-faster IT products and services involves a number of modern project management and software engineering practices and methods that can be collectively called "IT project management maturity." Three important basic project management and software engineering themes are embodied in this maturity model:

1. Do it right the first time
2. Do only manageable portions at a time
3. Do it in a reusable and adaptable manner

Figure 1.1. Marketing dimensions

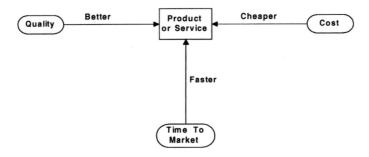

Figure 1.2. Products and processes

Figure 1.3. Changing shape of IT problems

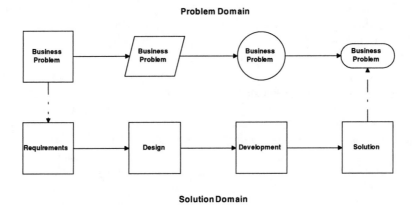

This method is illustrated in Figure 1.4, and each of these components will be discussed later in this book.

The project management processes, practices, and methods that are the key to this IT maturity model are based upon critical success factors. All too often in IT, project and line management do not allocate enough time to do the project work right the first time, but later they are forced to find the time and resources to do it over again. Completing

Figure 1.4. IT Project management maturity

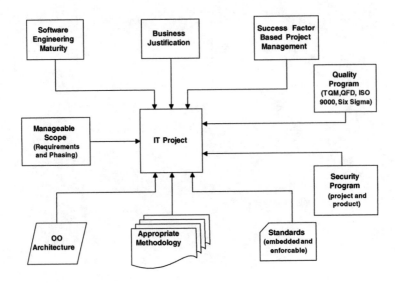

IT projects successfully the first time requires the identification and understanding of all the critical success factors of such projects. Once these factors are itemized and fully appreciated, then effective management and technical methods and metrics can be formulated for project performance, risk, and quality control.

Theoretically and statistically, project success probability decreases as the size of an IT project grows. Many factors, such as the interaction of project stakeholders and the interaction of technical components, increase in complexity in ratio to the square of the number of such items. Therefore, subdividing large IT projects into smaller parts decreases complexity and thus increases the likelihood of success; however, this subdivision needs to be consistent with the metrics and methods to monitor and control all identified critical success factors. In the next chapter, critical success factors for IT projects are identified and defined and, in later chapters, effective management and technical techniques for the measurement and control of these factors are presented.

Teamed-Based Workplaces

In the 20th century, management methods were largely based upon "command and control" techniques. These techniques evolved from ancient autocratic societies and military environments in which relatively few educated people lead large numbers of uneducated people. Management structures were developed to take much detailed information and to summarize that information up through a number of middle management levels so that decisions could be made in regard to different scopes and time horizons. Several management levels were formed at each of the business operational, tactical, and strategic decision points.

Today, however, in developed countries, management structures have changed and evolved due to a number of factors. One is that the economies of developed countries continue to shift from a manufacturing economy to a service economy. Another factor is that most corporate workers have become knowledge workers, where a computer or computer interface is an integral part of their job. And the other major factor is that IT is used extensively to gather and summarize the information flow from the point of origin to the eventual decision maker; IT is now often part of the decision process itself through decision support systems.

This evolution of management structures has resulted in a reduction of the number of middle management layers and the creation of team-based work at the lower levels. It used to be that a corporate organization chart might have management positions for supervisors (or foremen), unit managers, section managers, department managers, division managers, directors, and vice presidents. In a modern organization, there are much fewer levels, such as team leader (or project manager), director, and vice president (or CIO). Teams are given not only the work assignment(s) but also are given the responsibility (at least partially) for the work results. Management used to monitor employee performance by observing work activity and work results, hence the old expression *MBWA* (managing by walking around). But in the team environment, it is becoming the responsibility of teammates to observe *work activity* and the team leader to monitor *work results*. This creation of teams at the lower levels of the organization has proven very effective for maximizing employee performance, and where the nature of the work is the completion of projects, the team leader is called the project manager (PM).

IT has also shown that productivity is not necessarily related to proximity and, thus, work is being separated from the workplace. Many knowledge workers can do much of their work from places other that the company facility including working from home, or while traveling, or while at a customer or vendor location. In many cases, IT has made it possible for an individual to work for an organization and live anywhere.

Due to the tearing down of national barriers, the work of many companies and individuals is now on a global scale. Furthermore, IT has permitted the team based workplace to be extended to a global scale by the facilitation of virtual teams using electronic communication and collaboration tools such as e-mail, interactive Web sites with electronic forms, chat rooms, bulletin boards, instant messaging, and other forms of groupware. Even business processes, both intracorporate and intercorporate, have become Web-enabled. Virtual teams may be assembled quickly with the right mix of skills to address a particular problem or project, and then they may be disassembled just as quickly when the job is done. It is not atypical for an individual to be a part of many virtual teams simultaneously. In a virtual environment, managers only monitor work results and the old concept of managing work activity has almost disappeared. This does not mean that managers no longer interact with their staff, it is just that the mode of interaction has often become digital instead of face to face.

Some organizations have gone a step further and created the virtual organization, in which extensive use of IT is used to create an extremely flexible team- and project- based organization, which may need no physical facilities at all. A related concept is embedded in the term *virtual corporation,* which refers to a business strategy for allying complementary businesses via IT into a "symbiotic network" and allowing them to respond to customers as a single entity. The complete integration of IT into the work and virtual workplace is creating a number of strategies that include the word (or synonym) *instant* (Pearlson & Saunders, 2004, pp. 76-77):

- **Instant Value Alignment:** Understanding the customer so well that the customer's needs are anticipated.
- **Instant Learning:** Building learning directly into each employees work process and/or schedule ("just in time training").
- **Instant Involvement:** Using IT to communicate all needed information to vendors, employees, and so forth ("just in time inventory" and "supply chain automation").
- **Instant Adaptation:** Creating an environment enabling all teams to act instantly and to make timely decisions.
- **Instant Execution:** Designing business processes so that they have as few people involved as possible and reduce cycle times so that these processes appear to execute instantly.

To successfully function in this new IT-enabled instant world and workplace, managers must adapt and obtain the necessary knowledge and skills. Several years ago, The Gartner Group researched this topic, and their list of these management skills follow (York, 1999):

- *Understand project management*
- *Manage for results*
- Speak the language of business
- *Improvise with grace and harmony*
- Understand IT processes and business processes
- Make informed business decisions quickly
- *Know how and when to measure performance*
- Cultivate an environment of risk tolerance
- Communicate clearly, appropriately, and relentlessly

Computerworld also investigated this topic and called the new breed of IT team leaders "business technologists" and listed their ideal characteristics as (Brandel, 2001):

- Business and financial acumen
- *Understand tension between budget, operations, capital, expense, and head count*

- *Sensitivity to all the dimensions that influence a project*
- Both written and oral communication skills
- An understanding of relationship management
- *Project planning skills*
- *Performance monitoring skills*
- An understanding of the value of coaching
- A customer focused approach

In the preceding lists, those items that specifically deal with project management (as opposed to management in general) have been italicized; however, all these traits are necessary for effective project managers.

Projects and Project Management

A *project* is defined as "a temporary endeavor undertaken to create a unique product or service" (PMI, 2000). A project is undertaken when work is best accomplished through methods that fundamentally differ from those of everyday operations. A list of the key characteristics of a project can further clarify that definition:

- Temporary endeavor with a beginning and an end
- Often broken into subprojects (or phases)
- Creates a unique product or service
- Done for a purpose
- Has interrelated activities (tasks)
- Is an instrument of change

A project usually has certain aspects or key components which include project-related management, a common vocabulary, project-related methods and tools, teamwork, a plan, trade-offs (involving scope/deliverables, time, cost, and quality), identified requirements (needs) and unidentified requirements (wants or expectations), and stakeholders.

The *stakeholders* involved with a project may be many and possibly diverse in several respects including interests, needs, expectations, and priorities. Satisfying the stakeholders is one of the key objectives of the project and the project manager. Key stakeholders include the organization and people doing the work, who are called the "performing organization," and the people or organization benefiting from the work (and also usually paying for the work), who are called the "benefiting organization." These two organizations may or may not belong to the same corporation. This is illustrated in Figure 1.5. The benefiting organization, customer, and end user also may or may not be part of the same organization. The project manager is a key stakeholder, and this individual is almost always part of the performing organization. Another key stakeholder is the project sponsor (sometimes called the project champion), and this individual usually initiates or formalizes the idea of the project. It is extremely helpful if a project has support from high up in an organization, and the project sponsor is often part of upper management. Usually the project sponsor does not (and should not) play an active role in the day-to-day management of the project. Other stakeholders (shown in the diagram as "S") may be in either organization or be external to both.

Project management is "the application of knowledge, skills, tools, and techniques to the project activities in order to meet or exceed stakeholder needs and expectations from a project" (PMI, 2000). It involves the planning, organization, monitoring, and control of all aspects of a project and also the management, leadership, and motivation of all involved parties to achieve the project objectives within agreed time, cost, quality, safety, and performance criteria.

Project management in some form has existed for thousands of years, and it was likely used in the construction of the wonders of the ancient world. Modern project management, including the use of the engineering and management disciplines, started around the turn of the 20th century. "Around that time, managers of such projects faced pressure from proponents of scientific management to organize in a centralized way and control not just what was done but the details of how and when it was done" (Yates, 2000). Henry Gantt developed the Gantt Chart in World War I, and it was used in huge projects like the construction of the Hoover Dam in the 1930s. IT project management appears to go back to the 1950s, when the Critical Path Method (CPM) was developed by DuPont and Remington Rand/Univac.

However, it is not always necessary to use formal project management methods for important temporarily endeavors, and the British Computer Society (in the spirit of David Letterman's Top Ten List) itemizes the top 10 reasons **not** to use such formality:

10. Our customers really love us, so they don't care if our products are late and don't work.

9. I know there is a well-developed project management body of knowledge, but I can't find it under this mess on my desk.

8. All our projects are easy, and they don't have cost, schedule, and technical risks anyway.

7. Organizing to manage projects isn't compatible with our culture, and the last thing we need around this place is change.

6. We aren't smart enough to implement project management without stifling creativity and offending our technical geniuses.

5. We might have to understand our customers' requirements and document a lot of stuff, and that is such a bother.

4. Project management requires integrity and courage, so they would have to pay me extra.

3. Our bosses won't provide the support needed for project management; they want us to get better results through magic.

2. We'd have to apply project management blindly to all projects regardless of size and complexity, and that would be stupid.

1. We figure it's more profitable to have 50% overruns than to spend 10% on project management to fix them.

The Project Manager

The project manager (PM) is the leader of a team performing a project. The project manager and his team must identify the stakeholders, determine their needs, and manage and influence those needs to ensure a successful project. A key to stakeholder satisfaction is the diligent and accurate analysis of the stakeholders themselves as well as their stated needs and unstated expectations. A project manager should not just be handed a statement of work from upper management and then try to complete it; rather the PM should be deeply involved with the development of that statement of work. The roles of a PM are many, some of which include the following:

- Identifying the requirements and risks
- Making plans and organizing the effort
- Qualifying and possibly selecting project team, vendors, and other participants
- Communication among team, management, stakeholders
- Assessing the probability of occurrence of problems
- Developing solutions to problems (both in advance and on the spot)
- Ensuring that progress occurs according to the plan
- Deliverable management

Figure 1.5. Project stakeholders

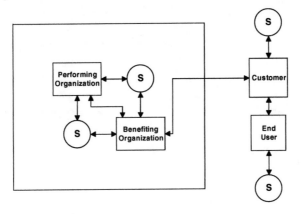

- Running meetings
- Acquiring resources for the project
- Influencing the organization
- Leading and team building
- Negotiation (external and internal)

The many elements of a PM's work were expressed in the "PM's Worldview," as shown in Figure 1.6 (Cooke-Davies, 2004).

It is the role of the project team members to do their assigned duties, complete their assigned tasks, and help each other. It is the role of upper management to define the goals of the project, support the project, and protect it from disruptive influences. Other project matters fall to the PM; thus, the prime role of the PM is as the integrator, communicator, and problem solver for the project team, upper management, the customer, and all other stakeholders. Project managers need a host of skills and knowledge of both business and technical matters, and this is particularly true in IT. Computerworld states:

Shouldering project management responsibilities isn't for the average Joe or the fainthearted. It requires people who have a relentless, or one might say obsessive-compulsive, attention to detail. They must also be thick-skinned individuals, willing to withstand verbal barbs, insults to their genealogy and possibly some old-fashioned assault and battery from people tired of being prompted for their part of the project. (Hall, 2004)

"It's a tough job with long hours and stress that needs someone who's a cross between a ballet dancer and a drill sergeant" (Murch, 2000). A well-known story (but of unknown origin) about PMs emphasizes their role:

A project manager, his chief software engineer, and lead network analyst were having a lunchtime stroll in the woods when they happened on a small brass lamp. They picked it up and rubbed it and a grateful genie appeared. When confronted with three of them, the genie granted the traditional three wishes, but only one wish to each of them.

The eager analyst went first and requested a South Sea Island with sweet music, swaying palm trees with a matching supply of lei-clad girls delivering endless Tequila Sunrises. "No problem" said the Genie, and with a quick flash and a cloud of smoke, the analyst disappeared.

Next came the software engineer, who merely wished to be locked in the sample room of the Coors Brewery with a guarantee of a self-regenerating liver. "No problem" said the Genie, and with a quick flash and a cloud of smoke the software engineer disappeared.

Then came the project manager. "No problem!" he said. "I want those other two back at their desks by 1:15."

IT Project Management

The evolution of flatter and team-based workplaces has progressed quicker and deeper in IT organizations than in the general corporate world. In addition, IT project management has some key differences and distinctions from project management in other fields. Some of these differences have to do with visibility, and this aspect alone makes IT projects more difficult that projects in other industries (McDonald, 2001). For example, the scope is hard to see—one cannot count the bricks, and quality is hard to see—it is not apparent if parts do not fit, do not work, cannot handle loads, cannot handle extensions, and are not compliant with standards. Here are other major differences and difficulties:

- The major cost is labor with high degrees of specializations
- There is a large difference in productivity rates of the human resources even in same job category
- There are multiple quality dimensions and criteria
- Cost and time estimation is more complex
- There are multiple architectures, methodologies, tools, et cetera, and these are constantly changing
- Projects have a high degree of complexity
- Projects may effect the entire organization or beyond
- Projects have a large amount of changes to requirements
- Projects usually have a high degree of significant risks, including
- New features
- New algorithms and methods
- New languages, platforms, architectures, and supporting tools
- New operating systems, telecommunications, interfaces
- New technology in general
- Measurement of return on investment (ROI) and other business metrics is difficult
- There are often unrealistic goals and pressures placed upon project managers and project teams to deliver software products better-cheaper-faster
- Today, IT projects often involve many outside parties as consultants and vendors
- Today, IT projects often involve offshore resources

Despite ongoing advances and innovations in project management, many projects fail; in IT, most projects still do not succeed. The Standish Group has been performing a study called CHAOS for about a decade. In 1994, their study found that only 16% of all IT projects come in on time and within budget (Cafasso, 1994); projects that are completely abandoned represent about 15% of the failures. The problem is so widespread that many IT professionals accept project failure as inevitable (Cale, Curley, & Curley, 1987; Hildebrand, 1998). In 2004, the IT project success rate in the CHAOS report was 28%, down from 34% in 2003, and IT projects were getting more expensive (Hayes, 2004).

The failure rate goes up as the size of the IT project increases; projects over $10 million have success rates of only 2%, projects between $3 and $10 million have success rates from 23% to 11%, and projects under $3 million have success rates from 33% to 46%. Even relatively small IT projects succeed only half of the time. However, the definition of success used here may be too restrictive and this is the topic of the next chapter.

The CHAOS report also lists the major causes of IT project failure, and over the years the top causes have been lack of end-use involvement; lack of executive support; poor project management and/or planning; unclear business justification; and problems with requirements, scope, methodology, and estimation (Standish Group, 2004). All of these issues (and other problem areas) are discussed in this book, and methods to mitigate such problems are illustrated.

Due to the difficulties in delivering successful IT projects, project management is viewed as one of the most valuable skills for IT professionals. The Project Management Institute (PMI) has a certification program for the project management discipline, and the highest level of certification therein is the project management professional (PMP). Citing a 2002 Foote Partners Study, Computerworld listed the certifications obtained by IT professionals, and which certifications were the most valuable in terms of percentage pay increases after certification (King, 2003). The three most valuable certifications in IT were

- PMI Project Management Professional (PMP): 15%
- GIAC Certified Intrusion Analyst: 12%
- Microsoft Certified Trainer: 12%

Figure 1.6. PM's worldview

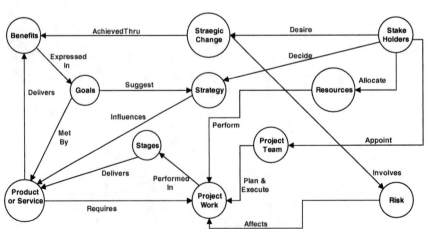

According to Sommerville (2003), there are three challenges to software engineering projects in the 21st century:

1. *The Heterogeneity Challenge:* Flexibility to operate on and integrate with multiple hardware and software platforms from legacy mainframe environments to the landscape of the global Web.
2. *The Delivery Challenge:* Ability to develop and integrate IT systems rapidly in response to rapidly changing and evolving global business needs.
3. *The Trust Challenge:* Being able to create vital (mission and/or life critical) software that is trustworthy in terms of both security and quality.

These are also three of the most critical issues for IT project management in general, and these issues are addressed throughout this book. Being able to build flexible and adaptable systems to address the heterogeneity and delivery challenge is crucial because more IT and related environmental matters are changing, and they are changing in an ever faster rate. In a similar vein, Computerworld's 2005 Executive Panel described an "evil triad" that has become the predominant future IT concern. That evil triad is poor security, unreliability, and increased complexity (Anthes, 2005).

With more powerful tools comes the potential for greater benefits including productivity increases, better cost and performance, and improved quality. However that power also brings a higher cost and damage potential when the tool is misused either accidentally or intentionally. IT is such a powerful tool, and that power in terms of computational speed is still doubling about every 18 months. Many other IT advances are also facilitating the possible misuse of IT, including,

*   Price for computational resources has dropped so low that even the smallest of organizations and countries can obtain massive power
*   Advances in data storage technology mean that huge amounts of data can be stored cheaply
*   Advances in data mining techniques mean that huge amounts of data can be analyzed in many ways
*   Advances in data networking mean that the cost and time of moving and accessing data has become very low, and that computers both inside and outside of an organization are increasingly connected

As a result of these advances which facilitate IT misuse, computer security incidents are growing rapidly. The number of domestic U.S. computer security incidents published by the CERT Coordination Center at Carnegie Mellon University has increased dramatically in recent years, as is shown in Figure 1.7. The number of these incidents has increased so much that CERT is no longer keeping detail information thereon.

Figure 1.7. Reported security incidents

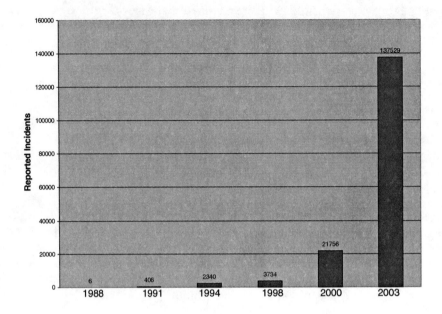

These are just the security incidents that have been reported. Because IT is so prevalent in all the products and services that organizations offer today and so prevalent in everything we do as individuals, the impact of these security problems is also quickly increasing. This problem could become enormous in the years ahead, and security breaches such as *Trojan horses* and *back doors* may already be in place within key software used by corporations and governments. The security issue in IT project management is twofold:

- Being able to shield the project work, project team, and other resources from security threats
- Being able to build adequate security protection into the product that is the subject of the project

In the future, the last of Sommerville's (2003) challenges previously listed may become as, or even more, important than the first two. Being able to run projects and build systems that are impervious to both internal and external security threats will become vital to the success of organizations and survival of free world governments.

References

Anthes, G. (2005, March 7). The dark side. *Computerworld*.

Brandel, M. (2001, January 1). Dual personalities. *Computerworld*.

Cafasso, R. (1994). Few IS Projects come in on time, on budget. *Computerworld, 28*(50), 20.

Cale, E. G., Curley J. R., & Curley, K. F. (1987). Measuring implementation outcome. *Information and Management, 3*(1), 245-253.

Cooke-Davies, T. (2004). Project success. In P. Morris & J. Pinto (Eds.), *The Wiley guide to managing projects*. Wiley.

Drucker, P. (2004). *The next information revolution*. Retrieved from www.versaggi.net/ecommerce/articles

Hall, M. (2004, February 16). Thieves among us. *Computerworld*.

Hayes, F. (2004, November 6). Chaos is back. *Computerworld*.

Hildebrand, C. (1998). If at first you don't succeed. *CIO Enterprise, Section 2*, 4-15.

Hundley, R., et al. (2004). *The global course of the information revolution: recurring themes and regional variations*. Retrieved from www.rand.org/publications/MR/MR1680/

King, J. (2003, February 10). Where certifications and paychecks meet. *Computerworld*.

McDonald, J. (2001). Why is software project management difficult ? And what that implies for teaching software project management. *Computer Science Education, 11*(1), 55-71.

Murch, R. (2000). *Project management best practices for IT professionals*. Upper Saddle River, NJ: Prentice Hall.

Paramount Pictures. (1986). *Top Gun*. Directed by Tony Scott.

Pearlson, K., & Saunders, C. (2004). *Managing and using information systems*. New York: Wiley.

PMI. (2000*). The project management body of knowledge (PMBOK)*. Newton Square, PA. ISBN 1-880410-22-2.

Sommerville, I. (2003). *Software engineering*. Boston: Addison-Wesley.

Standish Group. (2004). *Chaos chronicles*. Retrieved from www.standisgroup.com

Yates, J. (2000, August). Origins of project management. *Knowledge Magazine*.

York, T. (1999, January 18). Shift in IT roles ahead. *InfoWorld*.

Chapter II

Critical Success Factors for IT Projects

IT managers' careers will rise and fall based on their ability to deliver high quality projects on time.

(J. I. Cash, Harvard Business School)

A key factor leading to the continued failure in IT projects is the lack of identification and appreciation for all the major components of project success. Critical success factors are those things that must be done or handled properly for a project to be successful. A comprehensive model of critical success factors for IT projects permits the development of better management plans, processes, and metrics, particularly for risk, quality, and performance control. In this chapter, general critical IT success factors are identified and techniques for the management of those factors are introduced; later chapters then detail those techniques.

Definition of Success

Cost, time, and quality (often referred to as the *Iron Triangle*) have formed the prime basis for measuring project success for the last 50 years (Atkinson, 1999). However a number of authors in more recent years (Atkinson, 1999; Brandon, 2004; DeLone & McLean, 1992; Lim & Mohamed, 1999; Morris & Hough, 1987; Pinto & Slevin, 1998;) have suggested that other criteria are also important. Some of these other criteria may be less quantitative, more difficult to measure, and some of the criteria may be temporary in that their values may be much more important at some points in the project.

So what is meant by project success? Success needs to be defined *completely* so that the factors that lead to success or failure in a broad perspective can be identified. In the past, success has been too narrowly defined; this definition has typically been confined to scope, cost, and time issues. Handling these particular issues has been well addressed by methods such as earned value analysis (EVA), which have proven successful for accurate performance measurement and control (Brandon, 1999; Fleming & Koppelman, 1994, 1998); earned value is specifically addressed in later chapters of this book.

Originally, Schultz and Slevin (1979) discussed overall implementation success and identified three dimensions to success: technical (Does it work?), organizational validity (Is it what the users want?), and organizational effectiveness (Is it a cost effective solution?). Pinto and Slevin (1998) presented a widely used "10 Factor Model" for success factors involving project mission, management support, planning, client consultation, personnel, technical tasks, client acceptance, project control, project communication, and handling unforeseen issues (Pinto & Millett, 1999; Pinto & Slevin, 1992). Hawkins (2004) determined that the most critical success factors for ERP IT projects were adequate resources, shared and well communicated business justification, open communications, participation by all relevant levels of management, visible and continuous executive sponsorship, being in touch with those most affected, preimplementation training, and structured change management.

Klastorin (2004) illustrated project success in broader terms with the example of the movie *Titanic* (Paramount Pictures, 1997). When that movie was release in 1997, it was well behind schedule and cost almost twice the planned amount. It was, however, the first movie in history to gross over $1 billion, and it received the best picture award for that year.

Lim and Mohamed (1999) also raised the question of "What is a successful project?" and noted that different stakeholders involved with the same project may have different opinions about a project's success. One of their examples concerned the construction of a shopping center that was eventually completed to match the required quality standard, however with significant cost and time overruns. Some stakeholders were very unhappy, depending upon the type of contracts involved and who contractually bears the burden of the cost overruns (i.e., who pays for cost overruns). Other stakeholders (such as mall customers and the merchants renting space in the mall) were all pleased and saw the project as a great success. Lim and Mohamed defined two perspectives, the macro perspective, which involves all the stakeholders, and the micro perspective, which involves only the construction parties such as the developer and contractor(s). The macro perspective is relevant for all phases of a project from conceptualization, through construction, and then operation. The micro perspective is most relevant for the construction phase.

Completion and Satisfaction Criteria

Lim and Mohamed (1999) also defined two types of success criteria: completion and satisfaction. *Completion criteria* include contract-related items such as cost, time, and scope. *Satisfaction criteria* include utility (fitness for purpose), quality, and operation (ease of use, ease of learning, ease of maintenance, etc.). The macro perspective involves both; the micro perspective only involves completion perspectives. This is illustrated in Figure 2.1. Often, scope can be somewhat divided into a portion affecting completion (mainly stated requirements, or needs) and a portion affecting satisfaction (mainly unstated requirements and expectations, or wants). *This division of success criteria into micro and macro perspective types is very important in terms of project performance control and the effectiveness and cost thereof. This division provides for different review time periods, different review methods, and different project stakeholder involvement for the review of each type of criteria.*

Lim and Mohamed (1999) drew a clear distinction between "success criteria" and "success factors." The criteria are "a principle or standard by which anything is or can be judged"; factors are "any circumstance, fact, or influence which contributes to a result". Figure 2.2 illustrates this point. Factors for the completion criteria would typically include financial variables, process variables, resource variables (cost, availability, skill, motivation, etc.), management variables (project manager skill, line management support, etc.), and risk variables (weather, economy, technology, etc.). Factors for the satisfaction criteria would be those things that drive the satisfaction of the stakeholders.

Success criteria tend to be relatively independent of the type of project being measured. The factors are, however, very dependent on the type of thing being built (or accomplished). In the previous mall example, a factor for the satisfaction type criteria of utility might be "ample parking"; a factor for the operation component of the satisfaction criteria might be "ease of parking."

Generalization of Success Factors for IT

I proposed a more generalized model in an earlier work (Brandon, 2004), and in developing that generalized model for IT success factors, the success criteria were divided into the two dimensions of project success defined by Lim and Mohamed (1999). Next, the general criteria suggested by Lim and Mohamed were also used, and these criteria are relatively independent of project type. The third step was to determine the *factors that underlie these criteria for IT projects.*

Many authors have studied components of IT project success and risk. The original

Figure 2.1. Success criteria

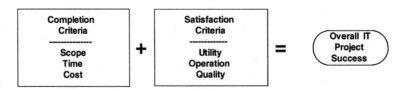

Figure 2.2. Criteria and factors

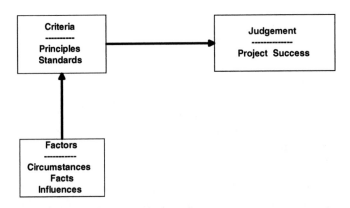

Standish Group (1994) study found that the three most common causes of project failure were: lack of user input, incomplete requirements, and changing requirements. Conversely they found that the three most important factors for success were user involvement, executive management support, and a clear statement of requirements. The European Software Process Improvement Initiative (ESPITI) performed a study in 1995 and noted that the major IT project failure factors were requirements specifications, managing customer requirements, documentation, quality, and project management methods. Hallows (1998) stated that the major causes of failure involved scope: poor original definition, poor management of scope, and unforeseen changes in scope.

Jones (1994) studied software risks in different IT environments and identified major issues and related metrics. For example, MIS software problems were "creeping" requirements (80%), excessive schedule pressure (65%), low quality (60%), cost overruns (55%), and inadequate configuration control (50%). McConnell (1998) developed a "survival test" for software development projects and detailed a number of success criteria within five categories. Pearlson (2001) assessed project success criteria by asking key questions to minimize risk: "Are we doing the right things?", "Are we doing it in the best way?", "How do we know how well we are doing?", "What impacts are we having on the business?", "Is the project cost-effective?", "Is there clear accountability for the project?", and "Are key assets protected?" In 2004, The Standish Group (1994) updated its list of IT critical success factors to include (Collett, 2005):

- User involvement
- Executive management support
- Clear business objectives
- Experienced project manager
- Minimal scope and requirements
- Iterative and agile process

- Skilled personnel
- Formal methodology
- Financial management
- Standard tools and infrastructure

Based on the detail study of these past works (both scientific parametric-based studies and the expert opinion of practitioners) combined with our own experience and research, we have developed a recommendation for the major IT project success factors, both completion and satisfaction. For the area of completion criteria, these major IT success factors have been identified:

- *Ability to Perform:* Includes having the necessary amount of resources needed and the correct resources to carry out the project plan. The ability to perform is also one of the Software Engineering Institute (SEI) "common features" in their Capability Maturity Model (CMM), which is discussed later in this book.
- *Commitment to Perform:* (Another CMM common feature) includes both project sponsor and upper management support (including organizational and environmental matters).
- *Methodology:* Involves the selection of specific IT software engineering processes (requirements analysis, systems analysis, design, development, documentation, testing, etc.) and how these processes will be organized, utilized, and integrated both amongst themselves and with the project management processes.
- *Verification:* Involves "built-in" quality or "defect prevention" and concerns the quality of the development *processes*, thus answering the question, "Have we built the product right?" Formally, verification is proof of compliance with requirements, specifications, and standards. Verification processes usually result in exception (bug) reports where compliance is not achieved.
- *Technology:* Involves the proper selection of applicable technology for use both in the product and in the process of building the product. It covers architecture, platform, language, tools, and supporting technology selection as well as issues of each including the maturity, stability, and support thereof.
- *Project Management:* Addresses the use of proper project management skills and knowledge in dealing with planning, schedule, cost, scope, risk, human resources, and stakeholders; this is what the Project Management Institute (PMI) calls "knowledge areas." Also included herein are the capabilities and experience of the project manager.

In the area of satisfaction criteria, these major success factors have been identified:

- *Business Justification:* Involves some type of cost-benefit model. Line management, users, and the project team must "buy-into" and support this model. Business justifications, financial models, and project feasibility are discussed later in the book.

- *Validation:* Involves the *product* that is the subject of the project and checks all user (customer) requirements (both stated and expected) and answers the question, "Have we built the right product?" Formally, validation is proof that the customer and end users are satisfied with the system. Proper user involvement is vital to this aspect of the development and/or integration process. Validation processes usually result in change orders when the user is not satisfied with an aspect of the product.

- *Workflow and Content:* Involves the effective integration of the new product into the organization and each user's workflow. Content includes all deliverable information including: documentation, help system, data, and media content (especially in the sense of modern and internet applications).

- *Standards:* Relate to compliance with applicable industry, corporate, and user (customer) standards in regard to both external (i.e. user interface) and internal issues (i.e. coding standards). Standards are also discussed later in this book under quality management.

- *Maintainability and Support:* Involves the inherent maintainability of the developed product and the willingness and timeliness of the developing (or support) organization in responding to the customer's concerns about usage or integrity (real or perceived) issues.

- *Adaptability:* Relates to the flexibility of the product to be adapted (successfully modified) for evolving changes in the environment in which the product is deployed; this includes both technical changes and business changes.

- *Trust and Security:* Relates to both the security built into the product and to the security of the process for building the product. Product security and trust involves the customer's willingness to fully utilize the system in all necessary modes without concern for compromise of any of the customer's assets including information assets.

Figure 2.3 summarizes our general modern model for IT success factors. In the last chapter of this book, we discuss project management from a strategic perspective and in particular the collective management of multiple projects. Probably the most effective method of modern strategic management is the Balanced Scorecard Method (BSC), which divides strategic metrics into four perspectives: financial, process, learning and growth, and the customer's perspective. Our general model uses just two perspectives for management at the individual project level (completion and satisfaction) and the reasons for that will become clearer with each chapter of this book. However, our completion criteria map to the BSC financial and process perspectives; and our satisfaction criteria map to the BSC learning, growth, and satisfaction perspectives.

The Slevin-Pinto Profile (Pinto & Slevin, 1998) discussed earlier has often been used to identify IT project success factors in order to focus management attention on the key issues. A more recent *Project Management Journal* article illustrates the application of such a profile (Finch, 1993). Figure 2.4 shows a mapping of our broader IT Success Criteria

Figure 2.3. Critical IT success factors

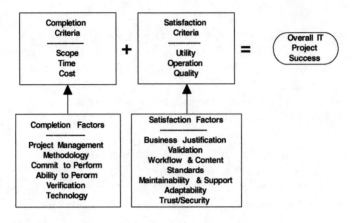

Figure 2.4. Success factors vs. Slevin-Pinto Profile

	Completion Factors						Satisfaction Factors					
	Project Management (KA)	Methodology	Commitment to Perform	Ability to Perform	Verification	Technology	Business Justification	Validation	Workflow & Content	Standards	Maintainability & Support	Trust/Security
Slevin-Pinto Profile												
Project Mission							X					
Top Management Support			X									
Project Schedule/Plan	SM/TM											
Client Consultation	CM	X										
Personnel	HRM			X								
Technical Tasks				X	X							
Client Acceptance	QM	X						X				
Monitoring and Feedback	TM/CM											
Communication	CM	X										
Troubleshooting	RM											

model to the Slevin-Pinto model. For the "Project Management" column, the PMI project management "knowledge area" is shown, and these are discussed later in this book.

Our critical IT success factors are for IT projects in general, and will be used throughout this book to formulate effective IT project management processes. If some of these factors are not relevant to a particular IT project (or if there are additional critical factors), then the processes, techniques, and metrics described later in this book can be modified accordingly.

Managing for Success

This book focuses on managing for success in modern times. Once the critical success factors for IT projects have been identified, then those factors become the foundation for effective performance management and management of other key project aspects as risk. Performance management involves the things we know we have to do; risk management involves the things we may have to do. This is illustrated in Figure 2.5.

This book introduces and develops the concept of splitting the traditional stage gate reviews (exit gates or kill points) based upon the critical completion and success criteria.

Figure 2.5. Success factors and performance/risk management

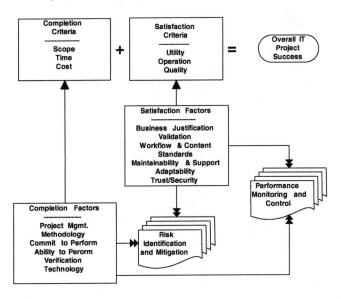

Figure 2.6. Dual stage gates and success criteria

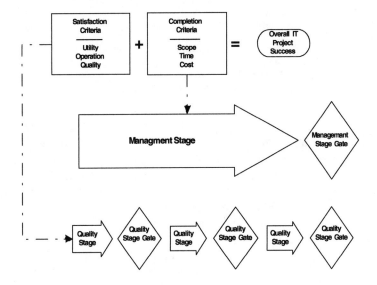

Figure 2.7. Risk framework and success factors

Risk Source Framework											
	Potential Hazards										
	Internal						External				
Threats to:	Product	Process	People	Organization	Other		Product	Process	People	Organization	Other
Completion Factors											
Project Management											
Methodology											
Commitment to Perform											
Ability to Perform											
Verification											
Technology											
Satisfaction Factors											
Business Justification											
Validation											
Workflow & Contents											
Standards											
Maintainability & Support											
Adaptability											
Trust/Security											

Figure 2.8.

Detail Coverage	
Success Factors	Book Chapter
Completion Factors	
Project Management	All
Methodology	5
Commitment to Perform	9,14
Ability to Perform	9,14
Verification	6,10
Technology	15
Satisfaction Factors	
Business Justification	3,10
Validation	6,10
Workflow & Content	10
Standards	5,10
Maintainability & Support	5,10
Adaptability	5, 10
Trust/Security	6, 10

Management stage gates are used for the completion criteria and are implemented via management by exception using earned value metrics at regular time periods so that the project can flow quickly with minimal management review delays. Quality stage gates are used to monitor the satisfaction criteria and their timing is event driven by the completion of preliminary product manifestations. This is outlined graphically in Figure 2.6 and discussed in detail later in the book. This dual gating process minimizes the time that both upper management and the project team spends in status meetings by splitting the review process into separate completion and satisfaction reviews with the occurrence of each based upon the need thereof. However, it ensures that customer involvement is sufficient in the project items that most concern the users.

With the success factor model becoming the foundation for other key project management areas (including quality, security, and risk), frameworks are developed for the detail processes of each management area. For example, a framework for risk identification and quantification is formulated as shown in Figure 2.7.

Chapter Summary

In this chapter the concept of critical success criteria has been developed, and critical success factors for IT projects have been identified and divided into completion and satisfaction groups. More detailed coverage of each critical success factor is contained in succeeding chapters of this book, and Figure 2.8 shows a rough mapping between success factors and book chapters. The notion of a dual stage gate process has been introduced for the comprehensive and effective management of these success factors, and later chapters will define metrics and control methods for both completion and satisfaction criteria.

References

Atkinson, R. (1999). Project management: Cost, time and quality, two best guesses and a phenomenon., *International Journal of Project Management, 17*(6), 337-342.

Brandon, D. (1999). Implementing earned value easily and effectively. *Essentials of Project Control,* 113.

Brandon, D. (2004, May). *A generalization of critical success factors for IT projects. Proceedings of the 2004 IRMA (Information Resources Management Association) Conference,* New Orleans, LA.

Collett, S. (2005, February 28). New project perils. *Computerworld.*

DeLone, W., & McLean, E. (1992). Information systems Success: The quest for the dependent variable. *Information Systems Research, 3*(1), 60-95.

European Software Process Improvement Initiative. (1995). *User survey report.* Bizkaia, Spain.

Field, T. (1997). When bad things happen to good projects. *CIO, 11*(2), 54-62.

Finch, P. (1993, September). Applying the Slevin-Pinto Project Implementation Profile to an information systems project. *Project Management Journal.*

Fleming, Q., & Koppelman, J. K. (1994). The essence of evolution of earned value. *Cost Engineering, 36*(11), 21-27.

Fleming, Q., & Koppelman, J. K. (1998, July). Earned value project management. *CROSSTALK, The Journal of Defense Software Engineering.*

Hallows, J. (1998). *Information systems project management.* AMACON, American Management Association.

Hawkins, P., et al. (2004). *Change management: The real struggle for ERP systems practices. Innovations through information technology.* Hershey, PA: Idea Group Publishing.

Hildebrand, C. (1998). If at first you don't succeed. *CIO Enterprise Section, 2,* 4-15.

Jones, T. C. (1994). *Assessment and control of software risks.* New York: Yourdon Press/ Prentice Hall.

Klastorin, T. (2004). *Project management: Tools and trade-offs.* Hoboken, NJ: Wiley.

Lim, C. S., & Mohamed, Z. (1999). Criteria of project success. *International Journal of Project Management, 17*(4), 243-248.

McConnell, S. (1998). *Software project survival guide.* Seattle, WA: Microsoft Press.

Morris, P. W. G., & Hough, G. (1987). *The anatomy of major projects.* New York: Wiley.

Paramount Pictures. (1997). *Titanic.* Directed by James Cameron.

Pearlson, K. (2001). *Managing and using information systems.* New York: Wiley.

Pinto, J., & Millet, I. (1999). *Successful information system implementation.* Newton Square, PA: Project Management Institute.

Pinto, J., & Slevin, D. (1992). *Project implementation profile.* Newton Square, PA: Xicom.

Pinto, J., & Slevin, D. (1998). Critical success factors across the project lifecycle. *Project Management Journal, XIX,* 67-75.

Schultz, R., & Slevin, D. (1979). Introduction: The implementation problem. *The Implementation of Management Science.* North-Holland.

Software Engineering Institute. Retrieved from www.sei.cmu.edu

The Standish Group. (1994). *Charting the seas of information technology—Chaos.* West Yarmouth, MA.

Chapter III

Project Selection
and Initiation

If everyone is thinking alike, then somebody isn't thinking.

(George Patton)

Careful selection of which projects to initiate is vital to the success of an organization. Project initiation represents a future commitment of both human and financial resources as well as of management attention. If a choice is careless or inappropriate, then the consequences may be severe and long lasting. In this chapter, methods for the proper selection and initiation of projects are discussed with regard to overall organizational goals and business justification.

Organizational Planning

Organizational planning and the associated decision processes occur at several levels of the company, including the operational level, the tactical level, and the strategic level. This is illustrated in Figure 3.1. The operational level is concerned with day-to-day activities in operating the business, including running the ongoing projects. The management focus at this level is on efficiency, productivity, and quality: managers make sure that things are done right. The tactical level is concerned with short-term planning (i.e., annually). The management focus at this level is on effectiveness, consistency, and accuracy; here, managers make sure the right things are being done. The strategic level is concerned with long-term planning (i.e., 5 to 10 years), and the focus is on competitiveness and the value of the organization's service and/or products as perceived by the customers and other stakeholders.

Most of this book is focused on the operational level, which concerns the planning, execution, and control of approved projects, thus addressing the question, "Are we doing our projects right?" Project managers play the leading role in this level of management. Chapter XVI examines the strategic level in regard to IT projects, including overall IT governance issues as they relate to project management, the management of broad issues that span multiple projects, and the adoption of special management structures for projects.

Chapter III, however, focuses on the tactical level of an organization and addresses the question, "Are we doing the right projects?" For those types of decisions, although project managers should be involved, business analysts and upper IT management play

Figure 3.1. Organizational management levels

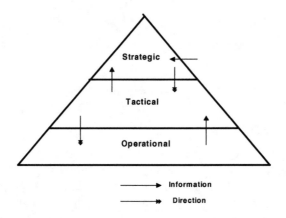

Figure 3.2. Book content vs. organizational levels

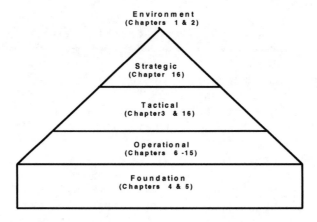

the lead role. The layout of this decision-rights–based content by book chapter is illustrated in Figure 3.2.

Project Initiation

Projects are initiated from the recognition that (a) there is a problem (or a specific need) to be addressed, and (b) that this problem can be addressed through a project to implement some solution. Problem needs must be quantified (eventually, in terms of requirements for IT projects) for a project to be formally initiated. The general process of refining "needs" into a problem statement is shown in Figure 3.3.

The party that recognizes the problem, the party that articulates the problem, the party that proposes the problem solution, and the party that performs the project may be different parties, either individually or organizationally. Project proposals are developed in the organization(s) in response to requests from managers (top down), from workers (bottom up), and from customers or other stakeholders (external). Proposals are generally reviewed by line management (which may request a detailed business plan), and if approved result in a project charter, which is the official go-ahead document. Project management (when selected and empowered) generally develops a scope statement, which eventually leads to functional requirements (what the proposed system will do), interface requirements, and technical requirements (how it will work). This is illustrated in Figure 3.4.

All the documents shown in Figure 3.4 contain a great deal of uncertainty. The problems and needs that are identified, and then articulated, are inherently fuzzy due to several common circumstances:

Figure 3.3. Project initiation

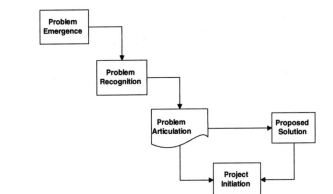

Figure 3.4. Scope and requirement development

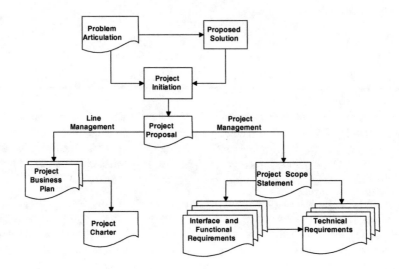

- The entire problem is like an iceberg; only a portion of it can be seen
- Customers (end users or benefiting organizations) may be somewhat ignorant or unclear about their true needs
- The needs change in time

In addition, the proposed solution (that is the subject of the project) may be identified prematurely. An end user cannot usually relate the problem to the proposed solution in abstract terms. Customers usually know what they do not want or need much better than they know what they do want or need, or how to best articulate the same. Customers needs to "see" the solution (or a manifestation thereof) before they can verify an effective match between their problem and the proposed solution. In addition, for large benefiting organizations, there may be multiple (and possibly conflicting) views of the problem and alternative solutions thereof. *Effective project management involves a recognition of uncertainty in all the initial documents and plans, and also involves methods and tools that adequately address these uncertainties.* In addition to initial uncertainty and uncertainty that develops as a project proceeds and takes on tangible forms, the end users may see new possibilities, and they may pressure the performing organization for changes and enhancements.

Project Proposals

Historically, IT projects have been justified on one or more of the three F's: fear, faith, or facts. The fear approach uses rational such as:

Our competitors are already developing such a system!

Upper management and shareholders will consider us behind the technology curve if we do not do this!

The faith approach uses rational such as:

Our competitors have done this and it is working for them!

This type of system is part of our IT infrastructure, and we cannot quantitatively justify it like we could an additional factory capital equipment item!

A facts-based project proposal would identify the specific benefits of such a project, the rough costs for developing the project's associated product, some information about the scope of the project, project and product risks and uncertainties, and the key stakeholders that may be involved. Benefits typically involve improving or solidifying an organization's financial position (additional revenue and/or reduced costs) through

Figure 3.5. Project proposal

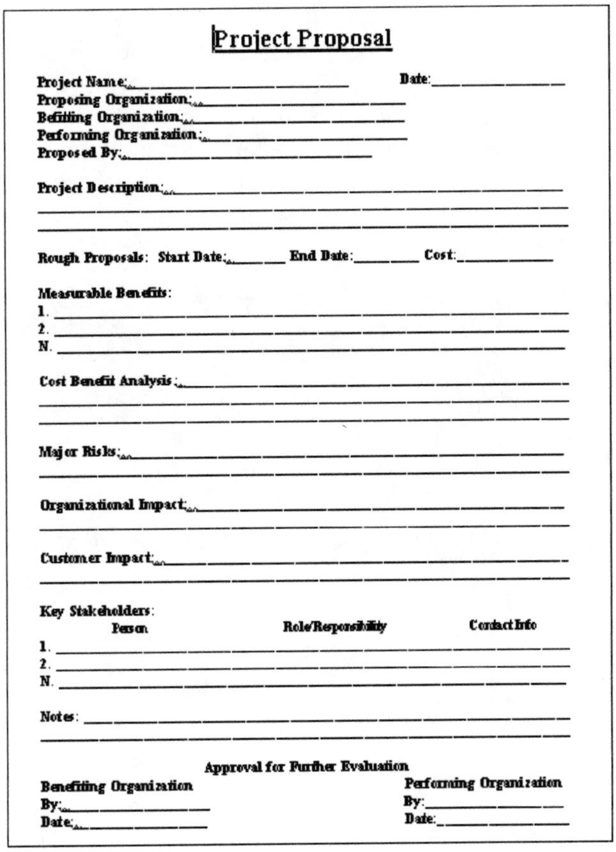

Project Proposal

Project Name: ______ Date: ______
Proposing Organization: ______
Befitting Organization: ______
Performing Organization: ______
Proposed By: ______

Project Description: ______

Rough Proposals: Start Date: ______ End Date: ______ Cost: ______

Measurable Benefits:
1. ______
2. ______
N. ______

Cost Benefit Analysis: ______

Major Risks: ______

Organizational Impact: ______

Customer Impact: ______

Key Stakeholders:
Person | Role/Responsibility | Contact Info
1. ______
2. ______
N. ______

Notes: ______

Approval for Further Evaluation

Benefiting Organization
By: ______
Date: ______

Performing Organization
By: ______
Date: ______

improvements to products and/or processes or new products (or services). Sometimes the benefit is not of a direct financial nature but is due to a compliance requirement of some external governing body. IT "benefits assessment" is neither specifically nor fully covered directly in this book; it is a very broad topic and part of the realm of general IT governance and management as opposed to IT project management. Finally, proposals should be formalized, and forms such as that shown in Figure 3.5 may be used.

Project Business Plan

After a proposal has been approved for further evaluation, a formal business plan should be required that elaborates (via extended research and analysis) all of the items shown in Figure 3.5, including a feasibility analysis and reviewing of alternative methods (and even alternative related project proposals). We say "should be required" because, in reality, many IT projects are funded without a further detail analysis due to organization issues including egos, power/politics, and who controls the purse strings.

With a more formal approach, IT projects would typically undergo feasibility analyses from at least three perspectives: technical feasibility, operational feasibility, and economic feasibility—in other words, Can we build it? Can we maintain it? and Can we make money on it? Economic feasibility typically involves numerical financial techniques. Other dimensions of feasibility may also need investigation for certain types of projects, such as schedule feasibility for a time critical contracting situation, legal feasibility for projects involving multiple companies and jurisdictions, and political feasibility when conflicting interests prevail within an organization or within stakeholders, or where the "balance of power" may change in an organization as a result of the project. The following is an example of the contents for a project business plan:

Project Business Plan

Table of Contents

I. Opportunity
    Background
    Problem Description/Customer Needs
    Market Window
    Proposed Solution
    Alternative Solutions
    Consistency with Organizational Strategy
    Critical Success Factors
II. Benefits
    Description of Benefits
    Mapping of Benefits to Problem Specifics
    Quantification of Benefits
    Measurement and Verification of Benefits
III. Resources (Schedule, Cost, People, other)
IV. Financial Analysis
    Benefit Cost Ratio
    Payback Period
    Internal Rate of Return

Financial Evaluation and Selection Methods

There are many numerical techniques used to evaluate the net benefit of a project. Most of these are financial in nature and rely on future estimates of revenues and costs. The most elementary technique is the simple *cost-benefit analysis,* which compares the cost to implement a project versus the benefit to be realized. For example, if we build a software system at a cost of $100,000 and it will save us $400,000 over the projected program's useful system lifetime of 10 years, the benefit-to-cost ratio would be 4 to 1. A simple return on investment (ROI) calculation can also be made as the ratio of the benefit minus cost over the cost; in this case 300% (300,000/100,000). Payback periods can also be similarly determined. For this example the payback period would be determined by dividing the cost ($100,000) by the annual benefit of $40,000 ($400,000 divided by 10 years) for 2.5 years. *Information Week* (D'Antoni, 2005) recently performed a study of payback periods on IT projects for U.S. companies, and results were as follows:

Less than 6 months—about 30% of projects

Within 1 year—about 35% of projects

Within 2 years—about 20% of projects

Within 3 years—about 15% of projects

The aforementioned financial metrics do not consider the absolute size of the investment or the benefit. Simple cost-benefit analysis is also problematic because it ignores the time value of money. When interest rates are low and short projects are under consideration, this may not be a serious shortcoming. However when interest rates are high (i.e., over 8%) and the projects under consideration are long (over several years), then *net present value* (NPV) techniques should be used. The formula for NPV (or discounted cash flow) is:

$$NPV = \sum (B-C)_t / (1+i)^t$$

Where $(B-C)_t$ is the benefit minus the cost for period t, and i is the interest rate (cost of borrowing money or opportunity cost for other uses of cash). For NPV, benefit minus cost is more formally revenue (cash in) minus expenditures (cash out). Figure 3.6 is an example of a NPV calculation done in a spreadsheet program. The cost column includes development and long-term total cost of ownership (TCO) values. TCO includes the incremental ongoing cost of support, operations, and maintenance (above the status quo). The column for discounted benefit minus cost is calculated from the application of the above formula. Even though the total benefit minus the total cost is $305,000, the NPV is only about $44,000 at an interest rate of 10%.

Another similar project financial evaluation technique is called the *internal rate of return* (IRR). This metric is better than NPV because it is not as sensitive to the uncertainties of future benefits and costs and to the future interest rates. The internal rate of return is the value of the interest rate that yields a zero value for NPV; this is sometimes called the return on investment. This can be calculated in spreadsheet programs by using built-in solver tools. Because, in reality, a quadratic equation is being solved, multiple IRR values could be found. Thus one must impose additional constraints on the solution (such as IRR is positive, or in a given range). Figure 3.7 shows the spreadsheet calculation for IRR on the previous example; the IRR here is about 13%.

Projects with the same net present value may have different internal rates of return. Consider the two cases shown in the spreadsheet of Figure 3.8. This is another reason that the IRR is a better way to compare competing projects.

Figure 3.6. NPV cost/benefit analysis

Year	Benefit	Cost	B-C	Discounted B-C
1	$0.00	$175,000.00	-$175,000.00	-$159,090.91
2	$0.00	$175,000.00	-$175,000.00	-$144,628.10
3	$50,000.00	$25,000.00	$25,000.00	$18,782.87
4	$100,000.00	$10,000.00	$90,000.00	$61,471.21
5	$100,000.00	$10,000.00	$90,000.00	$55,882.92
6	$100,000.00	$10,000.00	$90,000.00	$50,802.65
7	$100,000.00	$10,000.00	$90,000.00	$46,184.23
8	$100,000.00	$10,000.00	$90,000.00	$41,985.66
9	$100,000.00	$10,000.00	$90,000.00	$38,168.79
10	$100,000.00	$10,000.00	$90,000.00	$34,698.90
Total	$750,000.00	$445,000.00	$305,000.00	$44,258.22
		Interest = 0.1		

Figure 3.7. IRR calculation

Year	Benefit	Cost	B-C	Discounted B-C
1	$0.00	$175,000.00	-$175,000.00	-$154,728.74
2	$0.00	$175,000.00	-$175,000.00	-$136,805.61
3	$50,000.00	$25,000.00	$25,000.00	$17,279.80
4	$100,000.00	$10,000.00	$90,000.00	$55,001.46
5	$100,000.00	$10,000.00	$90,000.00	$48,630.33
6	$100,000.00	$10,000.00	$90,000.00	$42,997.19
7	$100,000.00	$10,000.00	$90,000.00	$38,016.58
8	$100,000.00	$10,000.00	$90,000.00	$33,612.90
9	$100,000.00	$10,000.00	$90,000.00	$29,719.32
10	$100,000.00	$10,000.00	$90,000.00	$26,276.76
Total	$750,000.00	$445,000.00	$305,000.00	$0.00
		Interest = 0.131011619		

Figure 3.8. IRR vs. NPV

Case 1

Period	Benefit	Cost	B-C	Discounted B-C
1	0	70	-70	-$60.87
2	0	50	-50	-$37.81
3	20	30	-10	-$6.58
4	90	0	90	$51.46
5	120	0	120	$59.66
			NPV:	$5.87
		Interest: 0.15		
		IRR: 0.17		

Case 2

Period	Benefit	Cost	B-C	Discounted B-C
1	0	20	-20	-$17.39
2	0	40	-40	-$30.25
3	20	50	-30	-$19.73
4	90	55	35	$20.01
5	120	12.95	107.05	$53.22
			NPV:	$5.87
		Interest: 0.15		
		IRR: 0.19		

Decision Trees

The financial aforementioned evaluation methods rely on future estimates of revenues and costs. As the uncertainty in these future estimates increases, the utility of these methods decreases. Decision trees are another project selection technique that considers the impact of uncertainty in the decision process. Decision trees are based on the Bayes (1763) rules of conditional probability, and they are typically implemented in a graphical and/or spreadsheet model.

The basis for decision trees goes back hundreds of years. In the early 18th century, an English philosopher and clergyman, Thomas Bayes, devoted his attention to a perplexing problem. Suppose there is a set of events, one of which must happen. It is possible to compute the chance that each will occur through the normal rules of probability. Now suppose that two or more of these events could give rise to the same observation. What is the probability that the observation came from a particular one of the events?

Bayes (1763) was so unsure of his rules that he did not publish them. His results were published by a friend, Richard Price, in 1763. The same results were later verified by the famous French mathematician Marquis de Pierre Simom LaPlace in 1774. His definition for *conditional probability* was:

P(AB)=P(B)P(A|B),

where P is probability, A and B are events, and | means "conditional." If A can occur if B does or does not (B' is not B):

P(AB')=P(B')P(A|B').

Then, because A can occur either way:

P(A)=P(AB)+P(AB')
P(A)=P(A|B)*P(B)+P(A|B')*P(B').

For example, there may be a severe winter. Let severe winter be event B, and the probability of B is 0.7. Let event A be the selling of over X units of product. If the winter is severe, the probability of selling mote than X units of product is 0.8. If the winter is not severe, the probability of selling more than X units of product is 0.5. What is the probability of selling more than X units, that is what is P(A).

P(A)=P(A|B)*P(B)+P(A|B')*P(B')
Now P(A|B')=1–P(A|B)
And P(B')=1–P(B)
P(A)=(0.8*0.7)+(0.5*0.3)=0.71

This analysis can also be represented graphically, as shown in Figure 3.9.

Decision trees are a form of graphical analysis used to select a decision based upon alternatives and their outcomes. The trees can also be implemented via spreadsheets as well as graphs. Each outcome has a probabilistic value. The components of a decision tree are:

"decision nodes"—represented by squares

"alternatives"—represented by circles

"states"—represented by ovals

Figure 3.9. Graphical representation of conditional probability

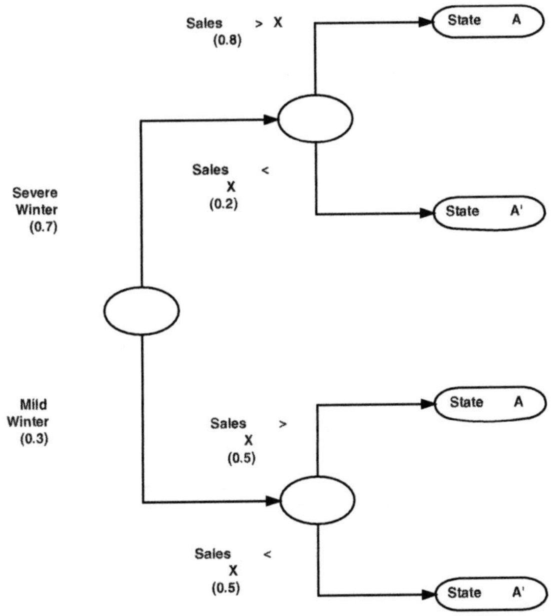

The states are known in the sense of their likelihood to occur or not to occur, and each state has an outcome measured in dollars of benefit. The alternatives have costs associated with them, as is illustrated in Figure 3.10. The Ps are the probability of occurrence of each state/outcome for each alternative, and the Bs are the benefit of each state for each alternative, and the Cs are the cost of each alternative. The sum of the Ps for each alternative is unity. The decision on which alternative to choose is based on the calculated EMV (expected monetary value) of each alternative. The EMV of each alternative is calculated by summing each benefit multiplied by its probability:

$$EMV_j = \sum P_{ji} * B_{1i} \text{ (where } i \text{ is the state and } j \text{ is the alternative).}$$

The overall EMV is the greatest EMV_j of each of the alternatives.

As we add additional layers to the decision tree, the overall EMV is "conditional" upon moving forward to the next level in the tree; here, the next phase of the project. As an example, consider the two-level tree in Figure 3.11 representing a two-phase project. The first phase is to develop a new software application and the second phase is to market that application. In that figure:

Cd = cost to develop

Cm = cost to market

Figure 3.10. Decision tree

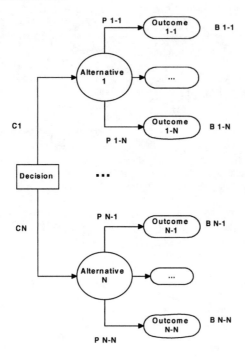

Pts = probability of technical success

Pbs = probability of market success

Bbs = benefit of business success

Bbf = benefit of business failure

The EMV of launching the new application *conditional* to the technical success of developing it is:

$$EMVb = Bbs * Pbs + Bbf * (1\text{-}Pbs) - Cm.$$

The overall EMV is:

$$EMV = EMVb * Pts + 0 * (1\text{–}Pts) - Cd =$$
$$Pts * (Bbs * Pbs + Bbf * (1\text{-}Pbs) - Cm) - Cd.$$

For example, if the probability of technical success is .80 and the probability of market success is .70, and the development cost is \$300,000 and the marketing cost is \$100,000, and the benefit is \$1,000,000 over the life of the application for a business success and \$200,000 for a business failure, then the EMV is only

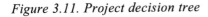

Figure 3.11. Project decision tree

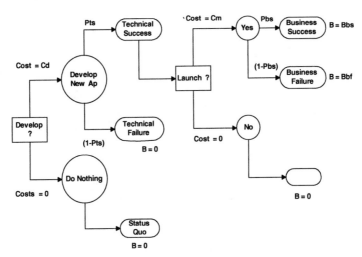

$$EMV = .8 * ((1000000*.7 + 200000*.3) - 100000) - 3000000 = \$228,000$$

as compared to a simple benefit minus cost of $600,000.

If the development time plus the time to market was several years and the interest rate was high, then one should use NPV in these formulas instead of simple benefit dollars. This is illustrated in the spreadsheet shown in Figure 3.12. Notice that now the EMV for this project has become negative.

The decision tree depicted in Figure 3.11 and Figure 3.12 could be extended both vertically to add other alternatives and horizontally to add additional phases. This is depicted in Figure 3.13. Here the project with the greatest EMV would be chosen (unless there are other factors to consider as discussed later).

The choice of which project (or projects) to initiate in Figure 3.13 is based upon the calculated EMV, which is based upon estimated costs, benefits, and probabilities of success in each phase. Other approaches can be used which do not rely on probabilities, but on a best case and worst case analysis for the benefit minus cost, or NPV. Here one employs a maximax, maximin, or equally likely approach. The maximax approach picks the maximum of the best case scenario; it is the most risky approach and would be used when the stakeholders were not adverse to risk (speculative). The maximin approach picks the maximum of the worst cases and this would be used with very risk adverse (timid) stakeholders. The equally likely approach averages the best and worst case scenarios. This is illustrated in Figure 3.14. Here we get three different choices based upon which strategy we follow.

Figure 3.12. EMV calculation

Year	Phase	Benefit		Cost		EMV	Discounted EMV
		Business Success	Business Failure	Develop Cost	Market Cost		
1	Develop	0	0	150000	0	-150000	-$136,363.64
2	Develop	0	0	150000	0	-150000	-$123,966.94
3	Market	100000	20000	0	50000	20800	$15,627.35
4	Market	100000	20000	0	10000	52800	$36,063.11
5	Market	100000	20000	0	5000	56800	$35,268.33
6	Market	100000	20000	0	5000	56800	$32,062.12
7	Market	100000	20000	0	5000	56800	$29,147.38
8	Market	100000	20000	0	5000	56800	$26,497.62
9	Market	100000	20000	0	5000	56800	$24,088.74
10	Market	100000	20000	0	5000	56800	$21,898.86
11	Market	100000	20000	0	5000	56800	$19,908.05
12	Market	100000	20000	0	5000	56800	$18,098.23
	Totals:	1000000	200000	300000	100000	228000	-$1,670.78

Probability of Technical Success: 0.8
Probability of Business Success: 0.7
Interest: 0.1

Figure 3.13. Multiphase project decision tree

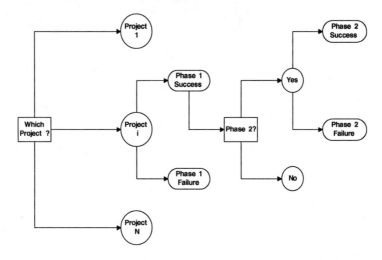

Project Scoring Methods

The aforementioned financial evaluation methods rely on future estimates of revenues and costs, either including uncertainty or not including uncertainty. Other methods of scoring that do not rely on entirely future financial estimates can be used in addition to or in replacement of the financial models. These other methods may consider purely strategic considerations or may involve a number of criteria including risk factors, environmental factors, sociological factors, and so forth. Stix and Reiner (2004) classified a number of IT project selection methods, as are represented in Figure 3.15:

B's—Bedell's Method

BSC—Balanced Scorecard

Figure 3.14. Maximax and minimax calculation

Alternatives	Best Case NPV	Worst Case NPV	Maximax	Maximin	Equally Likely
Project 1	1000000	-600000	1000000	-600000	200000
Project 2	600000	-100000	600000	-100000	250000
Project 3	500000	-50000	500000	-50000	225000
Project 4	700000	-300000	500000	-300000	200000
		Choice:	Project 1	Project 3	Project 2

Figure 3.15. Project scoring methods

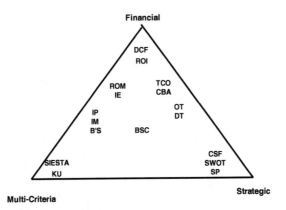

CBA—Cost Benefit Analysis

CSF—Critical Success Factors

DCF—Discounted Cash Flow

DT—Decision Trees

IE—Information Economics

IM—Investment Mapping

IP—Investment Portfolio

KU—Kobler Unit Framework

OT—Option Theory

ROI—Return on Investment

ROM—Return on Margin

SIESTA—"Siesta" Method

SP—Scenario Planning

SWOT—Strengths/Weaknesses

TCO—Total Cost of Ownership

Although less than 20 methods are illustrated in Figure 3.15, over 100 such methods currently exists (Stix & Reiner, 2004). Each of these methods has pros and cons, and each method is more applicable for certain types of IT projects and less applicable for other types of projects.

In an attempt to develop more holistic methods, many different scoring and ranking methods have been proposed that include less quantitative and more qualitative metrics for evaluating proposed projects. Most of these methods define a list of metrics with a corporate weighting assigned to each metric; the weightings sum to 100%. Then a score is given to each metric such as a value between 1 and 10 (not all methods use a linear scale). The definition of each metric is usually worded so that a high score is good and a low score is bad. As part of the definition of each metric, examples of the meaning of high and low scores should be specified. For example, in considering technical feasibility, a score of 10 may mean that "this type of project has been done in this organization successfully in the recent past," a score of 5 may mean that "this type of project has been done in similar types of organizations with success," and a score of 1 may mean that "we have not seen it done successfully anywhere yet." Statistically, it is best if the metrics do not interact too much, however in reality many metrics are going to indirectly affect other metrics. Typical metrics include:

Consistency with Organizational Mission and Goals (1 = *low*, 10 = *high*)

Technical Feasibility (1 = *low*, 10 = *high*)

Operational Feasibility (1 = *low*, 10 = *high*)

Economic Feasibility (1 = *low*, 10 = *high*)

External Risk (1 = *high*, 10 = *negligible*)

Internal Risk (1 = *high*, 10 = *negligible*)

Risk of Not Doing this Project (1 = *high*, 10 = *low*)

Internal Rate of Return (1 = *low*, 10 = *high*)

Capital Investment (1 = *very significant*, 10 = *little*)

Payback Period (1 = *long*, 10 = *short*)

Degree of Contracting/Outsourcing (1 = *much*, 10 = *little*)

Development Time (1 = *long*, 10 = *short*)

Geographical Dispersion of Team (1 = *much*, 10 = *little*)

Impact on Customer Base (1 = *little*, 10 = *much*)

Impact on Organization (1 = *little*, 10 = *much*)

Sociopolitical Impact (1 = *little*, 10 = *much*)

Environmental & Safety Considerations (1 = *very significant*, 10 = *little*)

Increase in Organizational Knowledge (1 = *little*, 10 = *much*)

Increase in Organizational Competitiveness (1 = *little*, 10 = *much*)

In this list, external risks involve factors outside of the performing organization such as market factors, regulatory factors, and the risk of working with a particular customer or benefiting organization (including the risks that the project is inappropriate for the customer's desired business objective). Internal risks involve the project team, the chosen technology, and other factors inside of the performing organization. These risks are itemized and analyzed later in the book. If a number of projects are being evaluated at one time, one can also use a forced ranking instead of a scale.

In older days, informal versions of this scoring and ranking were often called *murder boards* to eliminated projects from consideration which scored very low in one or more categories. Today, many organizations use modern group decision support software (groupware) to allow a number of stakeholders to come together in a virtual meeting room to score and rank projects. The groupware allows the stakeholders to voice opinions and to score each factor for each project in an anonymous manner. Many organizations today also have a project management office (PMO), which carries out project scoring and ranking directly or facilitates that process for stakeholders and/or line management. PMOs, managing multiple projects, and project portfolio management are discussed further in Chapter XVI.

Project Stage Gates

Project benefit analysis and scoring/ranking also needs to take place as a project proceeds as well as when a project is proposed. As a project proceeds, particularly for long projects, many factors may change, which could make this project less beneficial or make other projects more beneficial. Factors that may change include organizational factors, customer factors, or environmental factors. In Chapter II, project success factors were discussed and the dual stage gate notion was introduced (a dual gating process was shown in Figure 2.6). Management stage gates are place at regular time intervals (i.e., monthly or quarterly), and quality stage gates are placed at key delivery points for preliminary product manifestations (i.e., requirements documentation, use cases, paper prototypes, working prototypes, test results, etc.). There may be multiple quality stage gates within a management stage gate time interval, or vice versa.

The chosen project benefit metric(s) would be recalculated at each management stage gate using the earned value analysis (EVA) based estimate for the cost at completion; earned value is discussed in detail later in this book. The chosen benefit metrics might be any of those discussed previous such as IRR or scoring methods. It is important that these management reviews do not use sunk cost (how much has already been invested/spent) in determining whether a project should proceed or not; the only cost consideration should be the estimated cost at completion versus the benefit. Keeping a badly performing project alive by consideration of sunk cost is a trap into which many organizations have fallen.

In analyzing the chosen benefit metric(s), the satisfaction criteria needed would be those reported at the previous quality stage gate. Here the customer and other stakeholders have input into the decision as to whether a project should continue, be canceled, or be placed on hold. Canceling a project (as well as normal project close out) are discussed in detail later in the book. The customer's continued support for the project in terms of the overall benefit can be recalculated in light of the latest estimate for the total cost at

Figure 3.16. Stage gate evaluation

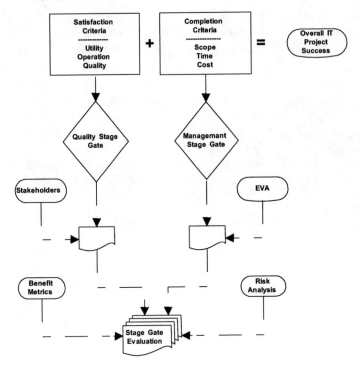

Figure 3.17. Stage Gate Review Form

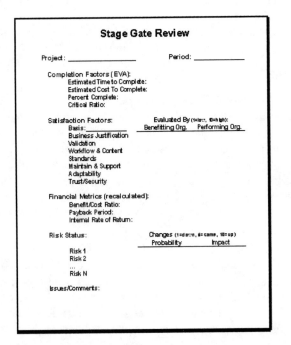

completion (EAC). Figure 3.16 illustrate this dual gating review process in regard to benefit metrics.

Figure 3.17 is an example of a stage gate review form. On this form the metrics from the earned value analysis as of a certain time period are recorded which indicate how the project is going from a progress and cost perspective. The next portion of the form concerns the satisfaction factors that are qualitatively evaluated by both the benefiting organization (typically users) and the performing organization (typically business analysts). The basis of the satisfaction scoring is also specified, which would be the last quality stage gate where a product manifestation was available, such as a prototype. Financial metrics are then recalculated based upon the current estimated cost to complete the project and the latest benefit projections. The risks that were identified and quantified at the start of the project are also reevaluated; risk analysis is covered in detail later in the book.

Chapter Summary

In this chapter, project initiation and the processes and documents involved with project evaluation from a business perspective were discussed and illustrated. Chapter VI continues with the life of a project after the organization has committed to perform said project. However, before getting to Chapter VI, Chapters IV and V discuss *project management* and *software engineering* from a disciplinary perspective, as these concepts and terms will be used throughout the remainder of this book.

References

Bayes, T. (1763). An essay towards solving a problem in the doctrine of change. In R. Price (Ed.), *Philosophical Translations of the Royal Society: Vol. 53* (p. 370). London, UK.

D'Antoni, H. (2005, February 28). Behind the numbers, tech investments take time to thrive. *Information Week.*

Stix, V. & Reiner, J. (2004, May). IT appraisal methods and methodologies—A critical literature review. *Proceedings of the IRMA (Information Resources Management Association) Conference*, New Orleans, LA.

Chapter IV

The Project Management Discipline

Those who cannot remember the past are condemned to repeat it.

(George Santayana)

Professional organizations that have developed around the world to foster the project management discipline (Morris, 2001) have recognized that a distinct skill set is necessary to ensure successful project managers, and these organizations are devoted to assisting their members develop, improve, and keep these skills current (Boyatzis, 1982; Caupin, Knopfel, & Morris, 1998). In this chapter, I discuss the methods, techniques, and standards that these organizations have formalized.

Project Management Organizations

The Project Management Institute (PMI) is the largest organization in the world devoted to project management. Other major international organizations include the Association for Project Management (APM), British Standard Institute (BSI), Engineering Advancement Association (ENAA) of Japan, Australian Institute of Project Management, and the International Project Management Association (IPMA). Each of these organizations has developed a set of project management standards as has the ISO (International Organization for Standards) with its ISO 10006 *Guide to Quality in Project Management*. These various project management standards can be compared using word size (Crawford, 2004):

PMBOK—56,000
APM BoK—13,000
IPMA ICB—10,000
ENAA P2M—36,000

The APM has developed a Body of Knowledge (BoK) of Project Management Competencies, which identifies 40 key competencies grouped as follows:

- *Project Management:* Covering the key elements that differentiate projects from general management
- *Organizations and People:* Detailing the main qualitative skills of a project manager
- *Techniques and Procedures:* Details the quantitative methods
- *General Management:* Covers industry specific concepts

The APM Body of Knowledge also provides a focal point for many of the programs run by the APM, including their Certification Programme, which assessing a person's competence in managing a project; the Course Accreditation Programme, which reviews training courses run by both commercial private training companies and higher education institutes; and the Project Management Capability Test, which assesses a person's knowledge in the APM Body of Knowledge.

The British Standards Institute publishes the *Guide to Project Management* (BS6079). This standard has been adopted by the British government and industry, and establishes commonly accepted terminology. The stated objectives of BS6079 are to provide guidance to

- General managers, to enable them to provide proper support for project managers and their teams;
- Project managers, to improve their ability to manage their projects;
- Project support staff, to help them understand project management issues and solutions; and
- Educators and trainers, to help them understand the project management environment and the context in which project management methods are deployed.

The International Project Management Association is a federation of national project management associations for several European countries. It publishes the IPMA Competency Baseline (ICB) in English, French, and German (it was first published in 1998). The content is similar to the APM BoK, but the organization is different and is termed the *Sunflower*. The IPMA encourages each national organization to form its own competency baselines, called "National Competency Baselines." There are now about 30 countries with NCBs throughout Europe, Egypt, India, and China.

The Engineering Advancement Association (ENAA) of Japan has also issued a project management body of knowledge: P2M (*A Guidebook of Project and Program Management for Enterprise Innovation*). Their PM standard is different from that of the PMI or APM, and is based on how project management can be used to increase business value for an organization and promote innovation. This P2M was a multiyear joint effort between the Japanese Project Management Forum (JPMF) and the Japanese Ministry of Economy, Trade and Industry (METI); it was supported by both the Japanese industry and government with a very significant contribution from academic research. The Japanese P2M is based on a tower structure. which, according to the Japanese Standard Committee, focuses on aligning project management to the business units (as opposed to the European and North American approach, which is dedicated to the management of a single project). The four areas of certification in the Japanese program are Objectives, Strategy, Value Management, and Finance.

Terminology, methodology, and, sometimes, concepts in project management. differ somewhat in these different organizations and in different parts of the world. In the United States, a concept may be commonly associated with a certain term and in other parts of the world a different term or terms may be used. Even within the United States, terms and concepts may differ in the federal agencies (i.e., NASA, DOD, etc.) versus the private sector. In this book we have tried to show alternative terms for the same concept and differing concepts used in similar ways.

Project Management Institute

The Project Management Institute (PMI) is the world's largest project management organization, with about 150,000 members in more than 125 countries. PMI has also established more than 200 local chapters around the world. The PMI Web site (www.pmi.org) records over 4 million visitors per year. Founded in 1969, PMI establishes project management standards, provides seminars and other vehicles for professional growth, promotes educational programs, funds and encourages research, and provides professional certification that many of the world's organizations desire for their project personnel. PMI produces a number of publications, including the *Project Management Journal, Project Management Quarterly, PM Network,* and *PMI Today.* This book will closely follow the PMI standards, however other and broader standards and concepts found in the other major project management organizations will also be included.

Project Management Body of Knowledge

PMI established its first body of knowledge in 1976, which around 1987 became *A Guide to the Project Management Body of Knowledge* (PMBOK; PMI, 2000). It was revised several times with major releases in 1996, 2000, and 2005; there are approximately 1.5 million copies of all PMBOK versions in circulation. The PMBOK embodies generally accepted best of practice procedures, methods, and general tools, which are derived by a structured consensus of its vast membership. The PMBOK an approved American National Standard (ANS) by the American National Standards Institute (ANSI). There is some overlap among project management best practices, general management practices, and practices specific to various fields, as illustrated in Figure 4.1.

The PMBOK's content is organized into processes, and each of the 37 key processes are defined as procedures that receive various input, produce various output, and use various methods (such as management techniques, mathematical techniques, statistical techniques, etc.), perhaps with the assistance of some general tools (typically, some type of software). These processes are shown pictorially in Figure 4.2.

These processes are grouped into five process groups that relate to how project work is managed:

1.   Initiation
2.   Planning
3.   Execution
4.   Control
5.   Closing

Figure 4.1. PMBOK components

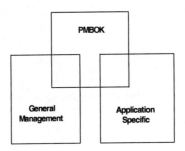

Figure 4.2. Process representation

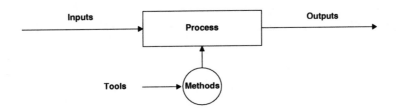

These processes are further subdivided into nine knowledge areas:

1. Integration Management [3 processes]
2. Scope Management [5 processes]
3. Time Management [5 processes]
4. Cost Management [4 processes]
5. Quality Management [3 processes]
6. Human Resource Management [3 processes]
7. Communication Management [4 processes]
8. Risk Management [4 processes]
9. Procurement Management [6 processes]

There are also overall project management activities The process groups are often called project management phases or stages, which are distinguished from project phases that are discussed later. Figure 4.3 shows the general sequencing of the process groups in the timeline for a project. In practice, however, there may be considerable overlap; that is, all initiation processes will not be complete before all the planning processes begin. Output from one process-group process will typically be the input to another process, either in the same process group or the next one in the sequence.

The overall organization of the PMBOK and the relationship among the processes, process groups, and knowledge areas is shown in Figure 4.4.

Large projects typically are broken down into phases, and the organization of those project phases is discipline specific and typically follows some type of methodology. Various types of IT methodology are detailed later in this book. Each project phase has a beginning and an end, and the five process groups are a part of each phase. Deliverables from one phase are typically inputs to the next phase; there may be phase overlap in some methodologies. Figure 4.5 shows how effort is generally distributed across project phases.

A typical phasing for very large IT projects might look like the following:

Figure 4.3. Process group interaction

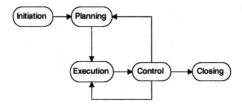

Figure 4.4. PMBOK process groups vs. knowledge areas

PMI Process Groups and Knowledge Areas					
	Initiation	**Planning**	**Executing**	**Controlling**	**Closing**
Integration		Project Plan Development	Project Plan Execution	Overall Change Control	
Scope	Initiation	Scope Planning	Scope Verification	Scope Change Control	Scope Verification
		Scope Definition			
Time		Activity Definition		Schedule Control	
		Activity Sequencing			
		Activity Duration Estimation			
		Schedule Development			
Cost		Resource Planning		Cost Control	
		Cost Estimating			
		Cost Budgeting			
Quality		Quality Planning	Quality Assurance	Quality Control	
Human Resources		Organizational Planning	Staff Acquisition	Team Development	
Communications		Communications Planning	Information Distribution	Performance Reporting	Administrative Closure
Risk	Risk Identification	Risk Identification		Risk Response Control	
		Risk Quantification			
		Risk Response Development			
Procurement		Procurement Planning	Solicitation	Contract Administration	Contract Closeout
		Solicitation Planning	Source Selection		
			Contract Administration		

Figure 4.5. Project phasing

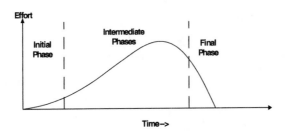

Feasibility, Proposal, Business Plan

Requirements Specification

Design

       Overall design

       External (user interaction) specifications

       Detail design

       "As designed" internal documentation

       Test plans

       Deployment and integration specifications

Implementation

       Coding

       Unit testing

       Module and Feature Testing

       User documentation

       "As built" internal documentation

Installation

       Conversion

       Training

       Network and site preparation

       Hardware install and integration

       Software install and integration

       Integration and acceptance testing

       Parallel operation

Operation and Maintenance (O & M)

As stated previously, in large phased projects the five process groups occur in each project phase, as is illustrated in Figure 4.6. For some industries and in some methodologies there may be overlap in project phases. IT may also have some project phase overlap,

Figure 4.6. Process groups in each phase

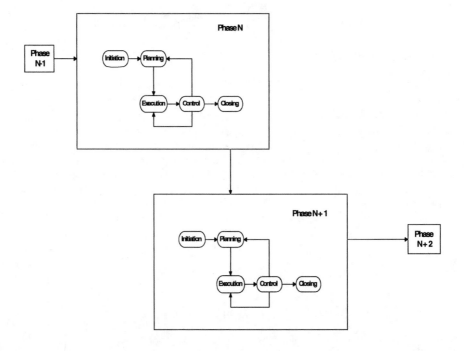

depending on the type of methodology adopted and the type of contracting arrangement; both of these aspects are discussed in more detail later in the book.

PMI's summarization of key activities by process group follow:

Key Initiation Activities

    Project feasibility (high-level ROI approximation)

    High-level planning

    Project charter document (memo, letter)

Key Planning Activities (order important)

    Develop scope statement

    Assemble project team

    Develop work breakdown structure (WBS)

    Finalize project team

    Do network type diagram (showing activity dependencies)

    Estimate cost and time, find the "critical path"

    Determine overall schedule and budget

    Procurement plan

    Quality plan

    Identify risks, quantify them, develop risk responses

    Other plans: change control plan, communications plan, management plan

    Overall project plan

    Project plan approval

    "Kickoff meeting"

Key Execution Activities

    Execute the project plan

    Complete work packets (activities)

    Information distribution

    Quality assurance

    Team development

    Scope verification

    Progress meetings

Key Control Activities

Overall change control

Performance reporting

Scope control

Quality control

Risk response control

Schedule control

Cost control

Manage by exception to the project plan

Key Closing Activities

Procurement audits and contract(s) close out

Product verification

Formal acceptance

Lessons learned documentation

Update all project records

Archive records

Release team

PMI established a certification program in 1984 for the project management discipline. The highest certification level is that of a PMP (project management professional). The requirements for an individual to be awarded that certification level include

- 4,500 hours of documented project management experience over 3-6 years
- BS/BA Degree and at least 35 contact hours in PM training
- Passing a very comprehensive 4 hour exam on the PMBOK
- Adherence to the PMI professional code of ethics

There are about 100,000 certified PMPs in the world. Those who have been granted PMP certification must demonstrate an ongoing professional commitment to the field of project management by satisfying PMI's Continuing Certification Requirements Program to retain their PMP status. In 1999, PMI became the first organization in the world to have its Certification Program attain International Organization for Standardization (ISO) 9001 recognition. The IPMA also has certification processes with four levels of certification: practitioner, professional, manager, and director. ENAA's P2M has three levels of certification: architect, manager, specialist (Crawford, 2004).

The PMP certification (or equivalent certification from another international organization) is now being required (or highly recommended) by many large corporations for one

Figure 4.7. Book contents and PMI process groups

PMI Process Group	Book Chapter
Initiation	III, V, VI
Planning	VI, VII, VIII, IX, X, XI, XII, XIII
Execution	XIII, IX, X, XI, XII, XIII, XVI
Controlling	XIV, XV, XVI
Closing	XI, XII, XVI

Figure 4.8. PMBOK and SDLC

PMBOK		SDLC	
Process Group	**Outputs**	**Stage**	**Outputs**
Initiation	Business Plan		
	Project Charter		
Plan	Overall Plan		
	Management Plan		
	Scope Statement	Definition	Project Plan:
			Communications Plan
			Change Management Plan
		Requirements	Requirements Document
	WBS Document		
	Network Diagram		
	Schedule		
	Resource Plan		
	Cost Plan		
	Procurement Plan		
	Quality Plan		
	Risk Plan		
Execute/Control	Performance Reports	Analysis	Overall Design Documents:
	Stage Gate Reviews		Use Cases
			Preliminary Users Manual
			Test Plan
		Design	Detail Design Documents:
			Menu/Navigation Design
			Screen Designs and Storyboards
			Report Designs
			Database Design
			Algorithms Design
			Prototypes
		Construction	Development Objects:
			Commented Code
			Test Scripts
			Help Screens
		Testing	Test Results Documents
			User Manual
			Training Material
		Installation	Install Documents
Closing	Project Close Out		
	Contract Close Out		
	Lessons Learned		

to become a project manager in their organization. Additionally many companies expect vendors to provide certified project managers for contracted work.

Chapter Summary

The formal discipline of project management was introduced and international organizations that foster the project management discipline were discussed. The PMI body of knowledge was illustrated (in later chapters the key processes and activities that are a part of each process group will be discussed in detail for IT projects). Figure 4.7 shows the chapters in which PMI process groups are covered.

In IT projects, there will be a correlation between the PMI process groups (and their outputs) and the chosen software engineering methodology (and its outputs). Chapter V discusses software engineering and IT methodologies; Figure 4.8 is an example of a correlation between PMI process groups and the classical software development life cycle (SDLC) of a single phase project.

References

Boyatzis, R. (1982). *The competent manager: A model for effective performance.* New York: Wiley.

Caupin, G., Knopfel, H., & Morris, P. (1998). *ICB IPMA competence baseline.* Zurich, Switzerland: International Project Management Association.

Crawford, L. (2004). Global body of project management knowledge and standards. In P. Morris & J. Pinto (Eds.), *The Wiley guide to managing projects.* Newton Square, PA: Wiley.

Morris, P. (2001, September). Updating the project management bodies of knowledge. *Project Management Journal.*

PMI. (2000). *The project management body of knowledge* (PMBOK). Newton Square, PA. ISBN 1-880410-22-2.

Chapter V

The Software Engineering Discipline

He who hurries cannot walk with dignity.

(Ancient Chinese saying)

Software engineering is vital for the proper planning of IT projects, although it is not a formal part of project management. The software engineering embedded in the acquired products will significantly affect long-term project success factors, even for IT projects that primarily involve software acquisition and integration instead of software development,. In this chapter I review software engineering and its relation to IT project management.

Software Engineering vs. Project Management

The project management and software engineering disciplines overlap considerably, as is illustrated in Figure 5.1. The Institute of Electrical and Electronics Engineers (IEEE) software standard 1490-2003 provides for the adoption of PMI Standard (PMBOK).

The IT industry has no one methodology, architecture, or set of standards; however, in other industries, there are typically established codes, frameworks, patterns, methods, and tools that are almost always used. For example, the home building industry has county building codes, frameworks for house patterns (ranch, colonial, Tudor, contemporary, etc.), subdivision guidelines and limitations, standard methods, and tools of the trades involved. The IT industry has a number of rapidly changing and evolving

Figure 5.1. Software engineering vs. project management

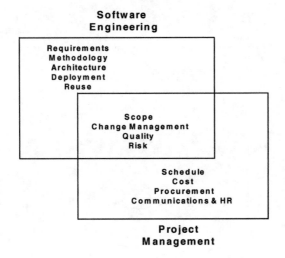

standards, frameworks, architectures, tools, and methodologies from which to choose. Therefore, before the project is planned in terms of breaking down and assigning to resources the scope/requirements, these other issues need to be addressed. Many of the problems in project management can be traced back to problems in methodology, architecture, reuse (lack of), and standards.

The term *software engineering* was coined by Bauer (1972) who was a principal organizer of the 1968 NATO conference on that subject. His definition of *software engineering* was "the establishment and use of sound engineering principles in order to economically obtain software that is reliable and works on real machines." The IEEE definition is "the application of a systematic, disciplined, quantifiable approach to the development, operation, and maintenance of software (IEEE Std 610-1990). The modern Webopaedia definition follows:

Software engineering is the computer science discipline concerned with developing large computer applications. Software engineering covers not only the technical aspects of building software systems, but also management issues, such as directing programming teams, scheduling, and budgeting.

Software Development Life Cycle Methodology

According to Webster's dictionary, *methodology* is "a system of methods." My definition for *methodology* is "organized know-how." The most common and established methodology used in building and/or integrating IT systems has been informally called the waterfall method and formally called the software development life cycle methodology (SDLC). This notion and term was first applied to IT systems by Royce (1970). The steps (illustrated in Figure 5.2) in this classical methodology are:

- Definition
- Specification (requirements)
- Design
- Construction (programming and unit testing)
- Testing (system and integration)
- Installation
- Operation and Maintenance

In theory these steps are not supposed to overlap or iterate. Some of the newer software methodologies are variations of or alternatives to the basic waterfall approach.

One hears many comments about the classical waterfall software development life cycle:

- The software development life cycle is the cornerstone of development!
- The life cycle is out of date!

Figure 5.2. SDLC waterfall

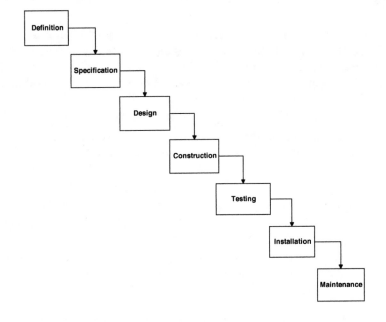

- Get good people and the life cycle will manage itself!
- There must be better and faster ways to build IT systems!

SDLC goals are to

- Do it right the first time!
- Meet customers' stated requirements!
- Have a timely completion!
- Complete within cost constraints!
- Build system with the necessary quality!

The *definition step* involves making a clear statement of goals, identifying why and how the proposed system will be better–cheaper–faster than the system it is replacing, and usually a overall/rough cost-benefit analysis. This phase is typified by frequent customer interaction, elimination of arbitrary constraints, negotiation and compromise on scope (features) versus time and cost, statement of assumptions, rough time and cost estimates, a rough project plan, and a signed go-ahead (i.e., the project charter).

The *specification step* involves a complete statement of scope (requirements), use case scenarios, preparation of preliminary user manual (external design specifications), detailed project plan (including work breakdown structure [WBS]), specification of needed resources, refined estimate of time and cost, refined cost-benefit analysis, and signed approval of requirements and user manual by stakeholders. However in practice the user's manual is rarely written at this stage. The reason the user's manual (or at least a draft) should be done at this step is so that some other dependent activities can begin, such as test planning and test scripts, making training plans and materials, and other dependent tasks, like internal or external marketing.

The *design step* involves resolution of critical technical issues, selection of architecture and platform(s), adoption of standards, assignment of staff, completion of external design (user interface design), design of critical data structure and database, internal design of algorithms and processes, Requirements Traceability Matrix, preliminary test script, final time and cost estimate, and a final cost-benefit analysis. Often the design step is divided into two steps; analysis (or overall design) and design (or detailed design).

The *construction step* involves the implementation of the design (i.e., via coding), unit testing, systems integration, draft internal documentation, and the completion of test scripts.

The *testing step* involves full scale integration and system testing, completion of user documentation, completion of training material, adoption of formal change control procedures, completion of the internal documentation, completion of installation manual and roll-out or phase-in plan. Testing is further discussed in Chapter X.

The *installation step* involves product roll-out, end-user training, producing lessons learned documentation, and defining procedures for handling operations, user support, and configuration management.

The *maintenance step* involves following and revising procedures for problem resolution and problem escalation, operations, backup and security, configuration control, and quality/performance monitoring.

At the end of each step there is usually a formal meeting in which a document is produced for the culmination of effort in that step. This document is reviewed by project management, the performing organization line management, and the benefiting organization (customer). If any of these stakeholders are not satisfied with the results of that step, the project can be terminated or the step repeated; the project will not proceed unless the stakeholders have given approval to move forward at each step. In theory this should result in a product that satisfies the initial requirements and the stakeholders. The following is what can, and often does, go wrong:

- User requirements are misunderstood, incomplete, not fully documented, or not fully implemented
- Requirements have changed
- Documentation is "unusable"
- System is difficult to use
- Training is ineffective
- Capacity or performance problems are present
- Audit and integrity problems are present
- "Bugs" and other quality issues are present
- Standards are not followed
- Estimation of workload is poor
- Project is managed poorly
- Budget is exceeded
- Not completed on time

These issues and others are discussed in detail in later chapters, along with the examination of root causes and remedies. Many in the field feel that the classical waterfall approach is too slow in today's fast-paced and rapidly changing world. Remember that only a small number of all IT projects result in fully working systems. Other projects are sent back for reconstruction, abandoned after delivery, or never completed. Therefore, how, *in general*, does one keep things from going wrong, even when a sound methodology is employed? These questions have to be answered:

- Are you committed to the methodology, or is it just words in a book gathering dust on the shelf?
- Do you have the ability to follow the methodology organizationally and with respect to resources?

- Does the methodology specify the things that need to be done?
- Do you measure via metrics or benchmarks things that have been done and done properly?

Under the Software Engineering Institute's (SEI) capability maturity model (CMM), which is detailed later in this chapter, these questions correspond to the "common features" of the maturity models:

- Commitment to Perform
- Ability to Perform
- Activities Performed
- Measurements and Analysis
- Verifying Implementation

Later chapters provide practical answers for the last three questions as they relate to specific project management and/or software engineering methods and tools. Figure 5.3 shows the IEEE/EIA Life Cycle Process definition as well as the definitions for support and organizational processes. (These processes are also covered in later chapters.)

Figure 5.3. IEEE/EIA life cycle process

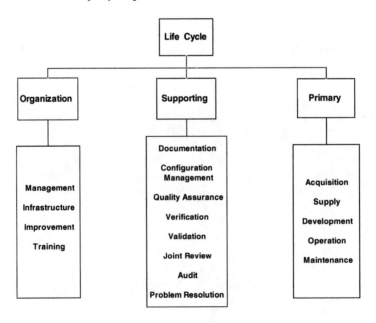

Management Stage Gates

The notion of stage gates can be traced back to phased project planning used decades ago by NASA for handling very large aerospace projects. These gates are attractive to management because they restrict investment in later stages until the anticipated return on investment is clarified and made more certain by earlier phases. Under this methodology, stages and gates divide the total effort into a series of consecutive stages, whereby gating criteria must be met before the project can move from one stage to the next. This is illustrated in Figure 5.4. The gating criteria involve the review of the defined outputs from the previous stage as well as metrics to justify that the project scope can still be completed within the time and budget constraints.

For IT projects, a traditional stage gate technique can be superimposed upon the chosen methodology. For example, combining the classical waterfall methodology with stage gates may result in the stage deliverables/outputs as shown in Figure 5.5.

At each stage gate, management would traditionally review the following:

- Defined output (stage deliverables)
- Completion status of activities
- Actual costs to date

Figure 5.4. Stage gates

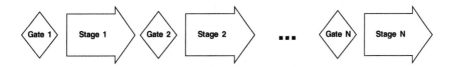

Figure 5.5. Stage gate outputs

Stage	Outputs
Definition	Project Plan
Requirements	Requirements Document
Analysis	Overal Design Documents:
	Use Cases
	Ext. Spec. (Prelim. Users Manual)
	Test Plan
Design	Detail Design Documents:
	Menu/Navigation Design
	Screen Designs
	Report Designs
	Database Design
	Algorithms Design
Construction	Development Objects:
	Code (incl. internal documantation)
	Test Scripts
	Help Screens
Testing	Test Results Documents
	User Manual
	Training Material
Installation	Install Documents

- Estimated cost at completion
- Estimated time to complete
- Updated risk analysis (i.e., the need for more or less reserves)

The stage gate technique can be used with any of the variations or alternatives to the classical waterfall discussed later in this chapter. For example, the stage gates can be set for each iteration if an iterative methodology is used. Another way to implement this approach is to set the gates at specific time periods, such as each month or each quarter.

This traditional stage gate process can slow down a project, however, due to the amount of review time at each gate. The events that comprise review time involves producing reports, sending reports to management, having management privately review reports, and then scheduling a public review meeting. Project cost is also higher due to the high cost of the people involved with a stage gate review. To overcome these disadvantages, a number of alternatives to the basic stage gate process have been proposed. These variations are called a number of names, such as fuzzy gates or exception gates, but the common goal is to have a process that is not slowed down by the gates, unless there is a significant problem.

As was discussed in earlier chapters, I suggest using a dual gating approach with a management stage gate at specific time periods (i.e., monthly or quarterly) wherein the earned value critical ratio is the dominant metric used for the go/no-go decision. This management gating technique is combined by a quality gating process, and there may be multiple quality gates within each management gate (or vice versa). The management gate focuses on the completion criteria and the quality gates address the satisfaction criteria. The quality gates review specific preliminary product manifestations in regard to the satisfaction factors of operation, utility, maintainability. A revised cost benefit analysis (based on latest earned value estimate at completion and revised benefit numbers) can also be included. *This combined gating process effectively and efficiently addresses all the project success factors discussed previously in this book.* Later chapters elaborate on earned value, quality management, metrics for all the success factors, and this type of gating process. Figure 5.6 illustrates this combined gating process and its relation to the project success criteria.

SDLC Variations and Alternatives

Because of the extensive and formal stakeholder review at the end of each step and the lack of overlap, the classical waterfall methodology can be slow in getting a software product to market. Also, the waterfall method becomes unstable if the initial requirements are significantly in error or change much. New technologies and global competition are quickly changing the business landscape, creating another problem. From the time a business problem is analyzed and a solution built, the "shape" of the original problem has changed significantly; thus, the developed solution no longer matches the original problem. This is illustrated in Figure 5.7. Project success rates show that large IT projects

Figure 5.6. Dual stage gates

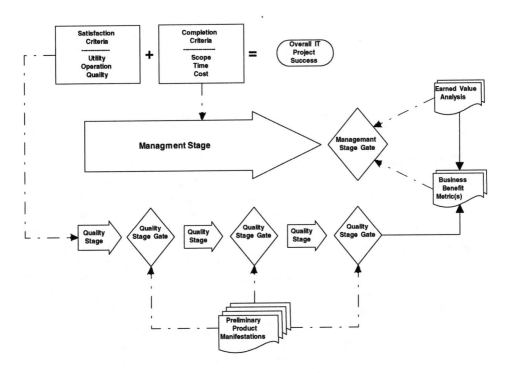

Figure 5.7. Changing shape of IT problems

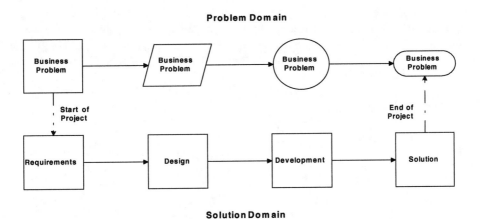

are getting harder to complete successfully (Standish Group, 2004). Projects over $10 million have success rates of only 2%, projects between $3 and $10 million have success rates from 23% to 11%, and projects under $3 million have success rates from 33% to 46%.

Because of these low success rates, a number of variations and alternatives have been suggested and tried, with varying degrees of success. Many of these approaches take large IT projects and break them down into smaller, more manageable pieces. However, there is no single silver bullet approach (Jones, 1994). Some of the software development life cycle methodology (SDLC) alternatives, to list a few, include Yourdon Structured Design, Ward/Mellor, Stradis, Spectrum, SDM/70, LBMS, Information Engineering, IBM AD/Cycle, Gane & Sarson Structured Analysis, DeMarco Structured Analysis, Anderson Method/1, Bachman, Agile and XP, and Clean Room. In this chapter, we will first discuss SDLC variations generically, and then discuss modern specific implementations.

The Overlap or Free-Flow Method allows any task to proceed as long as its dependent tasks are completed. Here the basic waterfall steps may have considerable overlap (this is illustrated in Figure 5.8). For example, even though the total-system design is not completed (or documented and approved), the implementation of those components whose design is completed may begin. This overlap is built into the dependency relationships in the work breakdown structure (WBS), which is discussed later in this book. One is betting that the total design (such as may be manifested in UML design drawings) will be approved. The concept is similar to optimistic record locking in an interactive database application. This technique works very well with the use of the dual stage gate approach of this book. This is also a good technique on contracts where incentives are available for early completion. Obviously risks are greater with larger projects and for projects where requirements can change significantly.

Evolutionary Development begins with only the user requirements that are very well understood and builds a first version. Often that first version is just a prototype. Analysis, design, implementation, and testing are done in a free flow overlapping manner without any formal review of documents. This first version is then taken back to the customer for review and definition of further requirements. Next the second version is built, and then taken back to the customer. This process continues until the customer is satisfied with a version and no further extensions are required. (This is illustrated in Figure 5.9.) Documentation, training, acceptance testing and other project completion activities are done at that point at which all (or most) of the customer's requirements have

Figure 5.8. Overlap method

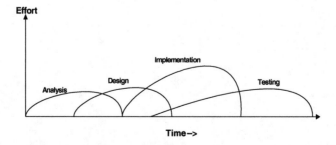

Figure 5.9. Evolutionary development

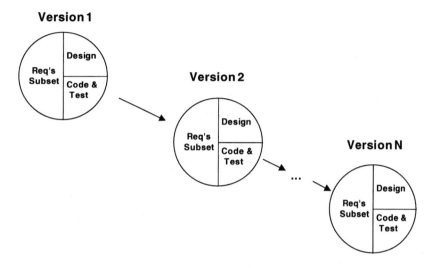

finally been included. This methodology is much faster than a waterfall approach and also somewhat quicker than the free-flow method. However, management visibility may be limited because little intermediate documentation is produced. Also, in a contracted environment (external or internal), a fixed price contract could not be used since the overall scope is not initially determined and priced. For a contracting environment, either a cost plus or time and material contract would have to be used. Contracting and procurement are discussed in a later chapter of this book. Also, internal design is often poor for evolutionary development because the entire scope is not visible from the beginning, and continually changing a system leads to a design that is less adaptable and harder to maintain. If the system is designed and built in a fully object-oriented manner, this problem may be minimized; object-oriented design is discussed later in this chapter.

Incremental Development begins with a determination of all the requirements, but only in a rough outline form. Next, those requirements are prioritized normally based upon those features that are most important from a business perspective. Because time is spent up front looking at all requirements a more appropriate overall platform, architecture, and design can be selected. This is particularly important for security requirements, because security cannot be an afterthought. Good security has to be built into the total product (and the methodology of constructing it), not bolted on afterwards.

After the initial requirements phase, development proceeds as in the evolutionary method. (This is illustrated in Figure 5.10.) Each increment typically represents a product portion that can be placed into service. Incremental development is not as quick as evolutionary development, but attempts to avoid the design problems caused by not knowing all the major requirements initially. However it suffers from the same contract type issues as the evolutionary method. Another potential problem is that the increments are based on the priorities of the requirements, and sometimes priorities may significantly

Figure 5.10. Incremental development

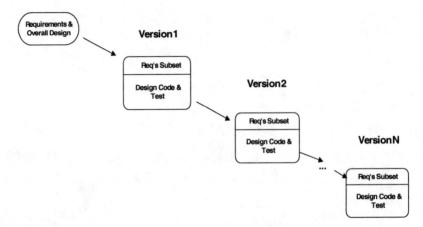

change during the time of developing the increments. Both the Rational Unified Process and Extreme Programming as well as several other new methodologies use this technique and these are discussed later in this chapter.

Bounding Box Development is similar to incremental development, except that each increment is not based on a certain scope (requirements subset) but is instead based on a measure of effort. If the effort put into an increment is constrained by calendar time then the term *timebox* is commonly used. (This is illustrated in Figure 5.11.) For contracted development (external or internal), the increments are usually based on a dollar (budget) amount. Thus this method does not have the contracting disadvantage that evolutionary or iterative methods have, but customers must be willing to contract for portions of the total system. However, because the amount of scope that will actually be completed in each increment is not known, each increment may not represent a product portion that can be placed into service.

Figure 5.11. Bounding box development

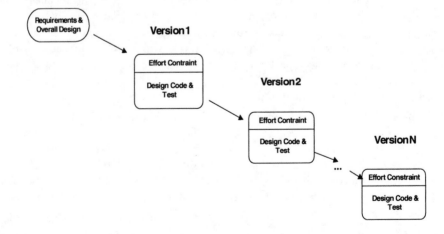

There is no one best methodology. An organization must select the methodology that is most appropriate for the type and size of the IT project at hand, the nature of the customer and stakeholders, the contracting environment, and the resources involved, both people and financial. Combinations of these methodologies can also be used such as in the Rational Unified Process which combines incremental and free-flow techniques. Figure 5.12 shows the primary advantage and disadvantage of each of the methodologies.

Development Acceleration

In addition to modifications of the basic SDLC, a number of other philosophies, methods, and tools have been proposed and tried, to compress all or certain steps in the SDLC.

Rapid Application Development (RAD) is a generic term for software development methods and tools that speed up the development process. It was commonly applied to products that automatically generated code to create user interface screens both of the character type and graphical type (GUI) starting in the 1990s. Products such as Clarion, FoxPro, Visual Basic, and PowerBuilder are examples of this era. Often these products also featured automatic report generation capabilities, and some products were devoted to this aspect such as Crystal Reports. So-called fourth-generation languages, such as Natural, were also part of this RAD landscape. Many RAD products were combined with databases such as Microsoft Access, and other RAD products could interface to stand-alone database products. Earlier RAD products built stand-alone PC applications or multiuser PC applications via LAN (local area network) file redirection (mapped drives). Later RAD products used SQL (structured query language) to create true client-server applications; however, almost all of these still required client machine configuration such as mapping drives, client installation of drivers, or other middleware. These RAD products did speed up considerably the implementation step for smaller applications, but they did not accelerate other development steps: requirements, analysis, design, and testing. For larger or more complex systems, automatic code generation is not powerful or flexible enough to meet application needs and programmers usually have to resort to traditional hand coding. Today, modern IDEs (integrated development environments), such as Dreamweaver, NetBeans, Eclipse, and Visual Studio, contain features including WYSIWYG (what you see is what you get), drop and drag screen generators, and

Figure 5.12. Methodology comparison

Method	Advantage	Disadvantage	Best For
Waterfall	Sound Development, High Quality	Slowest Method	Fixed Price Contract
Free-Flow	Faster Development	Risky for Unstable Requirements	Incentive Contracts
Evolutionary	Quick Development for Small Applications	Design Problems	Smaller Systems
Incremental	Quick Production of Partial Products	Contract Issues	Rapid Phased Deployment
Bounding Box	Quicker Development within Budget	Partial Products Uncertain	Budget Bound Organization

including, possibly producing, thin client Web applications, which do not require any client–machine configuration changes. *It is often said that RAD products speed up the easy part of the development; however, RAD products are very useful in creating prototypes and are particularly useful in incremental types of development methods.* RAD tools are constantly evolving with the fast-changing IT landscape, and RAD tool vendors are constantly being acquired by other IT vendors. Therefore, if one develops a product today, using a particular RAD tool, that tool may be obsolete or be in the hands of a different vendor tomorrow (with little or no remaining support).

CASE (computer aided software automation) refers to computer software systems that generally support several steps in the development process, usually including requirements, analysis, design, and possibly other steps such as coding, testing, documentation, and version control. Most CASE products are primarily geared towards the development of business software systems and central themes are a data dictionary and various design drawing and associated repositories. There are different types of CASE products, and these products can be classified in a number of ways. Some products support one particular methodology and others can support several methodologies; some support one particular computer language and some may support several languages. Some CASE products are called horizontal tools or workbenches or environments, and they provide integrated tools for the support of multiple development steps. A modern CASE environment consists of a number of tools operating on a common hardware and software platform; these tools may be from one or multiple vendors. This CASE environment also supports a number of different types of users: project managers, designers, programmers, database administrators, testers, technical writers, and so forth. The CASE environment is distinguished from a random tool set in that the environment facilitates the integration of those tools so that they can work together coherently without duplicating effort or information.

Today there are hundreds of CASE tools available, and perhaps many in each of the aforementioned categories. Commercial products include such names as Amadeus, Continuous, InConcert, Life*Flow, MATE, Process Continuum, Process Engineer, ProcessWeaver, ProcessWise, ProSLCSE Vision, and SynerVision. Although these products have provided significant development accelerations (up to 50% in some cases), *one must be careful not to let CASE replace a sound methodology, or all you will accomplish is to build the wrong system even faster.*

Prototyping involves creating a scaled-down model of the product to be built. The scaled-down model is usually live, in that it is implemented in software and has some degree of functionality; however, it may be only on paper (paper prototype). A prototype is not fully tested, does not implement all features/requirements, and typically does not address tasks/issues as database interaction, concurrency, transaction boundaries, scalability, security, recoverability, maintainability, reusability, and so forth. Speed and capacity are not issues here unless the prototype is specifically built to test those characteristics. Prototypes should be easily modifiable to explore different layouts, navigations, and behaviors; thus, today's prototypes are usually built with RAD/IDE type products. They can often serve as an external design for portions of the final system. The purposes of prototypes are to demonstrate feasibility, evaluate alternatives, clarify and flush out user requirements, and evaluate "user friendliness" and other qualitative aspects.

However, there are dangers in using prototypes. Often, a prototype can assume a life of its own. Sometimes when managers or customers see the prototype, they think that the product is close to being ready; they are not aware that the prototype is grossly scaled down and that some of the most difficult and time-consuming parts of the product are not in the prototype. *Despite these dangers, this author thinks that prototyping is a vital part of modern application development independent of whatever overall methodology is utilized.*

Paper prototypes, or *storyboards*, have many of the same advantages of live prototypes, but they do not have the aforementioned disadvantages of live prototypes, and they can be produced and modified quicker and cheaper. Paper prototypes can be constructed with paper and pencil, simple drawing programs, presentation software, or RAD products. The television and motion picture industry have used story boards for decades, but use in IT was minimal until the advent of Web applications. Storyboards essentially walk the user through the interaction between the end users and the system, and visually show that interaction through screen mock-ups of both input and output screens. After basic requirements are gathered and perhaps represented with use cases, storyboarding is the next logical step in clarifying or detailing those requirements and flushing out added requirements. Each interaction in a use case diagram could be simulated via a storyboard.

For example in the case of building modern Web-based applications, storyboards and simple user interface prototypes can be easily constructed with RAD products, like Dreamweaver. Even if the final Web product is going to use a Web server API (application programming interface), the tags and scripts (JSP, PHP, Cold Fusion, or ASP) can be added directly to the prototype HTML/XML/JavaScript code.

Joint application design (JAD) was formulated by IBM personnel in the late 1970s. In 1980, IBM Canada held several workshops to demonstrate the concept, and later in the 1980s, JAD was utilized in a number of companies. IBM defined JAD as an "interactive systems design concept involving discussion groups in a workshop setting." The purpose of JAD was to bring together developers and users in a structured environment for the purpose of obtaining quality user requirements. They believed this structured approach provided a better alternative to traditional serial interviews by analysts of the performing organization. The prime advantage of JAD is a reduction in the time it takes to complete a project. It improves the quality of the final product by focusing on the initial portion of the SDLC thus reducing the likelihood of errors that are expensive to find and correct later on.

JAD takes place in a structured workshop session. Representatives from the performing and benefiting organization meet in a room and discuss preset issues. Everyone gets a chance to speak, and questions are answered immediately—there is no telephone tag or waiting for memos or e-mails to recycle. JAD also seeks to eliminate the problems with traditional meetings by turning them into organized workshops, with facilitators, visual aids, agendas, deliverables, and feedback.

As JAD was used more in the 1990s, the term was broadened to include more collaborative efforts between the benefiting and performing organizations, including conflict management, brainstorming sessions, and motivational meetings. Sometimes the sessions were more like technical workshops, where participants focused on needs analysis and applied software tools in the process of gathering business requirements. Sometimes these sessions used RAD and CASE tools, and JAD usage expanded to functions other than the requirement gathering step in the software development life cycle.

Today, JAD is used in many steps of SDLC and is often defined as a system development methodology. In 20th century, JAD brought users and developers together in the same physical location, but today JAD is often held via virtual meetings. JAD meetings must be structured, and some guidelines include the following (Dennis, 1999):

- Have management support
- Use experienced facilitators
- Get the right people to participate and set their roles
- Set clear session objectives and deliverables
- Have a detailed agenda and stick with it
- Produce deliverables shortly after the session

I feel that clear and complete communication between the performing and benefiting organization is vital to the success of IT projects. JAD offers a valuable technique for effective communication particularly in requirements gathering. One must be careful to follow the above guidelines or these sessions may just waste more of everyone's time in meetings. There are also certain types of customers where access to customer personnel is very limited. *JAD sessions combined with review of prototypes are excellent way to solidify requirements early in a project.*

Modern SDLC Implementations

The Rational unified process (RUP) is based upon both the incremental methodology and the free-flow methodology discussed earlier. Instead of attempting to address all of a project's requirements, RUP produces software iteratively that addresses a compromised but known feature set and evolves the project over time (Jacobson, 1999; Kruchten, 1998). The difference between evolutionary methods and RUP, though, is that one identifies the requirements for the entire system, but only details the top 20% or so of architecturally significant cases during a single increment. This enables the determination of an appropriate architecture and design which will accommodate the remaining 80% of the requirements without compromising the integrity and quality of the total system. This is particularly important for security requirements, and a plug-in to the standard RUP, called CLASP (Comprehensive Lightweight Application Security Process), is available which, provides a structured way to address security issues in the software development process.

RUP specifies different roles for project participants. Before an architect ever gets involved, an analyst is building use cases and evaluating and prioritizing them with the customer. Before the coders begin implementation, architects work with analysts to identify the architecture which best satisfies requirements and constraints. UML tools are used to build a consistent model from requirements to detail design. RUP uses the free-flow methodology also in that there is considerable overlap in activities of different roles.

RUP is a phased approach that defines four distinct phases:

- *Inception:* Understanding the need, understanding the proposed system to address the need, making the business case for the proposed solution
- *Elaboration:* Selecting the architecture and developing the project plan
- *Construction:* Design, coding, integrating, and testing
- *Transition:* Installing the product on the target platform(s) and getting the user take ownership of the system

The key to RUP is iteration, both within each of the aforementioned phases and within the incremental production of version. Each iteration within a phase ends in a deliverable, and each increment results in a working product version. RUP defines static workflows, core workflows (business models, requirements, analysis/design, testing, deployment) and support workflows (change management, project management, environment and tools). However each of these static workflows is not associated with any one phase, and some degree of each type of workflow goes on within each phase.

The transition from phase to phase is not separated by a stage gate, and management control is not done by placing dates upon the phase boundaries. Management control is only done upon iterations. The project plan contains a list of proposed iterations (which is likely to change), and each iteration has an estimate (which is also likely to change). The proposed iterations are not assigned due dates, but decision points are set up in time (usually based upon weeks). At each decision point, a decision is made in regard to adding/removing resources, adding/removing iterations form the next release (version) of the product, or killing/holding the project. These decisions are based upon progress, cost, and/or earned value metrics. Thus a key part of the project plan is how risks will be managed; it is a plan of contingencies, as opposed to just a plan of activities. *RUP is not suitable for all IT projects. It is complex and difficult to quantify in a contracting arrangement. However for internal projects that are large and risky, and where quick deployment of partial products is necessary, it may be an appropriate choice.*

Agile programming (AP) is a name given to a growing number of lightweight methodologies with names like Crystal (Cockburn, 2001), Scrum (Schwaber, 2001), Adaptive (Highsmith, 2000), Feature-Driven Development (Palmer, 2002), Dynamic Systems Development Method (DSDM; Stapleton, 1997), and Extreme Programming (Beck, 1999). During the 1990s, there was such a need to quickly build new IT systems to take advantage of new technologies like Web applications and e-commerce, as well as the need to address the Y2K problem, that IT organizations began exploring these lightweight techniques. Lightweight methodologies do away with much of the SDLC process overhead that slow down developers, such as detailed formal requirements definitions and extensive documentation. Some feel that these new development approaches are based on the premise that if you hire competent programmers who always know what they are doing, then any problems they encounter are organizational and communications ones; and those are what the agile approach focuses on.

Although the various agile methods differ, they have some things in common. Most use an incremental free-flow approach, as does RUP. The common intent is to be agile, so one should embrace change and produce software that is adaptable; thus, most of these methods call for the use of object-oriented languages. Another common feature is a lot of contact time with users. Still another key focus is a focus on people, not processes, thus emphasizing team morale building. Most AP methods have some core principles, including the following:

- Use a simple design (the old military KISS principle)
- Design as you go, and keep refactoring the code
- Take small, incremental steps (when changing or adding code, take the smallest step possible, then test again)
- Stick to one task at a time (do not add code to accomplish two things at the same time)
- Use IDE and RAD tools
- Use only the techniques that really work for you

These methods may seem basic and obvious to many developers, but I know many programmers who never followed any of these principles. Some programmers, instead of modifying a module or class for a small change or addition, will spend a great deal of time writing the entire module from scratch. The advantages of these AP principles include the following:

- Faster reaction to changes in requirements
- Overall simplicity of the design
- Earlier coding is possible
- By refactoring the code, the most important parts get the most attention (no time invested in changing what does not need to be changed)
- Code in progress is always stable

Refactoring, one of the core development concepts, is a new word for cleaning up the code. More formally, refactoring improves the design and maintainability of code in small incremental steps confined to areas of current interest. One problem with refactoring, however, is that, when a programmer comes under pressure to finish quickly, he or she may not complete the refactoring work.

AP is relatively new, so the success and applicability of these methods is unclear. It is felt that AP is suitable for small projects and small teams; whether it has practical application for larger environments is still in question.

Extreme programming (XP) is a software development approach initially created for small teams on risk-prone projects with unstable requirements (Beck, 1999). Kent Beck, a programmer and project leader, developed XP while working on a long-term project to rewrite Chrysler's payroll application. XP is a form of AP based on a lightweight methodology. XP however, differs from most other agile approaches by being much more prescriptive. Like AP, XP is an incremental method with free-flow. XP advocates say the methodology (creating user scenarios and performing upfront feature testing) allows them to develop and deliver code more quickly with fewer bugs. XP is built around rapid iterations, an emphasis on code writing, and working closely with end users. The 12 basic practices of XP are:

1. Customers define requirements via use case scenarios ("stories")
2. Early on, teams release small increments into production
3. Teams use standard names and descriptions
4. Simple object-oriented coding is used
5. Designers write automated unit test scripts before coding
6. Refactoring is used extensively
7. Programmers work in pairs
8. Programmers have collective ownership of all code
9. Teams integrate and check code back into repositories frequently (no longer than 1 day)
10. Developers work only 40-hour weeks
11. User representative(s) remain on site
12. Programmers follow strict coding standards

Although XP in different forms has been used for a few years, many IT organizations have been reluctant to try it. A major issue is that some XP principles contradict longstanding IT policies. For example, XP specifies pair programming, in which two programmers sit side by side, working at a single workstation. Pair programming seems inefficient, but studies have shown that it is no less efficient that traditional programming and usually results in fewer code defects (Williams, 2000). Fewer defects eventually means quicker delivery. However, not all programmers want or are suited for pair programming. Very good programmers should not be encumbered with a sidekick. Many programmers like solitude—that is one of the reasons they choose to work as programmers. Often, programmers consider themselves masters of the trade, and two masters often cause conflicts.

Another problem with XP (like all AP) is its application in contract environments, and still another problematic issue for XP is that all code is generally open for programming pairs to review and alter. This can open up the team to integrity and security issues. As was mentioned previously in this book, internal security is becoming a prime concern for IT organizations, for internally developed code and, particularly, for outsourced programming. Further XP does not address downstream SDLC issues such as training and user documentation.

XP requires the benefiting organization to take a very active role in the development process, even to the extent that users are asked to write tests that will prove that requested functions work properly before they are coded (e.g., customers may write needed scenarios or features—one scenario per card—on index cards. Using index cards is far cheaper and faster than writing, editing, and reviewing a large formal requirements document.). Then, the developers estimate the time needed to build that feature, and, based on the estimates, the customer prioritizes the features. Next, the customer writes the test, and the developers write code that will successfully pass the test. Testing is normally automated, and test harnesses organize test scripts that related to particular functional areas. However, because testing is limited to "acceptance" type testing, full multilevel testing is seldom performed. This may lead to problems with unanticipated inputs, scalability problems, and security problems. This is discussed further in Chapter X.

Because XP requires constant communication between the benefiting and performing organizations (as well as among the developers), and because communication time and traffic increases in proportion to the square of the number of communicating parties, XP is not suited to large teams (Beck, 1999, advises limiting project teams to no more than 12 developers, working in pairs). As with JAD and AP methods in general, a customer may not be able to commit his or her resources to that much involvement.

Thus, XP has a number of specific advantages and a number of specific disadvantages. This is a hot debate topic in the IT world. On the one hand it is thought of as a great breakthrough, and on the other it is akin to "letting the inmates run the institution." XP is not for all IT organizations.

Cleanroom software development (CSD) as a process was developed by Harlan Mills (Mills, 1996) and involves the application of formal specification to software design. CSD can use any of the methodologies previously discussed, but the incremental approach is most often used. Requirements are turned into formal (sometimes mathematical) specifications (Prowell, 1999). These formal specifications are then turned into the final code through a series of correctness–preserving transformations. "Cleanroom treats software as a set of communicating state machines that separate behavior and implementation concerns" (Garbett, 2003). The code is statically checked via rigorous inspections, then system testing is done using statistical techniques. The testing team must be in a separate organization from the developing team. The Cleanroom Reference Model may be obtained online at the Software Engineering Institute (www.sei.cmu.edu/publications/documents/). Research results indicated that CSD produces code with fewer defects (less than 1 bug per KLOC) at no greater cost than traditional methods (4 to 50 bugs per KLOC; Linger, 1994). *However, CSD requires high-level experienced analysts and programmers. For that reason, CSD is best applied to mission-critical and/or life-critical types of systems that are built internally by expert programmers.*

Component-based software engineering (CBSE) is a development philosophy that utilizes existing software modules to build application systems. Any of the aforementioned methodologies may be utilized, but the requirements specification stage here may be longer due to the preparation of procurement documentation. CBSE is a formalized system of reuse at a high level, formalized in the sense of a business approach rather than at the software architecture level. Later in this chapter, reuse is discussed in more detail in regard to software architecture. CBSE is based on having a cadre of reusable modules or programs and some framework for integrating these modules. "IS shops that institute component-based software development reduce failure, embrace efficiency and augment the bottom line" (Williamson, 1997). CBSE can be applied at several levels of granularity. At the highest level is the COTS (Commercial Off-the-Shelf Software) approach, whereby commercial programs are purchased and integrated through a data exchange mechanism. Software acquisition is discussed in Chapter XII.

Web services is a recently evolving approach to CBSE using the Internet. Using this approach, different services are provided by different vendors in real time on their servers, generally at a per usage price. This new computing architecture is formally called SOA, or service oriented Architectures (Hall, 2003). Web services are based upon modern open standards; unfortunately some of these standards (SOAP, WSDL, UDDI, etc.) do not have adequate security built into them yet. Web services architecture uses SOAP (simple object access protocol) as a lightweight remote method invocation process. Older. more complex protocols for distributed object services are Microsoft's DCOM (distributed component object model), Java's RMI (Remote Method Invocation), and OMG's CORBA (Common Object Request Broker Architecture); RMI and CORBA are more secure than SOAP. Central repositories (registries) catalog which services are available and where. using the UDDI (Universal Description Discovery and Integration) protocol. Providers list the usage specifications of their services via the WSDL (Web Services Description Language) protocol. Web service applications can be created in a number of languages. with most written in Java, PHP, or Visual Basic-Net. Some think that the "service-oriented architecture" may become the core paradigm for software applications and integration (Eisenberg, 2004).

The advantages of the CBSE approach are speed of assembly and short-term cost. The disadvantages are that no strategic advantage is derived from the resulting product (nothing is proprietary, anyone can do it), compromise of requirements to meet capabilities of available components, vendor dependencies, possible performance issues, and security problems.

Object-Oriented Software

Object-oriented (OO) programming is a key part of many of the methodologies previously discussed, such as RUP, AP, XP, and CSD. Charles Darwin (1859) postulated that it was not the biggest, smartest, or fastest species that would survive, but the most adaptable. The same is true for application software. Applications must evolve, even before they are completely developed, because the environment under which they operate (business, regulatory, social, political, technical, etc.) changes during the time the software is designed and implemented (see Figure 5.7). In addition, there is the ever-present requirements creep, and even after the application is successfully deployed, there is a constant need for change. Conceptually, the concept of adaptable software is illustrated in Figure 5.13 (as compared to Figure 5.7).

Object-oriented software systems are inherently more adaptable and maintainable than traditional procedural software, and OO systems foster software reuse. "Object technology promises a way to deliver cost-effective, high quality and flexible systems on time to the customer" (McClure, 1996). In fact, out of all the aforementioned methodology variations and development acceleration techniques, OO is the only technique proven to be almost always effective in reducing *long-term* software development costs.

Modern OO design methods and programming languages are based on the concept of a class, which is a type of thing. Once a class is defined, it serves as a mold for making specific objects (instances) of that type. We could, for example, design a class for a student which would indicate the data properties (attributes) and functionality (methods) that is attributable to each specific student object. This is illustrated in Figure 5.14. Here we have defined a Rectangle class that has two properties: length and width, and

Figure 5.13. Software adapting to problem changes

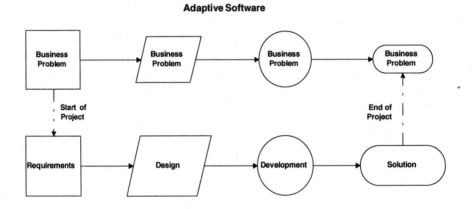

Figure 5.14. Class instances (objects)

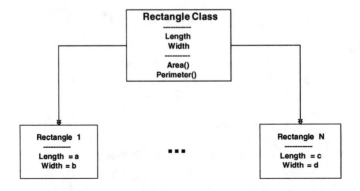

also two methods: Area and Rectangle. Every instance of a Rectangle (each object) will have specific values for length and width.

OO classes have a property called encapsulation, which is a way to protect the properties from unauthorized access from other code (functions) in a software system. This is illustrated in Figure 5.15, in which the width and length data is protected. To find the value for one of an object's properties, a "get" method must be used, and to change the value of an object's properties, a set method must be used. These methods can be coded with whatever access protection is necessary.

Figure 5.16 uses an UML (unified modeling language) diagram to show the main relationships involved in OO analysis, design, and programming. As well as the classification relationship (an object is classified as being an instance of a class), there are composition and inheritance relationships. An object can be composed (physically or logically) of other objects, and this composition is also a part of the class definition.

Figure 5.17 illustrates the inheritance relationship. Here we have introduced another class, Positioned Rectangle, which inherits from (is derived from) the Rectangle class. The Rectangle is called the base or super class, and the Positioned Rectangle is called the derived or subclass. A derived class has the same properties and methods as were defined in the base class, but more properties and methods can be included. In this example, the Positioned Rectangle adds two more properties and one more method.

Polymorphism is another property of OO systems, wherein a derived class can alter the behavior (code inside) of a method of the base class with the same name (signature: name and arguments). For some OO languages, the actual mechanisms involve more complex

Figure 5.15. Encapsulation

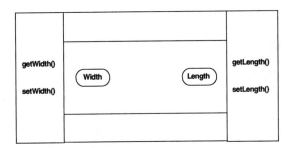

Figure 5.16. Object-oriented relationships

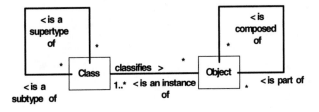

Figure 5.17. Class-based inheritance

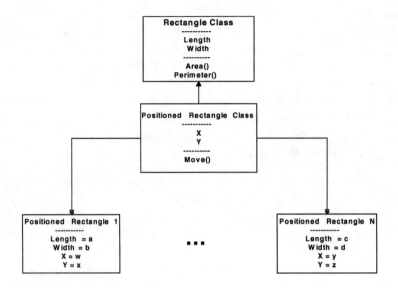

Figure 5.18. Polymorphism

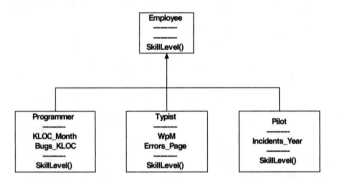

notions, such as virtual functions and/or late/early binding. This is illustrated in Figure 5.18, in which the skill-level function (e.g., which might return the skill level as an integer) has a different meaning in each of the three subclasses of Employee. The code in the skill-level function would be different in each of the three sub classes and presumably use the properties which could also be different in each subclass.

As an example of the power of OO systems in contrast to non-OO systems, consider the code for a payroll system. In this system, there are three types of employees: salaried, hourly, and commission based. So we would have three subclasses of Employee, each with its own version of the Pay function. This is illustrated in Figure 5.19.

Figure 5.19. Subtypes of employees

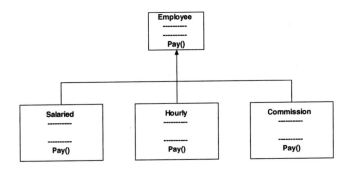

To perform the payroll operation in an OO system, we would walk through our database or data structure of employees and invoke the Pay function in each instance. In a non-OO system, we cannot use the same function name with different code therein, so in such a traditional non-OO language, we would have to use conditional code such as if, go-to, or switch/case constructs. We would need to say something like, If the employee were salaried, then invoke the salary-pay function. If the employee were hourly, then invoke the hourly-pay function. If the employee were commissioned, then invoke the comm-pay function. This may not seem important, but consider the evolution and maintenance problems.

Payroll may be just one of the operations in a huge human resources system of hundreds of thousand of lines of code. Many of the operations therein have conditional code, because the nature of the operation is different depending upon the type of employee. That particular conditional code is implemented within the operations, and conditional code is spread throughout the system. To make a change to the logic, you must first find all the conditional constructs that need to be changed. In an OO system, we just change the method in question in each class.

Now suppose we need to add another type of employee, one that is a piece-work laborer. With a non-OO system, we would have to go to possibly every conditional construct and add another case. Of course, we first have to find each one. With an OO system, all we have to do is add another class. OO systems are also safely modifiable, because when we add that additional class we are not involved with the other code in the system. In the non-OO systems, we have to examine and possibly modify much of the code in the system, and chances are (40%) that we are going to create a problem elsewhere while trying to solve the original problem.

SIMULA was the first object-oriented language (SIMULA I was developed in 1962-1965, and SIMULA 67 was developed in 1967). It was based somewhat on the ALGOL 60 programming language, and it introduced most of the key modern concepts of object-oriented programming, including objects, classes, subclasses, and inheritance. SIMULA was developed at the Norwegian Computing Center by Ole-Johan Dahl and Kristen Nygaard, and it quickly got a reputation as a simulation programming language. Later, it was found to possess interesting properties as a general programming language when the inheritance mechanism was used. In 1968, Edsger Dijkstra wrote his famous letter titled GO TO Statement Considered Harmful, and this letter was perhaps the first stone cast in the battle against spaghetti code. SIMULA compilers were developed for UNIVAC, IBM, Control Data, Burroughs, DEC and other computers throughout the 1970s.

SIMULA is still used around the world, but its main impact was the introduction of the modern OO programming principles. Alan Kay in 1970 was the person to coin the terms *object oriented* and *object-oriented programming*. His group at Xerox PARC (Palo Alto Research Group) used SIMULA as a platform for their development of Smalltalk (initially developed around 1973), extending object-oriented programming by the integration of graphical user interfaces and interactive program execution. In 1975, Marvin Minsky introduced frames in artificial intelligence (AI) programming, which were an ancestor to modern objects implemented later in languages such as C++. Brian W. Kernighan and Dennis M. Ritchie published *The C Programming Language* in 1978, after years of development. Although not object-oriented itself, C heavily influenced and formed the basic syntax and structure of most modern OO programming languages, such as C++, Java, C#, and PHP.

In the 1980s, at Bell Labs, Bjarne Stroustrup started his development of C++ (originally called "C with classes") by bringing the key concepts of SIMULA into the C programming language. In the 1980s, considerable resources were invested in the ADA language by the U.S. Department of Defense and in PROLOG via the Japanese Fifth Generation Computer Project. ADA had some basic OO capabilities and extended the Pascal language with strong typing, which reduced the occurrence of many types of programming errors. Many computer experts initially believed that ADA, PROLOG, and Smalltalk (with its Xerox and IBM backing) would fight for dominance in the 1990s, but as object-oriented programming became the dominant style for implementing complex programs with large numbers of interacting components (such as in GUI class libraries), more capable and flexible languages as C++ raced to the forefront. In 1989 the Object Management Group (OMG) was founded. It is committed to developing vendor independent OO specifications for the software industry.

In 1991 Sun Microsystems developed the Java programming language as part of a research project to create software for consumer electronic devices like TVs and VCRs. It contains many object-oriented programming features similar to C++ and was extended to easily handle Web and multimedia type of applications. In 1994, Rasmus Lerdorf created the initial version of Hypertext Preprocessor (PHP), an open-source Web server scripting language with object-oriented capabilities similar to C++ and Java. A number of other OO languages have some adopters (i.e., Eiffel, CLOS, SELF), however, with the current push to rewrite and convert applications to a Web-centric environment, even C++ is being replaced by more web enabled and standards embracing languages such as Java and PHP.

Because one uses a modern object-oriented language (i.e., C++, Java, or PHP) does not necessarily mean that one has written an object-oriented program. One can still build poor, non–object-oriented and nonreusable software with a fully object-oriented language.

Software Reuse

Today's software development is characterized by many disturbing but well-documented facts:

- The supply of qualified IT professionals is less than the demand
- The complexity of software is constantly increasing
- IT needs better-cheaper-faster software development methods
- Most software development projects fail (Standish Group, 2004; Williamson, 1997)

Granneman asked, "Why is this IT project so expensive?" (Granneman, 2004). His answer was that software is designed without much regard for future changes, even easily foreseeable changes. He suggested asking this question as part of the project design—Will this software need programming changes if:

- Business conditions change?
- Business partners change?
- Economic conditions change?
- Vendor relationships change?
- Banking relationships change?
- Products or services are added, changed, or discontinued?
- Business activity increases or decreases dramatically?
- The timing of how quickly information is needed changes?
- The source or destination of information changes?

"Reuse [software] engineering is a process where a technology asset is designed and developed following architectural principles, and with the intent of being reused in the future" (Bean, 1999). "If programming has a Holy Grail, widespread code reuse is it with a bullet. While IT has made and continues to make laudable progress in our reuse, we never seem to make great strides in this area" (Grinzo, 1998). "The quest for that Holy Grail has taken many developers over many years down unproductive paths" (Bowen, 1997).

Jones (1994) discussed the problem with the lack of reusability and itemized reusable material and the percentage of companies investigating and using the same. This is detailed in Figure 5.20. Although these numbers are somewhat outdated, the table illustrates the kinds of IT artifacts that can be reused and the relative percentage utilization of each. Jones also indicated that the amount of risk in a project is in inverse proportion to the amount of reuse. A root cause of the lack of reusability is that software development has evolved as a "craft" rather than as an engineering or manufacturing. The discipline of software engineering is an attempt to correct this historic evolution.

Figure 5.20. Reusable artifacts

Reusable Material	% Investigating	% Using
Architectures	1	1
Data	25	50
Designs	3	5
Code	20	50
Estimates	5	20
Human Interfaces	10	50
Plans	5	10
Requirements	2	10
User Documents	2	10
Test Cases	10	20

In his book, Jones (1994) itemized and discussed the risks from a lack of reusability in each of the above areas, and he indicated root causes, cost impact, and methods of prevention and control for each. Although outdated, many of the general principles still apply. "The bottom line is this: while it takes time for reuse to settle into an organization—and for an organization to settle on reuse—you can add increasing value throughout the process" (Barrett & Schmuller, 1999).

Radding defines several different types of reusable components in IT business systems (Radding, 1998):

- *GUI Widgets:* Effective, but only provide modest payback
- *Server-Side Components:* Provide significant payback but require extensive up-front design and an *architectural foundation*
- *Infrastructure Components:* Generic services for transactions, messaging, and database ... require extensive design and complex programming
- *High-Level Patterns:* Identify components with high reuse potential
- *Packaged Applications:* Only guaranteed reuse, however may not offer the exact functionality required

For all of the above types of reusable components, except packaged applications, OO programming is the most effective architectural and programming technique. Packaged applications and COTS software were identified and discussed earlier in this chapter. Reusing code has several key implementation areas: application evolution, multiple implementations, standards, and new applications. The reuse of code from prior applications in new applications has received the most attention. Just as important, however, is the reuse of code (and the technology embedded therein) within the same application. As stated earlier, applications must evolve even before they are completely developed, because the environment under which they operate (business, regulatory, social, political, technical, etc.) changes during the time the software is designed and implemented.

Another key need for reusability within the same application is for multiple implementations, the most common of which involves customizations, internationalization, and multiple platform support. For example, organizations whose software must be utilized globally might need to present an interface in customers' native languages and with a socially acceptable look and feel (localization). The multiple platform dimension of reuse today involves an architectural choice in delivery platforms (hardware and operating system) on both the client and server sides.

Corporate software development standards concern maintaining standards in all parts of an application and maintaining standards across all applications. For a computer system to have lasting value it must exist compatibly with users and other systems in an ever-changing information technology (IT) world (Brandon, 2002). Software reuse and OO programming as it relates to standards are covered in more detail in a later chapter of this book.

In most organizations, software reusability is a goal that is very elusive, "a most difficult promise to deliver on" (Bahrami, 1999). Radding stated, "Code reuse seems to make sense, but many companies find there is so much work involved, it's not worth the effort. ... In reality, large scale software reuse is still more the exception than the rule" (Radding, 1998). Bean, in "Reuse 101," stated that the current decreased "hype" surrounding code reuse is likely due to three basic problems:

- Reuse is an easily misunderstood concept
- Identifying what can be reused is a confusing process
- Implementing reuse is seldom simple or easy to understand (Bean, 1999)

Grinzo (1998) also list several reasons and observations on the problem of reuse, other than for some "difficult to implement but easy to plug-in cases," such as GUI widgets; a "nightmare of limitations and bizarre incompatibilities"; performance problems; "thorny psychological issues" involving programmers' personalities; market components that are buggy and difficult to use; fear of entrapment; component size; absurd licensing restrictions; or lack of source code availability.

Some organizations try to promote software reusability by simply publishing specifications on class libraries that have been built for other in house applications or that are available via third parties, some dictate some type of reuse, and other organizations give away some type of "bonus" for reusing the class libraries of others (Bahrami, 1999).

But more often than not, these approaches do not result in much success.

"It's becoming clear to some who work in this field that large-scale reuse of code represents a major undertaking" (Radding, 1998). "An OO/reuse discipline entails more than creating and using class libraries. It requires *formalizing* the practice of reuse" (McClure, 1996).

There are two key components to *formalizing an effective software reuse practice* (Brandon, 2002):

1.   Defining a specific information technology architecture within which applications would be developed and reuse would apply

2.   Defining a very specific object-oriented "Reuse Foundation" that would be implemented within the chosen IT architecture. Such a foundation is typically the combination of an overall framework and specific reusable patterns.

"If you want reuse to succeed, you need to invest in the architecture first" (Radding, *1998). "Without an architecture, organizations will not be able to build or even to buy consistently reusable components."* The major architectures today are Java Two Enterprise edition (J2EE), Microsoft's .Net, and open source LAMP (Linux, Apache, MySQL, PHP). Object-oriented frameworks are available from a number of vendors for each architecture, or an organization can create its own framework and patterns. Modern architectures may support one or more application servers, programming languages and IDEs (integrated development environments).

Application frameworks are a holistic set of specifications for the interaction and assembly of multiple reusable patterns. A pattern is the design of a core functional element such as the MVC (model-view-controller) pattern used for user interfaces. The boundary between architecture, framework, pattern, and programming language is blurry and not the same in different architectures. Examples of modern proprietary application frameworks include IBM's Websphere, Macromedia's ColdFusion and Flex, Sun's I-Planet, and BEA's Weblogic.

These reuse foundations (frameworks and patterns) are based on the key object-oriented principles of inheritance and composition. By establishing foundations like these, an organization can effectively begin to obtain significant reusability since programmers must inherit each of their classes from one of the established classes and they must only compose their classes of the established pre-built components. *As has been concluded by several authors, "A reuse effort demands a solid conceptual foundation"* (Barrett, *1999).*

Software Engineering Institute

The Software Engineering Institute (SEI; www.sei.cmu.edu/cmm) is a research institute funded by the U.S. Department of Defense (DoD), contracted to Carnegie Mellon University, which was started in 1984. The SEI receives tens of millions of DoD dollars on an annual basis. Their overall goal is to advance the practice of software engineering, and they are perhaps best known for their formulation of software engineering "maturity models." These models, called capability maturity models (CMM), define best practices—key practices (things to be done and ways of doing things) that organizations at different levels of software engineering "maturity" do.

A popular baseball analogy was first reportedly expressed by Watts Humphrey, known as the Father of CMM:

- *Immature Team:* When the ball is hit, some players run toward the ball and others stand around and watch, perhaps not even thinking about the game.
- *Mature Team:* When the ball is hit, every player reacts in a predefined disciplined manner. Depending upon the situation, the pitcher might cover home plate, infielders might set up a double play, and outfielders might back up their teammates.

The SEI has formulated a number of CMM over the years, including,

- SW-CMM: CMM for Software Development
- SA-CMM: Software Acquisition CMM
- P-CMM: People CMM
- SE-CMM: Software Engineering CMM
- IPD-CMM: Integrated Product Development CMM

The Software Capability Maturity Model (CMM for Software) was the first, best known, and probably used the most today. It defines five levels of software process maturity that determine effectiveness in delivering quality software:

- Initial
- Repeatable
- Defined
- Managed
- Optimized

It is primarily geared to large organizations and their contractors, however, many of the processes involved are appropriate to any organization, and if reasonably applied can be helpful. Organizations can receive CMM ratings by undergoing assessments by qualified auditors. *These ratings are useful to an organization for two reasons. First the assessment lets an organization know where it stands in terms of software engineering maturity as viewed by an independent source, and secondly the assessment (if very good) can be used by the organization in selling its services.* A description of each level follows:

- *Level 1 (Anarchy):* At this level, programmers generally do what they individually think best. Chaos, periodic panics, and heroic efforts are often required by individuals to successfully complete projects and successes is typically not repeatable. Cost, schedule, and quality are unpredictable. There is little formal planning or established programming practices. Overcommitment is common, and senior management does not understand application development/procurement.

- *Level 2 (Folklore):* Here programmers have experience developing certain kinds of applications. They have devised effective processes (policies and procedures in regard to project management, requirements, and configuration), and generally make time and cost estimates. Their strength depends upon doing the same kind of application, but they cannot adapt well to new applications, new methods, or new tools. Knowledge is only in heads of programmers.

- *Level 3 (Standards):* Here the corporate "mythology" is written down in a set of standards. These standard software development and maintenance processes are integrated throughout the organization and some sort of a software engineering process group is in place to oversee these processes. Groups may tailor the standards with approval, however the process has not been measured (by collecting data) or compared to other methods. Since it is not measured, programmers and managers debate the effectiveness of the metrics that are used to track productivity, processes, and products.

- *Level 4 (Managed):* Here project performance is predictable, and quality is consistently high. Metrics have been established, and hard data is collected to access process's effectiveness. Measurements are used to improve the product quality.

- *Level 5 (Optimized):* Here the focus is on continuous process improvement. The impact of new processes and technologies can be predicted and effectively implemented when required. Tools are available to automate collection of data, and measurements are used to improve the processes.

Each maturity level, except for the first, is broken down into key process areas. Each key process is described in terms of key practices. The key process areas at each level are:

Level 2 Key Process Areas [Basic Project Management]
        Requirements Management
        Software project planning
        Software project tracking and oversight
        Software subcontract management
        Software quality assurance
        Software configuration management

Level 3 Key Process Areas [Organizational Processes Standardization]
        Organization process focus
        Organization process definition
        Training program
        Integrated software management
        Software product engineering
        Intergroup coordination
        Peer reviews

Level 4 Key Process Areas [Quantitative Process Analysis - Metrics]
    Quantitative process management
    Software quality management

Level 5 Key Process Areas [Continuous Improvement of Entire Process]
    Defect prevention
    Technology change management
    Process change management

Note that the SEI CMM Level 2 key process areas encompass basic project management. We will look more into these level two processes in later chapters of this book. For convenience, the practices at all the levels are organized by common features, which address the level of implementation; these common features are:

- Commitment to perform
- Ability to perform
- Activities performed
- Measurements and analysis
- Verifying implementation

Note that these common features are embedded into our model for IT project critical success completion factors as described in Chapter II (in our model, verification assumes measurement and analysis).

The SEI is currently revising the software SW-CMM into a more comprehensive CMMI integrated model that will also encompass systems engineering and product development. Higher CMM levels have correlated with less software defects and higher cost savings (in terms of function points, which are discussed later in this book). Figure 5.21 shows these types of data, as published in *Computerworld* (King, 2003).

During the last 5 years, about 1,000 organizations have been assessed, and 27% were rated at Level 1, 39% at Level 2, 23% at Level 3, 6% at Level 4, and 5% at Level 5. Currently there are about 70 companies worldwide that are at Level 5 (King, 2003).

However, being at Level 5 does not guarantee that a company's internal implementation of these standards is best in class (King, 2003). The CMM standards describe what must be done, not how to do it. Remember also that "the CMM is a consensus among a particular group of software engineering theorists and practitioners concerning a collection of effective practices grouped according to a simple model of organizational evolution. As such, it is potentially valuable for those companies that completely lack software savvy, or for those who have a lot of it and want to avoid its pitfalls. At worse, the CMM is a whitewash that obscures the true dynamics of software engineering, suppressing alternative models" (Bach, 1994). A notable alternative model of software maturity is that of Jones: "Software Productivity Research" (Jones, 1994).

Figure 5.21. CMM levels and improvements

CMM Level	Defects per Function Point	% Improvement (from lower level)
1	0.750	---
2	0.620	17.33
3	0.475	23.34
4	0.228	52.00
5	0.100	56.00

Institute of Electrical and Electronics Engineers

The Institute of Electrical and Electronics Engineers (IEEE) is one of the world's largest professional organizations with over 350,000 members in over 150 countries. About one half of the IEEE members are outside of the United States, and that portion is growing more rapidly than the U.S. membership. IEEE publishes about one quarter of the world's literature within the technical fields it encompasses. The IEEE Computer Society is the largest of the 36 technical societies in IEEE, with over 100,000 members. The IEEE Computer Society is in the final stages of completing and approving a Software Engineering Body of Knowledge (SWEBOK). The knowledge areas to be covered include:

- Professional engineering economics
- Software requirements
- Software design
- Software construction and implementation
- Software testing
- Software maintenance
- Software configuration management
- Software engineering management
- Software engineering process
- Software engineering tools and methods
- Software quality

Most of the SWEBOK has already been documented within the various IEEE software standards, and many of these standards are discussed later in this book. These IEEE software standards include:

- 730-2002 IEEE Standard for Software Quality Assurance Plans
- 828-1998 IEEE Standard for Software Configuration Management Plans
- 829-1998 IEEE Standard for Software Test Documentation
- 830-1998 IEEE Recommended Practice for Software Requirements Specifications
- 982.1-1988 IEEE Standard Dictionary of Measures to Produce Reliable Software
- 1008-1987 IEEE Standard for Software Unit Testing
- 1012-1998 IEEE Standard for Software Verification and Validation
- 1016-1998 IEEE Recommended Practice for Software Design Descriptions
- 1028-1997 (R2002) IEEE Standard for Software Reviews
- 1044-1993 (R2002) IEEE Standard Classification for Anomalies
- 1045-1992, (R2002) IEEE Standard for Software Productivity Metrics
- 1058-1998 IEEE Standard for Software Project Management Plans
- 1058.1-1987 (R1993) IEEE Standard for Software Project Management Plans
- 1061-1998 (R2004) IEEE Standard for Software Quality Metrics Methodology
- 1062, 1998 Edition (R2002) IEEE Recommended Practice for Software Acquisition (includes IEEE 1062a)
- 1063-2001 IEEE Standard for Software User Documentation
- 1074-1997 IEEE Standard for Developing Software Life Cycle Processes
- 1175.1-2002 IEEE Guide for CASE Tool Interconnections-Classification and Description
- 1219-1998 IEEE Standard for Software Maintenance
- 1220-1998 IEEE Standard for the Application and Management of the Systems Engineering Process
- 1228-1994 (2002) IEEE Standard for Software Safety Plans
- 1233, 1998 Edition (R2002) IEEE Guide for Developing System Requirements Specifications (including IEEE 1233a)
- 1320.1-1998 (R2004) IEEE Standard for Functional Modeling Language - Syntax and Semantics for IDEF0
- 1320.2-1998 (R2004) IEEE Standard for Conceptual Modeling Language Syntax and Semantics for IDEF1X97 (IDEF object)
- 1420.1-1995 (R2002) IEEE Standard for Information Technology—Software Reuse—Data Model for Reuse Library Interoperability: Basic Interoperability Data Model (BIDM)
- 1420.1a-1996 (R2002) IEEE Supplement to Standard for Information Technology—Software Reuse—Data Model for Reuse Library Interoperability: Asset Certification Framework
- 1420.1b-1999 (R2002) IEEE Supplement to IEEE Standard for Information Technology—Software Reuse—Data Model for Reuse Library Interoperability: Intellectual Property Rights Framework

- 1462-1998 [Adoption of International Standard ISO/IEC 14102:1995(E)], Information technology — Guideline for the evaluation and selection of CASE tools

- 1465-1998 [Adoption of ISO/IEC 12119: 1994(E)], IEEE Standard Adoption of International Standard ISO/IEC 12119: 1994(E) Information Technology—Software Packages: Quality requirements and testing

- 1490-2003 IEEE Guide (©IEEE) — Adoption of PMI Standard—A Guide to the Project Management Body of Knowledge (©PMI)

- 1517-1999 (R2004) IEEE Standard for Information Technology—Software Life Cycle Processes—Reuse Processes

- 2001-2002 IEEE Recommended Practice for the Internet—Web Site Engineering, Web Site Management, and Web Site Life Cycle

- 1540-2001 IEEE Standard for Software Life Cycle Processes-Risk Management

- 12207.0-1996 IEEE/EIA Standard: Industry Implementation of International Standard ISO/IEC 12207:1995 Standard for Information Technology—Software Life Cycle Processes

- 12207.1-1997 IEEE/EIA Standard: Industry Implementation of International Standard ISO/IEC 12207:1995 Standard for Information Technology—Software Life Cycle Processes—Life Cycle Data

- 12207.2-1997 IEEE/EIA Standard: Industry Implementation of International Standard ISO/IEC 12207:1995 Standard for Information Technology— Software Life Cycle Processes—Implementation considerations

Other Software
Standards Organizations

There are about 50 other organizations worldwide that produce software engineering standards. Some of these are the International Organization for Standardization (IOS), the American National Standards Institute (ANSI), World Wide Web Consortium (W3C) for Internet-related standards, NIST which is an agency of the U.S. Commerce Department's Technology Office, space agencies such as NASA and military organizations such as the U.S. Department of Defense (DoD). The American National Standards Institute (ANSI) is a private, nonprofit organization that is the focal point for the U.S. voluntary consensus standards system. ANSI consists of approximately 1,300 national and international companies as well as many government agencies, institutional members, professional, technical, and trade organizations. ANSI facilitates a consensus amongst its members to foster ANSI accredited standards. A key part of the approval process is the fact that all members have the opportunity to participate in the standards development process.

However, the most dominant of these other organizations worldwide is ISO/IEC, the software engineering subcommittee of the International Organization for Standardization. The International Organization for Standardization (ISO, from the Greek *isos*, meaning equal) has set international standards (about 14,000 of them) in many areas for many years, including software engineering standards. ISO has over 180 technical committees, covering many industry sectors and products. The American Society for Quality Control (ASQC) handles the U.S. Technical Advisory Group (TAG), which offers its opinions to the overall ISO technical committees. Many ISO standards are shared ("adopted") by IEEE, and are so noted in the above list of IEEE standards. The ISO/IEC 12207 standard provides a total framework for the acquisition, supply, development, operation, and maintenance of software. In addition, the standard provides a methodology for managing software life cycle activities and a reference point for new and emerging engineering standards. ISO/IEC 12207 has been adopted/adapted by ANSI, IEEE, EIA, and DoD in the United States.

The European Software Institute is a major industry initiative, founded by leading European companies, to improve the competitiveness of the European Software Industry. To this end ESI promotes good software engineering and management practice. Since 1993, the Software Process Improvement and Capability determination (SPICE) project, launched within ISO, has been developing a framework standard for software process assessment. ESI, is a key partner in SPICE, and is taking the leading role in the European adaptation of SPICE.

Chapter Summary

Earlier in this book, the three challenges to software engineering in the 21st century were outlined (Sommerville, 2003):

- *The Heterogeneity Challenge:* Flexibility to operate on and integrate with multiple hardware and software platforms from legacy mainframe environments to the landscape of the global web
- *The Delivery Challenge:* Ability to develop and integrate IT systems rapidly in response to rapidly changing and evolving global business needs
- *The Trust Challenge:* Being able to create vital (mission and/or life critical) software that is trustworthy in terms of both security and quality

These challenges can be met by a careful integration of modern project management and software engineering principles and practices. This was illustrated in Figure 1.4 in Chapter I, and this chapter has discussed software engineering maturity, methodologies, and OO architecture. In Chapter VI, project scope, phasing, and requirements are discussed; later chapters of this book will further detail these other principles and practices. Throughout the book, critical IT project success factors are used as the basis for key project management processes as performance, risk, and quality control.

References

Bach, J. (1994, September). The immaturity of CMM. *American Programmer.*

Bahrami, A. (1999). *Object oriented systems development.* New York: McGraw Hill-Irwin.

Barrett, K., & Schmuller, J. (1999, October). Building an infrastructure of real-world reuse. *Component Strategies.*

Bean, J. (1999, October). Reuse 101. *Enterprise Development.*

Beck, K. (1999). *Extreme programming explained: Embrace change.* Boston: Addison-Wesley Professional.

Bauer, F. (1972). Software engineering. *Information Processing, 71.*

Bowen, B. (n.d.). Software reuse with Java technology: Finding the Holy Grail. Retrieved from www.javasoft.com/features/1997/may/reuse.html

Brandon, D. (2002). Achieving effective software reuse for business systems. In *Successful software reengineering.* Hershey, PA: Idea Group Publishing.

Cockburn, A. (2001). *Agile software development.* Boston: Addison-Wesley.

Darwin, C. (1859). *The origin of species by means of natural selection (or the preservation of favoured races in the struggle for life).*

Dennis, A. (1999, Spring). Business process modeling with group support systems. *Journal of Management Information Systems,* 115-142.

Eisenberg, R. (2004, April 17). Service-oriented architecture: The future is now. *Intelligent Enterprise.*

Garbett, S. (2003, August). Cleanroom software engineering. *Dr. Dobb's Journal.*

Granneman, M. (2004). Why is this IT Project so expensive? *Computerworld,* June 4.

Grinzo, L. (1998, September). The unbearable lightness of being reusable. *Dr. Dobbs Journal.*

Hall, M. (2003, May 19). The Web services tsunami. *Computerworld.*

Highsmith, J. (2000). *Adaptive software development.* New York: Dorset House.

Jacobson, I. (1999). *The unified software development process.* Boston, MA: Addison-Wesley Professional.

Jones, C. (1994). *Assessment and control of software risks.* Englewood Cliffs, NJ: Yourdon Press Computing Series.

King, J. (2003, December 8). The pros and cons of CMM. *Computerworld.*

Kruchten, P. (1998). *The rational unified process.* Boston: Addison-Wesley.

Linger, R. (1994). Cleanroom process model. *IEEE Software, 11*(2).

McClure, C. (1996). Experiences from the OO playing field. *Extended Intelligence.*

Mills, H. (1996). *Cleanroom software engineering.* Oxford, UK: Blackwell Publishers.

Palmer, S., & Felsing, J. (2002). *A practical guide to feature-driven development.* New York: Prentice Hall.

Prowell, S. (1999). *Cleanroom software engineering: Technology and process.* Boston: Addison-Wesley.

Radding, A. (1998, November 9). Hidden cost of code reuse. *Information Week.*

Royce, W. (1970). Managing the development of large software systems. *Proceedings IEEE WESTCON, IEEE Computer Society,* Los Angeles, CA.

Schwaber, K., & Beedle, M. (2001). *Agile software development with Schrum.* Upper Saddle River, NJ: Prentice Hall.

Sommerville, I. (2003). *Software engineering.* Boston: Pearson Addison Wesley.

Standish Group. (2004). *Chaos chronicles.* Retrieved from www.standisgroup.com

Stapleton, J. (1997). *DSDM dynamic systems development method.* Boston: Addison-Wesley.

Williams, L., & Kessler, R. (2000). Strengthening the case for pair programming. *IEEE Software, 17*(4), 19-25.

Williamson, M. (1997, May). Software reuse. *CIO Magazine.*

Chapter VI

Project Overall Planning

The will to succeed is important, but the will to prepare is even more important.

(Bobby Knight)

Getting off to a fast start in the right direction is important in any endeavor. This chapter discusses overall project planning and requirement analysis. These are two of the most important aspects of IT project management (Standish Group, 2004).

The Project Charter

In a previous chapter I discussed the project proposal and the project's business justification, which are often formalized in a project business plan. After these documents are approved, a formal project charter should be drafted. Whereas the project charter may be written by the project sponsor (project champion) or project manager (PM), the project charter is normally signed by general (upper line) management. The charter is the official go-ahead document for the project and indicates that funding and resources have been, or will shortly be, made available. The charter typically contains the following:

- Project title and description
- Project manager assigned and his or her authority level set (i.e., authority to set budget, schedule, staffing, procurement)
- Goals and objectives (what the project is to accomplish)

- Product (or service) description
- Applicable standards
- Assumptions and constraints

The charter should be signed by someone high enough in the organization so that everyone on the team will eventually report directly or indirectly to that person. Executives from both the performing and benefiting organization may sign off on the project charter, especially when both organizations are part of the same corporation. In larger corporations, IT project charters usually need the approval of the chief financial officer (CFO) and the chief information officer (CIO). The benefits of this charter are that it:

- Gives authority to the PM
- Formally recognizes the creation and existence of the project
- Outlines the objectives of the project

The charter should be broad enough that it will not require change during the project execution. Figure 6.1 shows an example of a simple project charter. If a project proposal or business plan is developed after the charter, the charter may also include financial information, such as the basic project budget and contingency funds.

Figure 6.1. Project charter

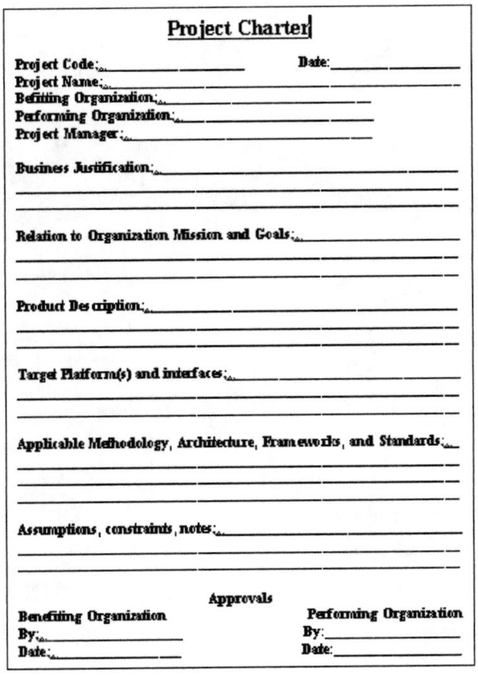

Project Charter

Project Code:______ Date:______
Project Name:______
Befiting Organization:______
Performing Organization:______
Project Manager:______

Business Justification:______

Relation to Organization Mission and Goals:______

Product Description:______

Target Platform(s) and interfaces:______

Applicable Methodology, Architecture, Frameworks, and Standards:______

Assumptions, constraints, notes:______

Approvals

Benefiting Organization
By:______
Date:______

Performing Organization
By:______
Date:______

The Project Master Plan

Once the project charter has been signed off and a PM has been assigned to the project, an overall project master plan is assembled by the PM and his or her staff. The word *assembled* is used here because, in most organizations that have formal project management, much of the initial master plan is boilerplate material in which existing templates for the subplans are used and customized for the project at hand. This is often coordinated by a project management office (PMO). The PMO is discussed in detail in Chapter XVI.

The master plan may be a simple one-page document, as is shown in Figure 6.4, but it is typically a collection of subplan templates, as is illustrated in Figure 6.2. Each of these subplans incorporate (or simply refer to) policies, procedures, and standards for the organization as a whole. The formality and detail of this master plan should be based on the size and complexity of the project, as is illustrated in Figure 6.3. The content and nature of each of these subplans is described and illustrated in later chapters of this book.

Figure 6.2. Project master plan

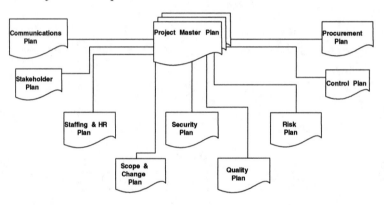

Figure 6.3. Master plan formality

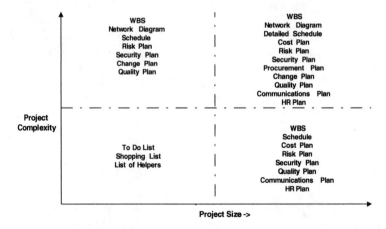

Figure 6.4. Project overall plan

Project Overall Plan

Project Code:_____   Date:_____
        Project Name:_____
        Befitting Organization:_____
        Performing Organization:_____
        Project Manager:_____

Rough Estimates: Start Date:_____ End date:_____ Cost:_____

Overall Product Deliverables – In Scope:
1. _____
2. _____
N. _____

Product Features – Out of Scope:_____
1._____
2._____
N._____

Key Milestones:
1. _____
2. _____
N. _____

Key Risks, Procurement, Security, and Quality Issues:_____
_____
_____

Key Stakeholders and Human Resources:
        Person   Role/Responsibility   Contact Info
1. _____
2. _____
N. _____

Communications and Reporting:_____
_____

Notes: _____
_____

Approvals
Benefiting Organization   Performing Organization
    By:_____   By:_____
    Date:_____   Date:_____

As the project unfolds and the scope is determined, the project-specific work and deliverables are incorporated into each of these subplans. This planning process, and the appropriate methods thereof, for IT projects are discussed and detailed in later chapters of this book.

The Software Engineering Institute's (SEI; www.sei.cmu.edu/cmm) CMM defines necessary Level 2 practices for software project planning:

- Are estimates documented for use in planning and tracking the project?
- Do the plans document the activities to be performed and the commitments made fore the project?

- Do all affected parties agree to their commitments?
- Does the project follow a written policy for planning a project?
- Are adequate resources provided for planning the project?
- Are measurements used to determine the status of the planning activities?
- Doe the PM review the activities for planning the project on both a periodic and event-driven basis?

The IEEE also has a standard for software project management plans: IEEE Std. 1058-1998. In their standard, the elements of such a management plan include:

Overview, references, and definitions
Project organization
    External interfaces
    Internal structure
    Roles and responsibilities
Managerial process plans
    Start-up (estimation, staffing plan, resource plan, budget plan)
    Work plan (activities, schedule, resources, budget)
    Control plan (requirements, schedule, budget, quality, reporting, metrics)
    Risk management plan
    Closeout plan
Technical process plans
    Process model
    Methods, tools, techniques
    Infrastructure plan
    Product acceptance plan
Supporting process plans
    Configuration management plan
    Verification and validation plan
    Documentation plan
    Quality assurance plan
    Reviews and audits
    Problem resolution plan
    Subcontractor management plan
    Process improvement plan
Additional plans

Modern IT projects should also have a specific security plan. Neither the current PMI nor IEEE standards include such a component in planning. The security issue in IT project management is twofold:

- Being able to shield the project work and project workers and other project resources from security threats
- Being able to build adequate security protection into the product that is the subject of the project

The first security item would also be included in the risk management plan, detailed in a later chapter of this book. A Gartner research report projected that IT project downtime due to security issues would rise from 5% in 2004 to 15% in 2008 for organizations that do not have a comprehensive security plan (Alexander, 2004). Such security plans should address both logical and physical security. However, it is no longer sufficient simply to "secure the perimeter" physically and logically; active security procedures need to be implemented for those objects already inside of the perimeter. Thus, security plans are also related to human resource (HR) planning in terms of procedures that may be necessary, such as personnel background checks; this is detailed later in the book. The second security item should be addressed (at least partially) in the software engineering that is embedded in the product, which is the subject of the project. *In today's IT environment, it is vital that both of these security points be fully addressed in the project planning.*

Project Calendars and Fiscal Periods

Before starting the project and the detail planning thereof, it is necessary to establish a project calendar. Such a calendar indicates the quantum of time used for both planning and reporting, as well as periods of nonwork, such as holidays and weekends. Some practitioners use scheduling systems whereby arbitrary time units can be used for task start and end dates. Also, some practitioners try to schedule IT resources down to the day or even hour. *For IT projects (and other types of professional work) this is inappropriate and ineffective; and as a result one may spend more time managing the schedule than managing the work.* IT human resources are largely professional types, they may work varying numbers of hours per day, they may be called upon to help another person or another project from time to time, and they may take off a day or two for whatever reason whenever they so chose. IT effort, time, and cost estimates involve considerable uncertainty, thus for all these reasons it is more effective to chose the project time quantum at a larger interval than 1 day;, periods of 1 week, 2 weeks, or a month are more appropriate.

In addition, the time quantum should match both the fiscal calendar of the organization and the accounting periods of the organization. This facilitates cost and completion reporting because such reporting can be incorporated into an existing payroll and/or timekeeping process. The time period of 1 week is the commonly used quantum for professional projects. This is discussed in more detail in later chapters of this book.

Figure 6.5 shows an example of a fiscal calendar for the first half of 2004. In this calendar, week numbers are used as the basis for planning and reporting, and these week numbers are numbered sequentially for the year, as 2004-06, which is in fiscal month 2004-02. When a specific task is defined and assigned resources, the task is scheduled for one or more fiscal weeks. Figure 6.6 shows such a fiscal calendar for the NASA Jet Propulsion Laboratory.

Kickoff Meeting

After the project charter has been approved and appropriately signed off, it is recommended to have an official kickoff meeting with the project team. This meeting has many benefits including finding out early if there are any major problems that have not surfaced already in the initial planning. Problems may include forgotten stakeholders or key team members, organizational issues, interpersonal issues, technical issues, environmental or regulation issues, or other constraints. Other alternative methods, plans, or approaches may also be discovered at this meeting. This first meeting allows team members to meet each other and builds enthusiasm, shared vision, and common goals and purpose. Things that should be done at this meeting include:

Figure 6.5. Project periods

Fiscal Year - 2004

Fiscal Month	Fiscal Week	Monday	Tuesday	Wednesday	Thursday	Friday	Saturday	Sunday
01	01	5	6	7	8	9	10	11
	02	12	13	14	15	16	17	18
	03	19	20	21	22	23	24	25
	04	26	27	28	29	30	31	1
02	05	2	3	4	5	6	7	8
	06	9	10	11	12	13	14	15
	07	16	17	18	19	20	21	22
	08	23	24	25	26	27	28	29
03	09	1	2	3	4	5	6	7
	10	8	9	10	11	12	13	14
	11	15	16	17	18	19	20	21
	12	22	23	24	25	26	27	28
	13	29	30	31	1	2	3	4
04	14	5	6	7	8	9	10	11
	15	12	13	14	15	16	17	18
	16	19	20	21	22	23	24	25
	17	26	27	28	29	30	1	2
05	18	3	4	5	6	7	8	9
	19	10	11	12	13	14	15	16
	20	17	18	19	20	21	22	23
	21	24	25	26	27	28	29	30
06	22	31	1	2	3	4	5	6
	23	7	8	9	10	11	12	13
	24	14	15	16	17	18	19	20
	25	21	22	23	24	25	26	27
	26	28	29	30	1	2	3	4

Figure 6.6. NASA JPL calendar

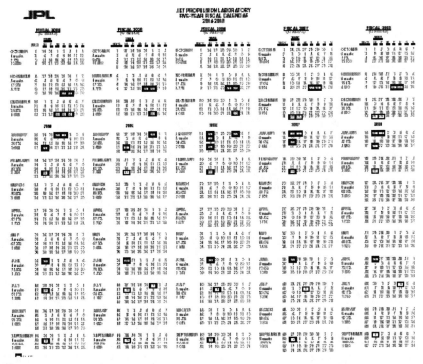

- Introduce the project sponsor or champion
- Establish clear leadership on the project
- Share then vision of the champion and other leaders
- Clarify and communicate goals and objectives to team and stakeholders
- Discuss overall project plan
- Review major milestones and deliverables
- Establish working relationships and lines of communications
- Explain relevant policies and procedures
- Get teams members to know one another
- Review status to date
- Review standards that will apply
- Establish responsibilities (individual and group)
- Make sure everyone understands his or her role and tasks
- Solicit questions and comments
- Document and follow up on questions that cannot be answered at this time
- Identify potential problems and risks
- Handle any other issues that may interfere with starting work
- Give team formal go-ahead to start work

For this meeting, one should follow the general guidelines for effective meetings; these guidelines are discussed in Chapter XIII.

Scope Management

A project's scope is the work to be done and the things to work on. This scope is enclosed within a multidimensional boundary line that separates those things that are part of the project from other things that are not part of the project. As part of defining this boundary line, one may itemized the things that are to be included in the project work and deliverables as well as to itemize those things that are not part of the project work. This itemization may be at a general level or a very specific level, or a combination thereof. The dimensions may include what, how, who, when, and other concepts used as metrics or definitions.

According to PMI's PMBOK (PMI, 2000), scope management involves the following processes:

- Scope Initiation
- Scope Planning
- Scope Definition
- Scope Verification
- Scope Change Control

Scope initiation, as discussed earlier, involves making sure that the project charter is approved and that the necessary financial and other resources are available to move forward with the project. Scope planning involves developing a written scope statement that is more specific than that included in the project charter. The scope statement usually further itemizes and defines the project objectives and includes the major features of the IT product(s) and other major deliverables.

For IT projects, the project scope is more extensive than the product scope. The *product scope* will be eventually be described by design documentation and includes the features and specific functionality of the software product(s) that is to be built, procured and/or integrated as well as appropriate standards and the chosen architecture. This is illustrated in Figure 6.7.

The *project scope* includes not only the product(s) but also all of the associated activities and deliverables. Some deliverables may be called for in the requirements, some deliverables are mandated by the organization's chosen methodology and/or standards, and some deliverables are called for in the contract between the performing organization and benefiting organization. The aforementioned project charter describes the project scope at a very high level, and often the charter may only describe the product scope.

Figure 6.7. Product scope

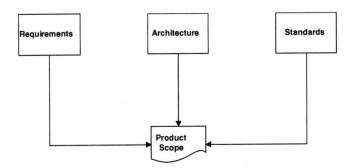

A separate deliverable definition document (DDD) may be produced, which lists every deliverable, the form of the deliverable (document, software, hardware, etc.), applicable standards, and approval levels. Items typically found in the DDD include:

- Requirements document
- Overall design document
- Paper prototype (storyboards)
- Detail design document
- Product prototype
- Users' manual (external specifications document)
- Internal specifications document
- Test plan and scripts
- The product itself
- Installation and operation document

The scope definition process involves determining the all the details embodied within the scope statement and DDD and then subdividing those details into smaller, more manageable components. For IT systems, this first major activity of determining the scope details is called requirements analysis, which is discussed later in this chapter. Those detail requirements must be subdivided further in order to effectively and accurately plan and control the project. The further definition (or breakdown) of scope is manifested in a work breakdown structure (WBS), which is defined by PMI as "a *deliverable oriented* grouping of project components which *organizes* and defines the total scope of the project" (PMI, 2000).

The WBS is typically arranged in a multilevel hierarchical manner, and the first level (Level zero) often corresponds to the project life cycle (phases: requirements, design, construction, etc.) and is fully specified before the project is further broken down; each level of the WBS is a further breakdown of the higher level. The lowest level defines the individual tasks, work packets, or activities. The development of WBS's for IT projects is discussed in detail in Chapter VII.

Scope verification is the process of formalizing the acceptance of the project by the stakeholders, particularly the benefiting organization (customer). It involves review of the work results (the final product or service) versus the scope definition (requirements). Scope verification

is typically done at the end of each project phase or, as suggested in this book, at quality stage gates; it involves requirements traceability, verification, and validation. Verification is a process related notion and is one of our critical completion success factors. It answers the general question, Have we done this process correctly? or, more specifically, Have we built the product correctly? Validation is a product-related notion and is one of our satisfaction critical success factors. It answers the general question, Have we done the correct process? or, more specifically, Have we built the correct product (the product the customer wanted)? Traceability of requirements means that every requirement is properly included in every preliminary product manifestation as well as in the final product; traceability is actually a part of validation. This is discussed in detail in Chapter X.

Scope change control is concerned with influencing the factors that cause change and controlling them to ensure that changes are beneficial. Change control also happens in retrospect to determining that a scope change has actually occurred and then handling the change in an appropriate manner. As part of this scope planning process, a scope management plan may be formally written that indicates how the scope will be further defined and then later managed in regard to scope changes. A scope change control process and system may be implemented that defines the procedures by which the project scope may be changed and often includes:

* Forms and other paperwork
* Tracking systems
* Approval levels
* Billing and or contract change procedures

The scope management plan also includes the processes necessary to make sure that all project work is addressed and extra work is not done. This extra work, which is outside of the project scope, is called gold plating and should not be done without the proper written approval of the benefiting and performing organizations. The goal of project management is to give the customer what they have asked for and expect, no more and no less. Most IT projects do not fully succeed, and so extra work should not be done; after all, one does not know that the customer actually desires that extra work or not, or if the customer will pay for that extra work. In this book, we address scope changes under the larger topic of "change management," which is discussed in detail in Chapter XI.

Requirements Analysis

One of the best and quickest ways to ensure problems or failure in an IT project is to have hastily gathered, ill-defined, incomplete, and/or poorly documented requirement specifications. Requirements are the details describing an IT product's features and other properties that are needed (and wanted) by the benefiting organization. Requirements should embody the features and capabilities of the IT product (application) and also the behavior and content of the application. The requirements analysis process involves several subprocesses, including:

- Requirement discovery
- Requirement organization and documentation
- Requirement prioritization and project phasing
- Requirement change management

Requirements can take many forms, and this is illustrated in Figure 6.8. One form is input specifications, which describe the content and form of the input to the application. Another form is output specifications, which describe the content and form of the output. For interactive systems, these input and output specifications are often combined into external specifications or interface requirements. The processing that the application will do is described in a set of functional specifications, and how that processing is done is specified in a set of technical or internal specifications. The external specifications will be externally observable in the application, and the functional specifications may be externally observable or implied from the output versus the input. However, the internal specifications may not be externally observable. Even though not externally observable, these internal specifications may be vital to the long-term success of the application, including its maintainability and adaptability. As discussed in Chapter V, many of these internal requirements can be embodied in the set of software standards adopted by an organization.

Figure 6.8. Types of requirements

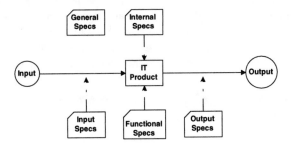

General specifications can involve any other properties of the application or the application's environment. As is illustrated in Figure 6.7, standards and target architecture may be separated from the application requirements, as the standards and architecture may be common to a number of applications, perhaps all the applications that are built/integrated by a particular organization. There is an IEEE standard for requirements (830), and that standard differentiates between product requirements and project requirements. Project requirements typically involve date/time and cost issues, and these are usually specified separately in contracts from the requirements or the statement of work (SOW); contract issues are discussed in Chapter XII.

Other general specifications may include grade and quality levels, portability, load and scalability, response times and other service levels, information content, security, and constraints such as the use of certain products or the use of general products as commercial off the shelf (COTS). Becoming more important in modern times is the need for security requirements to be detailed as early as possible. Security cannot be an afterthought, because good security has to be built into the total product (and the methodology of constructing it), not added on later. New legislation in various governments may be mandating added security-related requirements such as the Health Insurance Portability Act (HIPPA) and Sarbanes-Oxley Act (SOX) laws in the United States.

Requirement discovery is a process that involves a cooperative effort between the performing organization and the benefiting organization. This process may also involve other stakeholders with different needs and priorities. Chapter XIII deals with stakeholder identification and analysis, and how to handle different types of stakeholders. The IT personnel involved with requirement discovery are usually analysts such as business analysts, systems analysts, market analysts, or so-called requirements analysts. These analysts facilitate the flow of information from the users of the application to the builders of the application (designers and programmers). Thus these analysts need a combination of both people skills and technical skills; human resource and communication issues are also detailed in Chapter XIII.

Requirements must be consistent with the stated purpose of the overall system, and the PM must referee the requirements discovery process to make sure that suggested requirements are consistent with the project charter. Requirements should also be clear, complete, sufficiently detailed, doable, and testable. Just as it may be of little use to have a great solution to the wrong problem, it is of little practical use to build the wrong product very well. For this reason, requirements have to be clear (unambiguous), complete, and detailed enough so that the product, or at least a preliminary product manifestation, can be constructed. For example, a common nontestable requirement that often shows up in requirement specification is that the application should be user friendly. This is too subjective, and a testable version of this notion should be included instead, perhaps involving the types of human-computer interaction and the devices involved (mouse, keyboard, etc.).

There are many techniques of requirement discovery for IT projects, and these include:

- Informal conversations with end users and/or their management
- Structured interviews with end users and/or their management

- Collaborative working sessions between the benefiting and performing organizations
- Review of existing work flow and work processes
- Review of existing IT systems
- Review of existing external or internal documentation of processes and/or systems

Care should be taken to involve all of the stakeholders at some point in the total requirements process. Anyone who has an interest in the project and is not involved to some degree in the requirement discovery process could later cause problems. Again, stakeholder determination, analysis, and planning are discussed in detail in Chapter XIII.

A benefiting organization's requirements usually evolve during the planning and execution phases of a project. Requirements usually evolve from descriptions of the problem to descriptions of the solution; this is illustrated in Figure 6.9.

"The phenomenon is likened to a continuous application of Maslow's hierarchy of needs. Every time any need is satisfied, more needs appear" (Davis, Hickey, & Zweig, 2004). Often, end users cannot express in words what they want, but they may know what they want once they see it, or, conversely, they may know what they *do not* what when they see it. Showing the end users preliminary product manifestations is the best way to flush out all the real requirements, to further define the requirements, and to expedite this overall requirement evolution process. These preliminary product manifestations are part of the overall validation process, and those manifestations used depend upon the choice of methodology, as discussed in Chapter XVI. Typical manifestations include paper prototypes, working prototypes, and user's manuals. Users' review of these preliminary product manifestations is part of the quality stage gate process, which is described previously in this book and will be elaborated upon in upcoming chapters.

Figure 6.9. Requirements evolution

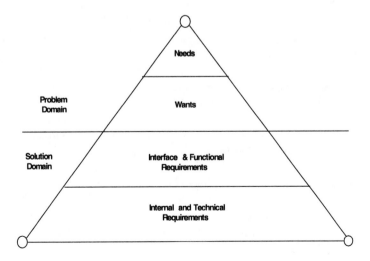

Organizing requirements in an effective and efficient manner can be difficult. One wants to cover as much detail as possible, but the resulting document must be clear. In addition, the time to produce the requirement document should not consume a high percentage of the project time and budget, and the document must not be overly burdensome to work with. Different organizations vary considerably in the manner and form of producing this document. Forms of the requirements document may be:

- No document at all (only in the minds of the users and developers)
- Simple checklist
- Spreadsheet
- Database
- Formal document
- High-level design documents (i.e., UML use cases)
- Specialized software product

Combinations of documents in this list may also be used. The degree of formality of this documentation process depends upon the software methodology chosen and the type of formal or implied contract between the performing and benefiting organizations. Whether the contracting situation between the performing and benefiting organization is formal or not, the requirements should be agreed to in writing by the line management of both organizations as well as the PM. Usually in the business world, "if it is not written, it never existed and/or was never agreed to."

As part of the validation process, requirements must be traceable through all preliminary product manifestations and in the final product and test plan thereof. Figure 6.10 is an example of a spreadsheet form of a requirements document that provides for each requirement: a brief description, a unique identifying code, a reference to a more detail description, and checks that each appears in the product manifestations. The spreadsheet may be sorted based on the contents of any column(s) such as priority, type, or appearance in the product manifestations.

Often, requirements are represented with high-level design documents. UML "use cases" are used more because their visual format facilitates communication with end users. A use case clearly shows the external aspects of a system. In the use case diagram, "actors," which may be humans or other IT systems, are shown as stick figures. The actors make requests of the system, provide information to the system, and receive information from the system. A rectangle, which represents the system's boundary, is drawn, and processes are shown as ovals within the rectangle. The processes respond to the actor's requests by either providing information back to the actor and/or changing the state of the system (information content of the system). An example is shown in Figure 6.11 with multiple processes. In addition to the drawing, there would be a simple text description for each interaction (line) between the actors (stick figures) and a process (oval) within the system (rectangle). These text descriptions embody both the interface specifications (what and how information is exchanged between the system process and the actor) and functional specifications (what the process is supposed to do); how the process works is not included in the use case. An excellent method of documenting external requirements is to combine the spreadsheet of Figure 6.10 with use cases, wherein the last column in each row of the spreadsheet references an interaction in a use case diagram.

Use cases (or a similar technique) are also a good discovery method because they keep unnecessary detail out of the requirement process. As previously stated, *how* the processes within the system work should usually not be part of the discovery process. The how of the process is determined later in the design stage (or detail design stage) of the project, including the definition of data requirements (database tables), classes, packages, algorithms, and so forth. A general misconception is that use cases are only used in object-oriented systems. Although I feel that object-oriented methods should always be used for new IT systems, use cases can be used just as effectively for non–object-oriented systems. Paper prototypes or "storyboards" are often used as a follow up to use cases or other forms of preliminary requirement documentation to further discover or clarify/detail requirements. These have many of the same advantages of live prototypes, but they can be produced and modified quicker and cheaper. Paper prototypes can be constructed with paper and pencil, simple drawing programs, presentation software, or RAD products. Storyboards essentially walk the user through the interaction between the end users and the system and visually show that interaction through screen mock-ups of both input and output screens. Each interaction in a use case diagram could be simulated via a storyboard.

Note that some software development methodologies may use little or no requirements documentation. Agile methods, discussed earlier in this book, use methods that require very close interaction between developers and end users to develop incrementally the application and to produce no formal and very little informal requirement documentation. Often the programmers use a test first approach to create automated testing scripts that embody the requirements in those test scripts. As discussed in Chapter V, these agile methods may have limited application.

After the initial requirements have been discovered and recorded, it must be determined which of those requirements will actually be included in the project or in the first phase of the project. First, the requirements must be prioritized, then very rough estimates of the time/cost of each requirement must be developed, typically using historical (or industry available) costs of similar work. In the requirements spreadsheet shown in Figure 6.10, another column could be added for the estimated cost and/or time. Detail cost estimation techniques are covered in Chapter VII. Both the benefiting organization and performing organization are integral to this process, which involves trade-offs and compromises between the project dimensions of time, cost, and scope. This requirement selection process may be done in a number of ways, and the particular manner in which it is accomplished is related to the chosen software engineering methodology and contracting arrangement to be used as

- Single-phase, fixed scope
- Multiphase, fixed scope per phase
- Multiphase, fixed time per phase
- Multiphase, fixed cost (budget) per phase

The first two methods are best suited to contract and bid situations, and the last two methods may be best suited to a type of incremental or iterative development methodology. Other issues may also factor into requirement phasing such as risks, market and application timing, interdependent applications, and available resources. In the requirements spreadsheet shown in Figure 6.10, another column could be added for the project phase; or separate spreadsheets (perhaps in the same workbook) could be used for each phase.

The final requirement process is "requirement change management." Requirements will evolve—some requirements will change, some will be removed, and others will be added. At some point in the initial planning process, the baseline requirements must be set (at least for the first phase), and after that, formal change control should be used. Formal change control is necessary for proper coordination between all the stakeholders, to make sure that all changes are needed and wanted, to review the total impact of changes, and to make sure that changes are properly included in the financial arrangements between the benefiting organization and performing organization. Changes to requirements should go through the same process as the original requirements, including written approval, cost/time impacts, project schedule revision, and traceability. Change control is discussed in detail in a later chapter of this book. The PM must make sure that all stakeholders know the full impact that changes may have on the project, and manage both the changes and stakeholders in the manner most beneficial to the project.

The Software Engineering Institutes Capability Maturity Model includes requirements management as a key process in its Level 2 maturity (www.sei.cmu.edu/cmm).

Level 2 Key Process Areas:

      Requirements Management

      Software Project Planning

      Software Project Tracking and Oversight

      Software Subcontract Management

      Software Quality Assurance

      Software Configuration Management

Figure 6.10. Requirements specification form

Requirements Specification

REQ ID	Description	Priority	Type				Traceability					Detail Reference
			External	Functional	Internal	General	Overall Design	Detail Design	Paper Prototype	Working Prototype	Test Plan	Users Manual	

The level 2 requirements management goals are:

- System requirements allocated to software are controlled to establish a baseline for software engineering and management use.
- Software plans, products, and activities are kept consistent with the system requirements allocated to software.

The key practices under each common feature for requirements are:

Commitment to Perform

The project follows a written organizational policy for managing the system requirements allocated to the software.

Ability to Perform

For each project, responsibility is established for analyzing the system requirements and allocating them hardware, software, and other system components

The allocated requirements are documented

Adequate resources and funding are provided for managing allocated requirements

Members of the software engineering group and other software-related groups are trained to perform their requirements management activities

Activities Performed

The software engineering group reviews the allocated requirements before they are incorporated into the software project

The software engineering group uses the allocated requirements as the basis for the software plans, work products, and activities

Changes to the requirements are reviewed and incorporated into the project

Measurement and Analysis

Measurements are made and used to determine the status of the activities for managing the allocated requirements

Verifying Implementation

The activities for managing the allocated requirements are reviewed with senior management on a periodic basis

The activities for managing the allocated requirements are reviewed with the project manager on both a periodic and event-driven basis

The software quality assurance group reviews and/or audits the activities and work products for managing the allocated requirements and reports the results

The ISO also defines standards for the requirement processes and these are detailed in ISO 9001:2000—Quality Management Systems—Requirements. These standards emphasize

- The requirement processes and the management of these processes
- The commitment and involvement of top management
- The customer focus
- The involvement of people
- Continual improvement of these processes
- The factual approach to requirement decisions

The IEEE also has developed standards for requirements. General system requirements are describe in IEEE Std. 1233-1998. Software requirements are detailed in IEEE Std. 830-1998: IEEE Recommendations for Software Requirements Specification (SRS). As stated in that document, a good SRS has the following benefits:

- Establish the basis for agreement between the customers and the suppliers on what the software product is to do.
- Reduce the development effort.
- Provide a basis for estimating costs and schedules.
- Provide a baseline for verification and validation.
- Facilitate transfer (of the software product).
- Serve as the basis for enhancement.

Figure 6.11. Use case analysis

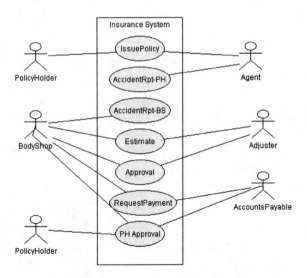

Their IEEE document also discusses the considerations for producing a good SRS:

Nature of the SRS
> Functionality
>
> External interfaces
>
> Performance (speed, availability, response, recovery, etc.)
>
> Attributes (portability, correctness, maintainability, security, etc.)

Environment of the SRS
> Include all needs
>
> Not include design or implementation details
>
> Not impose arbitrary constraints

Characteristics of a good SRS
> Correct
>
> Unambiguous
>
> Complete
>
> Consistent
>
> Ranked
>
> Verifiable
>
> Modifiable
>
> Traceable

Joint preparation of the SRS (customers, suppliers)

SRS evolution

Prototyping

Embedding design in the SRS (show design constraints not design specifics)

Embedding project requirements in the SRS (address the product not the process)

SRS templates are provided in this IEEE standard, and one such template is:

External interface requirements
> User Interfaces
>
> Hardware interfaces
>
> Software interfaces
>
> Communication interfaces

Functional requirements
> Mode 1

Functional requirement 1.1

...

Functional requirement 1.n

...

Mode n

Performance requirements

Design constraints

Software system attributes

Other requirements

As well as general purpose software tools such as spreadsheets, databases, and group decision support tools, there are a number of specialized software tools available to facilitate different portions of the requirement processes including discovery, organization/documentation, prioritization/phasing, and change control. Discovery tools allow users to enter data about possible requirements, sort and filter requirements based on their attributes, check for possible redundancies, and disseminate requirement information to stakeholders via various paper or electronic media. Prioritization tools allow users to enter priorities and other comments about each requirement (perhaps anomalously) either in a synchronous or asynchronous manner. Phasing tools allow users to finds set of requirements that match time and/or budget constraints based upon priorities and/or other factors. Examples of specialized requirements software include DOORS/ERS by Telelogic (www.telelogic.com/products/), Analyst Pro by Goda (www.analysttool.com/), RTM by Serena (www.serena.com), SpeeDev RM (www.speedev.com), RMS by TrueREQ (www.truereq.com), Catalyst Enterprise 3 by SteelTrace (http://steeltrace.com), RequisitePro from IBM/Rational (www-306.ibm.com/software/awdtools/reqpro/), ActiveFocus from Xapware (www.xapware.com), RIQTek (http://home.riqek.com), and Cradle from 3SL (www.threesl.com/). However, these specialized tools do not fully automate the overall requirement process, they simply facilitate certain portions thereof because all of these requirement processes involve attentive and careful personal interaction amongst stakeholders.

For further details on IT requirements, see *Managing Software Requirements* (Leffingwell & Widrig, 2000), *Software Engineering Requirements* (Thayer & Dorfman, 1999), and *Mastering the Requirements Process* (Robertson & Robertson, 1999).

Chapter Summary

In this chapter, initial and overall project planning has been covered. The process of IT requirements discovery and documentation has been discussed and illustrated. Once a complete and clear set of requirements has been documented and approved by all relevant stakeholders, detail project planning can begin; such detail planning is covered in upcoming chapters.

References

Alexander, M. (2004). Software development should include security plan. Retrieved from www.adtmag.com

Davis, A., Hickey, A., & Zweig, A. (2004). Requirements management in a project management context. In P. Morris & J. Pinto (Eds.), *The Wiley guide to managing projects.* New York: Wiley.

Leffingwell, D., & Widrig, D. (2000). *Managing software requirements.* Boston: Addison-Wesley.

PMI. (2000). *The project management body of knowledge (PMBOK).* Newton Square, PA. ISBN 1-880410-22-2.

Robertson, S., & Robertson, J. (1999). *Mastering the requirements process.* Boston: Addison-Wesley.

Standish Group. (2004). Chaos chronicles. Retrieved from www.standisgroup.com

Thayer, R., & Dorfman, M. (1999). *Software engineering requirements.* New York: Wiley.

Chapter VII

Developing the Schedule and Cost Plan

You got to be careful if you don't know where you're going, because you might not get there.

(Yogi Berra)

The Project Management Institute (PMI) project management process groups include initiation, planning, execution, control, and closing. In practice, however, the initiation processes of a project are often not part of a project for budgeting and control issues, but rather are charged to management and administration (M&A) or operations and maintenance (O&M) general ledger accounts. In some organizations, these charges are later reversed back to a project after it is decided to move forward with that project. Thus, only the planning, execution, and control processes become part of the project for accounting purposes; sometimes detail planning is part of a project but not overall planning. Similarly, the closing process group may or may not be a formal part of the project, and sometimes those processes are performed by an independent organization. This chapter is concerned with detail project planning, particularly the schedule and cost plan.

Detail Project Planning

After the requirements have been determined, documented, and approved, a detail analysis and breakdown of that project's scope are created. According to PMI.

Scope definition involves subdividing the major project deliverables (as identified in the scope statement and requirements document) into smaller more manageable components in order to:

- *Improve the accuracy of estimates*
- *Define a baseline for performance measurements*
- *Facilitate clear responsibility assignments. (PMI, 2000)*

These manageable components are organized into a work breakdown structure (WBS). According to PMI, the major activities (and the order in which they are to be performed) in project planning include the following (PMI, 2000):

- Develop scope statement
- Assemble project team
- Develop work breakdown structure
- Finalize project team
- Build a network diagram (showing activity dependencies)
- Estimate cost and time, and find the "critical path"
- Determine the overall schedule and budget
- Plan procurement
- Plan quality
- Identify risks, quantify them, and develop responses
- Other plans: change control plan, communications plan, and management plan
- Completion of an overall project plan
- Project Plan approval
- "Kickoff Meeting"

For a very simple project, however, one may only need a to-do list and a shopping list. The degree of project management formality has to be adjusted for the size and complexity of a project, as illustrated in Figure 7.1. For a large and/or complex project, all the above activities need to be done; but the order of these activities depends upon the manner in which IT departments estimate project costs and handle resource allocation and costing (particularly human resources).

Figure 7.1. Project planning formality

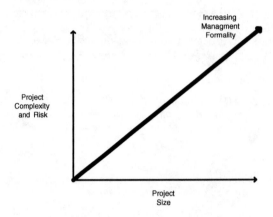

Developing the
Work Breakdown Structure

The concept and name of the WBS goes back to the U.S. Department of Defense (DoD) in the 1950s. The PMI definition of a WBS is "A *deliverable oriented* grouping of project elements that *organizes and defines* the total work scope of the project" (PMI, 2000). PMI is developing a practice standard for the WBS, which was only partially available during the writing of this book.

"The most important part of the planning phase is the development of the work breakdown structure" (Klastorn, 2004). *It is essential to develop a complete and well-organized WBS. Many project managers or coordinators spend too little time in developing the WBS and perhaps too much time in scheduling resources too precisely to WBS tasks. The WBS is the basis for all project planning and later performance monitoring; this is illustrated in Figure 7.2.*

For most projects, the WBS is typically arranged in a multilevel hierarchical manner, a so-called tree structure. The first level (Level zero, or top level) typically corresponds to the project phases. Each level of the WBS is a further breakdown of the previous level. Note that some authors refer to the top level of the WBS as Level 1 and there is only one code (node) at the top level, which represents the project in total. In the IT field, we are accustomed to starting our numbering at zero and consider the top node as our data structure name, not a WBS code (node). Note also that, although the WBS specifies the work to be done, it does not specify the order in which the work is to be done, nor does the WBS numbering indicate the order in which work items are to be done. The WBS numbering per se also does not indicate assignment of work to responsible organizational components, assignment of work to any resources, or the cost of any work item. The WBS can be schematically represented by a tree diagram, either horizontally, as shown in Figure 7.3, or vertically, as shown in Figure 7.4.

Figure 7.2. WBS uses

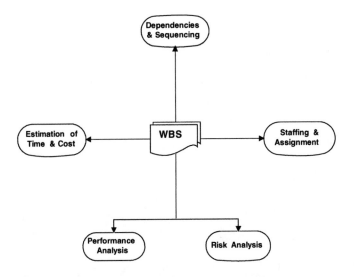

Figure 7.3. Horizontal WBS

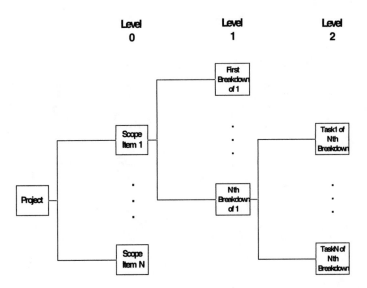

Figure 7.4. Vertical WBS

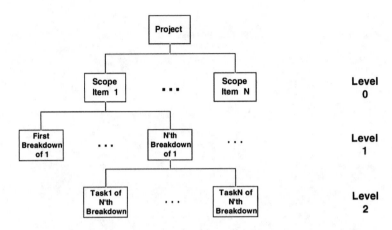

Text-based schematic representations are typically horizontal with indentation used for each level. Identification numbering of each WBS code typically uses a dot or dash notation. For computer sorting purposes, leading zeros are used so that each level of the WBS identification code uses the same number of digits. For example, with 12 codes at level zero, use "01" through "12", not "1" through "12".

  1.0 Scope Item 1

    1.1 First Breakdown of Scope Item 1

     ...

    1.N N'th Breakdown of Scope Item 1

      1.N.1 First Task of N'th Breakdown of Scope Item 1

       ...

      1.N.N N'th Task of N'th Breakdown of Scope Item 1

  2.0 Scope Item 2

   ...

The lowest level (when viewed as a vertical tree) defines the actual tasks, often called work packets. These work packets are also called activity WBS codes, as opposed to the WBS codes at the higher levels, which are called "control" codes. A control code has one or more lower level subsidiary code, each of which is either another control code or an activity code. Each activity code is associated with one and only one control code. ***Planned costs are posted only to activity accounts, and actual costs may be posted at any level, but the recommended approach is to gather costs at the activity level, also.*** The sum of the costs for a control code's activity codes are rolled up from is subsidiary codes to that control code.

Note that some authors consider the bottom level of the WBS as not a part of the WBS per se, because they consider tasks or activities to be part of the schedule not part of the WBS. In their view, WBS codes are only nouns or adjectives, and the schedule items are verbs. Also, in the early implementation of a WBS for earned value (discussed in a later chapter) by the U.S. DoD, the second lowest level of the WBS was called cost accounts (or control accounts), where each code corresponded to in intersection of the higher WBS level and a performing organization code; below that level of cost accounts were the work packets. In this early method, pricing was done at the cost account level and scheduling (including dependencies between packets) was done at the packet work level. In practice this is not always practical for several reasons including the fact that task dependencies may encompass multiple cost accounts. *In our more realistic and general purpose view, the tasks at the bottom level of the WBS are the activities that later get estimated, priced, assigned resources, and scheduled.*

There are several common methods of logically breaking down the scope of a project.

These methods not only logically divide the overall work, but also are relate to the way costs are accumulated for the project in an organization. Later in this book, we discuss cost gathering methods, constraints, and associated issues.

The organizational method divides the scope based upon the organization doing the work (performing organization), responsible for the work (responsible organization), or benefiting from the work (benefiting organization, usually the customer). This is illustrated in Figure 7.5. For the performing or responsible organization method, costs are gathered by the organization doing or delegating the work through its payroll, job costing, and/or accounts payable system. For the benefiting organization method, costs are usually gathered by a billing and accounts receivable system.

Figure 7.5. Organizational WBS

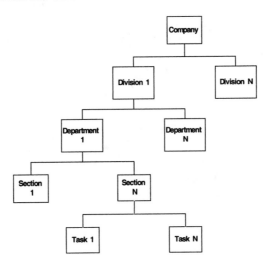

The product method organizes the scope based upon the logical or physical parts of a product, which is the subject of the project. This is illustrated in Figure 7.6. Here, costs are typically gathered based upon the part being worked upon and may be from a manufacturing/material resources/requirements planning (MRP) system. Because some scope may be related to nonspecific parts (overall management, operation, or services such as engineering design services), a totally product-based WBS is not common. Product-based WBSs are often associated with contracted work, such as with the U.S. government.

The functional (or task-based) WBS is based upon the work being done to carry out the scope of the project, and is illustrated in Figure 7.7. This type of organization is the most effective for measuring project performance as will be shown later in this book. Most organizations have some type of methodology for building the item that is the subject of the project, and the task based WBS usually follows that methodology in its logical layout.

Because none of these pure WBS methods reflect a logical structure by organization, product, or task, a hybrid WBS structure may be used, such as the one shown in Figure 7.8.

To account for the multiple dimensions of organization, product, cost category, and resources, other coding systems may be used for a project in addition to the WBS. These are used for both pure and hybrid types of WBS structures. These coding systems are

- *OBS:* The organizational breakdown structure is used to show organizational units of a performing or responsible organization. There may be an OBS for benefiting organizations also, but there is generally only one benefiting organization for the entire project (and the overall project code may include the benefiting organization code). Typically each task at the lowest level of the WBS (work packet) is associated with one OBS code for the responsible or performing organization.

Figure 7.6. Product WBS

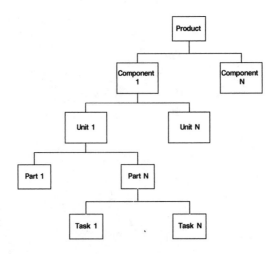

Figure 7.7. Functional WBS

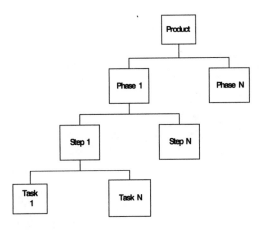

Figure 7.8. Hybrid WBS

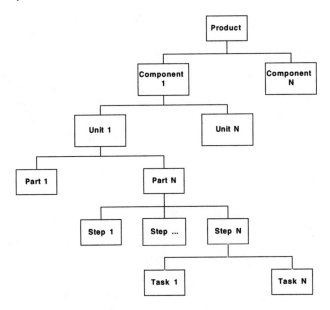

- *PBS:* The *part breakdown structure* shows the physical breakdown of parts. A PBS may be the "top" of a hybrid WBS, which has a task-based, lower level WBS. Alternatively, a PBS may be used as a code that is an attribute of some of the WBS codes (those that are specifically associated with one part).

- *RBS:* The *resource breakdown structure* is used to identify resources that are to be used on a project such as individuals (or labor categories). Typically each work packet is associated with one or more RBS codes. This is discussed later in this chapter.

- **CBS:** The *contractor breakdown structure* identifies outside (outside of the company or responsible organization) responsibilities for work or other services and may be used in a similar manner to the OBS (or the OBS may accommodate internal and external organizations). CBS codes are also commonly used for WBS codes at levels above the work packets to show outside delegation.

- **EOC:** The element of cost structure identifies the type of cost incurred or to be incurred such as labor, lease, travel, space allocations and other charges to a project.

- **GL:** The *general ledger* code is an accounting code to which charges are applied in the company's financial system. Typically, the GL code is determined (calculation or table lookup) automatically from other codes (typically the overall project code, the OBS, and the EOC).

In some organizations (i.e., the U.S. government) it is common to develop an organizational assignment matrix, which maps the WBS (down to the lowest level, excluding the work packets/activities) to the OBS. This may be called a responsibility assignment matrix (RAM), but that term is also commonly used for a mapping between the WBS and the RBS. Figure 7.9 shows a conceptual example of this matrix in a spreadsheet. The cells of the spreadsheet are typically the work packets (or a small set of interdependent work packets) and are called *cost accounts*, a term that originally came from the U.S. DoD Cost/Schedule Control Systems Criteria (C/SCSC), discussed in Chapter XIV.

The task or functional WBS is best for project performance measurement and control because the WBS is organized by the actual work to be done. This more clearly illustrated in Chapter XIV. The best approach for IT projects is to base the WBS tasks on the company's adopted methodology for software development, software acquisition, and/or software integration. Thus, an IT WBS is best developed from the project scope using adopted methodology with consideration for how the work will be allocated to organi-

Figure 7.9. Organizational assignment matrix

Organizational Assignment Matrix						
	OBS					
	1.1			2.0		
WBS	1.1	1.2	1.3	2.1	2.2	2.3
1.0						
1.1						
1.1.1	X					
1.1.2			X			
1.2.3					X	
1.2						
1.2.1		X				
1.2.2		X				
1.2.3				X		
1.3						
1.3.1						X
1.3.2						X
1.3.3	X					
2.0						
2.1						
...						

Figure 7.10. WBS development

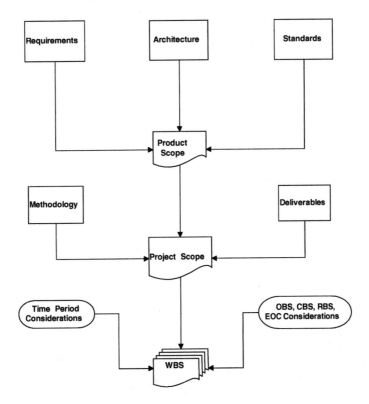

zational components and further broken down into manageable pieces. This is concep-tualized in Figure 7.10.

In using a methodology and task-based structure, it is common to use a PBS to create a hybrid WBS. The PBS for IT projects usually corresponds to software and/or hardware deliverables. There are two ways to structure such a hybrid WBS. The first is the methodology first method, as shown in Figure 7.11, and the second is the deliverable first method, as shown in Figure 7.12. The deliverables shown in these diagrams may consist of several levels, such as a level for major subsystems and a second level for the components of each subsystem (screens, reports, etc.).

The lowest level of the WBS represents the tasks to be done (work packages or activity codes). "The work package usually has a short-time span schedule (40 to 100 hours), is limited to one performing department, and has defined completion criteria" (Kiewel, 1998). *The size and nature of these work packets is very important in regard to project cost planning and control.* It is very important that they

- Are realistically and confidently estimable
- Cannot be (or should not be) logically subdivided

Figure 7.11. Methodology first WBS

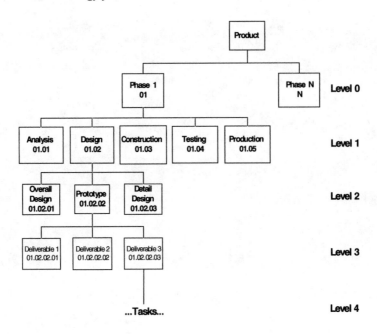

Figure 7.12. Deliverable first WBS

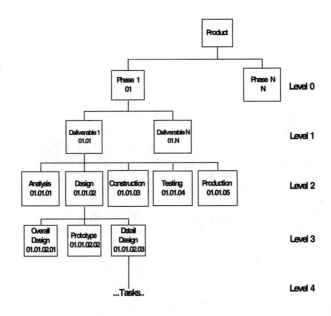

- Are to be assigned to one OBS/CBS code
- Can be completed relatively quickly (80 hours max rule of thumb)
- Have a meaningful and measurable conclusion and deliverable
- Have enough "visibility" so that progress and cost can be determined
- Can be completed without interruption (i.e., need for more info)

Each work packet should be assigned to one organization that is responsible for the work to be completed, so the packet would be associated with a single OBS or CBS code. If possible, it is also best to have each work packet assigned to a single resource (RBS code), although this may not be possible in some IT organizations where techniques such as pair programming are used. Different types of work should not be lumped into a work package; for example, design and coding should be in separate packages, particularly for estimation purposes, discussed later. A time period in a project calendar corresponds to the interval that is to be used for gathering project performance data, including hours expended and percent complete estimates. It is important that a work packet not encompass many such periods; the optimal situation would be for a work packet to correspond exactly to one time period. For performance analysis, progress estimates (% complete) and cost data should be available at each time period for each work packet (incurred effort and cost during that period). Work packets that are highly interdependent should be combined (if such is possible without extending the time of that packet beyond a few time periods) to reduce overall work packed interdependencies for scheduling. A *Work Packet Decomposition Checklist* was presented by Raz and Globerson (1998):

- Is there a need to improve the accuracy of the cost and duration estimates?
- Is more than one individual responsible for the work?
- Does the work content include more than one type of activity?
- Is there a need to know precisely the timing of activities internal to the work package?
- Is there a need to cost out activities internal to the work package?
- Are there any dependencies between the internal activities of the work package and other work packages?
- Are there any significant time breaks in the execution of the internal activities?
- Do resource requirements within the work package change over time?
- Do the prerequisites differ among the internal activities?
- Are there acceptance criteria applicable before the completion of the entire package?
- Are there any intermediate deliverables that can be used to generate a positive cash flow?
- Are there specific risks that require focused attention?

Figure 7.13. Web site development WBS

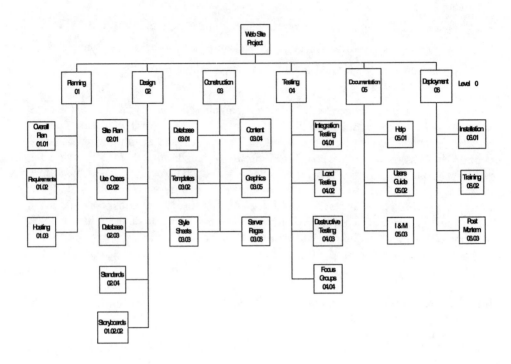

In addition to the formulation of the WBS itself, a WBS dictionary is often created by the project team and is typically used to control what work is done and when. It puts a clear boundary around each work packet:

- *Work Packet ID Info:* Code, name, element of cost
- *Assignments:* Performing organization, resource assigned to, customer contact
- *Time Information:* Start, length, end
- *Dependencies* (dependent WBS codes)
- *Detail Description* (both product/service and work)
- *Acceptance:* Quality criteria, testing required, approval by

As an example of IT WBS formulation, consider the case of a project for the development of a corporate Web site. A WBS based upon a typical software development methodology may appear as in Figure 7.13, which shows the first two levels (0 and 1) of the WBS developed for this project. Each Level 1 item expands into work packets at Level 2.

Software packages used in project management are discussed in Chapter XV, but a typical form to add a WBS code to a project appears in Figure 7.14 (from the Web-based

Figure 7.14. Form to add WBS code

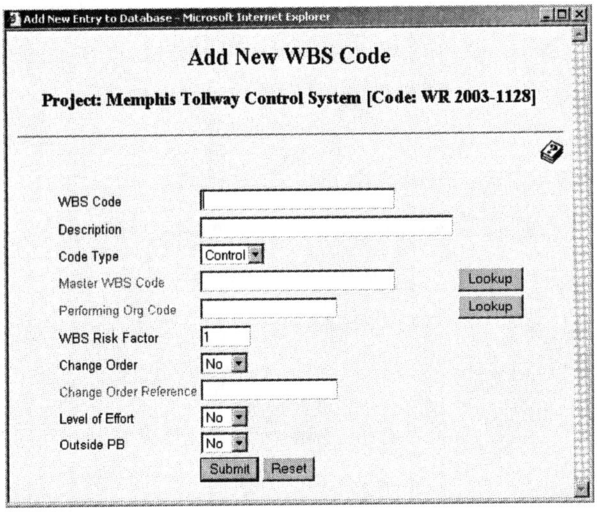
Add New Entry to Database - Microsoft Internet Explorer

Add New WBS Code

Project: Memphis Tollway Control System [Code: WR 2003-1128]

WBS Code
Description
Code Type: Control
Master WBS Code — Lookup
Performing Org Code — Lookup
WBS Risk Factor: 1
Change Order: No
Change Order Reference
Level of Effort: No
Outside PB: No
Submit | Reset

FiveAndDime system). Figure 7.15 shows a screen capture from a display of the Level zero WBS codes. Each Level 1 code expands into the Level 2 codes, which are the work packages for this project. For example, the Level 1 WBS code for Standards is shown expanded to the bottom level in Figure 7.16. Figure 7.17 is an example of another form; this one is used for quicker entry of subsidiary WBS codes, which by default inherit the OBS code of their master WBS code.

Task Estimation

After a WBS is formed, the next step is to estimate the amount of time it will take to perform each of the tasks at the lowest level of the WBS (work packets). Task estimation is still a problem area for IT projects. In a 2004 *Computerworld* survey, the question was asked in about 150 companies: "Do your project managers have the appropriate skills to develop accurate estimates?" The results were

- Sometimes: 47%
- Rarely: 27%
- Often: 19%
- Most often: 6%
- Routinely: 1% (Brandel, 2004)

Figure 7.15. Table of Level 0 WBS codes

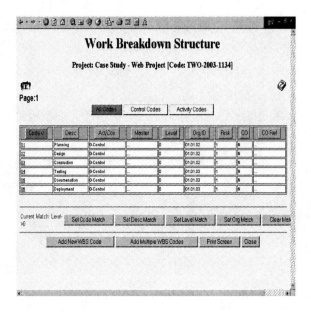

Figure 7.16. Table of Level 1 WBS codes

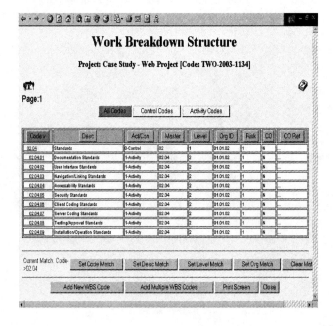

Figure 7.17. Form to add subsidiary WBS codes

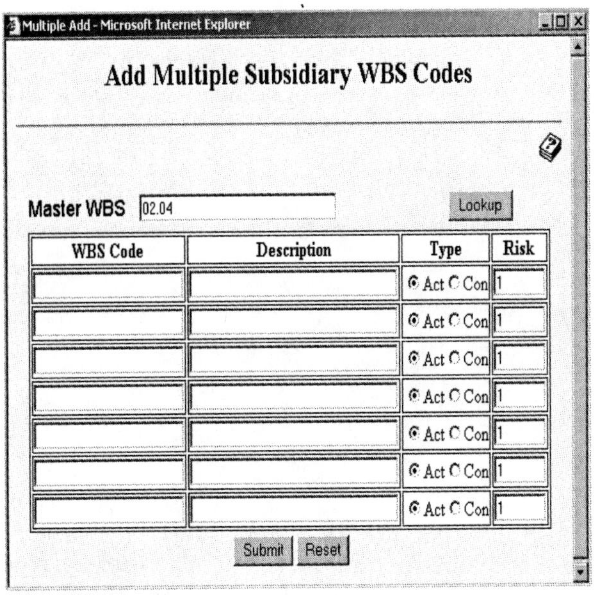

In many projects, particularly IT projects, the type of resource(s) needed for each of these tasks must be determined to estimate time and cost. Resource needs are usually specified generically at this point in the project, such as programmer/analyst Level 3 (PA3) or technical writer Level 2 (TW2). If the organization's resource breakdown structure is generically oriented, then a RBS(s) code may be assigned to the WBS codes at this point. Figure 7.18 is an example of a generic resources table that shows the "burdened" rate for each type of resource. The amount of time needed to complete a work packet should be a function of the type of resource and number of resources assigned; for example, we would expect that a PA3 would typically complete a programming task quicker that an PA2. Also, certain types of tasks may have "levels of difficulty" that could only be assigned to a resource above a certain level.

In many IT organizations, however, promotions from one grade level to another are based more upon "time in grade" than upon competency level, so there may not be much actual average productivity increase in moving up the grade scale. For that reason and others, in IT, the productivity rate varies widely between individuals, even in the same grade. This is a phenomenon that is perhaps peculiar to IT and a few other professional areas, such as engineering. As a contrasting example, in the construction area, most bricklayers have a similar productivity rate in terms of bricks per hour. Some IT organizations may specify the actual resources (i.e., by person) at this point in the project (or they may specify a "preferred individual" for a task), but typically, specific resource assignments come later in the project.

For IT projects, most packets involve only labor and the amount of work is usually estimated by using historical data, benchmarks, and/or some specific parametric tech-

Figure 7.18. Generic project resources

Generic Resources		
Code	Description	Burdened Rate
P1	Programmer 1	30
P2	Programmer 2	35
P3	Programmer 3	40
PA1	Programmer Analyst 1	45
PA2	Programmer Analyst 1	50
PA3	Programmer Analyst 1	55
SA1	Systems Architech 1	60
SA2	Systems Architech 2	65
SA3	Systems Architech 3	70
DB1	Database Analsys 1	50
DB2	Database Analsys 2	55
DB3	Database Analsys 3	60
TW1	Technical Writer 1	30
TW2	Technical Writer 2	40
SEC1	Security Specialist 1	40
SEC2	Security Specialist 2	50
TEST1	Test Specialist 1	30
TEST2	Test Specialist 2	40
PM1	Project Manager 1	60
PM2	Project Manager 2	70
PM3	Project Manager 3	80

nique such as lines of code, function point analysis, or number and type of requirements involved. Even if a parametric estimation technique or benchmarking is used, historical data (either internal or external to the organization) should be used for a reality check. Historical estimates for the effort required in the work packets usually come from informal estimates by individuals experienced with the specific type of work. If possible, estimates from the actual people who would be doing the work may prove the best, and it also provides a type of buy in from those individuals regarding the validity of the project estimates. A formal process such as the Delphi technique can also be used to gain better understanding and consensus among multiple experts on the effort required in IT tasks (Roetzheim & Beasley, 1998). This is an iterative technique and can take longer than informal methods, but usually produces better results.

Another form of estimation is analogous estimating or top down estimating. This technique uses prior similar projects, and then estimates the overall cost of the entire current project. Eestimates are then formed from that overall estimate for the first level of the WBS (Level zero) using a percentage breakdown from prior project experience. Then costs are broken down to the next lower level of the WBS, and so on. This technique is often used during project conception and selection but fortunately not typically used for IT projects for detail cost and time estimating. When this technique is used by upper management or PMs to set overall project cost, it can often result in unrealistic budgets and schedules for a project that will ultimately doom the project and/or demoralize the IT staff such that future projects will be at risk. PMs do not have a reputation for making accurate estimates of IT work by themselves. This may be true even if a PM came up through the technical ranks, since IT technology changes so quickly.

One or more benchmarks of task level work may be available from previous, similar projects, or actual benchmarks may be used. Often, prototyping and benchmarking efforts can be combined. These benchmarks may be used in a linear manner to estimate time for the tasks at hand. For example, we may know that a Web screen form with four fields took 2 hours to build and test, and that another Web form with eight fields took 3 hours to build and test. A linear relationship (two equations in two unknowns) would then predict the time to build and unit test such Web forms would be 1 hour plus the number of fields divided by 2. If there are many such Web forms to build, a "learning curve" relationship could be added, which is usually in a form as:

$$T(i) = T(1)*(a + (1-a)i^{-b}),$$

where $T(i)$ is the time to build the i'th form, $T(1)$ is the time to build the first form, b is the learning rate which is less than 1 (typically in the range of .01 to .1), and a is the incompressibility factor also less than 1 (typically about .5). Actual values of a and b can be calculated by how long it would take a programmer to build the first such form and how long it takes him to build a second and third such form. These values are then substituted in the formula (which is made linear via log functions) to determine the learning factor and the compressibility factor.

In practice, however, this scenario is oversimplified and there is usually more that one factor that influences the time to build an IT component. In the Web form example, each form field may have a different degree of complexity. For example, some fields may require validation, and they may require a new type of validation that is not already in our JavaScript validation library. Some fields may require simple lookups (i.e., drop downs) or more complex database lookup and/or validation, such as foreign key fields. In general, most parametric effort estimation models are a function of problem size and other adjustment factors (sometimes called "cost drivers").

In the early days of software application development (i.e., the 1960s and 1970s), the standard metric for the size and complexity of a software development task was measured in lines of code (LOC). Back then, business applications were written mostly in COBOL, and engineering/scientific applications were written mostly in FORTRAN. Although, it was always augmentable which lines counted and which lines were not counted (such as declarations and comments), and many such metric-based estimation techniques and databases were developed and found utility. The utility of such methods were the greatest where comparisons were made using the same language in the same platform and programming environment; also, the tasks being measured should be totally programming tasks (not involve testing and documentation or other related tasks).

The constructive cost model (COCOMO) was introduced in 1981 (Boehm, 1981). Based on a number of real software development projects, it presented parametric models correlating LOC to task effort. Using COCOMO, one first classifies the type of project into one of three categories: organic, semidetached, and embedded. Organic projects are relatively routine, embedded projects represents new endeavors for the organization, and semidetached are not new endeavors but are more complex than organic projects. There are also three points of application in a project: basic (applied early in a project), intermediate (after requirements are finalized), and advanced (applied after detail design). Basic COCOMO formulas were

Organic Projects: EFFORT = 2.4 * KLOC $^{1.05}$

Semidetached Projects: EFFORT = 3.0 * KLOC $^{1.12}$

Embedded Projects: EFFORT = 3.6 * KLOC $^{1.2}$

where KLOC is 1 thousand lines of code and EFFORT is expressed in person months. The intermediate model uses 15 cost drivers, including reliability needed, database size, complexity, experience and capability factors, schedule factors, and practices and tools maturity. The advanced model gets more detailed and sophisticated including phasing factors.

As languages multiplied and diversity and as fourth generation languages (4GLs), computer aided software engineering (CASE), and what you see is what you get (WYSIWYG) code generators became more common, these basic correlation metrics became less predictive. Other IT changes (such as a move away from mainframe batch processing to client-server real-time turnaround; more emphasis on software reuse, components, and OO software; and spending more time in design and less time in coding) also required new correlations. Other estimation techniques were developed, and COCOMO was expanded to COCOMO II (or COCOMO 2) for newer IT environments (Boehm, 2000). The original COCOMO model was also redesignated COCOMO 81. COCOMO II consists of three submodels, each one offering increased accuracy based upon the depth of planning/design. In order of increasing accuracy, these submodels are the applications composition, early design, and postarchitecture models.

With LOC estimation techniques, one still has to convert an application level component (such as a Web form) into an LOC number. This often can be done by looking at past coding artifacts. The concept of function point analysis (FPA) was proposed by IBM (Albrecht, 1979). This concept starts with application-level components. FPA tends to be relatively independent of language, coding style, and software architecture. A function point is defined as one end-user computational task, such as a query for an input. This notion is important because it allows a function point to be mapped easily into user-oriented requirements and components, but it hides internal functions.

Basic function points are categorized into five groups, or transaction types: files (internal logical file), outputs (external output), inquiries (external inquiry), inputs (external input), and interfaces (external interface). This is illustrated in Figure 7.19. In addition, each type of function point is rated as to it complexity: low, average, and high.

Complexity categories are assigned point scores, and a typical assignment might be *low* = 5, *average* = 10, *high* = 15.

The point score can vary based upon which of the five transaction types is involved. A file is typically a traditional disk file or a relational database table. The file's complexity is low if there are few attributes and it is complex if there are many attributes and groups. An interface is also typically a connection to a file or table, but one that is outside of the domain of this application. An external input provides for data to come into the application. It is typically a user input screen, but it can be any means of gathering input, such as from scanners. The external inputs generally alter the data in the files/tables via add, delete, or update functions; the number of files/tables affected determines the complexity level. An external output provides for data to exit the application boundary

Figure 7.19. Function point types

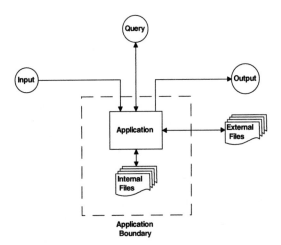

and is typically a report or an output screen; the number of files/tables from which the data comes determines the complexity. Queries first request and then output data across the application boundary but do not alter the state of the system (data contained in the files/tables); complexity is a function of the number of files/tables involved. Once all the application components are classified and rated for complexity, an unadjusted function point total (UFP) is calculated as shown in the spreadsheet template of Figure 7.20.

The next step in FPA is to calculate a value adjustment factor (VAF) based upon the presence (or lack thereof) of certain general system characteristics. Each of these general system characteristics is assigned a degree of influence from 0 to 5, with zero being *not present* to 5 being a *very strong influence*. These degrees of influence are then summed to get the total influence; this sum is then divided by 100 and added to a base factor (a typical base factor might be 0.65). General characteristics would include distributed data processing, online updates, transaction processing, multiple sites, and so forth. The total function points are then FP = UFP * VAF. For all the details and particulars for different IT environments, please see the standard practices for FPA methodology, which is found in the *IFPUG Counting Practices Manual* (IFPUG, 1996).

FPA can and should be done at several points in an IT project. An initial FPA can be done based on the overall scope statement; a more detailed FPA done later, based on the formal requirements definition; and again later, based on the WBS. FPA can also be done for change orders and to detect scope creep. Without some standardization of how the function points are enumerated and interpreted, consistent results can be difficult to obtain. For example, how are relational database views to be counted—one file/table, or many. Successful application depends on establishing a consistent method of counting function points and keeping records to establish baseline numbers for your specific systems. Training in FPA is available from many sources, and such training is recommended. There are also certification programs.

Figure 7.20. Unadjusted function point total

Type	Low			Average			High			Type Total
	# Comp	Scale	Points	# Comp	Scale	Points	# Comp	Scale	Points	
Files		12			16			20		
Inputs		7			12			18		
Outputs		5			10			15		
Queries		6			10			15		
Interfaces		10			15			20		
								Total-->		

The table is titled **Unadjusted FPA** with a **Complexity** sub-header.

Function point methodology has evolved over the years; the International Function Point User Group (IFPUG; www.ifpug.org/), formed in 1986, is the focal point for information on function point analysis (IFPUG, 1996). There is also a FPA user group for the United Kingdom, UFPUG. The original metrics have been considerably updated and refined to cover more IT application areas. Today, FPA has become widely used to estimate a software project's effort and duration, set productivity rates in function points per hour, determine support requirements, and to estimate system change orders. There is a large user community for function points; IFPUG has more than 1,200 member companies, and they cooperate in establishing an effective FPA program.

There are correlation tables to convert between function points and LOC in different IT environments, and this is called "backfiring" (Jones, 1995). Typical approximate values are shown in Figure 7.21.

COCOMO II supports the use of either/both function points or source lines of code. Early in the project, object points are used, which are similar to function points but broader and which basically represent an external object (such as a screen, report, or batch module) and their complexity. Each object generates a number of object points:

Screens – Simple = 1; Medium = 2; Difficult = 3;

Reports – Simple = 2; Medium = 5; Difficult = 8;

Modules – 10

There are guidelines for defining simple, medium, and difficult based upon the number of views used and database files/tables involved. The COCOMO II application composition (rough estimate) formulas using object points (OP) take the form of

EFFORT = NOP / PROD

NOP = OP * (100 - % reuse)/100

Figure 7.21. Function point backfiring

Language	LOC per Function Point
Machine Language	650
Assembly Language	300
Ada	70 - 80
Pascal	80 - 100
C	100 - 150
C++	30 - 50
Visual Basic	30 - 40
Java	25 - 50

PROD is the productivity that varies depending upon the maturity of the organization and the individual(s) involved; it typically ranges from 4 (very low) to 50 (very high). During the early design stage of a project, unadjusted function points are used. Once a specific architecture has been chosen, lines of code are used. The COCOMO II postarchitecture formulas take the form of:

$$\text{EFFORT} = \text{ASLOC}^{(AT/100)} / \text{ATPROD} + 2.5 * (\text{SIZE} * (1 + \text{BRAK}/100))^b \cdot \text{EM}_i$$

$$b = 1.01 + (\text{``SF}_j)/100$$

$$\text{SIZE} = \text{KSLOC} + \text{KASLOC} * \text{AAM} * (100 - \text{AT})/100$$

Where:

AT = % of components adapted

SF_j = scale factor

EM_i = effort multiplier

ASLOC = size of adapted components

BRAK = % code discarded due to requirements volatility

ATPROD = automatic translation productivity

AAM = adaptation adjustment multiplier

KSLOC = thousand lines of source code

KASLOC = thousand lines of adapted source code

There are a number of other estimation methods and formulas including the Software Lifecycle Model (SLIM, or Putnam Model), Price-S (Lockheed Martin Model), Waltson-Felix Model, Bailey-Basil Model, and the Doty Model. For a detailed analysis of these methods, see the DOD report by McGibbon (1997). For example a project of 100,000 lines of source code would be roughly estimated as shown in the following list by some of these models (assuming nominal effort multipliers and scale factors, no discarded code, and no adapted code):

COMOMO II – 500 person months

SLIM – 275 person months

Doty – 650 person months

Walston/Felix – 350 person months

Bailey/Basil – 175 person months (McGibbon, 1997)

There can be wide variation in predicted values for these different parametric models. Kemerer (1997) reported average errors of over 600% for COCOMO 81 models. For many of these estimation models, there are also estimation formulas for the schedule time as a function of the effort in person months, because the relationship between schedule time and person months tends to be nonlinear, particularly for large, complex projects. There are software programs available that implement the COCOMO II methodology, and these are available from both academic (USC) and commercial vendors. As of this writing, the latest version was USC COCOMO II.2001.0. For the latest in COCOMO II methodology, see one of the Web sites that maintain this information, such as http://sunset.usc.edu/research/COCOMOII or www.jsc.nasa.gov/bu2/COCOMO.html. Other estimating and costing software programs are available from a number of vendors, including www.softstarsystems.com/, www.galorath.com/, www.rcinc.com, www.pricesystems.com, www.marotz.com, and www.spr.com.

Whether historical estimates, benchmarks, or parametric models are used, there is a level of uncertainty in the estimates. For parametric models, there will be uncertainty both in the input to the model (size and other factors) as well as in the model itself. People tend to be overly optimistic, particularly in IT, about estimating the time required to do something. On the other hand, it is natural for the people who will actually be doing the work or responsible for the work (i.e., managers) to throw extra "padding" into an estimate. Program evaluation and review technique (PERT) is the most common method of dealing with uncertainties in task duration estimates. It assumes that these durations are random variables drawn from a beta distribution (Malcolm, Rosebooom, & Clark, 1959). Such a distribution is show in Figure 7.22. To calculate the PERT time for a task, three estimates are obtained: optimistic, pessimistic, and most likely. The PERT time (PT) is calculated as:

PT = (Optimistic + Pessimistic + 4 * Most Likely)/6.

The task variance and standard deviation is given by:

Variance = $(\text{Pessimistic} - \text{Optimistic})^2/36$

Standard Deviation = (Pessimistic – Optimistic)/6.

The beta distribution is typically not symmetric but it is unimodal. To find the combined variance from a group of tasks, we do not sum the individual variances, but instead sum deviation and take its square root. Many authors have investigated the accuracy and utility of PERT estimates and other techniques over the years, and there are other techniques that may be more accurate or useful in certain disciplines. However, for IT projects, the PERT estimate provides a reasonable method of estimating task times in the presence of uncertainty. Using our earlier example with Web forms, an optimistic value could be based upon the situation whereby none of the fields required any special handling (unusual validation or foreign key lookup), and the pessimistic value would be where each field required some type of special handling. It is important not to confuse the notions of pessimistic estimates with risk analysis, discussed later in this book. The pessimistic estimate is not made in regard to some unusual or catastrophic occurrence, such as a prolonged power outage, illness of the assigned programmer, and so on.

Task Sequencing and the Critical Path

Once a WBS is established and the effort involved in each work packet is determined, the next step is to sequence the tasks in the order they need to be performed. Task sequencing typically uses a network diagram, sometimes called a logic diagram, that shows how the project tasks (work packets) will flow in time from beginning to end of project. This sequencing can actually be done without knowledge of the effort involved in each task, and sometimes the sequencing is done before estimation. However, for the determination of a critical path, we must know how long it will take to do each task as well as the order in which the tasks can be done. How long it takes to do each task depends not only on the amount of effort of a task (typically measured in person hours) but also on how many people will be assigned to a task.

Figure 7.22. Beta distribution

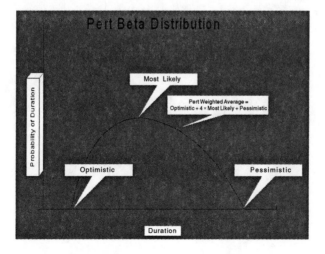

A network diagram is constructed by taking the tasks and putting them in the order they will be done, taking into account any dependencies. This process is called activity sequencing. Note that this process need not be done at the lowest level of the WBS, although it is typically done at that level to maximize the parallelism (the number of task that can be worked on simultaneously). When done at higher levels of the WBS, whole blocks of task may be dependent upon other blocks of tasks. For example, all of the implementation tasks may be dependent on the completion of all of the design tasks as in a strict waterfall methodology of software development. To maximize parallelism, and thus minimize overall development calendar time, it is more common to have the implementation and unit testing of one software module only dependent upon completion of the design for that one module (in reality one module's design may involve a number of design tasks such as its user interface, involved database tables, etc.). Eventually, all the software modules come together for integration testing, which would be dependent upon completion of the implementation and unit testing of every module.

The two general ways to do draw these network diagrams are activity-on-arrow and activity-on-node. The original critical path method (CPM) developed by Dupont and Remington Rand in 1957 used the activity-on-arrow method and used one time estimate only per task (as opposed to several estimates as in the PERT method). The more common method today is to show the activity on a node and the precedence diagramming method (PDM) is based on this representation. In the PDM method, nodes or boxes represent tasks, and arrows between the nodes show task dependencies. This is illustrated in Figure 7.23 with activities labeled A, B, and so on. There are four types of dependencies that may apply between two tasks:

1. *Finish-to-start:* A task must finish before another one can start.
2. *Finish-to-finish:* A task must finish before another can finish.
3. *Start-to-start:* A task must start before another one can start.
4. *Start-to-finish:* A task must start before another one can finish.

Figure 7.23. PDM method

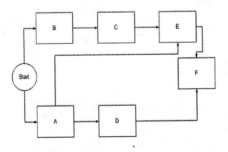

In the illustration, task E is dependent on tasks A and C. All, except the finish-to-start, are not commonly used and can be simulated by setting an earliest start date for a task, if necessary. There are no dummy activities in this method, and this method is easier to visualize than the activity-on-arrow method. Most modern project management software packages use this method.

In the activity-on-arrow (AOA) method, arrows are used to represent tasks, and ovals are used to relate tasks. Generally, only finish-to-start relationships can be used. This method was the one originally used with PERT. Dummy activities may be needed to show dependencies between tasks (often shown with a dotted line). This method does have a visual advantage in that the length of arrow can optionally be used for duration of task. Figure 7.24 illustrates this, and in that figure task D is dependent on E and C, and a dummy activity (no task identification letter) is used to show the dependence of D on E.

The critical path is the longest path(s) through a network diagram from the project start to project end. It can be found using either of the network diagramming techniques after the tasks are estimated; for the activity-on-arrow method, the critical path may run through a dummy activity. The critical path determines the earliest completion date for the project. It may change during a project, if task estimates are revised. There can be more than one critical path, and this is not desirable because it increases overall risk. Critical paths are calculated by most project management scheduling software systems and are done using dynamic or linear programming techniques (an example of using linear programming is found in Chapter XVI).

The amount of time a particular task can be delayed without delaying the entire project completion is called the total slack or float for a task. The float for the entire project is a fixed completion time minus the scheduled time (it may be negative). Tasks on a critical path typically have no slack (unless the project completion date is longer than the critical path activities). In the network diagram of Figure 7.25 (activity-on-node method), durations are shown in the nodes, and the critical path is shown using the bigger arrows. The length of this project is 35 time units, which is the sum of the tasks on the critical path.

Figure 7.24. AOA method

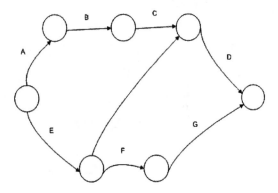

A forward pass through the network is used to calculate early-start and early-finish dates, and a backward pass (from the overall finish date) is used to determine late-start and late-finish dates. The float (total slack) for a task is the difference between the early-start and late-start dates for a task (or between the early-finish and late-finish dates, or the late-finish minus early-start dates plus task duration). Free slack is the amount of time a task can be delayed without delaying the early start of its successor task (minimum early-start time of all successor tasks minus early start of this task minus task duration). Most computer systems show total slack (float) time per task, and project managers use this number to know which tasks need to be most closely monitored and also in allocating scarce resources amongst multiple projects. Free slack can be used to determine how much a critical path task can be *crashed* before the critical path changes. If the fixed end date changes for a project, the critical path does not change; however, the overall project float may become negative. If the overall project float becomes negative (you are behind schedule), then the project manager would consider crashing or fast tracking (covered later in this book). In Figure 7.26, the floats are shown for the tasks that are not on the critical path. Note that the float for task A is 1, not 2, because delaying A by 2 units would not delay C, but the path through A and D to E would become longer than the path through B and C to E.

Lag is a necessary wait time between tasks; one adds lag time to a predecessor task to delay the start of a dependent task. For example, you must wait 2 days after pouring concrete before you can start to build the house frame. Another example, you must order certain materials 10 days before you need to use them. Lag is typically shown on the arrows on an activity-on-node diagram. Lead time is the amount of time you can overlap dependent tasks.

For time-sensitive IT projects, schedule compression can best be achieved by removing unnecessary coupling (dependencies) between tasks, thus allowing for more work on more tasks simultaneously. As discussed earlier in this chapter, this can be done with the proper choice of architecture, standards, and methodology. For example if requirement specifications, standards compliance, and end user documentation is done early in a project, then design and implementation can be done in parallel with integration test planning and end user training. Methodologies were discussed earlier in this book, and

Figure 7.25. PDM network diagram

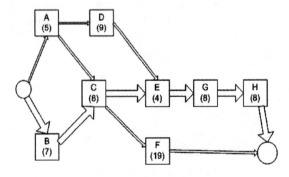

Figure 7.26. Network slack

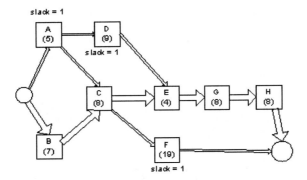

if modern free-flow incremental techniques are used instead of classical waterfall methods, then more work (WBS packets) can be done in parallel.

Scheduling

After all the tasks are sequenced, a schedule can be developed. The difference between a network diagram and a schedule is that a schedule is *calendar based* and takes into account the length of work weeks and holidays. The basic differences in these project management concepts are

- WBS defines "what"
- Network Diagram defines "how"
- Schedule defines "when"
- RAM defines "who"

If specific resources are assigned at this time, the schedule may also take into consideration resource availability (i.e., percent of their time devoted to this project) and resource absences for vacation and other time off. Many project management software packages can also level resources so that a resource is used an equal amount of time in each workweek. Adding specific resource issues to scheduling will generally lengthen a project's duration. The critical path on the schedule may also be different than the critical path in the network diagram due to resource availability and resource leveling. Graphic representations of schedules can be produced in expanded network diagrams and the nodes in such a schedule drawing may look like those shown in Figure 7.27; an example of such a diagram is shown in Figure 7.28.

Figure 7.27. Schedule nodes

Task Name	
Scheduled Start	Scheduled Finish
Actual Start	Actual Finish

Early Start	Duration	Early Finish
Task Name		
Late Start	Slack	Late Finish

Figure 7.28. Network diagram with expanded nodes

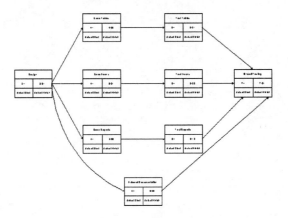

The typical graphical representation of a schedule, however, is the Gantt chart, which is the most commonly used graphic in project management. It was named after Henry Gantt, who first developed it during World War I with the U.S. Army. He was a mechanical engineer and management consultant and his charts were later employed on major U.S. infrastructure projects, including the Hoover Dam and the interstate highway system. An example is shown in Figure 7.29. The Gantt chart represents each task as a horizontal bar and is a time-line view of the tasks. This chart is a bar graph on which the length of each bar designates the start and finish dates for each task. Each task is labeled with its WBS code and description. There are many variations of the basic Gantt chart; more information may be added in extra columns or in the graphic area with the bars. In the graphic area there may be precedence relations, shading in the bars to show percent completions of the tasks, coloring of the bars to show tasks on the critical path, milestones (zero-length event markers), WBS hierarchy and envelopes, and so forth. A problem with the Gantt chart is that it portrays an even distribution of effort from the start of a task to the end of that task (particularly when a percent-complete shading of the bars is used). Another problem with the traditional Gantt chart is that it requires a lot of "real estate" on a computer screen or a printout for large projects. Figure 7.30 shows a Plan Gantt chart from the FiveAndDime system, which also shows planned cost in the bars; this is a Web-hyperlink-based system where one can click on WBS codes for added detail or to "drill down" to the next level of the WBS.

Figure 7.29. Gantt chart

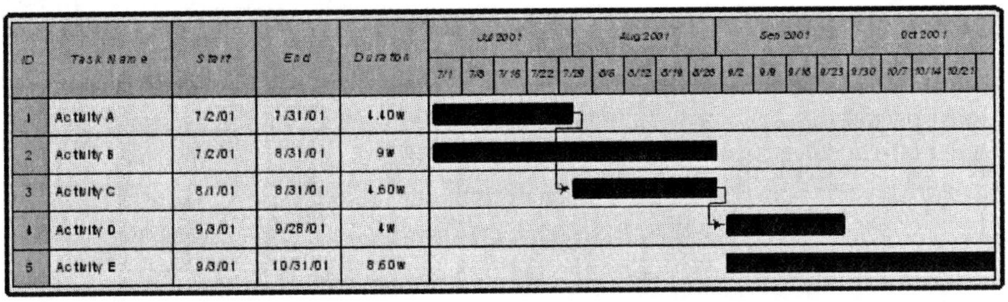

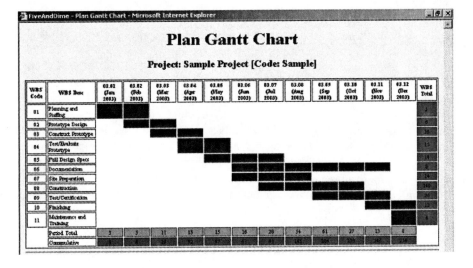

One must be careful, particularly with IT projects, in not overplanning a schedule. A
project manager should focus on managing the project, not managing the schedule. A
number of companies plan resource allocations using specific resource assignments and
plan down to the day. IT human resources are largely professional types, they may work
varying numbers of hours per day, they may be called upon to help another person or
another project from time to time, and they may take off a day or two for whatever reason,
whenever they so chose. As mentioned previously, estimates involve considerable
uncertainty, and productivity rates of individuals, even within the same category, vary
greatly in IT. These factors have always played a major role in IT project scheduling; one
of the best discussions of this goes back to Frederick Brooks's classic book, *The
Mythical Man-Month* (Brooks, 1975). Many companies have wasted valuable time with
dedicated project schedulers, who constantly modify the project schedule, trying to keep
up with individual resource availability. A rule of thumb for a work packet is to have one

Figure 7.30. Planning Gantt chart

timekeeping reporting period, which is 1 or 2 weeks in most organizations. Making resource assignments at that level (either specific or generic resources) is a more reasonable approach for IT projects. In other words, for each WBS work packet after the effort (in person hours) is determined, simply assign one or more individuals to that packet for the number of periods (weeks) necessary. Unrealistic schedules are one of the primary reasons for project crises and failures. According to Young (2003), seven things to do before one can create a realistic schedule are:

1.   Nail down the scope and requirements

2.   Prototype the biggest technical risks

3.   Create a model for the user interface

4.   Pay attention to industry-standard estimates for similar projects

5.   Let each person create an estimated task schedule for his own work

6.   Accept only observable, measurable status reports

7.   Subdivide all the tasks until each task takes 1 or 2 weeks to complete

Resource Assignment and Costing Methods

Resource assignment in IT is usually necessary to estimate the time duration of the work packets. In some industries, for some projects, time estimates may be independent of resource assignments. Resource assignment for preliminary task time and cost estimates is usually done generically, using a table, as was shown in Figure 7.18. The category rates may be averages for employees in that category, midpoints for the corporate salary bracket, contractor rates for contract labor, or some external average rate, such as that of a regulatory body or trade union.

At some time early in the project, the effort to staff the project begins. The initial staffing depends upon the time phased need of certain resources, the lead time to bring said resources onto the project, conflicting needs for said resources, and other related resource issues. The project may be reestimated (repriced) at that time if there is a significant difference in the rates for the actual resources versus the planned rates for those resources; for contracted projects, this depends on the terms of the contract. A responsibility assignment matrix (RAM) may be developed, which is similar to the organizational assignment matrix previously shown but shows the actual resources (mapping between WBS and RBS) as well as the organization; some organizations may maintain a single RAM for all projects. Figure 7.31 shows a window from the FiveAndDime system for adding resource information; FiveAndDime allows the adding of resources to the overall organization (such as for generic rate categories) and the adding of project-specific resources.

Figure 7.31. Form to add resource

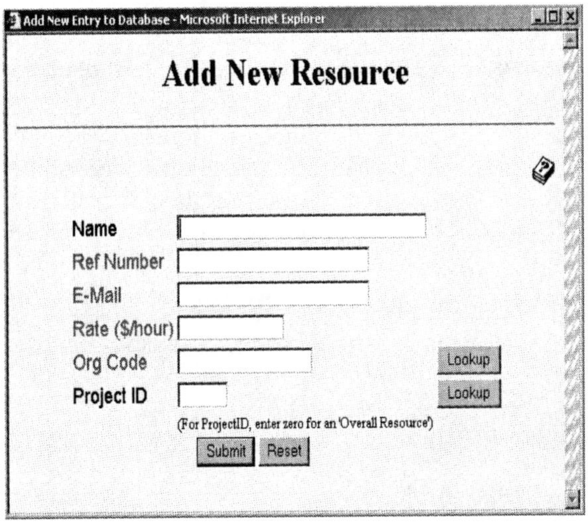

Assignment of actual resources to a project brings up the problem of resource leveling, that is making sure that a single resource is not overcommitted, not just to a single project, but between all projects in which that resource is involved. Some project management software programs can do some form of resource leveling within one project and some can do leveling between multiple projects. In either case, these automatic solutions may be far from optimum. The first step in resource leveling should be to obtain a report showing the planned time for each resource across all projects for the time span of interest. When a resource is overcommitted there are several possible solutions, including setting up task priorities, setting up a finish to start precedence between the tasks competing for said resource, getting the resource to agree to be overcommitted for a period of time (preferably in writing), and finding an alternative resource internally or via contracting or outsourcing.

As the project proceeds, actual costs accrue to the project. The costing of resources, particularly human resources, is one where confidentiality concerns may override concerns for accuracy of actual costs. The hours a person charges to a project and particular WBS codes are regularly reported. There are, however, a variety of ways to turn those actual hours into actual costs. Some organizations apply the actual burdened (including benefits, taxes, and possibly other factors) hourly cost of each individual. Although this approach to actual cost acquisition is the most accurate, it can reveal individual salaries. To solve this problem, many organizations use some type of average rates, which may be the same table used for cost estimating purposes. Another way to handle this problem for projects, where almost all the cost is labor, is to report and control actual costs in terms of person-hours instead of dollars; these details are discussed later in this book.

Developing the Cost Plan

After the schedule is developed, the estimated cost of each work packet is rolled up to the top level of the WBS to develop the cost plan. The cost plan, sometimes referred to as a cash flow analysis, shows the amount of money that has been planned to be spent as a function of time. This process is illustrated in Figure 7.32. Sometimes two such curves are developed, one with each work packet starting at the scheduled time, and another on which each noncritical task starts at the latest start time. If cash flow is an issue, one can choose between the two curves or, in a contract situation, one can base a payment schedule on one of the two curves.

Once the cost plan is accepted, it becomes the baseline for the project; baseline cost plans may be modified later as change orders are added. As an example, consider the following two-level WBS (Level zero is in bold) from an example appearing in the *Project Management Journal* (Brandon, 1998, 1999):

- *Planning & Staffing:* Project Plan, Resource Commitments
- *Prototype Design:* Requirements, Design
- *Construct Prototype:* Detail Design, Construction
- *Test/Evaluate Prototype:* Test Plan Development, Component Testing, Full Testing, Destructive Testing, Test Documentation
- *Full Design Specifications:* External Specifications, Internal Specifications
- *Documentation:* Internal Specifications, Required External Documents
- *Site Preparation:* Site Design, Site Construction
- *Construction:* Component Construction, Component Assembly
- *Test/Certification:* Test Plan Development, Component Testing, Full Testing, Destructive Testing, Test Documentation

Figure 7.32. Schedule and cost plan development

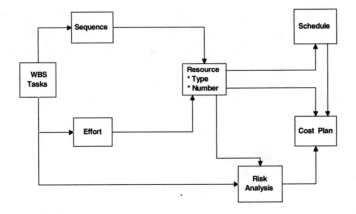

- *Finishing:* Component Finishing, Assembly Finishing
- *Maintenance Training:* Maintenance Personnel, Supervisory Personnel

The cost plan for this WBS (at Level zero) is shown in Figure 7.33, and a graph of the cost plan is shown in Figure 7.34. The cost plan becomes the basis for cost performance reporting as discussed later in this book. In developing a cost plan in most software project management programs each WBS work packet is associated with one of more resources and has a start date and a complete date. The cost calculated from the effort of the task (usually in person hours) and the rates of the assigned resource(s) is evenly spread from the start date to the completion date. In other types of project management software, time periods (work periods) are separate entities in the program and cost is associated with a time period and a work packet to form a plan item; in other words, a plan item is how much is to be spent in a particular time period for a particular WBS code.

Figure 7.33. Cost plan in spreadsheet

Project Cost Plan

WBS (Level 0)	JAN	FEB	MAR	APR	MAY	JUN	JUL	AUG	SEP	OCT	NOV	DEC	TOTAL
Planning & Staffing	3	2											5
Prototype Design		3	3										6
Construct Prototype			8	8									16
Test/Evaluate Prototype				5	10								15
Full Design Specs					5	6	3						14
Documentation						2	2	1	1	1	1		8
Site Preparation							8	3	3				14
Construction								20	50	50	20		140
Test/Certification										10	6	4	20
Finishing											8	4	12
Maintenance Training												4	4
Monthly Plan	3	5	11	13	15	16	28	54	61	27	13	8	254
Cumulative	3	8	19	32	47	63	91	145	206	233	246	254	

Figure 7.34. Cost plan graph

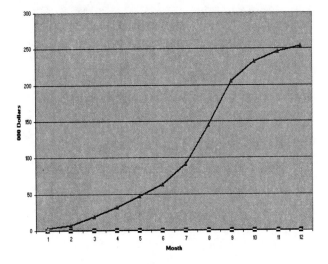

As was discussed in Chapter VI, in many organizations and in the U.S. government, standard calendars are set up based upon a work period of 1 week (for either a fiscal or calendar year). This later method provides for nonlinear distribution of WBS cost over time, easier handling of project overhead (level of effort) costs, and improved performance metric calculation (discussed later in this book). Figure 7.35, from the FiveAndDime systems, shows project work plan items for the current example, and Figure 7.30 showed a Plan Gantt chart which shows the individual plan items in a spreadsheet like chart.

This cost plan is sometimes called the *planned cost based on known work* and may include risk factors at the individual WBS work packet level. The inclusion of added cost based upon risk factors at the WBS work packet level (mainly estimation risk factors) and overall project risk is discussed in Chapter VIII. There may also be some unpriced additional work (real or suspected) added which brings the cost up to the expected work cost or the performance measurement baseline. The difference between the expected work cost and the planned cost based on known work is called the undistributed budget. The undistributed budget is for known work and sometimes used as a holding account until a formal contract change is made.

The project manager generally has responsibility to manage to the performance measurement baseline. In addition a management reserve may be added as a reserve for overall project risks including unforeseen work that is still within the overall scope of the project. The performance measurement baseline plus the management reserve adds up to the total project budget (or for a contract situation the negotiated cost). These provisions are part of the ANSI standard on Earned Value Management System guidelines (ANSI/EIA-748-1998), which is discussed later in this book and is illustrated in Figure 7.36.

For IT projects, costs other than labor may be present and these may or may not be allocated to the project. Contractor and consultant costs are usually part of the WBS and RBS structures. Other direct costs, such as hardware, software, training, entertainment, and travel, may made be part of the WBS or just added to the cost plan developed via

Figure 7.35. Cost plan table

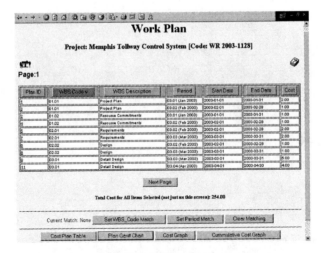

Figure 7.36. Hierarchy of contract cost

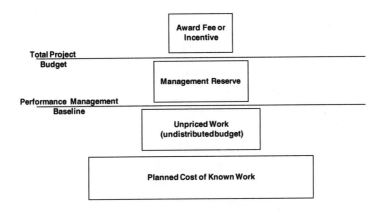

the WBS. Indirect, overhead, or level of effort types of cost may also be assigned to a project and become part of the project budget. These may be General and Administrative (G & A), Internal Operations and Maintenance (I & O), allocations (space, utilities, consumables, communications, etc.), nonproject time (general meetings, general training, etc.). In some organizations these costs are included in the burdened rates for the labor categories. In some organizations, these costs are given separate WBS codes. In projectized organizations, and even in traditional line management organizations, as more work becomes team and projected based, it becomes desirable to associate these costs with projects. If given separate WBS codes, their contribution to the cost plan is typically a linear spread over the project life.

Chapter Summary

The formulation of a detail schedule and cost plan has been discussed and illustrated in this chapter. WBS formulation, task sequencing, task estimation, scheduling, and costing methods have all been covered. The detail scope, time, and cost planning of this chapter forms the basis for other detail plans described in subsequent chapters including the risk plan, procurement plan, HR plan, quality plan, control plan, and change plan.

References

Albrecht, A. (1979, October 14-17). Measuring application development productivity. *Proceedings of the SHARE/GUIDE IBM Applications Development Symposium,* Monterey, CA.

Boehm, B. (1981). *Software engineering economics.* Upper Saddle River, NJ: Prentice Hall.

Boehm, B. (2000). *Software estimation with Cocomo II.* Upper Saddle River, NJ: Prentice Hall.

Brandel, M. (2004, August). Budgetary black holes. *Computerworld.*

Brandon, D. (1998). Implementing earned value easily and effectively. *Project Management Journal, 29*(2) 11-18.

Brandon, D. (1999). Implementing earned value easily and effectively. In J. Pinto (Ed.), *Essentials of project control* (pp. 113-134). Newton Square, PA: Project Management Institute Press.

Brooks, F. (1975). *The mythical man-month.* Boston: Addison Wesley.

IFPUG. (1996). *IFPUG counting practices manual.* Retrieved from www.ifpug.org/

Jones, C. (1995). Backfiring: Converting lines of code to function points. *IEEE Computer, 28*(11), 87-88.

Kemerer, C. (1987). An empirical validation of software cost estimation models. *Communications of the ACM, 30*(5), 416-429.

Kiewel, B. (1998, January). Measuring progress in software development. *PM Network,* 29-32.

Klastorn, T. (2004). *Project management—Tools and trade-offs.* New York: Wiley.

Malcolm, D., Roseboom, J., & Clark, C. (1959). Application of a technique for research and development program evaluation. *Operations Research, 7*(5), 646-669.

McGibbon, T. (1997, August 20). Modern empirical cost and schedule estimation tools. *DOD Data and Analysis Center for Software Report (DACS),* Air Force Research Laboratory.

PMI. (2000). *The project management body of knowledge (PMBOK).* Newton Square, PA. ISBN 1-880410-22-2.

PMI. (2004). *Practice standards for work breakdown structures.*

Raz, T., & Globerson, S. (1998, December). Effective sizing and content definition of work packages. *Project Management Journal,* 17-23.

Roetzheim, W., & Beasley, R. (1998). *Software project cost and schedule estimating: Best practices.* Upper Saddle River, NJ: Prentice Hall.

Young, S. (2003, August). Why IT projects fail. *Computerworld,* p. 44.

Chapter VIII

Risk Planning and Management

He who is not courageous enough to take risks will accomplish nothing in life.

(Muhammad Ali)

Success today in the business world (whether as an employee, manager, executive, or self-employed businessperson) involves taking some risks. The systems that are changing the world today are very risky, but the payback is enormous (DeMarco & Lister, 2003). One needs to know how to manage risk, however, including how to identify risk sources, quantify risk parameters, and develop plans to handle risk; these are the topics covered in this chapter.

Risks are inevitable in projects (particularly IT projects), *and if a PM does not practice sound risk management, that PM may constantly be in a crisis-management mode.* The high failure rate of modern *large* IT projects, such as those involving EAI/ERP, CRM, and SCM, is largely due to senior management and project management's failure to assess risks up front and to mitigate the causes of the greatest risks at the start of the project (Gibson, 2003). An adequate analysis of potential risks can significantly increase the likelihood of success for a project and can justify dollar amounts set aside for management reserves. "Risk management is increasingly seen as one of the main jobs of project managers" (Sommerville, 2003).

Project Risks and Opportunities

Risk is the possibility of suffering loss. In IT, the loss may involve increased costs, longer completion times, reduced scope, reduced quality, reduced realization of proposed benefits, or reduced stakeholder satisfaction. *Risk and opportunity are different sides of the same coin. Some IT projects advance the state of the art, and as such are more risky than those that do not. The opportunity for significant advancement cannot be done without significant risk.* "Risk in itself is not bad; risk is essential to progress, and failure is often a key part of learning. But we must learn to balance the possible negative consequences of risk against the potential benefits of its associated opportunity" (Van Scoy, 1992).

Many organizations around the world are involved with general project risk management and/or IT project risk management. Barry Boehm of the U.S. Air Force, while working with the Software Engineering Institute (SEI), set the stage for modern IT risk management (Boehm, 1991). According to the SEI, risk management is a software engineering practice with the following processes: assess continuously what can go wrong (risks), determine what risks are important to deal with, and implement strategies to deal with those risks. The SEI model for risk management is shown in Figure 8.1.

The ISO/IEC 17799-1:2000 Code of Practice provides a sequencing of the risk management process into subprocesses for context identification, risk identification, risk analysis, risk evaluation, and risk treatment. The IEEE 1540 standard on software risk management is being merged with the corresponding ISO/IEC standard. Figure 8.2 shows the IEEE 1540:2001 overall risk management process.

The Project Management Institute (PMI; 2000) Risk Management Processes are:

- Risk identification
- Risk quantification
- Risk response development
- Risk response control

This book will mainly follow the PMI process definitions. All projects have some degree of risk, and most IT projects have *considerable* risk. Risk can, however, be reduced (studies have found that risk can be reduced up to 90% [PMI, 2000]). A PM should be somewhat risk averse (avoids taking unnecessary risks), but to significantly reduce risks, one must start with thorough risk planning.

Figure 8.1. SEI risk management model

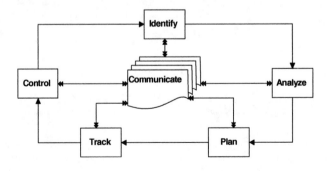

Figure 8.2. IEEE 1540:2001 risk management process

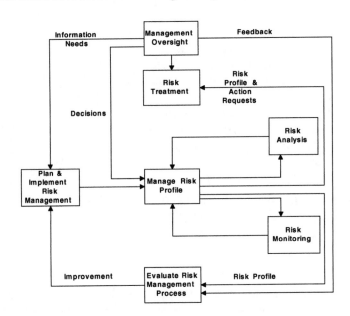

Risk management involves making plans and decisions in the face of uncertainty, and uncertainty is a state of nature, typified by the absence of information on a desired outcome. A *risk event* is a particular occurrence that could affect a project for good or bad. *Risk analysis* is the combination of risk identification and risk quantification. Therefore, *risk management* is the processes involved with identifying, analyzing, and handling risk. It includes maximizing the results of positive risk events and minimizing the consequences of adverse events.

Risk *context identification* is a step in the ISO risk-management processes. This context identification establishes the strategic, organizational, and risk-management environment.

Context identification is made through familiar business models like:

- *SWOT:* Strengths, weaknesses, opportunities, threats
- *Context:* Describes the system capabilities, as well as its goals and objectives and the strategies that are in place to achieve them
- *Target:* Describes the goals, objectives, strategies, scope and parameters of the activity, or system to which the risk management processes being applied
- *Assets:* Describes the identified assets and their dependencies
- *Security Requirements:* Describes the security requirements needed to preserve the identified assets

Risk context identification is typically focused on a particular management level: the entire organization, the IT organization, or the programs and projects,. Risk management for the entire organization involves threats and hazards to the organization as a whole. Risk management for the IT organization usually goes under the name "disaster planning" and involves threats and hazards to the IT assets, including hardware, software, and people. This chapter focuses on project-level threats and hazards that may affect the completion criteria or the satisfaction criteria identified earlier in this book. Most IT projects create or acquire software for deployment across one or a few servers and affect only part of an organization (i.e., few stakeholders). In EAI/ERM-type projects, however, the entire organization is affected (numerous stakeholders) and there are many more risk sources, including complex political, business value, expectations (requirements validation), security, workflow, and support issues (Maverick, 2003).

Good risk management is not a substitute for poor project planning! Risk management looks for things that might be a problem, whereas project planning (scope, cost, time, quality, etc.) identifies things that will definitely be problems and plans to make sure they do not happen (Young, 2003).

Risk Identification

The risk identification process normally considers the product description, scope, WBS, planning documents, historical information, and industry information to determine sources of risk, potential risk events, and risk symptoms. One must determine which risks are likely to affect the project (and the product that is the subject of the project) and the key characteristics of each risk. Ideally, risk identification should start during project initiation and should finish during project planning. In practice for IT projects, however, a risk analysis is typically done after project planning and before the final costing of the project. Risk identification cannot be fully completed until the WBS is created and most work, staff, and procurements have been specified. Then risks are further identified as the project proceeds and as change orders come in.

Project critical success criteria and factors were discussed previously in this book. In a broader sense, risk identification should start with these critical success factors of the project. These factors can be used to identify critical sources of risks that may arise from our satisfaction criteria and completion criteria. The critical success factors were determined by considering all stakeholders for a project, and risk source identification should also consider all stakeholders. For large IT projects that will create products that will significantly change organizations (such as how business processes are performed and the "balance of power" within an organization), the major risks may involve satisfaction criteria more than the completion criteria. "Business based project failures come from such things as not having new workflow processes [to go with the new product], not adapting the structure of the organization to the new ways of working, not revising incentives and rewards to emphasize the new goals, and keeping the old cultural practices in place even when they impede the new ways of working" (Gibson, 2003).

Risk identification is carried out by finding potential hazards and threats in different risk sources. What is the difference between a hazard and a threat?

*   The primary volcanic hazards are pyroclastic flows and surges, airborne fallout such as tephra clasts, ash (heavy accumulations and persistent), and lightning.
*   *The* threats posed to people *by these hazards are death or injury from inundation, fire, heat, missile impact, lightning strike, and ash ingestion.*
*   *The* threats to infrastructure, lifelines, and property *are destruction, damage, route obstruction, structural collapse, electrical malfunction, and pollution.*

For example, a board with a nail sticking out or it is a hazard that is more of a threat to people if the board is lying on the beach rather than lying in the street. Lying in the street this hazard may be more of a threat to cars than that same board lying on the beach. Risks/ hazards are often separated by such categories as:

*   *Business Risk:* Risk of a gain or loss
*   *Pure (Insurable) Risk:* Risk of a loss only

The sources of risk are further classified as:

*   *Internal:* Project variables (including managing the "normal" trade-offs in the project schedule, cost, quality, scope) and other factors inside an organization
*   *Technical:* Technology uncertainty or change
*   *External:* Factors outside of the organization
*   *Unforeseeable:* Only 10% of risks fall into this category

Internal and technical risks are often quantified at the WBS level for projects, whereas external and unforeseeable risks are quantified at the overall project level. A PM is generally responsible for internal and technical types of risk events. Sometimes issues dealing with the customer are classified as external, and sometimes they are classified as internal depending upon whether the customer (benefiting organization) is internal or external to the company. The same situation may be true of procurement, that it may be classified as internal or external; outsourcing risks are usually considered internal. Procurement and outsourcing are discussed in detail in a later chapter of this book. Some indicators of potential internal risks would be related to:

*   *Investment Size:* Size of project cost versus budget of benefiting or performing department (i.e., IT department)
*   *Project Size:* Time length of project compared to "cycle" time in that industry

- *Impact Analysis:* How broadly project results may impact organization, customers, industry
- *Business Risks:* New corporate organization, merger, new employees, new vendors/contractors
- *Political Risks:* Who internally cares about the project and their corporate influence and power
- *Performing Organization Risks:* Staff and management uncertainties

Some technical risks in IT projects would possibly be:

- New type of project
- New area of application
- New methodology
- New technology (platforms, languages, tools, algorithms, methods, etc.)
- New standards
- "Going where no project in this company has gone before"

External and unforeseeable risks are not usually the responsibility of the PM. Unforeseeable risks include natural hazards (such as weather events, earthquakes, etc.), market fluctuations, riots, fires, crime, war, and the like. Only about 10% of risks are unforeseeable (PMI, 2000). Some indicators of external risks would be related to:

- *Benefiting Organization (Customer) Risks:* Management and contact uncertainties
- *Procurement Risks:* Vendor issues
- *Political Risks:* Those who externally cares about the project and their political power
- *Compatibility Risks:* Alignment to current and new standards
- *Economic Risks:* Flexibility to changes in local, national, and global economic factors

One good way to start to identify risks is with a standard industry checklist or questionnaire. One such questionnaire from Pearlson and Saunders (2004) is:

- Are we doing the right things?
     Are project objectives clear?
     Will the proposed solution support business activities?
     What changes should be considered?

- Are we doing it the best way?

    Have alternative ways been explored?

    Are there new or emerging ways we should consider?

    What changes would increase the likelihood of success?

- How do we know how we are doing?

    What are the performance standards?

    Is there regular progress reporting?

    How will the staff give feedback?

- What impacts are we having on the business?

    To what extent have project objectives been achieved?

    Are the project clients satisfied?

    Is satisfaction improving or declining?

    Is support for the project improving, stable, or declining?

- Is the project cost effective?

    What significant business costs are influenced by this project?

    What is the trend of these costs?

    What significant variances from budget have occurred?

- Is there clear accountability for the project?

    Are the right people involved?

    Are lines of responsibility clear?

    Is senior management supportive?

    Is performance monitored and on track?

    Do all those involved with the project understand their roles?

- Are key assets protected?

    Will the IT infrastructure handle the deployment of this application?

    Is IT security adequate?

    Are risks identified and monitored?

    How are incidents reported and analyzed?"

A widely used checklist was given by Wideman (1992) who listed common general project risks and then specific risks by category: external unpredictable, external predictable, internal nontechnical, technical, and legal. Some of the items from his common general lists that are typical in IT projects are:

- This project is very different from previous ones we have done.
- The project scope, objectives, and deliverables are not clearly defined.
- Some or all technical data are lacking.

- The technical process is immature.
- Standards for performance are unrealistic.
- Design lacks engineering input.
- Prototype of key elements are missing.
- There is a higher than usual R&D component
- Other similar projects have not been successful.
- A wide variation in bids for support products and services.
- Some key subsystems are sole source bids.

Sommerville (2003) identified common risks to software development: staff turnover, management change, hardware unavailability, requirements change, specification delays, size underestimation, CASE tool underperformance, technology change, and product competition.

Another way to identify risk is via a framework. One such framework, defined by Marchewka (2003), began by examining risks involving project scope, quality, or budget. It then viewed risk influences for these items in terms of people, legal, process, and so forth. It then considers whether the risk is internal or external, what is known about the risk (frequency and impact), and where in the project timeline the risk will occur:

Scope
Quality
Schedule
Budget
     People
     Legal
     Process
     Environment
     Technology
     Organization
     Product
     Other
          Internal
          External
               Known risks (frequency and impact known)
               K-U risks (frequency known, impact unknown)
               Unknown risks (frequency and impact unknown)
                    Project conceptualization
                    Charter and plan

Execute and control

Closeout

Evaluation

The IEEE framework (taxonomy) is based upon identifying risk in three areas: product engineering, development engineering, and program constraints. Each category has subcategories, and each subcategory has specific areas (Carr, 1993):

- Product engineering

    Requirements

    Design

    Code and unit test

    Integration and test

    Engineering specialties

- Development engineering

    Development process

    Development system

    Management process

    Management methods

    Work environment

- Program constraints

    Resources

    Contract

    Program interfaces

This framework is very specific; for example, under product engineering/requirements, the areas are stability, completeness, clarity, validity, feasibility, precedent, and scale. Next questionnaires are developed based upon the three framework areas. The aforementioned IEEE report has specific questionnaires, and other related IEEE documents prescribe meeting and interview techniques to administer the questionnaires.

A more general framework suggested herein for IT projects is based upon the critical success criteria and factors introduced early in this book. Figure 8.3 shows a template for this risk source identification template.

Each cell in our framework table (intersection of a hazard and a threat) is a risk source arena. There may be more than one risk source in each cell. In practice, each cell is analyzed to identify sources of risk, and for each risk identified, a set of specific symptoms is listed. These symptoms are early warning signals that a risk event may be about to occur. Thus, the PM, project team, and line management can watch for these symptoms during the project execution.

Figure 8.3. Critical success-factor–based risk framework

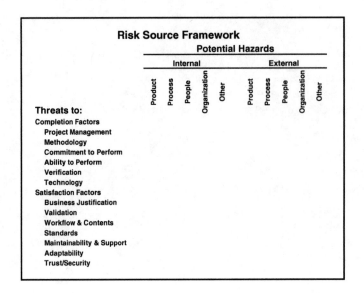

Risk Quantification

After the risks and their symptoms are identified, those risks need to be quantified and the stakeholders' risk tolerance levels determined. The risk quantification process will result in a list of opportunities to pursue, threats to respond to, opportunities to ignore, and threats to accept. Risk quantification may utilize several models, including

- *Hazard Frequencies:* Describes frequency estimates for the identified hazards
- *Threat Frequencies:* Describes frequency estimates for the identified threats
- *Consequence Estimates:* Describes consequence estimates for the identified hazards

The formal analysis of risk includes the following risk factors:

- The probability that the risk event(s) will occur
- The economic impact (money at stake)
- When the risk event(s) may occur (timing)
- How often are they likely to occur (frequency)

The first step in the analysis is determining the probability and impact. The two methods are commonly used are

- *Qualitative:* Expert opinion, project historical data, educated guess
- *Quantitative:* Parametric formulas, simulation, industry and/or application statistical data

Quantitative methods are certainly better (less subjective and more accurate) when the data are available and the use of that data is appropriate. Monte Carlo simulations using the network diagram and PERT estimates are sometimes used to simulate risk involving time and cost (gives a percentage probability that each task will be on the critical path).

The most common quantitative method is the expected monetary value (EMV) calculation. Probability and impact are used to calculate the EMV as:

EMV = Probability * Impact

EMV units may be dollars or some other loss scale. *EMV is very important to a PM in that it helps the PM prove his or her need for reserves!* The impact is typically in money or person hours. A single impact number may be used in the previous formula, or the impact may be calculated from a maximum impact (total loss) times the probability of that maximum value (Pi):

Impact = maxImpact * Pi

EMV = Pe * Pi * maxImpact (where Pe is the event probability)

Calculation of management reserves involves summing up the EMV for all the identified threats and opportunities. This is can be done in tabular or spreadsheet form, as shown in Figure 8.4.

A less precise quantitative method uses the base formula but expresses both impact and event probability on a scale (such as from 1 to 10) or as a rough percentage. This method, though less precise, may be more applicable, particularly in IT projects in which impact and probability are harder to estimate in an absolute sense. The impact for each risk is the fraction of the project overall budget that is directly affected by that risk. A relative EMV is calculated for each risk by multiplying the probability of the risk by the impact

Figure 8.4. EMV determination

Risk/Opportunity	Impact	Probability	EMV
Threat 1			
...			
Threat N			
Opportunity 1			
...			
Opportunity N			
Total	-----	-----	xxx

(amount of the budget at risk). The relative EMVs may be summed to calculate a management reserve for risk mitigation:

$$\text{Management Reserve} = \sum \text{Probability}_i * \text{Impact}_i$$

For example, if there are two risks, and the first risk affects 50% of the project budget with a probability of 20%, and the second risk impacts 30% of the project budget, with an probability of 15%, then he management reserve would be 14.5%. Another similar method is based upon a risk matrix, which gives a grade to the intersection of risk probabilities and impacts. This is shown in Figure 8.5. Each risk is assigned a grade and then is ranked accordingly.

Tolerance levels (the amount of risk that is acceptable) should be determined for each stakeholder (or each type of stakeholder). Those tolerance levels are later used in developing the risk management plan, specifically what types of risk events may be accepted versus those risk events that need to be averted, deflected, or mitigated. A project's stakeholders may be daredevils, or they may be timid. If they are daredevils, they will assume risks and will not be too upset if a risky decision proves to be the wrong choice; however, if the stakeholders are timid, they will be upset about decisions that involve any significant degree of risk. The R-Variables control the stakeholders view of risk: Regret/Resent [pain], and Rejoice [rejoice] (Piney, 2003). By knowing the stakeholders well, or by interviewing them, one can determine risk tolerance. A formal utility function can also be developed, as is illustrated in Figure 8.6.

Piney (2003) defined different zones for the utility function graph that indicate different ways risks may need to be analyzed to determine stakeholder tolerance. The dead zone indicates threats and opportunities for which no response is developed. A table or spreadsheet may be prepared listing threats and opportunities for which responses need to be developed, as is shown in Figure 8.7.

As stated previously, internal and technical risks are often quantified at the WBS level for projects, whereas external and unforeseeable risks are quantified at the overall project level. Figure 8.8 shows a screen from the FiveAndDime system that provides for project-level risk factors for internal and technical risks (the project risk factor—how risky is this work) and for external risk (the customer—how risky [difficult] is this customer to work with). These risk factors are applied to cost estimates. Further on in this chapter, a specific example is given to illustrate one way to calculate these factors. Figure 8.9 also shows a screen from the FiveAndDime system for a WBS item in which there is a risk factor at the WBS level (how risky is this item of work).

Figure 8.5. Risk grading

Probability	Low	Impact Medium	High
Low	1	2	3
Medium	2	3	4
High	3	4	5

Figure 8.6. Risk utility function

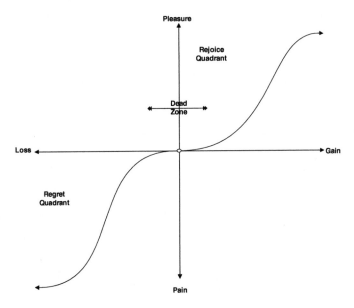

Figure 8.7. Response matrix

Risk/Opportunity	EMV	Priority	Respond ?
Threat 1			
...			
Threat N			
Opportunity 1			
...			
Opportunity N			
Total	**xxx**	-----	-----

Risk Response Development

Once the threats and opportunities have been categorized (opportunities to pursue, threats to respond to, opportunities to ignore, and threats to accept), the risk responses are formulated and the risk management plan is completed. The risk management plan usually specifies the overall management reserve. This is illustrated in Figure 8.10.

Figure 8.8. Project form (showing project risk factors)

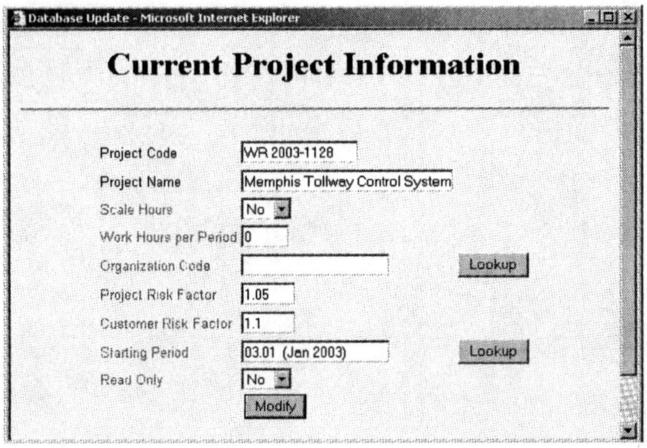

Figure 8.9. WBS form (showing WBS risk factor)

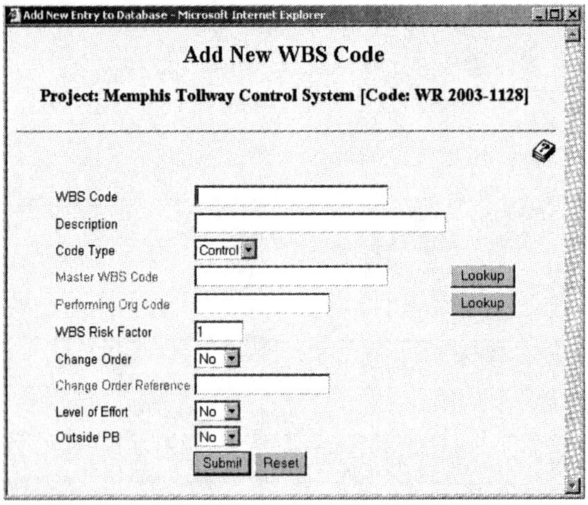

Figure 8.10. Risk plan development

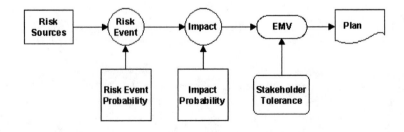

There are several types of risk response plans (often called "mitigation strategies"):

- *Avoidance:* Eliminate the cause of the event(s) or reduce the EMV via reducing probability
- *Mitigation:* Reduce the EMV via reducing the impact of the risk event
- *Acceptance:* Accept the risk (take no preventive action)
- *Deflection:* Assign (transfer) the risk to another party

Avoidance reduces the EMV by reducing (or setting to zero) the probability. The main methods used here are safety- and prevention-related techniques, which are employed in the early stages of a project. Prevention measures are available for almost all IT risks and include such methods as employee retention and motivation incentives, buying parts of a system instead of building all of it, use of contract labor for nonconfidential parts of the system, parallel design and construction of alternative algorithms, platform independent implementation techniques, use of open source software, using reusable components, and using object-oriented techniques. These methods have been discussed in earlier chapters of this book. For avoidance to be effective, one must identify the root cause of potential risk problems. One method is the Ishikawa Diagram (commonly called the *fish bone* or *cause-and-effect* diagram), which is illustrated in Figure 8.11.

Mitigation reduces the EMV by reducing the impact; these methods are:

- **Contingency Plans:** "Planned mitigation"; alternative means to do something should a certain risk event occur; "contingency reserves"
- **Workarounds:** A method devised to handle risk when the risk event happens ("unplanned mitigation")

Figure 8.11. Cause and effect diagram

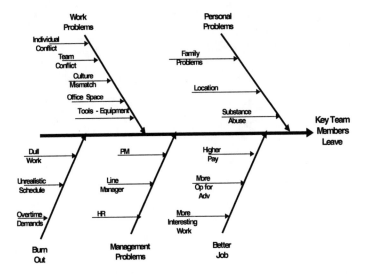

A bullet analogy (extended here), concerning being the target of a gunshot, was presented by Wideman (1992):

Mitigation (workarounds):
>> Move out of the way
>> Deflect the bullet
>> Repair the damage done by the bullet

Mitigation (planned):
>> Wear a bulletproof vest

Avoidance (reduces the probability of being shot at):
>> Carry a visible gun yourself
>> "Play dead"
>> Take steps to avoid being confronted by someone with a gun

Avoidance is usually a better measure than mitigation, but it is not always cost effective or possible. One can chose mitigation, avoidance, or both; however, one is not in control of the bullet. One could also ignore the risk by assuming that the likelihood is very low or that the impact is very low (bullets cannot hurt me). Mitigation techniques may be planned but are not typically implemented until the risk event is imminent or has occurred. This is illustrated in Figure 8.12. Well-planned projects have more contingency plans than workarounds; the opposite is the case for poorly planned projects. Avoidance and mitigation usually cost money to implement, and reserves are formulated. Reserves are the amount of time and cost added to a project to account for risk, also called management reserve. PMI recommends at least 10% (PMI, 2000). Using PERT and Monte Carlo simulations, one can calculate the reserve needed at the task level and then total these amounts for the entire project. However, in practice, less-precise methods are typically used because the data available for the analysis are less precise.

Figure 8.12. Risk plan components

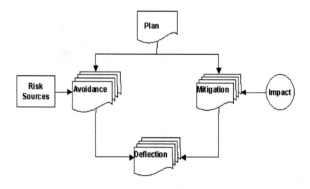

Deflection attempts to transfer the risk (part or all) to another party via:

- *Insurance:* Exchanges most of a risk of a probabilistic event(s) for a certain fixed cost
- *Outsourcing:* Let someone more capable or experienced do the work
- *Procurement/Contracts:* Buy/rent the needed expertise, equipment, material, software, and so forth

Deflection transfers and reduces the risk, but does not eliminate it. As discussed in a later chapter of this book on procurement and outsourcing, there are considerable risks in outsourcing. Hallows (1998) lists such subcontractor risks as:

Technical

 Competent resources not assigned

 Lack of familiarity with project or product

 Methodology not proven

 Poor project management techniques

 Technical disconnects due to distance of relationship

Operational

 Subcontractor staff goes out on strike

 Subcontractor lands a higher priority project

 Distance leads to business and operational disconnects

 Transportation causes problems

 Customs causes problems

Financial

 Subcontractor goes bankrupt

 Subcontract holds up deliverables due to contract or payment disagreements

 Subcontractor uses your schedule to extract extras

 Subcontractor reduces quality

Jones (1994) lists the major risk factors (and a percentage of projects at risk) in contracting and outsourcing arrangements as:

- High maintenance costs (60%)
- Friction between contractor and client personnel (50%)
- Creeping user requirements (45%)

- Unanticipated acceptance criteria (30%)
- Legal ownership of software and deliverables (20%)

These risks can be minimized by thoroughly qualifying the vendor, requiring the vendor to have the proper certifications, having the proper contract (with regard to terms, legal language, length, etc.), handling security issues, and requiring the vendor to report costs and progress using earned value methods (discussed later in this book).

The table in Figure 8.13 lists common risks for IT projects and possible avoidance and mitigation measures.

Figure 8.13. Common IT project risks

Risk	Avoidance	Mitigation
Incomplete requirements; Insufficient user involvement	Document clearly all requirements and get customer approval; utilize prototypes; make sure your analysts are talking to the right customer personnel; establish formal change control system	Involve users in documenting and approving requirements; use prototypes to flush out requirements; involve users with testing and documentation
Customer is difficult to work with	Assign higher risks and increase reserve; request customer management contact for conflict resolution; determine if the problem is with your personnel or customer personnel; have very good legal contracts	Document all customer interaction; frequently involve customer with requirement analysis, prototype review, design review, and test review
Lack of standard architecture	Obtain software engineering expertise; adopt standard architecture; adopt relevant IT standards; consider open source software	Depending upon depth into project, adopt and enforce relevant standards; use more prototypes
Inaccurate task estimating; Unrealistic task estimates	Use parametric estimation technique and compare with historical data and estimates by those who will do the work	Re-estimate remaining work if original estimate were not done in a quantitative manner and/or if multiple estimation techniques were not used; see cost overruns below
Inexperienced or poor PM	Set up apprentice PM program in organization; require PMI (or equivalent) certification for all PM's (for projects over a certain size); set up a PMO in organization	Project plans, controls, and issues reviewed by internal or external certified PM consultants; upper management review of PM choice
Insufficient staff; recruiting problems, staff illness	Prioritize requirements and phase project; use contract labor; outsource part of work; buy components	Use contract labor; outsource part of work; request extension from customer
Dependency on key team member(s)	Special recognition, position, incentives for these key persons; identify backup employees or contractors	Additional incentives to motivate the key members to stay thru project completion

Figure 8.13. Common IT project risks (cont.)

Risk	Avoidance	Mitigation
Scope creep, requirements changes	Have user sign off on requirements and change order plan; contingency funds for unforeseen changes; more use of prototypes	Document all change requests; Prioritize requirements and phase project; Charge customer for changes and develop new baseline schedule and cost plan
Vendor problems (lateness, quality issues, etc.)	Have a formal procurement process that results in qualified vendors, good legal contracts, and a "win-win" situation for both buyer and seller	Negotiate issues with vendor and use whatever measures are available within your contract (see book chapter on procurement)
Cost overruns (not due to scope creep)	Use earned value metrics (see book chapter on performance measurement); employ multiple estimation techniques, employ PERT estimation	Voluntary uncompensated overtime, scope reduction, project phasing, buy components
Lateness (not due to scope creep)	Use earned value metrics	Crashing, fast tracking, contract resources, scope reduction, project phasing
Quality problems	Carefully set and enforce standards, utilize modern object oriented architectures, use proven technology, plan for thorough testing; use Quality Function Deployment (QFD) to involve customer; use extensive prototyping	Increase prototyping and testing, verify standards adherence, use QFD
Team problems: low productivity, burn out, low morale	HR to interview backups, identify contractors; "team building" measures	"Team building" measures; re-assign people to different tasks or projects; utilize backup personnel or contractors
Weak upper management support	Strong quantified business justification for project; thorough project charter signed off at high level in organization	Revisit business justification with upper management; seek other support in organization; regular reporting of project progress and cost

The final risk-management plan documents information about the identified risks and how each risk is be handled. It may also include information about noncritical risks (risks not needing a response development) so that they can be revisited (during project execution) if necessary. An excellent risk management plan is a sign of an experienced PM versus an inexperienced PM.

Risk Plan Example

As a very simple example, consider the case of a company that plans to develop a software system, and has the following steps in its risk management plan:

- Identify the risks via the success factor framework, its lessons learned and industry historical data
- Grade each risk on a scale of 1 (*low*) to 10 (*high*), based on the probability of occurring
- For each risk, list the symptoms
- Grade each risk on its impact (percentage of budget affected) from 0 (*no impact*) to 10 (*total*); a value of 10 in this instance means that the entire project budget is at risk
- Calculate the relative EMV (impact times probability divided by 100)
- Identify the response to be taken for each risk (deflection, avoidance, contingency plans, workarounds)

In identifying the risks, the PM and his or her team review the published lists of the most common reasons why projects fail, both in general and for IT projects in particular. Jones (1994) studied software risks in detail, and his list of the most serious software risks are:

- Inaccurate metrics
- Inadequate measurement (of software development costs)
- Excessive schedule pressure
- Management malpractice (PM experience)
- Inaccurate cost estimation
- Silver bullet syndrome
- Creeping user requirements
- Low quality
- Low productivity
- Canceled projects

Another well-known list for software risks in IT projects is called "CHAOS," from the Standish Group (2004), which has surveys for several years from 1994 to 2004:

- Lack of executive management support
- Insufficient user involvement
- Inexperienced project manager
- Business objectives not clear
- Minimization and compromise of scope
- Lack of standard software architecture/infrastructure
- Lack of clear statement of requirements
- Lack of formal methodology

- Poor estimates
- Lack of proper planning
- Unrealistic expectations
- Scope minimized
- Lack of project "ownership" by team
- Team not hard working and focused
- Vision and objectives unclear
- Incompetent staff
- Improper setting of milestones

This Standish risk list represents the ranking of the problems in their 2000 report, although other years had a different order to the issues, for example in 2004 user involvement was first and executive support was second. Here is another list of risks from the ETP Group (O'Connell, 2002):

- The goal of the project is not defined properly
- The goal of the project is defined properly, but then changes to it are not controlled
- The project is not planned properly
- The project is not led properly
- The project is planned properly, but then is not resourced as planned
- The project is planned such that it has no contingency
- The expectations of the project participants are not managed
- The project is planned properly but then progress against that plan is not monitored and controlled properly
- Project reporting is inadequate or nonexistent
- When projects get in trouble, people believe the problem can be solved by some simple actions (e.g., work harder, extend the deadline, or add more resources)

Here is yet another list, from Tennant (2002):

- Poor planning
- Lack of resources (money and people)
- Constant reorganization and scope changes
- Lack of management support
- Poor communications
- Too much infighting and disputes
- No clear definition of roles and responsibilities

- Lack of clear objectives or scope
- Failure to recognize warning signs
- Unrealistic expectations

Another list is available from PCI Global (2002):

- Lack of timely approvals
- Delay in funding
- Surprise audits
- Defective materials
- Mistakes trigger rework
- Vendors do not deliver on time
- Key staff member is pulled off project
- Management institutes a "hiring freeze"
- Member of the team is absent too much
- Member of the team resigns
- Changes in specifications

This example in Figure 8.14 is a new and difficult type of project for the company, and the project team identifies the following risks: employee burnout, poor project management, insufficient resources, general employee turnover, key programmers leave, scope creep, overly low task estimates, and nonfeasable choice in technology (i.e., "immaturity"). Using these identified risks, the project team prepares a risk-management plan in

Figure 8.14. Example risk analysis

Risk	Prob.	Budget Impact	Relative EMV	Symptoms
Employee "burnout"	2	1	.02	Low Morale, lateness
Poor project management	1	5	.05	Lateness, cost overrun, earned value issues
Insufficient resources available	3	1	.03	Lateness, staffing problems
Employee turnover	2	1	.02	People leaving
Key programmers leave	2	4	.04	Key people leave
Scope "creep"	3	1	.03	Lateness (project level); additional scope
Task estimates are too low	2	3	.06	Lateness (task level), earned value issues (task levels)
Poor IT architecture choice	1	2	.02	Prototype time lengthens

Figure 8.15. Example risk plan

Risk	Response
Task estimates are too low	Closely monitor against actual costs to see if project needs to be phased or scope reduced
Poor project management	PM and team address specific issues, Upper Mgmt. involvement
Key programmers leave	Provide added incentives to key people to at least stay until project completion
Insufficient resources available	Phase project or request more $
Scope "creep"	PM steps in to "phase" project and deal with customer
Employee turnover	HR to interview backups, identify potential contractors
Employee burnout	Re-assign people to different tasks or projects
Poor IT architecture choice	Re-evaluate architecture choice, use more prototyping

a tablular format. The columns include information about probability, impact, EMV, and the symptoms for each risk.

The team next ranks the risks by EMV and then determines the response (in this example there is a need to respond to each threat); this is shown in Figure 8.15. The management reserve is calculated at about 27% (sum of relative EMVs). To complete their risk plan, the following information is recorded for each risk:

- Complete definition of the risk
- Why the risk is important to the project
- The impact, probability, and EMV
- The planned response(s)
- Who is responsible for recognizing and tracking the symptom(s)
- Who is responsible for the response(s) and recording results thereof
- What resources are needed for the response(s)

Risk Response Control

Risks need to be monitored continuously during the execution of a project by looking at the risk symptoms and seeing if any risk events have occurred or are about to occur. In fact, one of the most important items to address during project team meetings is risk. If any planned risk events occurred, then the risk management plan must implement the called-for response (i.e., contingency plans); or, if any unplanned risk events occur, then a workaround must be found. New risks or risk events may have also surfaced, or there may be a change in the risk ranking due to changes in probability or impact amount; some previous noncritical risks now become important. In Chapter IX, I review corrective actions and workarounds for projects that have schedule and/or cost problems, including such methods as fast tracking and crashing.

When risk events happen, they should be recorded in a project risk log, which describes the risk, the circumstances of its occurrence, the risk response taken, the degree of success of the response, the estimated cost of the event, and how the team thinks such risks could be better handled in the future. This log becomes part of the lessons-learned documentation at project closeout (project closeout is discussed in Chapter XI).

Rita Mulcahy (2003) listed the most common stumbling blocks in risk management:

- *Risk identification is completed without knowing enough about the project.*
- *Project risk is evaluated using only questionnaire, interview, or Monte Carlo techniques and thus does not provide a detailed, per task analysis of risk.*
- *Risk identification ends too soon resulting in a brief list (about 20) rather than an extensive list (hundreds) of risks.*
- *Risk identification and risk quantification are blended resulting in risks that are evaluated or judged when they come to light. This decreases the number of total risks identified and causes people to stop participating in risk identification.*
- *The risks identified are general rather than specific (e.g. communication rather than poor communication of customers needs regarding installation of system xxx caused two weeks of rework).*
- *Whole categories of risks are missed such as technology, cultural, or marketplace.*
- *Only one method is used to identify risk rather than a combination of methods. A combination helps ensure that more risks are identified.*
- *The first risk response strategy identified is selected without looking at other options and finding the best option or combination of options.*
- *Risks are not given enough attention during the project execution stage.* (Mulcahy, 2003)

Chapter Summary

Risk management and the planning thereof have been discussed in this chapter. The project risk-management process interacts with the other project management processes (as defined by PMI, 2003) in such a manner as to create or minimize risks. This is illustrated in Figure 8.16. Procurement and outsourcing activities in any phase of an IT project introduce additional risk, and these topics are covered more extensively in Chapter XII. *Thus, how well the other project management processes are done affects the risk introduced into the total process.*

Figure 8.16. Planning influence on risk

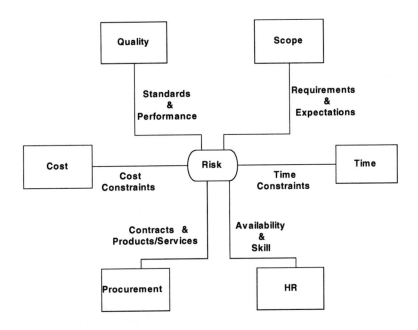

The project management office (PMO; discussed in detail in Chapter XVI), should be the organizational focal point for risk policies, procedures, frameworks, templates, and checklists. Risk factors (probability and impact) need to be evaluated not only initially but throughout the project. Earlier in this book, success criteria and stage gates were discussed. The stage gate evaluation process should include an updated analysis of risk; this overall process was shown in Figure 3.16 in Chapter III. Example forms for this stage gate evaluation were also illustrated earlier in the book, and based on that form each risk was reexamined.

For another excellent analysis of IT and software-related risks, see *Assessment and Control of Software Risks* (Jones, 1994). Jones itemizes the most common and most serious software risks and for each risk discusses: definition, severity, frequency, occurrence, susceptibility and resistance, root causes, associated problems, cost impact, methods of prevention, methods of control, support (product, consulting, education, periodical, standards, and professional associations), effectiveness of known therapies, cost of therapies, and long-range prognosis. Some of the details in this book are outdated at this point in time, although the general observations and recommendations are still very relevant. PMI also has a risk management special interest group (SIG; www.risksig.com/). The PMI Risk Management SIG offers forums for the exchange of ideas on topics in this area. Products like FiveAndDime have risk management built into the total PM system, but there are software products that are used only for risk management and interface to various PM software tools and or spreadsheet programs: Pertmaster (www.pertmaster.com), RiskTrak (www.risktrak.com), Crystalball (www.decisioneering.com), Primavera's P3-MonteCarlo (www.primavera.com/products), Decision Products' RiskDriver(www.riskdriver.com/), Palisade's @RISK (www.palisade.com), and Risk+ and RiskRadar (www.iceincUSA.com).

References

Boehm, B. (1991). *Software risk management.* Upper Saddle River, NJ: IEEE.

Carr, M. (1993). *Taxonomy-based risk identification* (Tech. Rep. No. 93-TE-6). Pittsburgh, PA: CMU/SEI.

DeMarco, T., & Lister, T. (2003). *Waltzing with bears: Managing risks on software projects.* New York: Dorset House.

Gibson, C. (2003). IT enabled business change: An approach to understanding and managing risk. MIS *Quarterly Executive, 2*(2), 104-115.

Hallows, J. (1998). *Information systems project management.* American Management Association.

Jones, C. (1994). *Assessment and control of software risks.* Englewood Cliffs, NJ: Yourdon Press Computing Series.

Marchewka, J. (2003). *Information technology project management.* Wiley.

Maverick, G. (2003, November). EAI project management. *Business Integration Journal,* 48-50.

Mulcahy, R. (2003). *Risk management, tricks of the trade for project managers.* Minneapolis, MN: RMC.

O'Connell, F. (2002). *Reasons why projects fail.* Retrieved from www.etpint.com/whyfail

PCI Global. (2002). *Crises events in projects.* Retrieved from www.pciglobal.com

Pearlson, K., & Saunders, C. (2004). *Managing and using information systems.* New York: Wiley.

Piney, C. (2003, September). Applying utility theory to risk management. *Project Management Journal.*

PMI. (2000). *The project management body of knowledge (PMBOK).* Newton Square, PA. ISBN 1-880-410-22-2.

Sommerville, I. (2003). *Software engineering.* Boston: Pearson Addison Wesley.

Standish Group. (2004). *Chaos chronicles.* Retrieved from www.standishgroup.com

Tennant, D. (2002, July 7). *Reasons why projects fail.* PMI.

Van Scoy, R. L. (1992, September). *Software development risk: Opportunity, not problem* (CMU/SEI-92-TR-30, ADA 258743). Pittsburgh, PA: Software Engineering Institute.

Wideman, R. (1992). *Project and program risk management.* Newton Square, PA: PMI Press.

Young, S. (2003). Why IT projects fail. *Computerworld.*

Chapter IX

Project Execution and Control

If you can't measure it, you can't manage it.

(Peter Drucker)

In fairy tales and traditional romance movies, the story ended when the prince found his soul mate, married her, and rode off with her into the sunset. The ending caption said: "They lived happily ever after." Well, we know that real life is not quite that simple; after the marriage comes the most difficult (and, one hopes, interesting) part. Similarly, a great project contract and plan is of little consequence without constant monitoring and control. Once the project is planned and underway, the project manager cannot simply ride away and assume that everything will go according to plan.

To insure success, many project matters need to be monitored; if a matter deviates from the plan, then some form of control must be exerted to bring the situation back in line with the plan. In this chapter I discuss the many matters that need to be monitored for IT projects, how best to monitor each matter, and what type of control actions may be appropriate for each.

The Control Process

The basic control process used in project management is the same process used in most engineering and business systems. It is based on the definition and establishment of key measures, and those measurements are then compared to some desired values or standards to formulate algebraic formulas, usually called metrics. If the difference between the measurement and the desired value exceeds some threshold, then corrective action (feedback) of some type is invoked, and the degree of corrective action may be a function of the size of the difference (and/or the integration [accumulation] or differentiation [rate] thereof). The measurements may be of process outputs or of the process itself, and the measurement level may be process-related (generally, how things are being done) or product-related (generally, what things are being built). This is illustrated in Figure 9.1.

The project control processes go on during the execution of the project. The execution of the project is carried out primarily by the project team members, and the control of the project is carried out primarily by the project manager. PMI defines several processes that support the overall process of project execution (PMI, 2000), that is, activities that should be taking place while the team does it work:

- Information dissemination (i.e., reporting)
- Team development
- Scope verification
- Quality assurance
- Procurement activities (solicitation, source selection, contract administration)

The Software Engineering Institute's (SEI; www.sei.cmu.edu/cmm) CMM also implies necessary practices (Level 2) for project tracking and oversight:

- Are the project's actual results compared with estimates in the plans?
- Is corrective action taken when actual results differ significantly from the plan?
- Are changes agreed on by all affected parties?
- Does the project follow a written policy for tracking and control of activities?
- Is someone assigned specific responsibilities for tracking work products and activities?

Figure 9.1. The control process

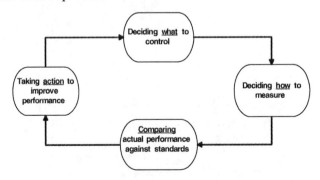

- Are measurements used to determine the status of the tracking activities?
- Are activities for tracking and oversight reviewed with upper management?

What to Control

Once the decision is made to measure and control project matters, the next question is, What to control? PMI (2000) defined several processes that support the overall process of project control:

- Scope change control
- Schedule control
- Cost control
- Quality control
- Risk response control

For most projects, the consumption of resources (time and cost) is always controlled, and the previous list of supporting processes adds the control of scope, risk, and quality. Other matters need to be considered, however, for effective management of IT projects. The Standish Group Reports (called "CHAOS"), which are based on large surveys in years from 1994 to 2004 (Standish, 2004), provide some guidance. The reports list the leading causes of IT project failures as:

- Lack of executive management support
- Insufficient user involvement
- Inexperienced project manager
- Business objectives unclear
- Minimization and compromise of scope
- Lack of standard software architecture/infrastructure
- Lack of clear statement of requirements
- Lack of formal methodology
- Poor estimates
- Lack of proper planning
- Unrealistic expectations
- Scope minimized
- Lack of project "ownership" by team
- Team not hardworking and focused

- Vision and objectives unclear
- Incompetent staff
- Improper setting of milestones

The order of the Standish list represents the ranking of the problems in its 2000 report. The list in other years ordered the issues differently; for example, in 2004, user involvement came first and executive support was second. This list suggests that other matters that need to be tracked include management support, requirements verification and validation, user involvement and attitudes, project management practices, business objectives and vision, technology issues like architecture and infrastructure, methodology, and project team attitudes.

Another qualified source for matters that should be controlled in IT projects is the "Seven Core Metrics in the rational unified process (RUP), which was discussed in Chapter V (Royce, 1998):

- Work and progress
- Budgeted cost and expenditures
- Staffing and team dynamics
- Change traffic and stability
- Breakage and modularity
- Rework and adaptability
- Mean time between failure and maturity

All these project matters that need to be controlled (as suggested in the three previous lists) are already included in the general model for IT project critical success factors. This is a general model, and therefore some of these factors may not be relevant or important for any particular project or some other peculiar factors may need to be included. Figure 9.2 shows a spreadsheet that organizes these items, specifies key measurements for each, and indicates the book chapter(s) that provides detail coverage thereof. Each of these areas is briefly defined in Figure 9.2 and discussed in more detail with specific techniques in other chapters of this book.

Measurement of Completion Factors

Once it has been decided which project matters need to be controlled, the measurements that need to be made must be decides upon. Figure 9.2 indicates the measurements for our critical success factors of IT projects, and we will first examine the completion factors.

Figure 9.2. Book content and success factor

Project Control		
Success Criteria	**Metrics**	**Book Chapter**
Completion Factors		
Project Management		
Schedule (Time)	EVA SPI	XIV
Cost	EVA CPI	XIV
Progress	Percent Complete, EVA CR	XIV
Scope	CO Approved/CO Submitted	XI
Team Morale	Surveys & Interviews, Staff Attitude, Turnover	XIII
Stakeholder Morale	Surveys & Interviews	XIII
Risk	Planned vs Unplanned Mitigation	VIII
Methodology		
Change Introduction	$ CO/ $ Budget	V, X
Change Resolution	CO Completed/CO Approved	V, X
Commitment to Perform		
Sponsor Support	Interviews	XIII
Upper Management Support	Interviews	XIII
Ability to Perform	Current Budget, Budget Horizon	VI, X
Verification		
Defect Introduction	Defects per 1000 LOC (by phase)	V, X
Defect Resolution	Defects Reported/Defects Corrected	v
Technology		
Process	Productivity (LOC per person hour)	V
Product	Product-related metrics	V
Satisfaction Factors		
Business Justification	ROI, IRR, Payback Period	III, X, XVI
Validation		
Stated Requirements	Requirements Document Approval	VI
Unstated Requirements	Preliminary Product Manifestation Review	X
Acceptance Testing	Acceptance Exceptions (Changes & Defects)	X
External Quality Dimensions	Product-related Metrics	X
Workflow & Content	Preliminary Product Manifestations Review	X
Standards	Compliance Audits and Inspections	V, X
Maintainability & Support	Comment Ratio, LOC per CO, Code Walkthrough	V, X
Adaptability	Reuse %, Avg Time per CO, Code Walkthrough	5, 10
Trust/Security	Security and background checks	XII, XIII
Process Security	Security incidents, lost time	VI
Product Security	Intrusion testing	VI, VIII, X

Project management addresses the use of proper project management skills and methods in dealing with each of the nine PMI knowledge areas. The following is a list of subdivisions

- *Schedule, cost, and progress* control has been traditionally handled via Gantt chart analysis and budget-vs.-actual cost metrics. A much better method of measure-

Figure 9.3. Earned value analysis

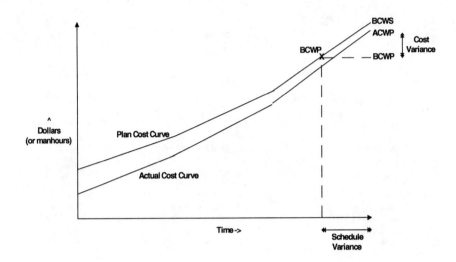

ment and analysis is earned value analysis (EVA), detailed in Chapter XIV. EVA uses three measurements and provides three key metrics: cost performance index (CPI), schedule performance index (SPI), and critical ratio (CR). These metrics can be used to estimate project time to complete and cost at completion. The three measurements are budgeted cost (BCWS), actual costs (ACWP), and earned value (BCWP); these are illustrated in Figure 9.3. Earned value is a function of the progress measured in terms of "percentage complete" of each WBS task.

- *Scope control* comprises the management of project change for the benefit of the project and resulting product. A PM must avoid *scope creep* and *gold plating*, and depending upon the contract situation, must make sure that all changes are estimated, priced, and billed. A key metric is the ratio of approved change orders to the total requested change orders. If the majority of change order requests are being approved (as opposed to being denied or deferred to another phase/version), then either changes are being accepted that are outside of the initial scope or the initial scope was ill defined. Change control is discussed in detail in the chapter on change management.

- *Team morale* and the morale of other stakeholders can be monitored through various types of interviews or surveys. The quality stage gates technique, discussed throughout this book, provides one opportunity for such monitoring. Other indicators of team morale problems include poor attitudes and complaints about the project and assignments, staff turnover, unplanned overtime, and low productivity.

- *Risk management* comprises the identification, quantification, and mitigation of potential risks to the project. This was discussed in detail in Chapter VIII, including specific metrics and techniques for IT risks. The key measure of risk planning effectiveness is the number of planned versus unplanned mitigation (workarounds).

Methodology comprises the selection of specific IT software engineering processes (requirements analysis, systems analysis, design, development, documentation, testing, etc.) and how these processes will be organized, utilized, and integrated, both among themselves and with the project management processes. (Chapter V discussed these subjects.) If the methodology chosen is inappropriate for the project, then there will be a high percentage of the project cost for changes and corrections. For measurement purposes, these costs can be subdivided into the following areas:

- *Change introduction* can be measured by the money (or person hours) in change orders relative to the total budget. Values over 10% may indicate the need for a different methodology or smaller increments if an incremental methodology is already in use. As discussed previously, large IT projects have lower success rates than smaller projects because the complexity grows according to the square of the number of items (people, requirements, technologies, etc.) involved. Excess change causes the project to grow and become more complex.

- *Change resolution* can be measured by the ratio of completed change orders to total change orders submitted and approved. As a project draws towards completion, the curve of completed change orders should approach the curve of approved changed orders, as is shown in Figure 9.4. If these two curves do not start to converge, then the change process is out of control due to an inappropriate choice of methodology.

Commitment to perform comprises upper management support for the project from both the project sponsor and upper management. It can best be measured by personal interviews and dialog as the project proceeds. In many organizations, this involves "politics," to which either the PM and/or the project sponsor must be a party.

Figure 9.4. Change orders

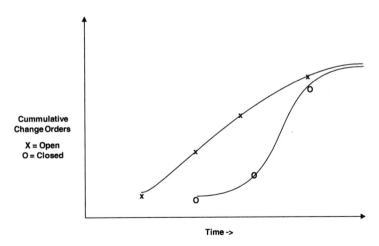

Ability to perform is having the amount of resources needed and the correct resources to carry out the project plan. The key measurement in this area involves budgetary matters including both the current fiscal period budget and the budget horizon for longer term projects and multi-phase projects. In this area the PM must work with the project sponsor and upper management to make sure that continued funding for the project is included in strategic planning forecasts.

Verification involves built-in quality or defect prevention and concerns the quality of the development *processes*, thus answering the question, "Have we built the product right?" Formally, verification is proof of compliance with requirements, specifications, and standards. Verification processes usually result in exception (bug) reports, in which compliance is not achieved. For measurement purposes, this is implemented via internal testing and inspection and can be subdivided as follows:

*   *Defect introduction* measures the defects relative to the size of the development effort, the common measure being defects per 1,000 LOC (KLOC). The basis for the KLOC may be the total LOC or just the LOC in new code, not including any "reused" code ("included" code). If the basis is the total code, greater reuse will mean a lower defect introduction rate. Current industry values average between 2 and 5. Defect introduction should also be analyzed based upon where the defect was originally introduced (requirements, design, coding, testing, etc.); this is discussed in more detail in Chapter X.

*   *Defect resolution* measures the number of defects reported versus the number of defects corrected, and may be measured in terms of numbers or cost (i.e., in money or in person hours). Similar to the situation with change orders, as a project draws toward completion, the curve of corrected defects should approach the curve of found defects, as is shown in Figure 9.5. If these two curves do not start to

Figure 9.5. Defects

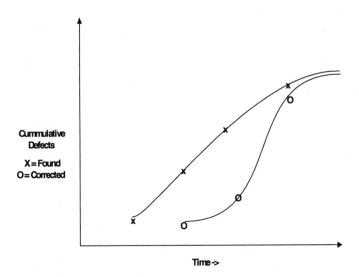

converge, then the defect situation is out of control due to the lack of built-in quality or an inappropriate choice of technology.

Technology comprises the proper selection of applicable technology for use in both the product and in the process of building the product. It covers architecture, platform, language, and supporting technology selection as well as issues of each, including the maturity, stability, and support thereof. It can be subdivided into the following:

- *Process* comprises the technology used to construct the product, and a key measure is productivity rate, usually measured in function points and/or KLOC per person, per hour, or per day. Design processes typically use function point-based metrics, and coding processes typically use KLOC metrics. Depending upon the chosen programming language, most programmers average anywhere from 25 to 100 KLOC per day (code developed prior to integration testing), with an average value of 50 to 60.

- *Product* comprises the technology built into the product, including the choice of platforms and other dependent software. There are a number of product-related metrics, including recoverability, scalability, and portability. Another key metric is whether the product is (or can be) based on open source components (runs on or utilizes open source products, such as Linux, Apache, MySQL, etc.).

Measurement of Satisfaction Factors

In a similar manner, the satisfaction factors can be examined to determine the necessary key measurements:

Business justification comprises the selected type of cost-benefit model(s), as was discussed earlier in this book. The business justification should be revisited and measured during the project to ensure that the assumptions in those models are still correct and relevant. This is part of the quality stage gate analysis process.

Validation comprises the *product,* which is the subject of the project and checks all user requirements (both stated and expected) and answers the question, "Have we built the right product?" Formally validation is proof that the customer and end users are satisfied with the system. Validation processes usually result in change orders when the user is not satisfied with an aspect of the product. Proper user involvement is vital to this aspect of the development and/or integration process.

- *Stated requirements* (needs) are initially manifested in some type of requirements document, as was discussed earlier in this book. Additional requirements are formalized via the change order approval process. The requirements are also included in more tangible forms in other documents, such as a users manual.

- *Unstated requirements* (wants and expectations) are best discovered via user review of preliminary product manifestations, such as use cases, design drawings, paper prototypes, and live prototypes. Unstated requirements were discussed in detail in Chapter V, and are part of the quality stage gate analysis.

- *Acceptance testing* is the final and formal measure of user satisfaction with the product (see Chapter X for more details on acceptance testing).

- *External quality dimensions* are a part of validation, even though they may not be a formal part of the contract or the acceptance testing. External quality dimensions must be addressed for the long-term success of the product and the performing organization. Included herein are measures such as usability, reliability (does the product do it right all the time), robustness (product can handle invalid/unusual data and usage), responsiveness and efficiency (with respect to speed, storage, clicks, keystrokes, and other resources), testability, auditability, and capacity/scalability.

Workflow and content comprises the effective integration of the new product into the organization's (and each user's) workflow. Content includes all deliverable information, including documentation, help system, data, and media content (especially in the sense of modern and Internet applications). The measures for this aspect of the project are the degree to which the deliverables corresponding to these items have been completed and the degree of the customer's satisfaction with such manifestations of the product.

Standards relate to compliance with applicable industry, corporate, and user (customer) standards in regard to both external (i.e., user interface) and internal issues (i.e., coding standards). (See Chapter X for more details on standards.) The measures for this item are compliance audits and inspections, which may be exhaustive or selective ("spot" checks).

Maintainability and support involves the inherent maintainability of the developed product and the willingness and timeliness of the developing (or support) organization in responding to the customer's concerns about usage or integrity (real or perceived) issues. For IT projects that succeed, 70% of the total life-cycle cost of the product is spent in the maintenance phase; thus, maintainability is extremely important. Maintenance programmers also spend about half of their time studying the existing code (Standish, 1984). Therefore, if the code is easy to read and easy to understand, support costs are lower. One traditional but important metric is the ratio of comment statements to executable statements in the code. For well-written 3GL code, this ratio should be about one comment line per every one to three code lines. Periodic code walkthroughs are also necessary to ensure the quality of the comments and the quality (and standards compliance) of the code. Another measure of maintainability is the lines of code affected per change order. More comprehensive metrics in this area include both the lines of code affected and the lines of code examined per change order.

Adaptability relates to the flexibility of the product to be adapted (successfully modified) for evolving changes in the environment in which the product is deployed; this includes both technical changes and business changes. Design and code walkthroughs are necessary to ensure proper object-oriented techniques. One key measure is the ratio of the total code that has been reused (from object-oriented libraries and packages). The percentage of reused code should be over 50 for most projects in modern IT environments. This metric can be misleading if one imports simply because that code is part of the overall imported module, but that code is not actually used. Modern object-oriented implementations usually have ways to measure only the code that is part of the executable program. One cannot assume that the cost for reusing code is always negligible. Another important measure is the average time (person hours) per change order, because adaptable systems are able to be changed faster.

Trust and security relates to both the security built into the product and to the security of the process for building the product. Security must start with the project stakeholders, particularly the people involved in designing, building, and testing the product; these individuals (both employees and contractors) should undergo complete security and background checks.

- *Process security* metrics would include counts and severity of security incidents that occur during the project. A related metric would be lost time due to security problems.

- *Product security* involves the customer's willingness to fully utilize the system in all necessary modes without concern for compromising any of the customer's assets, including information assets. This type of security must be built into the product, and the metrics involve special intrusion testing in regard to security holes.

Measuring and Reporting

To avoid spending more effort on measure and control than can possibly be gained in return, appropriate measures are necessary. The metrics for a project must be selected carefully and appropriately for the size and complexity of the project. Once the desirable measures are selected, the next step is to find the best way to obtain those measurements. It is important, particularly for projects involving professionals, to have measurements that are noninvasive and consume very few additional resources. If possible, the measures should be a byproduct of normal work or of other normal and required processes, such as basic time/attendance and/or status reporting. For IT projects, many of the measures can be obtained automatically by the choice of methodology and technology and the supporting tools thereof; this is illustrated in Figure 9.6. For most IT organizations, the chosen system of measurements is put into place for all projects performed by that organization; certain metrics for small or simple projects may be excepted. A project management office (PMO) often coordinates this overall measurement system and its supporting tools and techniques (PMOs are discussed in Chapter XVI).

The reporting process consists of taking the information from established metrics and summarizing some of that information for some stakeholders; not all measures are

Figure 9.6. IT project metrics

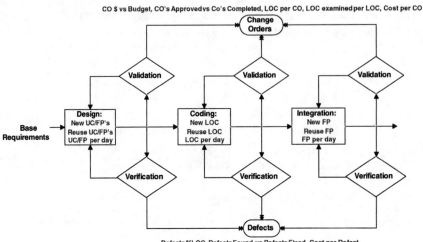

reported to all stakeholders. A communication plan indicates specific information that is reported to certain stakeholders, and included how and when that information is reported. (Communications and stakeholder management is discussed in Chapter XIII.) Although not all information is reported to all stakeholders, there may be organizational policies and procedures or contract provisions that dictate certain reporting requirements; however, the PM should always follow the following key principles in reporting progress and other measures:

- Honesty is the best policy!
- Bosses hate surprises!
- Bad news does not get better with age!
- Document all issues and problems!

A simple progress report form is shown in Figure 9.7. Problematic projects require closer monitoring than nonproblematic. Some warning signs of "runaway" projects were given in PM Network (Block, 1999):

- Inadequate project planning
- Faulty task management
- Poor reporting and communications
- Infrequent status reports
- Insufficient documentation
- Abrupt schedule changes

Figure 9.7. Project status

Project Status

Project Code:_____   Report Date:_____
Project Name:_____
Befitting Organization:_____
Performing Organization:_____
Project Manager:_____

Business Evaluation:_____
_____
_____

Milestones Met:
1._____
2._____
N._____

Earned Value Metrics
Actual Cost:_____   Planned Cost _____   % Complete:_____
Budget Variance:_____   Earned Value:_____   Critical Ratio: _____
CPI: _____   BAC: _____   EAC:_____   ETC:_____
SPI: _____   Estimated Completion Date: _____

Risks Status:_____
_____
_____

Explanations/Notes_____
_____
_____

Corrective Actions Necessary:_____
_____
_____

Approvals
Benefiting Organization   Performing Organization
By:_____   By:_____
Date:_____   Date:_____

- Project disorganization
- Muddled business objectives
- Extreme project complexity
- Escalating costs
- Too many project team meetings

Stage Gate Implementation

As suggested earlier, the use of a dual stage gate approach to project performance reporting and control. This is illustrated again in Figure 9.8. Multiple quality stage gates may be within one management stage gate or vice versa. This dual gating process minimizes the time that upper management and the project team spends in status reporting meetings by splitting the review process into separate completion and satisfaction reviews with the occurrence of each, based upon the need thereof. However, it ensures that customer involvement is sufficient in the project matters that most concern the users.

Figure 9.8. Dual stage gates

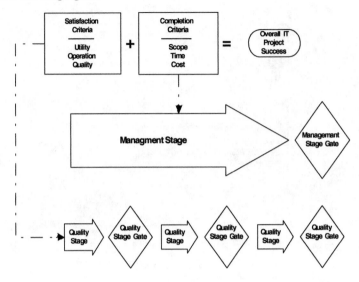

Figure 9.9. Stage gates and stakeholder involvement

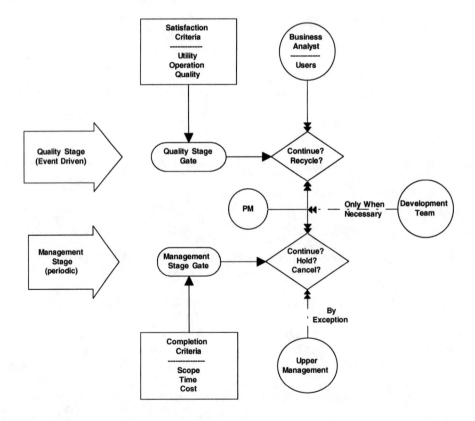

Management stage gates handle the completion criteria, and these stage gates can be set at fixed time intervals or upon completion of a major project phase. For methodologies in which phases overlap, or when using incremental or iterative approaches, the management stage gates can be set between increments or iterations, or upon fixed-time increments, such as 1 month. To minimize the time and cost associated with formal management reviews, it is recommended that the management stage gates happen at regular time intervals but that they take place only on an exception basis, when key metrics (such as EVA indexes) indicate problems. At the management stage gate, completion metrics are reviewed (either exhaustively or by exception) and a go/kill/hold decision is reached. This is illustrated in Figure 9.9.

Quality stage gates address the satisfaction factors that are examined by relevant stakeholders for that gate via focusing on a particular preliminary product manifestation; the review does not make a go/kill/hold decision but rather a go-forward or recycle type decision. Figure .9.9 illustrates these distinctions. These concepts are discussed in more detail in Chapter X.

Corrective Actions

Measurements are compared to some desired values or standards to determine deviations and differences. If the difference between the measurement and the desired value exceeds a threshold, corrective action of some type may be necessary. In project management, the need and amount for corrective action depends upon the direction and magnitude of the deviation. Deviation rates and accumulations may also factor into the type and magnitude of the chosen corrective action as well as the point in the project that the deviation is discovered.

Controls need to be appropriate for the type, size, complexity, and organizational environment of the project, or one may spend more on the effort to control than can possibly be gained in return. A PM cannot assume the job is finished when he or she has implemented the controls. In addition, accurate results may not be obtained unless the project team and other subordinates also buy into the controls. Some controls are needed, particularly in IT, and one should:

- Keep them as simple as possible
- Control only what needs to be controlled
- Minimize the additional work of data acquisition and processing for the controls
- Let the project team and other employees in on the controls and the overall purpose thereof

In general, the PM uses the measures and controls to track and review but does not intervene directly unless there is a problem. Corrective actions are management prerogatives that are available to a PM (and upper management), based upon the type of organization (functional/hierarchical, projectized, or matrix, as is discussed in a later chapter), the position of the project manager, the organization culture, HR policies, possible union rules, and the governing laws of the state or country. Some corrective actions may be operational, some tactical, and some strategic.

Managing a project involves the trade-off of some key variables, in particular, scope, time, and cost. There is an old expression in project management that says, "Do you want it good, fast, or cheap—pick any two." If the project is behind schedule, one can consider adding additional resources (people, money, etc.). This will cost additional money, which may be acceptable if the project is below cost or if the customer is more concerned with schedule than cost (contract permitting). Changing resources and obtaining better-cheaper-faster resources may also be considered, but there will be a cost and delay for the changeover (and added risk), and if it is late in the project or if it is a relatively short project, the net benefit may be minimal. If the customer is more concerned with cost than schedule, the schedule can be extended by adding more time, contract permitting. Another alternative is to reduce the scope by deleting features, by moving features into a future phase (or version), or moving features into the maintenance phase. Still another alternative is to reduce quality by:

- Increasing tolerances (safety margin, backup, etc.)
- Reducing testing
- Forcing the testing onto users
- Not fixing all the defects

These measures usually increase the long-term cost of a product, but some software companies often use these techniques.

Duration compression is another technique that can sometimes be used to correct schedule problems. There are two types of duration compression: crashing, which may be combined with reductions in scope and/or quality, and fast tracking. Both of these methods usually increase project risk. Crashing involves allocating more resources to the critical path tasks; according to PMBOK, "Taking action to decrease duration by analyzing a number of alternatives to get the maximum compression for the least amount of cost" (PMI, 2000). Resources may be taken from noncritical path tasks if resource types

Figure 9.10. Task crash evaluation

Task	Duration	Crash Time Savings	Crash Cost	Crash Risk
A	15	2	3000	HIGH
B	10	2	9000	LOW
C	4	1	1000	LOW
D	8	1	2000	HIGH
E	12	3	8000	NONE

are same or similar. This may result in higher costs; however, for many tasks (particularly IT tasks), increasing resources may not speed up those tasks. A common analogy applies: It takes one woman 9 months to have a baby; the process cannot be accelerated by putting nine women on the job for 1 month. According to Brook's Law, adding manpower to a late IT project makes it later (Brooks, 1995).

As an example, consider the project-critical path tasks shown in Figure 9.10. If one had to cut 3 months time off the project and the schedule was most important, followed by cost and then risk, then tasks A and C would be crashed. Instead, if one had to cut 3 months time from the project, and schedule was most important, followed by risk and then cost, tasks E would be crashed.

Fast-tracking is starting tasks that fall later in the project schedule before their predecessors are completely finished and/or reducing lag times. This also typically increases project risks. For traditional waterfall methodologies, fast-tracking may include starting one phase before its predecessor phase is completed (i.e., starting coding before the completion of detailed design). Fast-tracking to some extent is already a part of overlap, iterative, and incremental methodologies, which are discussed in Chapter V. Consider the small project schedule shown in Figure 9.11. Any task on the critical path that has a predecessor task could be fast-tracked by starting it before the predecessor was completed (if it was physically possible to do so); here, task B, C and/or G.

Many other corrective actions may be available to PMs that may improve the productivity or resourcefulness of the PM's project team members and thus reduce time or cost, or improve quality. These actions include employee/contractor disciplinary actions (negative reinforcement), employee/contractor incentives (positive reinforcement), and "pep talks" and other motivational techniques. A PM must maintain the strong commitment of stakeholders throughout the project, and these human resources issues are discussed in detail in Chapter XIII. Of course, upper management may also choose to change the PM.

There may be systematic problems in the project due to the choice of methodology, technology, or tools. Defects introduced early in the overall development process are more expensive to correct than defects introduced later. For this reason it pays to focus defect prevention during the early processes, such as requirements and design. An analysis, such as the one shown in Figure 9.12, examines where the defects are introduced versus where they appear.

Figure 9.11. Network PDM diagram

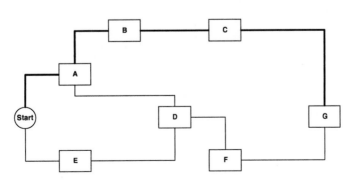

Figure 9.12. Defects by stage

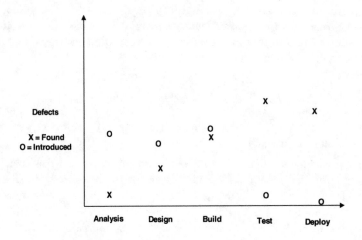

Figure 9.13. Cause and effect diagram

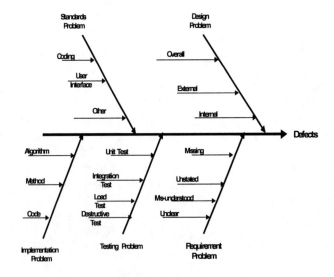

For systematic problems, one first needs to find the root causes. Fishbone diagrams, as is shown in Figure 9.13, are a good way to analyze these types of problems in detail so that an eventual solution will be discovered.

Chapter Summary

In this chapter, project performance control and corrective action techniques were defined and discussed. Performance metrics for each critical success factor were identified and illustrated. PMs must often be clever and innovative to solve difficult project control problems. A common analogy is that upon running into a "brick wall," a PM must examine all alternatives and find a way to go over, under, or around that wall. Cockburn (as cited in King, 2004) stated in *Computerworld*: "A core part of the job of project manager is coming up with inventive ways to get out of incredibly constrained situations."

References

Block, T. (1999, April). The seven secrets of a successful project office. *PM Network*.

Brooks, F. (1995). *The mythical man month: Essays on software engineering, 20th anniversary edition*. Boston: Addison-Wesley.

King, J. (2004, February). Project management in the trenches. *Computerworld*, p. 16.

PMI. (2000). *The project management body of knowledge (PMBOK)*. Newton Square, PA. ISBN 1-880410-22-2.

Royce, W. (1998). *Software project management—A unified approach*. Addison-Wesley.

Standish Group. (2004). *Chaos chronicles*. Retrieved from www.standisgroup.com

Standish, T. (1984, September). An essay on software reuse. *IEEE Trans on Software Engineering, Vol.SE-10*(5).

Chapter X

Managing Quality

Well done is better than well said.

(Benjamin Franklin)

Quality is defined by PMI as conformance to requirements, specifications, standards and fitness for use (PMI, 2000). Part of this definition is mostly quantitative, namely the requirements, specifications, and standards (assuming that these three things have been carefully and correctly itemized), but "fitness for use" is mostly qualitative. Because of this qualitative portion of the definition, the quality of the product which is the subject of the project may be an area for potential conflict between the performing organization and benefiting organization. *In fact, as a project proceeds, quality is the most difficult area to keep on track, not because of its complexity, but because the project team may compromise it when a crunch arises* (Hallows, 1998).

Quality Management

Quality is more than just conformance to requirements. A good set of requirements is often difficult to devise for IT systems. If there are defects in the requirements (which there usually are), one could conceivably have a high-quality system that is useless. In addition, simply meeting the requirements will not guarantee that the customer or end users are satisfied with the product. Quality must also be distinguished from grade. A low-grade product may have just as much quality as a high-grade product. Different grades of a product are generally created for different classes of service, and they generally have different unit prices.

Most people think of bugs when they think of quality in the context of IT systems. The term *bug* was originally coined by Dr. Grace Hopper, who developed the COBOL language. She had found that a computer crash was due to a moth that lodged inside of the hardware. For large IT systems of 1,000 function points or more, total defects will average five bugs per function point (Jones, 1994). Even with high-quality software development, for every 500 or so lines of procedural C-like code there is one bug (Linger, 1994). Your electric razor has dozens of bugs, your TV may have hundreds of bugs, and your car may have thousands of bugs. Most of these bugs are encountered only when a certain set of circumstances arises. Software bugs cost as much as $60 billion annually, as estimated by the National Institute of Standards and Technology. Inside sources reported that Microsoft Windows 2000 was released with 63,000 potential defects (Foley, 2000; ZDNet, 2000). Software bugs increase in number in our modern world as our dependency on IT deepens and our reliance on automation and embedded software grows.

In addition to bugs, however, the basic definition of *quality* needs to be further extended when we consider completion criteria and satisfaction criteria. A more complete definition of *quality* for IT projects should include:

- Conforms to requirements and specifications
- Meets "customer expectations"
- Is defect-free
- Is highly usability
- Is consistent with adopted standards
- Is reliability (does it do it right all the time)
- Is robust (can handle invalid/unusual data and usage)
- Is testable
- Is auditable
- Is maintainable and readable
- Is secure
- Is recoverable
- Is appropriately documented (external and internal)
- Is efficient (with respect to speed, storage, clicks, keystrokes, and other resources)
- Is platform independent (portability)
- Is flexible and adaptable

A less specific but official list of quality attributes is found in IEEE 83: portability, reliability, efficiency, accuracy, error, robustness, correctness. Another official list of quality attributes is found in ISO 9126: functionality, reliability, usability, efficiency, maintainability, and performance.

Poor quality can result in a number of undesirable events and states, including increased costs, low morale in both the performing and the benefiting organization, lower stakeholder satisfaction, increased risk, lost business, and lower project business benefits, whereas meeting quality standards generally results in increased morale, lower risk, higher stakeholder satisfaction, and meeting project benefit expectations. *Quality in IT projects has a long-term effect.* Sometimes the effects of poor quality may not be noticed until well after an IT product is built and deployed. Often, an IT product will perform in a satisfactory manner but may not be economically maintainable or adaptable. For an IT project that is successful (and remember that most IT projects do not succeed), most of the long-term costs will be in the maintenance phase (about two-thirds of the life-cycle costs).

A PM needs to understand what quality looks and feels like for his or her project. *It can be disastrous if the PM of an IT project does not understand how quality manifests itself in the application area for his or her project!* Team members need the same understanding and appreciation, and if lacking appropriate training should be supplied. Quality management is the overall process required to ensure that the above IT quality metrics are achieved; this overall process includes the following three subprocesses: quality planning, quality assurance, and quality control. Figure 10.1 defines these three processes (PMI, 2000).

Quality Planning

The main focus on quality used to involved product inspection (checking items after development). Deming (1982) and others showed that quality could be improved more by preventative measures such as improving production processes rather than by postproduction inspection. With the advent of modern quality philosophies, companies have begun to spend more on planning and prevention. It was found that the cost of using prevention was less than the cost of quality nonconformance. A rule of thumb states that for every dollar spent on prevention, the cost of repair is reduced by $3 to $10 (Jones, 1994). Often, management is less concerned with prevention, because solving problems is a high-visibility effort with immediate rewards, whereas preventing problems has low visibility. Both conformance and nonconformance incur costs; the different cost issues of each are shown in Figure 10.2. Thus, the total costs involved with quality can be expressed as (Campenella, 1999; Crosby, 1979):

Figure 10.1. Quality processes

Quality Planning	Quality Assurance	Quality Control
Define quality for the project and how it will be measured	Take measurements; determine if measurements are appropriate	Compare measurements to plan and take corrective action
Planning project phase	Execution project phase	Controlling project phase

$$\text{Cost}_{\text{quality}} = \text{Cost}_{\text{conformance}} + \text{Cost}_{\text{non-conformance}}$$

Complete quality planning comprises the design and plans for preventative measures (built-in quality) and product testing.

Nonconformance costs are classified as internal or external. Internal costs are incurred when the performing organization finds the defect, and external costs are incurred when the benefiting organization finds the defect. External costs are typically greater than internal. *The cost of correcting defects in IT systems is a function of when the defect is introduced and when the defect is discovered.* Defects introduced early and found late in the development process are the most expensive to correct. Consider the example methodology in Figure 10.3 for developing Web applications. Defects introduced in the requirements stage but not found until deployment may mean that all intervening steps have to be repeated in some degree. Defects introduced during program development (programming bugs) and found during integration testing will require the repetition of much fewer steps.

Figure 10.2. Cost of conformance and nonconformance

Cost of Conformance	Cost of Non-Conformance
Quality Planning and Training	Rework and Delay Costs
Effectiveness Studies	Wasted Effort
Validation and Verification	Warranty, Refund, Contract Penalty, and Legal Costs
Benefit Surveys	Loss of Customer Goodwill and Market Share

Figure 10.3. Web application development methodology

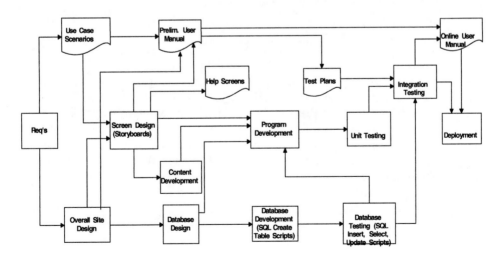

Defects generally can be traced to five origins (Jones, 1994): requirements, design, coding, documentation, and bad fixes. It can cost 40 to 1,000 times more to fix a defect found late in the development cycle (Gause & Weinberg, 1989). Up to eighty percent of a typical software product's development time may be spent correcting errors not found early in the project (McConnell, 1997). In U.S. Department of Defense's (DoD) studies conduct by Hughes, it was found that it cost 100 times more to fix a problem that is not recognized until the application is released. A large number of errors are not found until the product is released and put in general use (about 22%) and most errors are introduced in the definition/requirements phase (about 55%). When defects are eventually fixed, there is a 40% change that other errors will be inadvertently introduced (for non-object-oriented software). Thus, the initial focus for IT project quality should be on prevention or built-in quality. Building in quality involves establishing defined rigorous procedures for how something is built or assembled. The discipline of software engineering is largely concerned with this topic, and this was covered in an earlier book chapter. For IT systems, this dimension of quality manifests itself mainly through: IT standards, requirements gathering techniques, design techniques, implementation techniques, and maintainability, adaptability, and reuse methods. Jones lists primary software defect prevention techniques as (Jones, 1994):

- Formal quality plans
- Use of joint application development (JAD)
- Use of prototyping
- Structured analysis and design techniques
- Reusable code and designs
- Software quality assurance teams
- Total quality management (TQM) methods
- Quality function deployment (QFD) methods
- "Clean room" development methods
- Quality measurement programs
- Reviews and inspections
- Use of defect estimation and measurement tools

The term *verification and validation* (V&V) has emerged in recent years and has been applied to software development projects; IEEE 1012-1998 is the new standard for V&V. Definitions from an IT perspective differ among authors concerning exactly which project activities are verification activities and which are validation activities; and some types of activities have ingredients of both. Formally, verification is proof of compliance with requirements, specifications, and standards. Verification is primarily concerned with built-in quality and is a *process-related notion* that asks the question, "Are we building the product in the correct manner?" Answering that question requires both the internal testing of the product and the inspection of processes. For IT projects, inspection involves primarily design walkthroughs, code walkthroughs, and method and tool evaluations. These are often called *peer reviews* because peers are involved and typically provide more valuable feedback that management in these activities. These *defect prevention methods* can have a high defect removal rate of about 60% (Jones, 1994).

Formally, validation is proof that the customer and end users are satisfied with the system. Validation is a *product-related notion* that asks the question, "Have we built the correct product?" Answering that question requires inspection and acceptance (external) testing of the product, which for IT systems mainly comes at the end of the development cycle. Prior to the acceptance testing, which is typically performed by the benefiting organization (sometimes for contract compliance), there is normally several levels of internal testing (verification), including unit testing, integration testing, load testing (capacity), timing tests, destructive testing, and intrusion testing (security). Testing is discussed in more detail later in this chapter.

All validation need not be at the end of the development process. There are a number of procedures that can be carried out early in the overall process to help guarantee that the correct product is being built. These procedures involve getting the benefiting organization and other stakeholders more intimately involved in the review of preliminary product manifestations; this methodology is discussed in detail later in this chapter.

A part of the effort to build in quality for IT systems is to identify the major quality problem areas and then find the root causes of these problems. The Pareto chart is a classic quality engineering diagram that helps focus attention on the most critical problems of a project by presenting information in order of priority; this is illustrated in Figure 10.4. The philosophy is based on the old 80/20 rule (80% of the problems come from 20% of the activities). For a PM, instead of solving each problem as soon as it occurs, the Pareto diagram helps put the problems into perspective so a PM's time can be focused first on the key issues.

Figure 10.4. Pareto chart

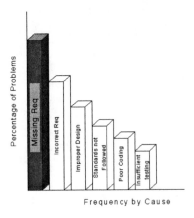

Quality Assurance

Quality assurance is done primarily during the execution of a project. Planned measurement systems are analyzed to see if all measurements are necessary or if more measurements need to be established. Overall project performance is regularly analyzed to make sure the project will satisfy the required quality standards. *For IT projects, quality metrics should be defined in three areas: process, product, and perception; these three areas should encompass the critical success factors identified earlier in this book.* For IT maturity models such as the SEI CMM model, maturity levels involve improvement of both the product and the process of building the product. Project control was covered in Chapter IX, and some of the control metrics identified and discussed in that chapter that are also quality related and are shown and classified in Figure 10.5. As well as product and process quality metrics, some metrics involve environmental factors into which the product is to be deployed.

Figure 10.5. IT quality metrics

Quality Metrics

Success Criteria	Metrics	Product	Process	Environment
Completion Factors				
Project Management				
Team Morale	Surveys & Interviews, Staff Attitude, Turnover		X	X
Stakeholder Morale	Surveys & Interviews		X	X
Verification				
Defect Introduction	Defects per 1000 LOC	X	X	
Defect Resolution	Defects Reported			
	Defects Corrected		X	
Technology				
Process	Productivity (LOC per man hr)		X	
Product	Product related metrics	X		X
Satisfaction Factors				
Business Justification	ROI, IRR, Payback Period	X		X
Validation				
Stated Requirements	Requirements Document Approval	X		
Unstated Requirements	Preliminary Product Manifestation Review	X		
Acceptance Testing	Acceptance Exceptions (Changes & Defects)	X		
External Quality Dimensions	Product Related Metrics	X		X
Workflow & Content	Preliminary Product Manifestations Review	X		X
Standards	Compliance Audits and Inspections	X		X
Maintainability & Support	Comment Ratio, LOC per CO, Code Walkthrough	X		
Adaptability	Reuse %, Avg Time per CO, Code Walkthrough	X		
Trust/Security				
Process Security	Security incidents, lost time		X	
Product Security	Intrusion testing	X		

The product which is the subject of the IT project may also need to meet a certain *service level agreement* (SLA), which could even be part of the project contract. A SLA specifically defines the "quality" of service that is to be provided by the product within a certain deployment environment. Items typically found in SLAs are:

- Response time upper limits
- Percentage of log-ins or calls not answered first time
- Downtime maximum percentages (i.e., "99% uptime")
- Maximum downtime interval

The Software Engineering Institute's (SEI; www.sei.cmu.edu/cmm) CMM defines the necessary Level 2 practices for software quality assurance:

- Are quality assurance activities planned?
- Do these activities provide objective verification that software products and activities adhere to standards and requirements?
- Are the results of quality reviews and audits provided to affected parties?
- Are issues of non-compliance that are not resolved within the project addresses by upper management?
- Does the project follow a written policy for implementing quality assurance?
- Are adequate resources provided for performing quality assurance activities?
- Are measurements used to determine the cost and schedule status of quality assurance activities?
- Are these activities reviewed with upper management on a regular basis?

Quality Control

Quality control involves analyzing the measurements, comparing them to the plan, and taking corrective action if necessary, such as eliminating the cause of unsatisfactory performance. Analyzing the measurements typically involves quality control tools, such as statistical methods, control charts, trend analysis, and other flowcharting methods. Trend analysis may also involve using mathematical techniques to forecast future outcomes based upon historical values. Trend analysis is often used in IT projects to monitor technical performance metrics, such as how may defects have been introduced and detected and in which stages of the project. Finding many defects in later stages such as integration testing or user acceptance testing is an indication of earlier quality problems in analysis or design. This is illustrated in Figure 10.6.

Figure 10.7 shows another useful type of trend chart that of cumulative defect occurrence and correction. For this type of analysis, one hopes to see the gap between cumulative

Figure 10.6. Defects introduced and found

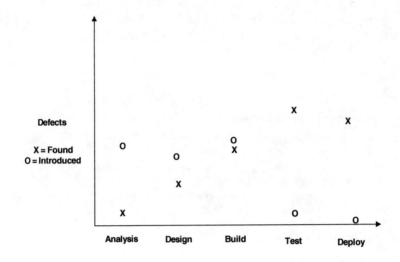

Figure 10.7. Cumulative defects

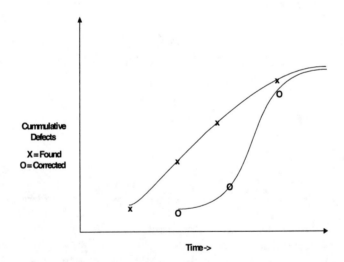

defects found and cumulative defects corrected closing as the project proceeds. If that gap (between the two curves) is becoming wider, then there is a problem in getting timely fixes to the defects.

A very useful technique for finding root causes of projects is the Ishikawa or Fishbone diagram (also called cause-and-effect diagrams). These diagrams show how various causes or potential causes (and their subcauses) relate to cause the overall problem. These diagrams also help stimulate project team thinking. Figure 10.8 shows this type of diagram for the problems involved with requirements analysis.

Figure 10.8. Requirements cause and effect diagram

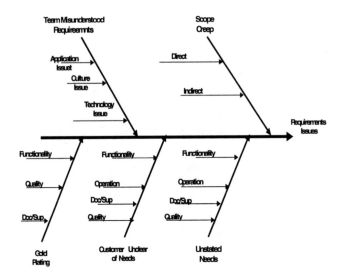

Figure 10.9 shows another diagram of this type for analyzing the problem of software defects.

Jones (1994) lists the eight *root* causes of quality problems as:

- Lack of an understanding of what quality means for software
- Inadequate defect prevention
- Inadequate use of reviews and inspections
- Insufficient or careless testing
- Lack of quality measurements
- Lack of understanding by project management that quality is critical to completion metrics and user satisfaction
- Excessive schedule pressure leading to reduced quality efforts
- Unstable and ambiguous user requirements

Often detailed and structured, *quality audits* are conducted upon project completion to evaluate both the software engineering and the project management processes in regard to quality aspects, and these become part of the project lessons-learned documentation.

Figure 10.9. Defects cause and effect diagram

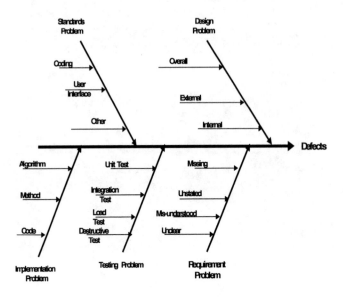

Software Testing

Techniques to build quality into software systems have been quite successful over the last several decades. The average software defect rate declined from about 8 per KLOC (thousand lines of code) in the 1970s to 5 per KLOC in 1990 ("The Quality Imperative," 1991). *However, when software is created using the most rigorous of methodologies and quality standards (producing 1 or 2 defects per KLOC), there will still be a significant number of defects in the product prior to testing. Software testing and defect correction typically takes between 30% to 60% of project development time and budget.* Complex application developments can spend more than half of their total program effort on testing. When a time crunch arises in a project, often the full testing of a product is compromised. A generally accepted rule is that testing costs will be 25% of the total development costs (Brown, 1998).

There may be times that testing is not necessary; the Software Program Managers Network has identified these circumstances (Brown, 1998):

- When the responsibility for failure can be shifted to someone else
- When the impact or significance of any problem is insignificant
- When the software does not have to work
- When no one is or will be using the system
- When the project has already failed .

Figure 10.10. IEEE standard for software unit testing

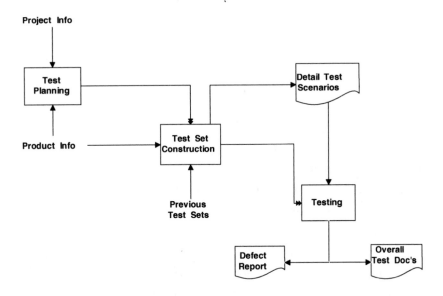

Testing should be a multilevel process with different types of testing in different stages of the project. Single stage testing is about 30% effective, but multilevel testing can achieve a much higher efficiency (Jones, 1994). Testing should also be included for software components that are purchased or otherwise acquired.

Unit testing is typically done by the developers and is a process to make sure that each software module performs properly relatively independently from other modules. Input, output, and interface operations are typically simulated. Unit testing is typically mostly white-box ("structural") testing where knowledge of module internals is utilized to insure that each source code statement and path through the code is exercised, possibly as a function of different external and database conditions. Often, test harnesses are created for each module, which is a set of specific tests for that module. These harnesses are checked into the source code version control system, and they are usually automatically repeated for each change to that module. For cleanroom software engineering discussed earlier in this book, unit testing is not done by the coders but by separate testers; the coders review each others code and walk through the execution paths. The economic benefits of this clean room approach to unit testing are debatable. The unit testing of a module is typically included in the work breakdown structure (WBS) task to build that module.

Integration testing involves testing the entire system working together; this is often called an "end-to-end" or system test. This type of testing should not be done by the developers, but by an independent testing group. The project WBS should have separate WBS code(s) for integration testing. This testing process is typically composed of three phases: test planning, test set construction, and test execution. Figure 10.10 from the

IEEE Standard for Software Unit Testing (IEEE/ANSI STD 1008, 2002) illustrates these three testing phases.

The activities in each phase include the following (IEEE/ANSI STD 1008, 2002):

- Test planning
    - Plan the general approach
    - Plan resources and schedule
    - Determine test environment(s)
    - Determine features to be tested
    - Refine the general plan
- Test set construction
    - Design the set of tests and associated procedures
    - Implement that design (build test scripts)
- Testing
    - Execute the test sets
    - Check for correct behavior and results
    - Evaluate the test results, effort, and other relevant metrics
    - Document results

A test plan document is usually produced not only for the testing group, but also to be read by other interested stakeholders. It would include such items as:

- Identification of IT product and version
- Background of product/version including purpose
- Prior versions including revision history
- Purpose and objectives of this testing
- Reference to other product documents (i.e., requirements, design, etc.)
- Relevant standards
- Project team and stakeholder identification and contact info
- Test organization contact info
- Test resources (people, training, access to other people, hardware, space, etc.)
- Test environment(s), platforms, locations, and conditions
- Assumptions and dependencies
- Test scope and focus
- Relation to other validation activities
- Testing outline

> Testing data and other setup
>
> Test metrics
>
> Testing tools
>
> Test scripts

- Detail test procedures
- Test reporting, documentation, deliverables

A key part of this test process is the construction of the test sets, sometimes called test scripts. The test scripts should be based upon the product requirements either directly or via the use case scenarios and storyboards (screen design or "paper prototypes"); this is illustrated in Figure 10.11. *If the test scripts are taken from the use case scenarios, then the likelihood is much greater that the testing will involve features and code paths that are more important to the customer. Testing is expensive, so one does not want to waste time testing features that no one will use or cares little about. However, if the test scripts are not taken directly from the requirements, there still needs to be a check that each requirement is included somewhere in the test scripts (requirements traceability was discussed earlier in this book).*

These test scripts indicate specifically how the product is to be tested and what the expected results are at each point in the test. For example, in testing a form to add a new entity to a database, the script would indicate exactly what was to be typed into each field on the form, including typing of invalid entries (for which the product should give meaningful error messages). In conjunction with the generation of test scripts, there may be a need to generate test data. The ideal situation is to have the test data created as part of running earlier test scripts. However, to allow more testing to go on in parallel, the test data may need to be created before running the test scripts; also, for volume testing, huge amounts of data may need to be generated. The test environment also has to be defined and set up, and this environment may involve one or more platforms on both the server and client sides. For example, in building a modern Web application, one may need to test

Figure 10.11. Requirements-based testing

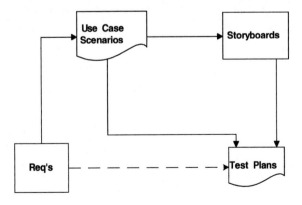

using both Microsoft and Unix/Linux type servers, possibly from different vendors and versions; and one may need to test using multiple client configurations (browser types, browser versions, screen size/resolution, and PC/MAC).

The running of test scripts can often be automated by direct programming or by using a software-testing product; this is discussed later in this chapter. When running the test scripts, each failure, defect, standard deviation, concern, or suggestion for improvement must be noted in the test documentation. Failures may arise from a number of causes, and the test plan should indicate procedures for dealing with each of these causes:

- A fault in the test script
- A fault in the test data (including meta data [table/view definition, constraints, etc.])
- A fault in the test environment
- A fault in the implementation (i.e., coding bug)
- A fault in the algorithm
- A fault in the design
- A misunderstanding of the requirement

The ANSI/IEEE STD 829-1983 IEEE Standard for Software Test Documentation is a standard for the documentation produced in the testing phases. For each failure, detail documentation should be produced that would include items such as:

- Product name and version
- Location of defect within product
- Environment and platform info
- Related processing info (database conditions, etc.)
- Assigned/generated defect ID number
- Date/time
- Status (new, previous, etc.)
- Complete information about the failure (including screen shots, etc.)
- How to reproduce the problem (if reproducible as opposed to "random")
- Estimated severity of the problem
- Cause of defect (if known or suspected)
- Tester info (name, contact, organization, etc.)

When the defects were deemed fixed and/or rerested, that information would be appended to the aforementioned record (retest info, status, etc.). When developers indicate that a defect has been corrected, there is a need to retest. Defect corrections (and possibly other requested changes) are generally "batched" together to produce a new version of the software product. Integration/system testing is then repeated for that new version. This retesting process is called "regression testing," and a key issue is how many of the original test scripts need to be repeated. One can simply repeat just the tests for new features and those that produced defects in the previous version, or alternatively, run all the tests again. Any specific fix cannot correct the defect (or partially correct it), but can also introduce other defects. The safest choice therefore would be to run all the tests again; this is often not a feasible choice in terms of time and cost, unless the testing has been considerably automated.

After integration testing, which focuses on features, there may be separate testing for loads, scalability, and timing. Timing may be a function of the load for "wall clock" measures of completion or response times, or it may be measured in the number of "clicks" or "keystrokes" needed to complete a task. These types of tests may be necessary to ensure compliance with SLAs during production operation. Destructive testing may also be carried out separately or in conjunction with the integration testing. A certain amount of destructive testing should be included in both unit testing and integration testing such as the effect of incorrect or missing user input. In destructive testing, one tries to destroy or compromise the integrity of the system via input errors, usage errors, executing features out of sequence, violating security measures, and intentionally tricking the system. Most integration testing utilizes black-box (behavioral) testing, in which only the external specifications of the product are used. However, destructive testing may involve types of "white-box" testing, in which knowledge of module internals is utilized. Separate auditability tests may also be run particularly for business applications in which both forward and reverse traceability is tested. Forward tracing follows the entry of a transaction through the system to where it is posted to account/entity totals. Reverse tracing takes account totals and works backward to display the transactions that make up that account total.

Acceptance testing, which involves the benefiting organization (i.e., the customer), is often carried out after integration testing. The project contract may require that acceptance testing be done; this testing is sometimes performed exclusively by the benefiting organization. Normally, acceptance testing is implemented on a much smaller scale than integration testing, and it represents a sampling of features and conditions. After (or instead of) acceptance testing, the product might be produced for alpha testing for use with a limited set of friendly users. If alpha testing is successful, beta testing is implemented, which involves a larger and not necessarily friendly group. Beta testing, involving many users (i.e., 1,000 or more), can achieve testing efficiencies of about 75% (Jones, 1994).

The Software Program Managers Network defines eight levels of software testing from white-box unit testing through final site black-box production testing (Brown, 1998). Each level has a focus, organizational responsibility, documentation basis, test type, and test activities. Their 10 commandments of testing are as follows:

1. Black-box test that validates requirements must trace to approved specifications and be executed by an independent organization

2. Test levels must be integrated into a consistent structure

3. Do not skip levels to save time or resources; test less at each level

4. All test products, configurations, tools, data, and so forth, need configuration (version) control

5. Always test to procedures

6. Change must be managed

7. Testing must be scheduled, monitored, and controlled

8. All test cases have to trace to something that is under configuration (version) control

9. You cannot run out of resources

10. Always specify and test to criteria

Extreme programming (XP) was discussed earlier in this book, and extreme testing is a key part of that XP methodology. Developers are expected to write unit test scripts first before the application is constructed. Test scripts are under source control (version control) along with the source code. The customers are expected to be a part of the project team and to help develop scenarios for the test scripts, at least acceptance scripts, if not all testing scripts. QA and test personnel are also expected to be a part of the project team.

Most testing of IT systems is still done manually. However, automated testing can often produce better results at a cheaper price. Newer, automated tools cover all phases of the testing process, including planning. The Quality Assurance Institute conducted benchmarks comparing manual and automated testing methods and found an overall reduction in person time of 75% (QA Quest, 1995). Reduction in the actual test runs was 95%, with little savings in the test planning phase. Automatic testing, along with saving time and cost (after an initial learning curve in time and dollars), has these further advantages (Brown, 1998):

*   Test repeatability and consistency
*   Expanded and practical test reuse
*   Practical baseline suites

Automatic testing tools really come in handy when one has to repeat the same tests for a number of different client and/or server platform environments, as is the case with modern Web and e-commerce applications. Automated testing is also very useful when load testing is necessary with a high volume of users, transactions, and/or data. However, there are situations in which automatic testing is less useful, such as situations in which human judgment is necessary, and it is difficult to define criteria in a quantitative manner. Usability testing is one such area (usability of documentation as well as the product), and another area is "localization" particularly of global e-commerce applications.

There are a number of software testing products available to automate all or portions of the testing process: QAWizard (www.seapine.com), TestQuest (www.testquest.com), e-Test (www.empirix.com), HighTest (www.vtsoft. com), ApTest (www.aptest.com), QES (www.qestest.com), TestComplete (www.automatedqa.com), QACenter (www.compuware.com/), and TestWorks (www.soft.com/TestWorks/). Some testing products are for specific environments (i.e., Web applications, windows applications, Java applications, etc.), some are for specific products (i.e., SAP, Peoplesoft, etc.), some are for specific problems (i.e., "memory leaks," bounds checkers, uninitialized variables, type mismatch, nonconformance to coding standards), and some are general purpose. For a list of current open source testing tools see OpenSourceTesting (www.opensourcetesting.org/). There are also a number of special purpose programs available for defect tracking as: Bug-Track (www.bug-track.com), ElementTool (www.elementtool.com), and TrackStudio (www.trackstudio.com).

Evaluating, selecting, procuring, and learning a test tool can be a significant expense and perhaps be a project in itself for an IT organization. Activities that are part of this effort include a needs analysis, a business justification for the procurement and implementation costs, a study of the available appropriate tools, implementation of the tool, and personnel training on the tool. These tools are difficult to evaluate and it is possible that it will take 6 months to discover that the tool will not fit the application (Hendrickson, 1999). "Try before you buy" is the best philosophy here. For example, with modern GUI applications, simple playback tools are inadequate, because if a single GUI widget is changed on a screen, then the whole script may have to be changed. For GUIs, more complex tools are needed that allow one to associate specific GUI widgets with specific series of valid/invalid script entries. Organizations should not underestimate the time and cost necessary to learn to use a specific tool, or the effort in setting up the tool for the application at hand (which typically involves test script programming). Dustin (1999) listed some lessons learned in test automation, including:

- Various tools used throughout the life cycle do not integrate easily
- Duplicate information had to be kept
- The testing tool drove the effort
- The staff was very busy learning to write the scripts
- Elaborate test scripts are developed, duplicating development effort
- Script creation is cumbersome
- The test tool(s) were introduced too late
- Training in the tools was too late
- Some testers resisted tools
- Expectations of early payback were not realistic
- Tool(s) had problems recognizing third party GUI controls
- Lack of test development guidelines
- Tool(s) was intrusive, and required "inserts" into code
- Reports reproduce by tool(s) was useless
- Tools were selected before overall system architecture was determined
- Upgrade to new tools had compatibility problems
- Tool(s) database was not scalable

There are also companies that offer testing and Q/A services, such as Systemware (www.sysemware.com). Several Web sites are available that provide links to numerous testing resources (tools, books, articles, etc.), such as the Software Q/A Test Resource Center (www.softwareqatest.com), the Software Testing and Quality Engineering Network (www.stqe.net), and Testing and Quality Engineering Magazine (www.stqemagazine.com).

Quality Stage Gates

User acceptance testing is a validation activity that comes late in the development process but not necessarily at the end. There are activities that can be carried out earlier in the overall process to help guarantee that the correct product is being built. These activities involve getting the benefiting organization and other stakeholders more intimately involved in the review of preliminary product manifestations. Sometimes these types of activities are called "static testing" because they do not actually involve running the system (final product). The cooperative review of these preliminary product manifestations are called quality stage gates. Management stage gates were discussed earlier in this book, and applying management stage gates to the classical waterfall methodology (and variations thereof) was also illustrated. Figure 2.6 in Chapter II illustrated my notion of dual gates.

Multiple quality stage gates may fall within one management stage gate or vice versa. At the management stage gate, the completion criteria are reviewed (either exhaustively or by exception), and a go/kill/hold decision is reached. Management stage gates can be set at fixed time intervals or upon completion of a major project phase. For methodologies in which phases overlap, or when using incremental or iterative approaches, the management stage gates can be set between increments or iterations or upon fixed time increments, such as 1 month. To minimize the time and cost associated with formal management reviews, it is recommended that the management stage gates occur at regular time intervals but that they take place only on an exception basis when key metrics (such as EVA indexes) indicate problems.

For each quality stage gate, the satisfaction factors typically are reviewed by focusing on a particular preliminary product manifestation by relevant stakeholders for that gate; the review does not make a go/kill/hold decision but rather a go-forward or recycle type decision. Figure 10.12 illustrates these distinctions.

Whereas the management stage gates review completion factors (i.e., actual costs to date, earned value, estimated cost at completion, completion status of activities, estimated time to complete, updated risk analysis, and need for more or less reserves), the quality stage gates focus on satisfaction factors as utility, operation, maintainability, auditability, and a revised business justification (i.e., revised cost-benefit analysis based on latest cost estimate and revised benefit numbers). Different stakeholders may be present at the two types of stage gate reviews, to minimize the cost and time of key individuals. Preliminary product manifestations that should be reviewed by concerned stakeholders would include requirements document, use case scenarios, preliminary

Figure 10.12. Dual stage gates

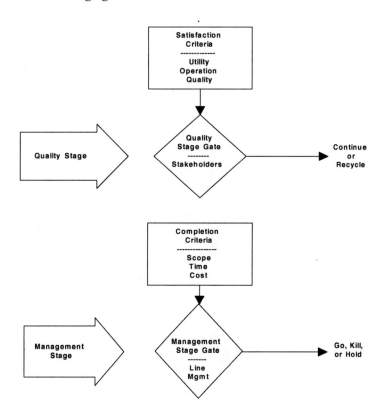

user manual, storyboards ("paper prototypes"), screen/report designs, and working prototypes. Wiegers (1999) reported a return on investment of up to 800% for requirements reviews. Figure 10.13 shows an example of how the quality gates might be set up for the classical waterfall methodology.

Figure 10.14 is an example of a stage gate review form. On this form, the metrics from the earned value analysis of the last management gate (typically at certain time period intervals) are recorded, which indicate how the project is going from a progress and cost perspective. The next portion of the form concerns the satisfaction factors, which are qualitatively evaluated by both the benefiting organization (customer) and the performing organization (project team). The basis of the satisfaction scoring is also specified, which would be the last quality gate in which a product artifact was available, such as a prototype. The risks that were identified and quantified at the start of the project are then reevaluated. The information on this form is then typically reviewed by line management of both organizations (either regularly or by exception) to determine if the project should continue.

Figure 10.13. Event driven quality stage gates

Stage	Outputs	Quality Gates
Definition	Project Plan	X
Requirements	Requirements Document	X
Analysis	Overal Design Documents:	
	Use Cases	X
	Ext. Spec. (Prelim. Users Manual)	X
	Test Plan	
Design	Detail Design Documents:	
	Menu/Navigation Design	X
	Screen Designs/Storyboards	X
	Report Designs	X
	Database Design	X
	Algorithms Design	
	Prototypes	X
Construction	Development Objects:	
	Code (incl. internal documantation)	
	Test Scripts	
	Help Screens	X
Testing	Test Results Documents	X
	User Manual	X
	Training Material	X
Installation	Install Documents	X

Figure 10.14. Stage gate review form

Stage Gate Review

Project: ________________ Period: ____________

Completion Factors (EVA):
- Estimated Time to Complete:
- Estimated Cost To Complete:
- Percent Complete:
- Critical Ratio:

Satisfaction Factors: Evaluated By (1=low, 10=high):
- Basis:__________ Benefitting Org. Performing Org.
- Business Justification
- Validation
- Workflow & Content
- Standards
- Maintain & Support
- Adaptability
- Trust/Security

Financial Metrics (recalculated):
- Benefit/Cost Ratio:
- Payback Period:
- Internal Rate of Return:

Risk Status: Changes (1=down, 6=same, 10=up)
Probability Impact
- Risk 1
- Risk 2
- ...
- Risk N

Issues/Comments:

Quality Programs

There are a number of modern quality programs sponsored by national and international organizations. These organizations foster quality by defining certain general or specific approaches to achieving quality and/or by setting standards for quality. Earlier in this book, the Software Engineering Institute's Capability Maturity Models (SEI CMM) and the Project Management Institute's Body of Knowledge (PMI PMBOK) were discussed. Quality assessment methods for IT (specifically software development) were also discussed, including the SPICE (ISO/IEC 15504), TickIT, CobiT, and ITIL approaches. These organizations foster quality by defining rather specifically the best practices for each of these overlapping disciplines. These best practices are the things organizations need to do in order to produce quality products via properly managed projects. Although the things that need to be done are itemized, exactly how to do them is left up to the discretion of the individual organization and/or PM. In this section we look at more general quality programs.

Total quality management (TQM) is a business philosophy that encourages organizations and their employees to focus on quality and finding ways to make continuous improvements to the organization's products/services and practices. TQM gained popularity in the United States in the 1990s after successful implementation by Ford, Boeing, and other major corporations. TQM is based on earlier work from around the world (particularly in Japan after World War II) by Shewart, Demming, and Ishikawa. The six principles of TQM are:

*   Customer focus
*   Focus on process as well as results
*   Prevention versus inspection
*   Mobilize the expertise of the workforce
*   Fact-based decision making
*   Feedback

The cornerstones, however, of TQM are continuous improvement, employee empowerment, and customer focus. Continuous improvement (or *kaizen*) is a continuous process of making improvements, typically by small steps. In Japanese, *kai* means to alter and *zen* means to make better. Employee empowerment means to allow employees to make suggestions on how to improve processes, because they are the people most intimate with the process, not their supervisors. TQM is based on the tenet that most employees want to be involved in improvement and to do their jobs well. TQM fosters teamwork among employees to identify quality issues and corrections. An application for the Malcolm Baldrige Award[1] may be made by companies that have fully implemented TQM and quantified the benefits thereof.

Quality function deployment (QFD) was founded in Japan in the late 1960s by Professors Shigeru Mizuno and Yoji Akao. Statistical quality control had become prevalent in the

Japanese manufacturing industry, and these quality activities were being integrated with the teachings of Ishikawa and Feigenbaum, which later became known as TQM. Mizuno and Akao sought to develop a quality assurance method that would design customer satisfaction into a product before that product was produced. The first major application was in Bridgestone Tire, in Japan, which used a Ishikawa ("fishbone diagram") to identify each customer requirement (effect) and to identify the design the process factors (causes) needed to control and measure it. With continued success, these fishbone diagrams of customer needs and expectations were refashioned into a spreadsheet or matrix format, with the rows being desired effects of customer satisfaction and the columns being the controlling and measurable causes. At about the same time, Ishihara introduced the value engineering principles that described business functions necessary to assure quality of the design process itself. QFD emerged as a combination of these two methods to ensure comprehensive quality design system for both product and business process (Akao, 1990). QFD reached the United States and Europe in the 1980s when the American Society for Quality Control published Akao's work and invited Akao to give QFD seminars in America. Today, QFD is used extensively in the United States, Japan, Sweden, Germany, Australia, Brazil, and Turkey. QFD is somewhat different from other quality principles in that it focuses on both customer-stated and unstated requirements. It seeks to maximize positive quality aspects, such as ease of use, fun to use, interesting, etc. QFD key principles are (Mizuno & Akao, 1994)

- Understanding customer requirements
- Quality systems thinking + psychology + knowledge/epistemology
- Maximizing positive quality to add value
- Comprehensive quality systems for customer satisfaction
- Strategies to "stay ahead of the game"

The International Organization for Standardization (ISO) also defines a set of quality management principles called ISO 9000, which encompasses much of TQM. Within the U.S. DoD, 2167A represents a similar set of principles and requirements. The latest version of ISO 9000 (ISO 9000:2000) is composed of these management principles:

- *Customer Focus:* Keep the customer's need at the forefront
- *Quality Focus through Leadership:* Leaders must always be concerned with quality and foster a similar attitude in their followers
- *People Focus:* Management must keep all stakeholders involved and foster open and honest communication
- *Process Focus:* Production and project activities should be viewed as a process so that process optimization techniques can be applied
- *Systems Approach:* Interrelated and dependent processes should be viewed as a system so that system optimization principles can be applied across all such processes

- *Continuous Improvement:* The organization should strive to continually improve its systems and processes via metrics and goals
- *Quantitative Decision Making:* Decisions should be based upon information and methods to formally analyze that information
- *Symbiotic Relations with Suppliers:* Relations with vendors should create value for both organizations for the long-term success and quality of both organizations

Organizations may seek ISO 9000 certification to prove that they have implemented these quality management principles and the business processes to support same. ISO 9000 certification can be sought under one of three programs: ISO 9001, ISO 9002, or ISO 9003. ISO 9001 is the certification that typically applies to IT organizations because it is for organizations that have design and development processes as well as production and support. If an IT organization does not do design and development (such as may be the case where all projects involve integration of off-the-shelf products), then ISO 9002 may apply. *The process standards for the ISO certifications basically make sure that organizations have and follow their own quality procedures; they do not define the quality procedures.* Companies desiring such certifications typically conduct a detailed self assessment first, then seek formal approval by a third party which is registered to conduct such audits. It has been suggested that jumping through the ISO hoops can be an expensive and depressing process for organizations as opposed to the application for a the TQM Baldrige award, which is more uplifting (Jones, 1994).

A bit more quantitative and specific quality program is *Six Sigma.* This program was started by Motorola in the 1980s and received considerable attention after very successful implementations by General Electric (GE) in the 1990s. Sigma (σ) is Greek and is the standard deviation in the normal distribution. This statistical distribution is the most common, and it is used in quality analysis, such as for measurement variations; it is illustrated in Figure 10.15. The *standard deviation* (sigma) is a measure of how far a point is from the mean (half of the distribution is on each side of the mean). Sigma ranges are

Figure 10.15. Normal distribution

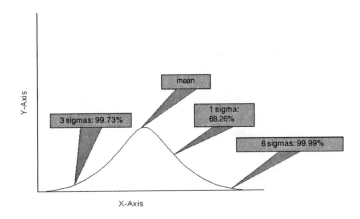

- 68.26 % of the distribution is within one sigma
- 95.46% of the distribution is within two sigma
- 99.73% of the distribution is within three sigma
- 99.99% of the distribution is within six sigma

For six sigma, about 99.99% of the products (or lines of code) are without defects. Inversely, for a metric like defects per million, the six-sigma level is only 3.4 defects per million.

Like other quality programs, Six Sigma focuses on processes; metrics are set up to measure defects per opportunity (DPO). A defect is essentially anything that results in stakeholder dissatisfaction. Defects are measured as early as possible during development rather that after the product is produced. For IT development, this involves setting up metrics at each stage in the development process: requirements gathering, analysis, design, implementation, testing, and deployment. Six Sigma differs from earlier quality programs (like TQM) in that it is not quality just for the sake of quality but specifically for the sake of the customer. The customer defines the defects. Once customers have defined what is most important to them, such as speed in completing the on-line ordering process, the organization determines which activities most affect its ability to speed up that process. Those selected activities become critical-to-quality (CTQ) activities (Shand, 2001). The Six Sigma program is composed of 12 steps (Harry & Schroeder, 2000):

Measure
1.   Select critical-to-quality (CTQ) activities
2.   Define performance standards
3.   Validate measurement system

Analyze
4.   Establish product capability
5.   Define performance objectives
6.   Identify variation sources (root causes)

Improve
7.   Screen potential causes
8.   Discover variable relationships
9.   Establish operating tolerances

Control
10   Validate measurement system
11.   Determine process capability
12.   Implement process controls

The basic Six Sigma process identifies CTQ activities, finds root causes for potential problems with those processes, discovers quantitative relationships between cause and effect, sets up metrics to measure causes, and controls the causes of the potential problems so that the effects remain within the six-sigma level. To implement Six Sigma requires a significant investment in a very specific training program.

Recently, *Computerworld* has defined many of these quality programs and summarized their degree of abstraction and specific IT relevance, as is illustrated if Figure 10.16 (Athens, 2004).

Software Development Standards

Quality programs and best practices focus mainly on processes, and most are fairly general rather than specific. Quality programs do not always handle the long-term effects of quality problems, particularly in IT projects. Issues like maintainability, adaptability, and reuse are not fully addressed in quality programs, particularly in customer-focused programs (because these aspects may never be seen by the customer). Standards focus mainly on product criteria, and standards can also be established to deal with the long-term effect of quality. *One of the best ways to ensure quality in IT processes, products,*

Figure 10.16. Quality programs

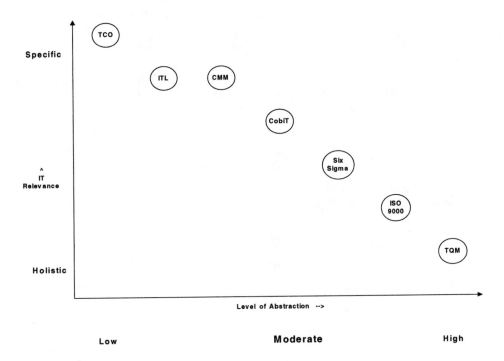

and projects is by setting standards within the IT organization at the highest relevant level. Standards are formal documented specifications for how processes are to be specifically executed, how products are to be built, and/or how products are to perform.

There are many areas of technical standards. Some of the most common and important for IT development involve requirements, design, coding, database, testing, internal and external documentation, user interface, and other external interfaces. The IEEE has many important software engineering standards, and the ones most relevant in the quality area are:

- IEEE Standard for Software Quality Assurance Plans
- 829730-2002-1998 IEEE Standard for Software Test Documentation
- 982.1-1988 IEEE Standard Dictionary of Measures to Produce Reliable Software
- 1008-1987 IEEE Standard for Software Unit Testing
- 1012-1998 IEEE Standard for Software Verification and Validation
- 1012a-1998 IEEE Standard for Software Verification and Validation—Supplement to 1012-1998
- 1061-1998 (R2004) IEEE Standard for Software Quality Metrics Methodology
- 1228-1994 (2002) IEEE Standard for Software Safety Plans
- 1465-1998 [Adoption of ISO/IEC 12119: 1994(E)], IEEE Standard Adoption of International Standard ISO/IEC 12119: 1994(E) Information Technology-Software packages: Quality requirements and testing

Details of these standards are available on the IEEE Web site (www.standards.ieee.org). Other relevant IT standards are also available from the American National Standards Institute (ANSI) and the International Organization for Standardization (ISO); IEEE, ANSI, and ISO standards overlap in many areas and often correlate directly to each other. These are all fairly general standards which must be made specific for each organization, and perhaps for each platform and programming language. Consider, for example, an organization's coding standards, which may include such items as:

- Naming conventions for variables (static and instance), constants, classes, functions/methods, and so forth.
- Use and placement of constants (i.e., in one place such as a resource file, C++/PHP abstract class, or Java interface)
- Use of object orientation (inheritance, composition, polymorphism, interfaces)
- Use of comments and internal documentation
- Use of indentation and "white space"
- Use of parenthesis for expression evaluation order
- Conditional versus logical expressions
- Proximity of decisions and actions

- Iteration versus recursion
- Code density (i.e., one code line per statement) and readability
- Function/method sizes (i.e., only one logical function and under 100 lines of code)
- Types of classes (delegation, adapter, inner, anonymous, etc.)
- Access protection (public, private, package, protected, etc.)
- Minimization of coupling (friends, object arguments, etc.)
- Error handling (input checking, exceptions, etc.)
- Overloading (function, operator, etc.)

For communicating and enforcing standards, many companies probably still rely on some type of printed standards manual. For some companies, this is a large multivolume set of bound documents. Other organizations, who may or may not have such extensive standards manuals, do periodic "code walkthroughs," which have peers and/or managers examine samples of each programmer's code to make sure they are following the company standards. Some software engineering methodologies have a degree of code walkthrough built into the methodology, such as in pair programming, in XP.

The testing process is another way to make sure the programs have the desired "look and feel." Here, the results are easily viewed but not the underlying methods. Weinschenk (1997) stated that "in order for your guidelines to be successful, people must know they exist and be encouraged to use them." She outlines a list of several management actions which foster effective standards implementation.

The only way to really make sure that standards are being followed from both an external and internal perspective, however, is to require developers to utilize components in which the relevant standards have already been embedded (Brandon, 2000). The method of component utilization varies with the programming language and programming style from simple "include" techniques (such as a COBOL copy books, SHTML server-side includes, or PHP requires) to the object-oriented techniques of inheritance and composition that were discussed earlier in this book.

As an example, consider the user interface, which is often the key part of a modern IT application. There has been a lot of attention on user interface approaches and standards ever since Apple Computer was successful with the first commercial graphical user interface (GUI; Collins, 1995). Many books and some movies have been made concerning the technical, business, and social issues of the GUI saga. For a computer system to have lasting value, it must exist compatibly with users and other systems in an ever-changing IT world. Even if a system by itself is excellent, the fact they it may have a different look and feel to other systems in use will eventually spell its doom.

Companies building software systems, whether for their internal use or for resale, must build products that are compatible with other systems. As stated by Weinschenk and Yeo (1995), "interface designers, project managers, developers, and business units need a common set of look-and-feel guidelines to design and develop by. Coming up with these guidelines can be a long and difficult process. New GUI applications can't be held up for eight months while a task force argues about guidelines." There have been many books written on the subject of proper user interface design in general (Fowler, 1998; Galitz, 1997; Wood, 1998), and there are also books specifically devoted to certain platforms, such as Microsoft Windows (Cooper, 1995; Microsoft, 1995). Appendix A of Weinschenk's (1997) book also presents a list of user interface standards; *there are more than 300 items listed there.*

To enforce standards and to provide a flexible and adaptable programming base, an IT organization should adopt or develop a foundation for standards implementation. Figure 10.17 illustrates the concept of one such standards foundation with a unified modeling language (UML) diagram (Brandon, 2000).

In this example, an application is composed of a number of Application Windows. Each Application Window (i.e., PHP program, Java Server Page, Java Applet) is derived (inherited) from the Corporate Standard Window. The Application Window implements the GUI Standards Interface (or a window from which the Application was derived has implemented this interface). By interface, it is meant a Java interface or a C++ or PHP abstract class. The Application Window is composed of the Corporate Standard GUI Components. These standard components use the Corporate GUI Standards and these components may be derived from HTML/XML GUI objects, MFC, Java AWT, Java Swing, or third-party class libraries as long as these class library sources have been extended (customized) to use the data in the Corporate GUI Standards.

As well as implementing all the desired corporate standards, the standards foundation classes can also be constructed to encapsulate security mechanisms. If all application input is forced to take place through the standard foundation classes, then rogue programmers or contractors will be less likely be able to build-in "back doors," "Trojan horses," "time-bombs," and other illicit mechanisms into the system being developed. The standard foundation classes would be built and inspected by trusted sources, and those classes to be imported by other coders would be made final.

Figure 10.17. Standards foundation

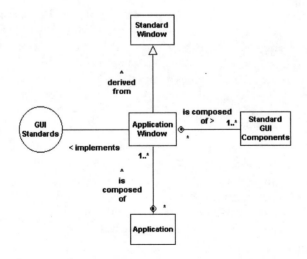

Figure 10.18. Standards implementation via window inheritance

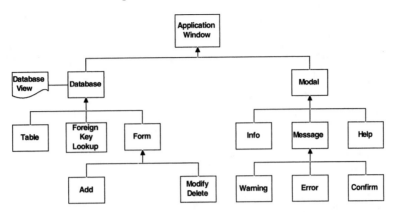

Whereas Figure 10.17 shows a conceptual standards foundation, Figure 10.18 is an example of a typical implementation (via object-oriented inheritance) of a corporate standards foundation for windows in a business database type application. Each window would be further subclassed; for example, the general table would be subclassed for different entities such as employees, vendors, and so forth.

Chapter Summary

Earlier in this book, the many IT project management challenges were identified. These challenges can be met by a careful integration of modern project management and software engineering principles and practices. This was illustrated in Figure 1.4 in Chapter I; this chapter has discussed the quality aspects of project management. Critical IT project success factors were used as the basis for key quality metrics. A quality management plan for IT projects should include both verification and validation, and both of these processes should be on going throughout the project and controlled via a technique such as the quality stage gate process described herein. Other key quality topics were also discussed in this chapter, including the many types and methods of software testing, software development standards, and quality organizations and programs.

References

Akao, Y. (1990). *Quality function deployment: Integrating customer requirements into product design* (G. Mazur, Trans.). New York: Productivity Press.

Athens, G. (2004, March). Model mania. *Computerworld*.

Brandon, D. (2000). An object oriented approach to user interface standards. *Challenges of information technology management in the 21st century* (pp. 753-756). Hershey, PA: Idea Group Publishing.

Brown, N. (1998). *Little book of testing: Vols. I & II*. Chesapeake, VA: Software Program Managers Network.

Collins, D. (1995). *Designing object oriented user interfaces*. Boston: Benjamin/ Cummings.

Cooper, A. (1995). *About face*. Boston: IDG Books.

Crosby, P. (1979). *Quality is free*. Princeton, NJ: McGraw-Hill.

Deming, W. (1982). *Out of the crisis*. MIT Press.

Dustin, E. (1999, September/October). Lessons in test automation. *Testing & Quality, 1*(5).

Foley, M. (2000, February 11). Can Microsoft squash 63000 bugs in Windows 2000. *Smart Reseller*.

Fowler, S. (1998). *GUI design handbook*. McGraw-Hill.

Galitz, W. (1997). *The essential guide to user interface design*. New York: Wiley.

Gause, D. & Weinberg, G. (1989). *Exploring requirements: Quality before design*. New York: Dorset House.

Hallows, J. (1998). *Information systems project management*. New York: American Management Association.

Harry, M. & Schroeder, R. (2000). *Six Sigma: The breakthrough management strategy revolutionizing the world's top corporations*. New York: Doubleday.

Hendrickson, E. (1999, May-June). Making the right choice. *Software Testing and Quality Engineering*.

IEEE/ANSI STD 1008. (2002). *IEEE standard for software unit testing*. Piscataway, NJ: IEEE Computer Society.

Jones, C. (1994). *Assessment and control of software risks*. Englewood Cliffs, NJ: Yourdon Press Computing Series.

Linger, R. (1994). Cleanroom process model. *IEEE Software, 11*(2)

McConnell, S. (1997). *Software project survival guide*. Seattle, WA: Microsoft Press.

Microsoft. (1995). *The Windows interface guidelines for software design*. Microsoft Press.

Mizuno, S. & Akao, Y. (1994). *QFD: The customer-driven approach to quality planning and deployment* (G. Mazur, Trans.). Newton Square, PA: Quality Resources.

PMI. (2000). *The project management body of knowledge (PMBOK)*. ISBN 1-880410-22-2.

QA Quest. (1995, November). *The newsletter of the Quality Assurance Institute*. Orlando, FL.

The Quality Imperative. (1991, Bonus Issue, Fall). *Business Week.*

Shand, D. (2001, March 5). Six Sigma. *Computerworld,* p. 38.

Weinschenk, S. & Yeo, S. (1995). *Guidelines for enterprise wide GUI design.* New York: Wiley.

Weinschenk, S., Pamela J., & Sarah Y. (1997). *GUI design essentials.* Wiley.

Wiegers, K. (1999). *Software requirements.* Seattle, WA: Microsoft Press.

Wood, L. (1998). *User interface design.* Boca Raton, FL: CRC Press.

ZDNet. (2000, February). Retrieved from www.zdnet.com

Endnote

[1]   The Malcolm Baldrige National Quality Award (presented by NIST – National Institute of Standards and Technology) was created by Public Law 100-107, signed into law on August 20, 1987. Principal support for the program comes from the Foundation for the Malcolm Baldrige National Quality Award, established in 1988. The award is named for Malcolm Baldrige, who served as Secretary of Commerce from 1981 until his tragic death in a rodeo accident in 1987.

Chapter XI

Change and Closeout Management

You must welcome change as the rule, but not as your ruler.

(Denis Waitley)

Change is a fact of life for most projects, particularly IT projects. *The biggest single cause of project overruns is changes in scope* (Hallows, 1998). Change can be for the good or the bad, but change is to be expected, and change has to be managed. This chapter is concerned with that management process.

Project Changes

Resistance to change is usually rooted in fear of the unknown as PMs and people in general prefer stability and predictability. However, in order for a project to survive, PMs must deal with changes effectively. Many projects fail not in their goals and directions, but in their plan (or lack of a plan) for dealing with changes. Not having a formal change control system "guarantees a project will be plagued by chaos, errors, permanent damage, low productivity, and unmanageable software evolution" (Brown, 1998). *Formal change control is vital in projects involving an external performing or benefiting organization so that one organization can be appropriately compensated for the additional effort.*

Change can arise for many reasons; in IT projects, the leading sources or indicators of change are:

- The customer (benefiting organization) is unsure of their needs
- The customer is unsure as to how the needs should be delivered
- The performing organization is unclear to the details of the customer's needs
- The performing organization is not sure how to do the work
- The deployment environment has changed
- Planned methods or algorithms prove unsuitable
- Better methods of building or deploying the system have come forward
- The business case for the project has changed
- Market demographic and/or geographic shifts
- The sociopolitical environment for the project has changed
- The corporate environment has changed (reorganizations, mergers, acquisitions)

Changes in a project can come in any part of the project from early planning through project closeout; in IT projects, most changes come later in a project such as during implementation, testing and deployment. *Changes coming later in a project are usually much more expensive than if that need for a change were identified earlier.* A change in one part of the project deliverable may cause changes in many other parts of the project as well. So, as was discussed earlier in this book, it is very important to take steps early to flush out user requirements and potential changes. Validation of the preliminary product manifestations with quality stage gates using methods as prototypes, use case walkthroughs with customers, and design reviews with appropriate stakeholders will minimize changes later in a project.

Project change management usually concerns changes to scope, but other changes also need to be managed. Normally, change control systems are set up to deal with only scope and deliverable change; other project change is usually handled via risk management, as was discussed earlier in this book. Scope management in general includes the processes necessary to make sure that all project work is addressed and that extra work is not done. Scope change control should be planned and procedures defined early in the project (charter, SOW, contract, overall project plan). Change control is concerned with the following (PMI, 2000):

- Influencing the factors that cause change control to ensure that changes are beneficial
- Determining that a scope change has occurred
- Managing the actual changes when and if they occur

In the IT environment, the term *change control* can be confusing because those words are often applied to the control of changes to program source code and/or changes to a target hardware/software deployment platform. In this book, the control of source code and related artifacts will be called version control, and the control of hardware and dependent software components on the deployment platforms will be called configuration control; both of these topics will be discussed later in this chapter. In this book, the term *change control* refers only to change control at the project level; however, a change in a project requirement or deliverable may trigger corresponding version or configuration changes.

Establishing a Change Control System

A project scope change control system defines the procedures by which the project scope may be changed and typically includes forms, tracking systems, and approval levels. An illustration of such a form is shown in Figure 11.1. It should be integrated with a system that logs and documents all project changes. A code or number should be assigned to each proposed change whether the change is proposed internally (i.e., project team member) or externally (i.e., customer). This degree of formality is usually imposed after a segment of the methodology is initially completed. For example, formal change control of the design work is normally implemented after the initial design is completed. The pros and cons of the change should be analyzed and discussed in terms of all project parameters including cost and time consequences, and what other changes may be necessary (or desirable) due to this change. The propose change may or may not be within the project budget, or may or may not be part of the undistributed budget.

The discussion of suggested changes normally takes place at a regularly scheduled meeting of a change control board, which has members from both the performing

Figure 11.1. Change order form

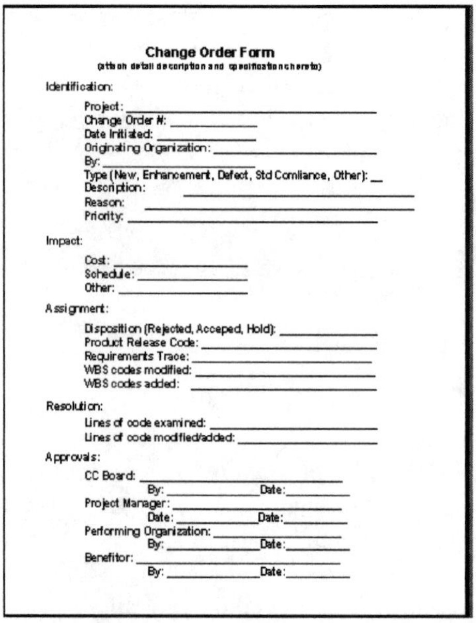

Change Order Form
(attach detail description and specifications hereto)

Identification:

Project: __________
Change Order #: __________
Date Initiated: __________
Originating Organization: __________
By: __________
Type (New, Enhancement, Defect, Std Comliance, Other): __
Description: __________
Reason: __________
Priority: __________

Impact:

Cost: __________
Schedule: __________
Other: __________

Assignment:

Disposition (Rejected, Acceped, Hold): __________
Product Release Code: __________
Requirements Trace: __________
WBS codes modified: __________
WBS codes added: __________

Resolution:

Lines of code examined: __________
Lines of code modified/added: __________

Approvals:

CC Board: __________
By: __________ Date: __________
Project Manager: __________
Date: __________ Date: __________
Performing Organization: __________
By: __________ Date: __________
Benefitor: __________
By: __________ Date: __________

organization and the benefiting organization. It is also advisable to include representatives from other major stakeholder groups. Representatives should be educated into the process that they are about to become a part of. To maximize the benefit of these meetings and minimize the meeting time lost by attendees, the meetings should not be too frequent, briefing packages should be sent to representatives in advance of the meeting, and changes should be sorted and bundled into product functional areas. Often, many small changes can be analyzed and discussed as one change set or release. Defects and noncompliance to requirements and/or standards normally do not go through formal change control, however in some organizations the change control board may be advised of such issues during the project. *Sometimes there is a fine line between a change to the scope and noncompliance to the original requirements; and of course this may cause conflict between the organizations involved.* It is best to document all such issues and their resolution even if that information will not be turned over to the change control board.

If the change is approved by the board, then there may be certain required additional levels of approval necessary in the line management of the performing and benefiting organization. Often if a change is within the undistributed budget, then higher approval is not required. After approval, a new work breakdown structure (WBS) work packet is created (or an existing packet modified) to reflect the change and a new project baseline cost plan and schedule is created; for externally contracted work, a contract change may also be required, which is called a "change order." Figure 11.2 shows an example of change control information (change control number) associated with WBS work packets. Usually it is better to create a new WBS work packet that will be a replacement (or in addition to) another packet; for replacements, the old packet has its planned cost set to zero (or to the amount already spent on it if work on it was already started).

Figure 11.3 illustrates a typical overall procedure for handling project changes. After a change request is initiated, a decision is made as to whether the requested change is actually part of the original (baseline) scope or not. This decision may be made by the CC board or upstream from the board by project management. Those change requests that are encompassed by the baseline scope are sent to work control to be incorporated

Figure 11.2. Form to add WBS Code (showing change info)

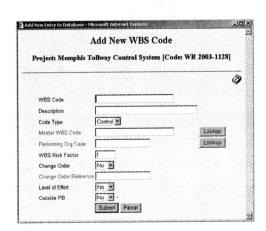

Figure 11.3. Change control process

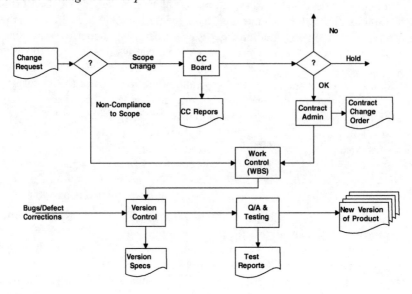

into the WBS. Those change requests that are for additional work are sent to the CC board for study. The board studies the request in light of benefit versus project impact and makes a decision to implement the change or not. If the decision is to implement, then contract administration may need to price the new work and issue a contract change order. If the contract change order is approved (by benefiting and performing organizations), then the change goes to work control. Scope changes and corrective changes are typically batched into product versions which go through version control (discussed later) and Q/A.

Figure 11.4 shows a useful type of trend chart for cumulative change orders opened and cumulative change orders closed (approved for implementation or rejected). For this type

Figure 11.4. Cumulative change orders

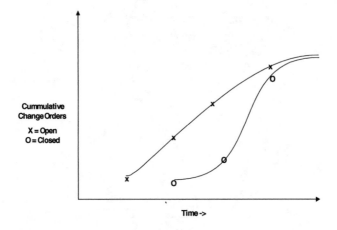

of analysis, one hopes to see the gap between open change orders and closed orders closing as the project proceeds. If that gap (between the two curves) is becoming wider, then there was a problem in the project scope definition. For IT projects that succeed, 70% of the cost of the product is in the maintenance phase; thus, maintainability is extremely important. A measure of IT product maintainability is the lines of code affected per change order. A comprehensive metric in this area includes both the lines of code affected and the lines of code examined per change order, because in implementing a change, programmers spend about half of their time just examining the existing code. Both of these metrics are included in the sample change order form of Figure 11.1.

Version Control

Version control is primarily a process for making sure that multiple developers do not override each others changes to source code modules. It typically involves manual or automatic check-in/check-out procedures for these modules. Version control may apply to IT project artifacts or deliverables other than just source code including various forms of documentation (including design documents) or system content. In a modern software engineering process, where requirements and design as well as implementation are captured in rigorous notations early in the life cycle, formal version control is applied to all of these artifacts (Royce, 1998). Version control systems typically document changes in terms of who, what, why, and when changes were made, as well as keeping developers from stepping on each other toes. Version control systems may also maintain information on who can make and/or approve what type of changes and maintain archive copies of all versions of artifacts, handle naming and numbering rules, thus providing traceability of the software and related artifacts throughout the product's life cycle. Version control systems typically manage changes to source code and related artifacts both due to project level changes (requirement changes and additions) and due to internal changes such as bugs or needed redesigns. Modern version control products also coordinate changes so that builds of a particular version use the appropriate and current modules. Traditionally the building process for a software product involved compilation and linking operations; however, today, with modern Web-based systems, there may not be any linking or any compilation. However, there are still processes (Java bytecode production, encryption [HTML, JavaScript, PHP], obfuscate, etc.) that need to be performed in making the transition from the source code the developers use to the code that is placed on the production server(s).

The major components of a version control management system are (Brown, 1998)

Item Identification

      Product identifiers (names and numbers)

      Product artifact identifiers

      Identification of product acceptance criteria

      Identification of changes

>Identification of releases

Change Control

>Change criteria

>Revisions

>Procedures

>Organizational review

Status/Accounting

>Product description records

>Change status records

>Verification records

>Authorizations and approvals

Audits

>Formal Qualification Reviews

>Physical Audits

>Functional Audits

There are number of commercial products available for version control some of which are server based and some are peer-to-peer based, these include QVCS (www.qumasoft.com), CS-RCS (www.componentsoftware.com/), Code Co-op (www.relisoft.com/), Surround SCM (www.seapine.com/surroundscm.html), and CodeMatrix (www.codematrix.com/). There are also a number of free, shareware, or open source products available (www.thefreecountry.com/programming/versioncontrol.shtml).

Configuration Control

Control of interdependent software modules and hardware components on client and server platforms is typically called configuration control. However, sometimes the term *configuration control* is applied to both *version control* (as discussed previously) and *deployment platform configurations.* For a client server application, there may be many interdependent software modules each of which requires particular versions of the other modules to operate. This may include the operating systems, database management systems, device drivers, communication protocols, and many middleware software components. This is further complicated because there may be many versions of a particular software interdependent modules in time and/or in features. For example, a software product may be in its fifth version, with eight different customizations installed on thousands of customers' computers, where each customer may have a different version and customizations.

With the advent of Internet applications, a single network protocol (TCP/IP), and thin clients, organizations were able to eliminate all of their configuration control issues on the client side (because the only application level client software required was a browser). In addition, many configuration control issues on the server side were also eliminated since once the new version of an application was placed on the server it was downloaded to clients when they first accessed the system (downloaded HTML, JavaScript, CSS, and image or other multimedia files). However, with the need (or opportunity) to sell goods or services globally now, configuration control issues have resurfaced in a different form since the web content may have to be "localized" for different languages, countries, and demographics.

Scope Creep

Scope creep is very common in IT projects. Customers should get what they asked for and expect, no more and no less. Giving the customer extra work is called gold plating. However, because the majority of IT projects do not succeed, you should never do additional work for the customer because you may not be compensated for it, and you do know for sure that the customer actually wants the work done. Scope creep is so common because it is natural for project team members to want to please their customer, and much of the communication between project team members and customer personnel takes place without any involvement of the PM. It is also not uncommon for a project member (particularly in IT and in other technical work) to want to explore technical details beyond the task boundaries. The PM must make sure that all the stakeholders know what is encompassed in the scope and also what is *not* part of the project scope; this distinction is best made early in the project. *The project team members (and PMs) have to be educated (and reminded) about the need to prevent scope creep and for formal change control.*

The Software Program Managers Network (Brown, 1998) lists best practices for change and version control:

- Make change management everyone's job
- Create an environment and process that enables change management
- Define and document the process, then select a tool set to support it
- The change control staff should consists of individuals with technical expertise to support the development and maintenance of the product
- The change plan and procedures need to be developed and documented in the same way that the development plan is created at the start of the project

They also establish the following rules for successful change management (Brown, 1998):

- The change management system must "own" the product information
- Early identification and control of products and artifacts is essential

- The change management process and procedures must be simple and supported by the methods and tools used in the product development
- The actions of the change control board must be documented
- Change control must be a primary focus and integrated into the organizational culture
- All information that is placed under change control must be "promoted" via a quality (stage) "gate"
- All proposed changes must be properly classified (as to the type of change)
- All releases of code and artifacts from the library (check-outs and check-ins) must be recorded
- It is essential that the change control system be continually aware of the status of the products/artifacts under control and of the relationship of one product/artifact to another
- The worst way to establish change control is to buy a tool set and then to fit your process to the tool

The Software Engineering Institute's (SEI; www.sei.cmu.edu/cmm) CMM defines necessary Level 2 practices for software configuration management (change control):

- Are change control activities planned for the project?
- Has the project identified, controlled, and made available the software products through the use of configuration management?
- Does the project follow a documented procedure to control change and configuration?
- Are standard reports on the software baseline distributed to affected parties?
- Does the project follow a written policy for implementing change control activities?
- Are project personnel trained to perform those change control activities?
- Are measurements used to determine the status of change control activities?
- Are periodic audits performed to verify that software baselines conform to the documentation in which they are defined?

There are also industry standards (IEEE 828) and military standards (MIL-STD 973, 2549) that can be used as further guidelines in setting up change, version, and configuration control systems. Software systems are available to aid in the control of project change management. As well as features built into general project management software systems such as FiveAndDime, there is software dedicated to project change management such as TrackWise (www.sparta-systems.com), SeaPine (www.seapine.com/cmsuite.html), Software Planner (www.softwareplanner.com), and ChangeManagementExpert (www.change-management-expert.com/).

Project Closeout

Management must, at some point, stop taking change orders, and the project must officially end. Additional requests for changes can be deferred to a successive version of the product or deferred until the product is officially transferred to the operation and maintenance phase. The original contracting arrangement (written or implied) will often determine (or suggest) the time a project should end. This is usually after all the original scope is completed plus important change orders that must be done before the product is placed in service. In many IT projects, coming to closure may be difficult:

- Sometimes a project will continue when funding is available, even when the budget and schedule is far exceeded; this is often due to management's misunderstanding of "sunk costs" and/or a lack of a clear original business justification.
- Sometimes it is difficult to call an end to projects when the benefiting organization stills wants more changes (and is willing to pay for them) and the performing organization wants to do the work.
- Sometimes the buyer (which is often the benefiting organization) will not sign off for official acceptance until some issue(s) is resolved.
- Sometimes the project team wants to continue because some of them may be concerned about: future assignments, significant scope has not been completed yet, documentation deliverables have not been completed, and bugs or problems are still present (even though they may not yet have surfaced in testing).

Project closeout can be a very hectic time and can also be a time of distress or excitement for different stakeholders. The PM must take care that all tasks and issues are fully and properly finished. Team members may worry about future work after the project is complete or they may be overly eager to get on with the next project. But unless the projected is ended, and a new one started if necessary, the work being done will no longer match the original goals and business justification.

Projects may come to successful completion and end normally or they may be terminated abnormally. A project may end normally (perhaps within time and budget constraints) even though management may decide not to use the product (put it into operation). This decision may be for a number of reasons, including:

- The product is no longer needed or wanted by the end users.
- Economic conditions have change, and the business value can no longer be realized.
- The product cannot be operated in an economically feasible manner.
- Resources have run out.
- The product is not sufficiently secure.
- The product cannot be economically maintained.

- The product is not sufficiently "usable."
- The product has major design flaws.
- The product is riddled with bug.
- The product does not comply with current standards or regulations.
- The project sponsor ("champion") no longer supports the effort.
- Other alternative products have proven more effective.

These conditions could have also occurred at a stage gate review, and the project could have been prematurely canceled or put on hold. This criteria are part of a quality stage gate review as defined in this book, and organizations can save considerable amounts of money and effort by discovering any of these problems before the project fully completes.

Whenever a project is canceled or put on hold, the PM should consult with key stakeholders and administrative offices (e.g., legal, HR, and procurement/contracting offices) to determine the impact of the cancellation and mitigating actions that may be necessary. To minimize organizational impact on both the performing and the benefiting organizations, a formal cancellation plan may be needed, and all stakeholders should be informed of the cancellation at the appropriate time and in the appropriate manner. The cancellation plan should also include steps to salvage reusable components.

When the project is completed, either normally or abnormally (hold or cancel), some key activities that should be performed include:

- Procurement audits and contract(s) closeout
- Product validation and verification, including change orders
- Confirmation of deliverables
- Formal inspections and compliance verification by regulators
- Formal acceptance and sign off" by buyer or benefiting organization
- Notification of completion to all stakeholders
- Formal "turnover" to operations/customer
- Postproject review and lessons learned documentation
- Itemization of change orders that were not done (deferred or rejected)
- Updating and closing project time, cost, and other records
- Properly archive of all records and artifacts
- Turnover relevant information to PM of next phase/version of product
- Acknowledgment of support of key stakeholders
- Acknowledgment of outstanding contributions
- Releasing project resources, including financial accounts and security items
- Formally releasing team

Project closeout forms or checklists are often used. Figure 11.5 is an example of a simple project closeout form. In some organizations, project closeout is divided into three parts: administrative closeout, contract closeout, and personnel closeout. Administrative closeout is done by the PM and project team in conjunction with line management of the performing organization and ensures that all project matters, including all billing, have been completed. Contract closeout is done by the procurement office and ensures that all contracts are properly completed, all vendors are paid, and all inventory issues are settled.

Personnel closeout is done by the HR office, which handles final personnel evaluations (typically done by the PM), return of checked-out equipment and other items, and final security issues. Project team members (groups or individuals) need to be properly released when their role on the project is over. If they are released in a proper and timely manner, costs will be reduced by not having to make work for them until they are reassigned to other projects. This also improves morale by reducing uncertainty about future project assignments or work opportunities. A final team meeting should be held so that all closing activities can be coordinated and a post mortem done that answers the following questions:

- Was the business justification realized (or does it appear that it will be realized)? If not, why not?
- What processes, methods, tools, techniques, and resources worked well?
- What processes, methods, tools, techniques, and resources did not work well?

Figure 11.5. Project closeout form

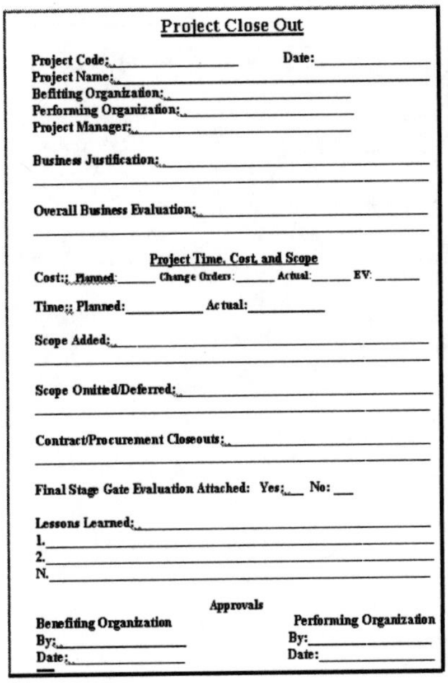

Project Close Out

Project Code: ______ Date: ______
Project Name: ______
Befitting Organization: ______
Performing Organization: ______
Project Manager: ______

Business Justification: ______

Overall Business Evaluation: ______

Project Time, Cost, and Scope

Cost:: Planned: ___ Change Orders: ___ Actual: ___ EV: ___

Time:: Planned: ______ Actual: ______

Scope Added: ______

Scope Omitted/Deferred: ______

Contract/Procurement Closeouts: ______

Final Stage Gate Evaluation Attached: Yes: __ No: __

Lessons Learned: ______
1. ______
2. ______
N. ______

Approvals

Benefiting Organization
By: ______
Date: ______

Performing Organization
By: ______
Date: ______

- What risks events occurred, and how they were handled?
- What risks events did not occur? Why not?
- What artifacts and components can be reused?
- What in general should be done differently on the next such project?

All these questions must be answered and documented. In addition, this documentation must be formulated in such a manner that it will actually be used. The answers to this post mortem can be entered into a lessons-learned software system. This process, as well as knowledge management in general, is discussed further in Chapter XVI.

A final stage gate review would be necessary if a stage gating process was used. An example of a stage gate review form is illustrated in Figure 11.6. This final quality stage gate review provides the final view of the project's critical success factors: completion and satisfaction. Whether or not a final stage gate report is used, it is common for a final project closeout report to be created. That final report includes the information shown in Figures 11.5 and 11.6, including final progress, time, and cost. Often a separate closeout meeting is held with the benefiting organization and possibly with the end users. In this closeout meeting, the end users are introduced to the operation and support people with whom they may work in the future. Often the performing organization uses this meeting as an opportunity to introduce or discuss the possibility for product extensions or enhancements. For successful projects, many organizations also have a celebration party for the project team and other key stakeholders. For unsuccessful projects, many organizations have an outside independent auditor review the way the project was managed.

Figure 11.6. Final stage gate review form

Final Stage Gate Review

Project: ________________ Date: ________________

Completion Factors:
EVA SPI:
EVA CPI:
EVA Critical Ratio:

Satisfaction Factors: Evaluated By (1=low, 10=high):

	Benefitting Org.	Performing Org.
Business Justification		
Validation		
Workflow & Conent		
Standards		
Maintain & Support		
Adaptability		
Trust/Security		

Financial Metrics:

	Planned	Expected
Cost		
Benefit		
Benefit/Cost Ratio:		
Payback Period:		
Internal Rate of Return:		

Risk Status:

	Occurred (y/n)	Impact	Mitigation
Risk 1			
Risk 2			
...			
Risk N			

Chapter Summary

In this chapter, project general change management has been covered, particularly for IT projects version control and configuration control. A serious problem for IT projects is always "scope creep," and this topic was also covered. Project closeout and related topics were also included and illustrated.

References

Brown, N. (1998, November). *Little book of configuration management.* Software Program Managers Network.

Hallows, J. (1998). *Information systems project management.* American Management Association.

PMI. (2000). *The Project Management Body of Knowledge (PMBOK).* Project Management Institute. ISBN 1-880410-22-2.

Royce, W. (1998). *Software project management.* Addison-Wesley.

Chapter XII

Procurement and Outsourcing

A pessimist sees difficulty in every opportunity; an optimist sees the opportunity in every difficulty.

(Winston Churchill)

Many IT projects involve the purchasing of goods and/or services, and some IT projects are mostly procurement activities, at least from a cost perspective. Between one quarter and one third of all U.S. software projects involve contractors or subcontractors (Jones, 1994). With the increase in IT outsourcing and of outsourcing offshore, there is an increasing need for very formal procurement management.

Procurement

PMI defines *procurement* as the processes required to acquire goods and services from outside the performing organization; it breaks procurement down into the following procurement management processes (PMI, 2000):

- Procurement planning
- Solicitation planning
- Solicitation
- Source selection

- Contract administration
- Contract closeout

The Software Engineering Institute (SEI) addresses software acquisition, and there is a separate capability maturity model for software acquisition (SA-CMM); however, in discussing procurement herein, I will follow the PMI process outline. Project management in a contracted situation is more involved and more difficult:

- The PM must deal with another company's procedures and systems
- Problems (in scope, cost, schedule, quality) are not as visible
- Solutions to problems take longer to implement
- The PM must rely on the accuracy and timeliness of vendor reports
- The PM must have a very good relationship with vendor
- Risks are more and greater, thus sound risk management is vital

Risk management in general was discussed earlier in this book, and subcontracting risks were identified and discussed in that chapter. Outsourcing magnifies procurement risks and other corporate risks and this is discussed separately later in this chapter.

Procurement typically involves contracts, and most contracts are formal agreements that contain the relevant requirements/specifications for the goods and/or services to be exchanged. Contracts are enforceable within courts of the specified jurisdiction and, legally, a contract must:

- Contain an offer to provide something specific by one party
- Contain an acceptance of that offer by the other party
- Specify consideration—payment in the form of money or something else
- Involve parties with "legal capacity" (separate competent legal parties)
- Be for a "legal purpose" (that which is to be provided must not be illegal)

The contract also typically includes business terms and conditions and things referred to in the bid documents, such as marketing literature, specifications, drawings, request for proposal (RFP) information, scope statements, and the like. A contract supercedes any memos or conversations, either before or after the contract is signed. Most IT contracts are atrocious, poorly written, and short on details. The faults lie largely with technology buyers (Hoffman, 2004), so project managers (PMs) need to be fully involved in the procurement process and work with their buyers and/or procurement offices to ensure a successful procurement and contract.

A PM should be named before the procurement process begins. Procurement is actually one form of risk mitigation and the PM should be in control of what is to be procured and how it may affect schedule, cost, quality, and other project issues. Depending upon the organization, either the PM or a procurement (or contracting) officer may handle the process. In either case, the PM must have an understanding of the needs and risks of the project and communicate these to the procurement officer. Because the PM should be aware of the terms of project contracts, the PM must understand contracts and procurement. An organization may have a centralized procurement office that handles all contracts. The advantages of having such a procurement office are that there is more expertise and experience in contracting, and standardized methods and forms are in place. The disadvantages are that people are not dedicated to the project, and it may take more time to get the officer's attention.

The overall procurement procedure is shown in Figure 12.1. *Procurement planning* involves a make-or-buy decision, and then for the buy decision, creation of a statement of work (SOW). *Solicitation planning* involves the creation of the RFP or other form of procurement document and associated evaluation criteria. *Solicitation* involves the distributing and advertising the RFP and answering questions of potential bidders. *Source selection* involves the selection of a vendor and execution of a contract. *Contract administration* involves the review of reports and correspondence from the vendor, review of the work, approval of payments as required, and the handling changes. *Contract closeout* involves verification that work was completed in a satisfactory

Figure 12.1. Procurement processes

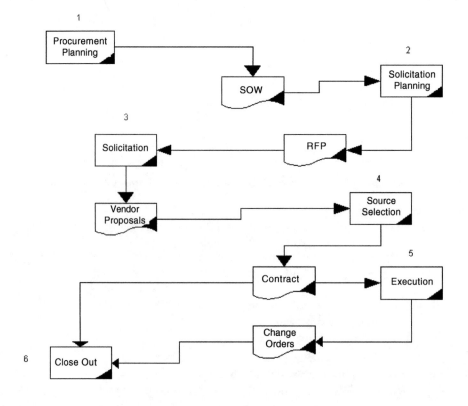

manner, formal acceptance of the work and related deliverables, and gathering and filing all supporting paperwork.

Procurement Planning

The procurement planning process starts with a description of the needed product and/or services, goes through a make/buy/lease decision process, and then develops a draft statement of work. The make versus buy/lease decision involves which services or products are best bought externally instead of done internally. *Best* is measured in terms of improved risk, cost, time, and quality. It may be better to "make" if one has idle capacity, the need to retain control (i.e., for strategic advantage), or if confidential information is involved. It may be better to buy/lease if the process to produce the product in question is not a core competency of the organization. In considering procurement, one must quantify not only the initial price but the total cost to manage the procurement and any long-term operational or maintenance issues.

Procurements usually involve contracts, and deciding which type of contract to use is part of procurement planning. There are several contract types, although any individual contract may not fall exactly into one of these standard categories. These types have different ways of assigning risk between the buyer and seller (vendor), and also may establish incentives for the seller to complete the contact faster or cheaper. The contract type a buyer uses is usually based upon standards in that industry, the type of goods/services, amount of risk the buyer can tolerate, how well defined the scope is, or amount of change to scope anticipated. The three main types of contract are:

- *FP:* Fixed price (or FFP, Firm Fixed Price)
- *CR:* Cost reimbursable
- *T&M:* Time and material

A key distinction of the contract types involves which party (buyer or seller) bears the risks of cost overruns. In a fixed-price (FP) contract, which is the most common type of contract, one price is agreed upon by the parties and the seller assumes the most risk. A purchase order (PO) is a simple form of a FP contract that is unilateral (signed only by the buyer); the PO is typically used for simple purchases of standard stock items. In a fixed price incentive fee (FPIF) contract, an incentive is added, typically to get the job done quicker or cheaper. An example would be $100,000 fixed fee, with an incentive of $5,000 for every week completed before the contract end date. There may also be a sharing ratio (x/y), in which the buyer gets x% of the cost savings (overage) and the seller gets y% of the cost savings. For FP contracts a ceiling cost may be included. Another variation typically used for long-term contracts is the fixed price economic price adjustment (FPECA), which allows for periodic price increases typically tied to material prices or economic indicators.

In a cost reimbursable (CR) contract the buyer assumes the most risk. The vendor's costs are reimbursed plus some profit; costs typically include all costs, including management and administration (M&A). There are various contract variations that determine the method of calculating vendor profit:

- *CPFF (Cost Plus Fixed Fee):* The profit (fee) is a fixed amount
- *CPPC (Cost Plus Percentage of Costs):* There is no incentive for the vendor to control costs (the U.S. government cannot enter into these types of contracts)
- *CPIF (Cost Plus Incentive Fee):* Buyer pays all costs plus a defined fee, in addition there are incentives to increase (decrease) the fee if costs are minimized and/or schedule is improved; there may be a sharing ratio (x/y), where the buyer gets x% of the cost savings (overage) and the seller gets y% of the cost savings

In a T&M contract, the buyer has some risk, depending upon whether the time or the material cost is greater for the job. The buyer reimburses the vendor for material (either actual cost or a specified rate for each type of material), and the buyer typically pays for time at a specified rate (for each type of worker). The rate for labor includes the seller's profit. This contract type is typically used for professional services: architects, lawyers, engineers, and programmers. The buyer incurs more risk when the work is done at the vendor's location because actual work time is harder to oversee. Figure 12.2 illustrates the pros and cons of these contract types.

The statement of work, sometimes called scope of work is written to describe the work to be done under the contract. There are several common forms of SOWs, and the appropriate form depends upon standards in a particular industry, nature of the services/ products, and type of contract. Commonly, the SOW legally becomes part of the contract. SOWs typically contain specifications, drawings, plans, requirements, functionality and other descriptions. There are several forms of the SOW:

Figure 12.2. Pros and cons of contract types

	FP	CPFF	T&M
Pros	Lowest risk. Vendor must control costs. Price known. Easier to manage.	Lower cost than FP. SOW may be less detailed.	Simpler SOW. Easy to manage. Good for "professional services" for people at your site under your direction.
Cons	Highest price. SOW must be more detailed. Changes may be expensive. Vendor may compromise quality or scope.	Most risk. Price unknown. Must audit vendor's costs. More costly to manage. Seller has less incentive to control costs.	Possibly high rates for the people. Difficult to control the amount of time used when the people are not at your location and/or under your direction.

- *Design:* Describes how the product is to be built
- *Performance:* Describes what the resulting product should do
- *Functional:* Defines the purpose of the product and key characteristics

There is normally a relationship between contract type and type of SOW. For an FP contract, the SOW must be very complete and detailed; a design form of SOW usually is used. Often the SOW is done by a design firm, such as an architectural firm. For a CR contract, the SOW is typically not as complete or detailed, and may be a performance or functional SOW. In this case, the buyer realizes there may be considerable additions or changes to the SOW. For T&M work, the SOW is typically brief and could take any of the three forms, but it is more often design or functional. The buyer typically hires bodies for some professional service of a relatively short time period. Figure 12.3 illustrates this relationship.

During procurement planning, and before the draft SOW is completed, there should be a form of Procurement Management Plan completed that clearly states:

Goods/service to be procured

Time period desires/constraints (start, milestones, end)

Contract issues:

Type of contract

Type of SOW

Expected cost (should cost)

Other important project-related contract terms (not legal issues)

Solicitation Planning

After the procurement management plan and draft SOW is completed, solicitation planning begins. The output from solicitation planning will be bid documents, evaluation

Figure 12.3. Procurement documents

Procurement Documents	Form of SOW	Type of Contract
RFP	Performance or Functional	CR
RFQ	Functional or Design	T&M
IFB	Design	FP

criteria, and a final SOW. Bid documents are the papers assembled to describe to vendors the products or services the buyer needs. Bid documents should allow vendors to make suggestions or alternatives that will provide for a better or cheaper procurement and also allow buyers to better compare the vendors. The bid documents usually include:

- SOW
- Buyer identity and corporate information
- Instructions for preparing and delivering proposals
- Vendor evaluation criteria
- Pricing worksheets
- Preliminary contract terms and conditions

There are several forms the bid documents take:

- *Request for Proposal (RFP):* Request a detailed report on how a job will be done and often who (generically or specifically) will be doing the work
- *Request for Quotation (RFQ):* Usually used to request a rate for professional services
- *Invitation for Bid (IFB, or RFB):* Requests one price for total job, perhaps with a breakdown or with rates for specific extras

An RFP usually indicates to a vendor that the buyer is interested in high-quality work, whereas an RFQ or IFB may indicate that the procurement will be mainly price driven. Evaluation criteria are often included in bid documentation, particularly for RFPs, and typically includE:

- Financial capacity and history of vendor
- Understanding of SOW
- Contract price and life-cycle costs
- Ability to perform (skill sets of people doing the work) and certifications held
- Management approach including project management
- Vendor suggestions and alternatives

Sometimes a procurement is awarded to a seller without competitive biding; this may be used when:

- The project is under extreme schedule pressure
- The vendor has unique qualifications

- There is only one vendor for the product or service
- Other mechanisms exists to make sure vendor prices are competitive

A *single-source procurement* means that there is a preferred seller, and a *sole source procurement* means there is only one supplier for this product or service. *Whenever a procurement is made without competitive bidding, there may be suspicion of compromise to procurement integrity; one has to be extremely careful in such a situation to completely document the reasons for not going through the full competitive process.*

Solicitation

The next step in the procurement process is to begin the solicitation process. In this process, the bid documents are sent to prospective vendors, and eventually proposals are received from these vendors. Vendors may be selected from a number of sources, including listings of qualified sellers in industry publications. Some of these lists may contain vendors that have been pre-qualified by virtue of some past performance, examination, or certification. SEI CMM, ISO, PMI, and other specific network, database, security, or programming certifications are very relevant in IT procurement.

A bidder's conference is often used, which may involve one or more meetings held with prospective vendors to make sure that they understand the procurement documents. The vendors have the opportunity to answer questions; such questions and answers should be written up and distributed to all vendors (whether attending the conferences or not). These conferences are quite important in complex and/or large procurements to obtain the correct pricing for the scope at hand. After the bidder's conference, there is generally a period of due diligence, where both buyer and seller investigate and validate the information provided by the other party, including financial information about each organization.

In order to gain the attention of more sellers, buyers can advertise their procurement. The U.S. government (and many other government bodies) is required to advertise certain procurements in certain publications. Generally, each industry area has trade journals that have sections devoted to such ads.

Source Selection

The next step in the procurement process is source selection, which involves the review of vendor proposals, the selection of a vendor, and the execution of contracts. First proposals are reviewed for completion and timeliness, and the proposals may be rejected entirely or the vendor asked to resubmit depending upon bid document stipulations. Complete proposals are reviewed in detail and "scored" using the established evaluation criteria. Screening criteria (minimum standards), vendor past performance, comparison of vendor's proposed cost versus a "should cost" value may be used to shorten the list of vendors receiving a full evaluation and scoring. A short list of vendors may be selected for a detailed presentation, site visit, or other fact finding initiatives. Upon preliminary selection, a letter of intent may be issued; however, this letter is not legally binding.

Once a specific vendor is selected, then negotiation begins on contract price and terms. The objectives at negotiations are to develop and protect a good and honest relationship with the vendor and to agree on a fair price for the product/service with reasonable terms. In negotiations it is important to arrive at a win-win situation; if not, one party may try to get back at the other party for what they lost in the negotiations. Price is usually negotiated first, and a final revised proposal representing a last and best may be offered by the vendor. Typical things discussed in negotiations for IT type contracts are price and incentives, payment schedule, work schedule and milestones, work locations and oversight, security issues, standards, responsibilities and penalties, management methods, technical methodology, reporting requirements, documentation requirements, contract change procedures, testing methods and metrics, and ownership of tangible and intangible products and byproducts.

The next step in this process is the execution of contracts. A PM should be involved as a consultant here, but this step needs to be the responsibility of the procurement office, purchasing department, and legal department. Vendor's responses to RFPs (which become part of the contract) are usually written by the sales people of the vendor and written in such a manner to close the deal; important details are avoided. Hoffman presents a list of things to do in contract negotiation (Hoffman, 2004):

- Align the finalization of contracts with the end of vendor's fiscal quarters.
- Include provisions for acceptance testing for both functionality and performance.
- Make sure that software does not include intellectual property of another vendor.
- Have a source-code escrow clause in the contract.

Risk management was discussed in Chapter VIII, and there are more and greater risks involved in activities that involve procurement. As part of risk management planning, risk identification and contingency plans need to be made for most procurements (Perkins, 2002). These include

- Estimating the probability of failure on the part of the vendor, both performance failure and business failures (going out of business, bankruptcy, acquisition, etc.)
- Assess the impact of potential failures
- Evaluate current treatment of vendor
- Protect yourself contractually
- Protect work continuance
- Regularly monitor the vendor work performance and corporate performance

Contract Administration and Closeout

The administrative portion of procurement involves review of the vendor's reports and work results to ensure compliance with contract provisions in regard to scope, quality, time, and cost. Vendor payments may be tied to one or more of these performance dimensions. Contract exception issues should involve both the PM and the contracting officer. A major portion of contract administration particularly in IT contracts involves coordinating contract changes. A portion of the contract should have specified change procedures. The PM is responsible for his or her company's change control system and the interface with the vendor's change control system. Change management was discussed in Chapter XI.

At the completion of a contract, all of the contract artifacts must be gathered and logically and physically filed (contract, contract changes, contract formal reporting, letters, memos, etc.). This provides a basis for information to settle any disputes (legal or otherwise) that may arise from the contract work. This is similar to project closeout, but with more attention to detail in regard to documentation. Lessons learned (postcontract evaluations) should be held and documented for use in future contract matters. Sometimes there may be procurement audits. These are structured reviews of the entire procurement process. The objective may be to identify successes and failures that can be used in other projects (or in other procurements on this project) or to look for suspected wrongdoing on the part of the PM, procurement staff, or project team members.

SEI SA-CMM

The Software Engineering Institute has a model of software acquisition called the Software Acquisition Capability Maturity Model (SA-CMM). It is a model for benchmarking and improving the software acquisition process. The model has a similar structure to the Capability Maturity Model for Software (SW-CMM) but is tailored to the needs of individuals and groups who are planning and managing software acquisition.

Each maturity level indicates an acquisition process capability and has several key process areas (KPAs). Each KPA has goals, common features, and specific activities. The common features are commitment to perform, ability to perform, measurement and analysis, and verification. The KPAs for each level are:

- Level 2: Repeatable (basic project management)

    Planning

    Evaluation

    Contract tracking and oversight

    Project management

    Requirements development and management

    Transition to support

- Level 3: Defined (process standardization)
  - Training program
  - Acquisition risk management
  - Contract performance management
  - Project performance management
  - User Requirements
  - Process definition and maintenance
  - Solicitation
  - Software acquisition planning
- Level 4: Quantitative (quantitative management)
  - Quantitative acquisition management
  - Quantitative process management
- Level 5: Optimizing (continuous process improvement)
  - Acquisition innovation management
  - Continuous process improvement

Outsourcing

A trend in recent years has been to outsource some or all of IT resources, activities, or projects. Software development is often totally or partially outsourced to software

Figure 12.4. Outsourcing analysis

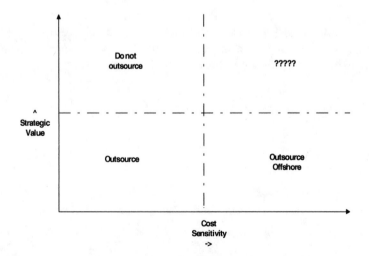

subcontractors. There are many factors driving this outsourcing trend, but the major ones are reducing costs by using cheaper labor pools and the fact that highly qualified IT staff are often expensive and difficult to find and retain in the United States and other highly developed countries. Also, by bringing in outside expertise, management can focus less on IT development and operations and more on their key business goals. Outsourcers are specialists, and should understand how to manage IT staff and other resources more effectively. Outsourcers may have larger IT resource pools that can provide greater capacity on demand.

Outsourcing is primarily a major means of cost control that allows an organization to focus on its core competencies. Figure 12.4 shows the traditional decision space for an outsourcing decision. The classic outsourcing model was to outsource only processes that did not give away competitive advantage. Processes that were not strategic but that were cost sensitive (cost of labor is very important) were considered for outsourcing to locales were labor was very cheap.

A new model sometimes outsources competitive advantage functions, if these are completed by outside experts with the proper confidentiality agreements, security safeguards, and legal foundation. *Selective outsourcing* is the decision process that chooses which IT capabilities to retain in-house and which to outsource. *Software Development Magazine* lists the factors that make good outsourcing project candidates (Strigel, 2004):

- Not much innovation required
- Close collaboration not required
- No critical or strategic code
- Limited need for specialized domain knowledge
- Minimal dependencies on other projects
- Stable hardware and software platforms
- Clearly defined requirements, performance goals, and acceptance criteria
- Internal management and domain expertise available to the supplier

CIO Magazine also listed the type of work that will likely be outsourced as opposed to the type of work that will not (Koch, 2004):

Going:

> Highly defined, noncollaborative programming
>
> Commodity help desk
>
> Legacy maintenance

Staying:

> Collaborative, creative programming
>
> Project management
>
> Requirements analysis

Design

Business process consulting

Processes requiring ultra–high-service levels

Security risk processes

The Software Engineering Institute's (SEI; www.sei.cmu.edu/cmm) CMM also considers outside contracting and defines necessary Level 2 practices for software subcontract management:

- Is a documented procedure used for selecting subcontractors?
- Are changes to subcontracts made with the agreement of all affected parties?
- Are regular technical interchanges held with subcontractors?
- Are the results and performance of the subcontractors tracked?
- Does the project follow a written policy for managing subcontractors?
- Are the people responsible for managing subcontractor appropriately trained?
- Are measurements used to determine the status of subcontract management activities?
- Are the subcontract activities reviewed with the PM on a regular basis?

An organization can outsource activities to another company within the same country or outsource to companies in other countries. Outsourcing to other countries is called *offshore outsourcing* or just *offshoring*. *Insourcing* involves using the company's own employees. *Offshore insourcing* involves using employees of that company who live in another country. There are a number of ways companies utilize labor markets to reduce manpower costs, and the following table lists some of the common terms for these options:

Outsource	Insource
On Shore	On Shore
Offshore	Offshore
Near Shore	Near Shore
Best Shore	Best Shore

All of these options involves trade-offs in terms of cost, quality, creativity, risks (organizational, security, economical, political, legal), loyalty, and career-path development. Almost one half of all U.S. CIOs used offshore outsource providers in 2004, and two thirds plan to send work overseas. The Gartner Group predicted that by the end of 2004, 1 in every 10 IT jobs with U.S.-based companies would be staffed offshore. Eighty-six percent of the 100 plus U.S. IT executives surveyed by *CIO Magazine* in 1993 said they already outsourced offshore application development, and 26% offshore their call

Figure 12.5. Programmer salaries

Country	2003	2015
United States	74, 486	85,000
Germany	39,879	65,000
England	38,450	67,000
France	37,250	65,000
Japan	30,338	35,000
Russia	7,540	25,000
India	6,350	20,000
China	5,852	10,000
Thailand	1,760	8,000

Figure 12.6. Outsourcing market share

Country	Market %
India	57.8
United States	5.6
Germany	2.8
Australia/Oceania	2.6
United Kingdom	2.3
China	2.1
Mexico	2.0
South America	1.9
Africa	1.4
Other European Countries	13
Other Asian	8.5

centers; all predicted their offshore outsourcing to rise. Gartner further estimated that by 2005, 30% of the top global 2,000 companies would have a sourcing strategy encompassing near-shore or off-shore solutions (Datz, 2004). A quick comparison of programmer salaries and projected salaries around the world (Figure 12.5) explains the push to offshore software projects.

India leads the world in attracting offshore outsourcing IT work, with almost 60% of the total global market; the distribution is shown in Figure 12.6 (Greenspan, 2003).

India is also the largest producer of movies in the world, because movie production is being outsourced from Hollywood to Bollywood in India. India has the second largest English-speaking technical workforce in the world, however India's middle class is estimated at only 0.35% of their total population (approximately 350 million out of 1 billion).

Corporations are always looking for a cheaper source of labor , so India may be close to the peak of their market penetration, especially because salaries are rising quickly in India and the turnover rate is becoming large. Some IT organizations are looking closer to home to minimize travel, communications cost, and, possibly, risks; for U.S. companies, Canada and Mexico, and even cheaper markets in the United States (such as Oklahoma) are being given a second look. Ciber Corporation, based in Colorado, has picked Oklahoma City as its first "made in America" application development center (Frauehheim, 2005).

Figure 12.7. Outsourcing analysis

Country	Assessment	Political Risk	English	Salaries
India	Leader	Moderate	Good	4 – 12K
China	Up and Comer	Low	Poor	4 – 12K
Thailand	Rookie	Low	Poor	4 – 12K
Malaysia	Up and Comer	Low	Fair	4 – 12K
Vietnam	Rookie	Moderate	Poor	Under 4K
Singapore	Up and Comer	Low	Fair	Over 12K
Philippines	Leader	Moderate	Good	4 – 12K
Ireland	Leader	Low	Good	Over 12K
Russia	Up and Comer	Moderate	Poor	4 – 12K
Poland	Up and Comer	Low	Poor	4 – 12K
South Africa	Up and Comer	Moderate	Good	Over 12K
Israel	Leader	Moderate	Good	Over 12K
Brazil	Up and Comer	Moderate	Poor	4 – 12K
Argentina	Rookie	Moderate	Fair	4 – 12K
Canada	Leader	Low	Good	Over 12K
Mexico	Up and Comer	Moderate	Poor	Over 12K

Many organizations today are performing a formal risk analysis (discussed later in this chapter) and trying to diversify their outsourcing locations (not "putting all their eggs in one basket"). *CIO Magazine* recently ranked 24 countries in regard to key outsourcing characteristics (Datz, 2004; see Figure 12.7).

Whether outsourcing on- or offshore, there are many disadvantages and potential problems to consider, such as:

- Possible abdication of control
- High switching costs—hard to get out of an outsourcing arrangement once one is begun
- Lack of internal technological innovation (loss of creativity)
- Loss of local candidates for career path vacancies
- Loss of worker corporate loyalty
- Outsource provider does not have complete visibility into organizational needs and culture
- Possible loss of ownership
- Loss of work results (possibly due to political instability)
- Privacy problems with data
- Security problems

Potential security problems are enormous in outsourcing and particularly in offshore outsourcing. Offshore outsourcing services—which, unlike software development, typically require the transfer of personal data—grew to about $2 billion in 2003. Consider the potential for compromise of vital trade secrets and possibly the ability for an organization to operate at all when a large percentage of an organization's software code is written offshore. As stated in *Computerworld*, "How do you keep customer data, or the powerful algorithms that give your systems a competitive edge, from being sold to the highest bidder?" (Betts, 2004). *CIO Magazine* listed six steps to making a smart outsourcing decision (Overby, 2004b):

- Resists the instinct to either rule out or not outsourcing based upon initial reactions
- Involve corporate and business units early in the discussion and analysis phase
- Take at least 6 months to study the issues
- Engage outside experts to help study the situation
- Consider the impact on employees
- Once a decision is made, remember that it needs to be revisited as conditions change

The long-term disadvantages of outsourcing professional work (such as IT programming and design) are only beginning to appear. Programmers often form the foundation for the career ladder to higher level IT jobs because programming develops both essential quantitative analysis skills and understanding of the business process that are the subject of the development. Without that large corporate foundation to select from, where will companies find the competent knowledgeable people to fill vacancies in higher level IT (and other business segment) positions? As stated in *CIO Magazine*: "As the former deputy CIO of Proctor and Gamble learned, it's crucial to retain enough work in-house to train the next generation of IT leaders" (Smith, 2004). The business process of compensating professional people for work has always involved more than just code for money; this is illustrated in Figure 12.8.

For these reasons, many large successful IT organizations do not even consider outsourcing. Such is the case with the retail giant Wal-Mart, whose CIO once stated that "we'd be nuts to outsource" (Sullivan, 2004). About 21% of IT executives surveyed in 2004 by management consulting firm DiamondCluster International said they had prematurely terminated offshore arrangements in the prior 12 months (*Network World*, 2004). *Computerworld* reminded readers of the "mythical man-month" principle, which

Figure 12.8. Employee compensation

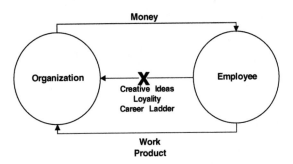

says that "you cannot compress the time it takes to complete software by throwing more bodies at it—the brute force programming techniques with low cost coders from India and elsewhere" (Hall, 2004). Research has shown that 80% of organizations have suffered problems ranging from time and cost overruns to nonadherence to specifications and requirements when outsourcing IT projects (Meta Group, 2004). For offshore outsourcing, "while 93% of business technologists surveyed recently by *Software Development* magazine say the work that's going offshore is either important or critical to their companies' operations, 56% say what's coming back is worse than what could be achieved in-house and, in the worst cases, unusable." (TechWeb, 2004).

Twenty percent of outsourcing deals do not produce cost savings; in fact, 10% of those deals actually wind up increasing costs (Network World, 2004). Claims of 80% savings in cost are exaggerated and do not consider all the cost in offshore outsourcing. A more likely number is 20%, and that takes years of effort and a huge up-front investment (Overby, 2003). CIO *Magazine* developed methods to calculate the total cost of offshoring (TCO), which included cost items and factors (of base contract value) for best and worst case historical data. This is shown in Figure 12.9 (Overby, 2003). As is shown in Figure 12.9, hidden costs range from about 15% to 60%

Software Development magazine lists seven steps that help make outsourcing projects work (Strigel, 2004):

- Choose the right partner
- Choose the right type of project
- Choose the right phase of the project
- Manage communication
- Write detailed specifications
- Manage changes
- Manage the project

In terms of partner selection, some suggestions on how to avoid vendor pitfalls in outsourcing include the following:

Figure 12.9. Hidden outsourcing costs

Cost Item	Best Case	Worst Case
Vendor Selection	.002	.02
Transitioning Work	.02	.03
Layoffs and retention	.03	.05
Lost Productivity/ Cultural Issues	.03	.27
Improving Development Process	.01	.10
Managing Contract	.06	.10
Total Hidden Costs	.152	.57

- Do not focus solely on price—vendor markup is about 30%
- Thoroughly evaluate outsourcers' capabilities and certifications (i.e., SEI CMM)
- Work to establish "strategic alliances"
- Use multiple, best-of-breed suppliers
- Choose an outsourcer whose capabilities complement your own
- Base choice on corporate cultural fit as well as expertise
- Develop skills in contract management and procurement

An item on the list concerns the certifications of the vendor, and verifying technical and business competencies is important. However, just as important, and missing from this list, is a comprehensive security assessment of both the outsourcing organization and each and every person that will be involved with the work. Security clearances and complete background checks should be in place for anyone doing IT work or having any kind of access to IT resources. Such clearances and checks have become vitally important for both work that is outsourced as well as the use of foreign labor internally, such as via work and/or study visas.

One key indicator of vendor competence is the SEI CMM maturity level discussed earlier in this book. Today, many U.S. government agencies in addition to the DoD require companies that bid on their contracts have a CMM Level 3 or higher. Some corporations that outsource to India in particular require that software developers have a CMM Level 5, the top level (Koch, 2004). However, some outsource vendors lie about their CMM scores, appraisers cheat and are bribed, and there is no organization that verifies CMM maturity claims. Koch listed 12 critical questions to help validate CMM claims (Koch, 2004):

- Who was the appraiser?
- What part of the company was tested?
- How long ago was this done?
- How long did it take the company to move from one level to another?
- Where is your evidence of continuous improvement?
- Who runs the quality group?
- Was the appraiser from inside or outside the organization?
- Where are the reports?
- What types of projects were assessed?
- Did the appraiser consult on the projects being appraised?
- How many project managers who were assessed at Level 5 will be on your project team?
- How does the company train new people to be CMM Level 5?

Figure 12.10. Outsource management

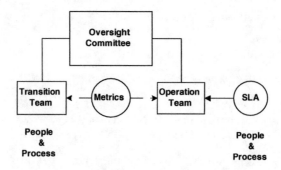

Another list of outsourcing pitfall avoidances is from Gomolski (2002):

- Know your strengths—Outsource your weaknesses, not your strengths
- Do not completely write off IT infrastructure—Own your processes
- Know what you are outsourcing
- During vendor selection, do not shop based on price alone
- Stay engaged with the work and the vendor

Staying engaged with the vendor involves the marriage of people and process from both organizations, both during the transition and during the operation (or maintenance) phases. This is illustrated in Figure 12.10.

Software Development magazine listed 12 warning signs that an outsourcing arrangement may be headed for trouble (Wieggers, 2003):

- Schedule status reports are late, incomplete, or do not correlate with observations
- Unqualified staff are being assigned to the project
- The acquiring organization is not actively managing the relationship with the vendor
- Unrequested requirements (gold plating) are being implemented
- Schedule reviews are postponed or do not take place
- Decisions are not made in a timely manner
- Incomplete deliveries are received
- Processes are being bypassed or not working
- Project tracking charts for earned value are missing
- Cost and deviations have no explanations
- Early milestones are missed

Proper legal foundations (confidentiality, nondisclosures, noncompete, hiring restrictions and other agreements with vendors and individuals) are vital in outsourcing. Renegotiation clauses in these contracts are also very important. Gartner reported that 85% of all outsourcing contracts signed since 2001 would be renegotiated within 3 years because the original contracts did not serve the organization's long-term needs (Gartner Group, 2004). "To a CIO, outsourcing contracts may look like another procurement, but they are much riskier" (Melymuka, 2004). "You're writing a contract for a service that is impossible to describe, that will change over time, that will make you dependent on the service provider, and for which termination is not an option." Specific contract problem areas listed by *Computerworld* are unresolved issues, fuzzy scope, tasks missing from scope, exclusivity, damage waivers, decreasing technology costs (being locked into total costs), complex benchmarking, lock-in to provider, ownership of intellectual property, ceding control of people, and ignoring termination issues (Melymuka, 2004). An *Information Week* survey listed the worst situations companies have faced with outsourcing (Gareiss, 2002):

- Takes more management time that expected
- Does not meet performance specifications
- Unexpected add-on costs
- Does not meet savings projections
- Systems cannot change quickly when strategy changes
- Lack of promised knowledge transfer
- Lack of innovation
- Conflicts over intellectual property

Earlier in this book I discussed software engineering and modern methodologies such as free-flow, incremental methods, agile, and extreme programming. These newer methods are difficult to use in an outsourced arrangement (Iverson, 2004). Thus, outsourcing will limit one's choices in methodologies and techniques. Maintaining a project's knowledge base and continuity is more difficult with an outsourcing arrangement, particularly offshore outsourcing. Foreign employee turnover in offshore outsourcing countries is around 30% and growing. *CIO Magazine* offered a list of 10 key steps in dealing specifically with knowledge transfer between a company and its outsourcing foreign partners (Overby, 2004a):

- Start with a pilot
- Include contract provisions for minimal continuous staffing of critical positions
- Create a knowledge transfer "roadmap" with roles and responsibilities
- Require offshore workers to shadow one's own employees during transition
- Map outsourcer's responsibility to the individual role, not to the team level
- Train outsourcer's people into your processes and terminology

- Conduct classes into language and culture issues
- Keep at least 20% of offshore staff on site as liaisons
- Send a home country based manager to the offshore location
- Rotate on shore and offshore staff

In today's business world, offshore outsourcing may appear to be a competitive necessity for many companies. But it is not always the best option. You should weigh a number of factors before you make such a move. Among them are (Iyengar, 2004)

- *Cost:* Take into account the *total* cost of the move. It may save you some money and increase your competitiveness but some costs may not be readily apparent. Do not forget to consider elements such as physical and system infrastructure, telecommunications, and management overhead.
- *Protection of Intellectual Capital:* You should expect greater difficulty in managing the loss of intellectual property (IP) and the retransfer of IP in offshore situations.
- *Understanding of Local Business Requirements and Culture:* Providers often lack executives on site who can interact effectively with your higher level executives.

"In addition to performing due diligence in assessing factors like these, be sure that your internal debate takes into account the concerns of all your key stakeholders. Offshore outsourcing can be profitable but only if you develop a sourcing strategy that weighs and then diminishes risks" (Iyengar, 2004). For those in IT concerned with functions of their department being outsourced, *CIO Magazine* listed eight steps to take to "outsourceproof" your IT organization (Koch, 2004):

- Focus on collaboration with the business organization
- Compete on process (such as the SEI CMM)
- Develop a standard enterprise architecture
- Sell service levels
- Reeducate your staff (both state of the art tech skills and collaboration)
- Create career paths from tech ranks into collaborative and project management areas
- Augment, don't replace (use outsourcing for overload situations)
- Get transparent (clearly show cost and time)

Deciding what activities to outsource and where and how to outsource them is an exercise in risk management and portfolio optimization. "In an outsourcing relationship, only enterprises that can effectively manage risk will be able to address the issues that will inevitably arise and prevent a successful outcome" (Murphy, 2003). Gartner listed some risk categories and compares the degree of risk of internal software development versus

Figure 12.11. Internal vs. outsourced risk factors

Risk Category	Internal Development	Outsourced Development
Cost Effectiveness	2	4
Business Value Failure	1	4
Operational Failure	4	2
Slow to Operation	5	2
Political Resistance	1	3
Future Flexibility Inhibited	0	4
Management Complexity	5	5

Figure 12.12. Outsourcing analysis by SDLC phase and business process

SDLC	Finance	HR	CRM	Sales	Manufacturing
Requirements					
Analysis					X
Design					X
Build/Buy	X	X	X		X
Test			X		X
Integrate			X		X
Operate			X		X
Maintain					X

Figure 12.13. Outsourcing risk portfolio analysis

Task	Country 1 Cost Factor	Risk Factor	...	Country N Cost Factor	Risk Factor
1					
2					
3					
4					
5					
6					
...					

outsourced development (Murphy, 2003). This is illustrated in Figure 12.11, where 0 is *low risk* and 5 is *high risk*.

Each software development life cycle (SDLC) process can be examined for each business process. The objective is to maximize the cost savings at a tolerable risk. For example, Figure 12.12 shows certain portions (tasks) of different business processes which may be outsourcing candidates.

The choices here may be based upon the magnitude of the cost of each task, the criticality of that task to business continuation, and the potential for security compromises for each area. In a formula it may be represented as:

Outsource Potential Cost = Cost - $EMV_{business}$ - $EMV_{security}$

$EMV_{business}$ = Business Loss * Frequency

$EMV_{security}$ = Security Impact * Frequency

Business losses can occur in a number of ways and some were listed earlier as business value (ROI) not met, operation/implementation delayed, and so forth. Security losses can similarly occur in a number of ways as compromise of customer privacy, compromise of company competitive information, loss of company resources, loss of customer good will, and so forth. Here cost and EMV are measured in dollars per time period. Next one would take each one of these candidate outsourcing tasks and look at the cost and risks of outsourcing each in different locations. This is illustrated in Figure 12.13. Here one wants to maximize the product of cost times risk factor summed over all tasks to be outsourced. The additional constraint is for diversification, and that constraint may specify that no country gets more than so many tasks or so many dollars. The optimization process is similar to maximizing the return and minimizing the risk of a stock portfolio with certain diversity constraints.

As outsourcing matures, mutations of the standard business arrangement are occurring to mitigate some of the inherent problems with offshore outsourcing. One arrangement is being called cosourcing, where work and management is shared between the buyer and the offshore vendor. The five recommendations listed in *MIS Quarterly* for developing successful cosourcing arrangements are as follows (Kaiser & Hawk, 2004):

- Understand where cosourcing is applicable
- Define and develop the appropriate in-house IT competencies
- Build trust but avoid building a binding relationship
- Foster mutual understanding of ethnic and corporate cultures
- Map out a progression to cosourcing

The key to successful cosourcing is the establishment of a dual project management hierarchy. Figure 12.14 shows one successful implementation (Kaiser & Hawk, 2004):

Figure 12.14. Cosourcing implementation

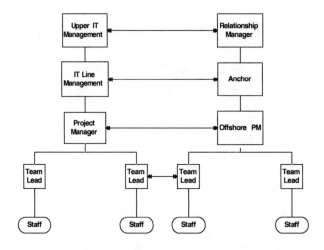

One of the most bitter debates at this point in U.S. history is the extent to which outsourcing is responsible for some of the current labor-market problems. Given the potential impact of outsourcing on the domestic and global economies, this issue has become a "political football." Responding to a survey on this prominent issue, 66% of U.S. workers believe that offshore outsourcing of jobs is harmful for the economy (Hudson Global Resources, 2004). In the last 3 years, offshore programming jobs have nearly tripled while at the same time U.S. undergraduate computer science majors have dropped by 30% (Chabrow, 2004). India is now graduating 75,000 IT students, compared to 26,000 in the United States. India is the largest recipient of offshore outsourcing jobs, with about IT 50,000 jobs per quarter. About 80% of the jobs coming into India are from the United States. The U.S. Department of Labor has reported U.S. IT job loses at 5,000 per quarter. Thus without offshore outsourcing, there would be considerable IT growth rate in the United States. Other highly developed countries are experiencing the same effect.

The other side to this argument is that offshore outsourcing helps domestic companies save money and thus avert layoffs in other types of jobs. It is difficult to determine a clear, accurate measure of how many total U.S. jobs are being lost to outsourcing, or how many might be lost in the future. Out of the current 140 million jobs in the United States, about 900,000 may have been lost already with up to 6 million lost through this year (2004); another 14 million U.S. jobs are at risk (Center for American Progress, 2004) *Computerworld* predicts that by 2015, 3.3 million white collar jobs will move offshore; of that number, about 500,000 will be IT jobs (Hoffman & Thibodeaux, 2003). Service jobs and IT jobs are at risk in all major developed countries. In the United Kingdon as many as 50,000 jobs moved offshore in 2003; Germany and Sweden are feeling political pressure as well. Up to 25% of IT jobs in developed countries may move offshore by 2010 (Gartner Group, 2004). *America is the only developed nation that does not have protectionist legislation that provides disincentives for companies that use imported and offshore cheap foreign labor.* However, that may change in the future; as of February 2004, 27 bills designed to restrict offshore outsourcing had been introduced into the U.S. Congress. Similar bills have passed or been introduced into legislatures of the individual U.S. states. Both federal and state bills range from full restriction, to preferences for local companies, to limits on work permits and visas (i.e., H-1B and L-1).

Offshore outsourcing has caused a considerable backlash in the United States from both employees and customers. Eighty-four percent of buyers and 82% of providers in the IT sector are now concerned about this negative backlash from their employees (King, 2004). Fifty-eight percent of American workers believe that companies that outsource work that could be done by Americans should be penalized by the U.S. government (ELA, 2004). A Harris Poll stated that 53% of Americans felt it is un-American to send U.S. jobs overseas (St. John, 2004). Twenty-four percent of customers indicated that they will stop doing business with a vendor if they outsource support offshore, regardless of the quality of support (Bodem, 2004). Sixteen U.S. states have introduced "right-to-know" bills that require corporate call-center employees to disclose their geographic location to customers.

Corporate CEOs, however, are certainly benefiting from outsourcing. Studies show that CEO salaries at the 50 U.S. firms outsourcing the most (IBM, Intuit, etc.) increased by 46% in 2003 compared to 365 other large U.S. firms which had an increase of only 9%

(Frauehheim, 2004). From 2001 to 2003, the CEOs of these top 50 outsourcers earned $2.2 billion while sending an estimated 200,000 U.S. jobs overseas. With outsourcing, the CEO-to-worker wage gap is rising again (after two years of narrowing), with a ratio in 2003 of 301:1.

Chapter Summary

This chapter covered general project procurement and the formal procedures and documents used in procurements, such as the statement of work, request for proposal, and contracts. The different types of procurement documents were discussed along with types used in certain situations and with what types of contracts. In particular for IT projects, the subject of outsourcing was also covered. In the last century, outsourcing was mostly a simple cost-cutting maneuver used for noncritical labor intensive functions. *In the 21ˢᵗ century, outsourcing has become a strategic initiative that can drastically transform an organization. In a rapidly changing global IT intensive marketplace, the pressure is on to cut even deeper into one's business for outsourcing opportunities. Take the wrong slice or get it wrong, then undoing the outsourcing arrangement will be a most formidable and expensive task; take the right slices and do it right, and the reward may be very significant. In either case, the security risks and the risk of permanently losing key expertise and creativity for the organization and for an entire country are enormous.*

References

Betts, M. (2004, November 15). Outsourcing dangers. *Computerworld.*

Bodem, W. (2004, August). Service excellence research group report. Retrieved from www.serviceXRG.com

Center for American Progress. (2004, March 16). *Outsourcing statistics in perspective.* Retrieved from http://www.americanprogress.org/

Chabrow, E. (2004, August 16). By the book. *Information Week.*

Datz, T. (2004, July 15). Outsourcing world tour. *CIO Magazine.*

Einhorn, B. (2003, July 30). The quest for Asia's outsourcing crown. *Business Week Online.*

ELA. (2004). *Equipment leasing association,* June survey. Retrieved from www.ChooseLeasing.org

Frauehheim, E. (2004). *For CEO's, offshoring pays.* Retrieved August 31, 2004, from http://zdnet.com

Frauehheim, E. (2005, January 14). Outsourcing to Oklahoma? *CNET News.*

Gareiss, R. (2002, November 18). Analyze the outsource. *Information Week.*

Gartner Group. (2004, March). Successful outsourcing relationships. *Proceedings from the Gartner Symposium/ITxpo,* San Diego, CA.

Gomolski, B. (2002, May 17). Don't be naïve about outsourcing. *Computerworld.*

Greenspan, R. (2003, September 10). *Going to the (out) source.* Retrieved from www.clickz.com/stats/markets/b2b

Hall, M. (2004, November 15). Offshoring revives man-month myth. *Computerworld.*

Hoffman, T. (2004, August 23). Attorney says sloppy IT deals all too common. *Computerworld.*

Hoffman, T. & Thibodeau, P. (2003, April 28). Exporting IT jobs. *Computerworld.*

Hudson Global Resources. (2004). Retrieved from www.hudson resourcing.com

Iverson, J. (2004, May). Extreme outsourcing. *Proceedings of the 2004 IRMA Conference,* New Orleans, LA.

Iyengar, P. (2004). *Factors to weigh before going offshore.* Retrieved from http://outsourcing.weblog.gartner.com

Jones, C. (1994). *Assessment and control of software risks.* Englewood Cliffs, NJ: Yourdon Press Computing Series.

Kaiser, K., & Hawk, S. (2004). Evolution of offshore software development: from outsourcing to cosourcing. *MIS Quarterly Executive, 3*(2).

King, J. (2004, July 12). Damage control. *Computerworld.*

Koch, C. (2004, March 1). The CMM hype. *CIO Magazine.*

Koch, C. (2004, October 15). How to outsource-proof your IT department. *CIO Magazine.*

Melymuka, K. (2004, March 22). Outsourcing gothas. *Computerworld.*

Meta Group. (2004). Retrieved from techupdate.zdnet.com/source/Meta_Group

Murphy, J. (2003). *Evaluating and mitigating outsourcing risk.* Gartner Group.

Network World. (2004). Retrieved from www.networkworld.com

Overby, S. (2003, September 1). The hidden cost of offshore outsourcing. *CIO Magazine.*

Overby, S. (2004a, July 15). Lost in translation. *CIO Magazine.*

Overby, S. (2004b, November 1). One outsources, the other doesn't. *CIO Magazine.*

Perkins, B. (2002, December 9). Developing a supplier contingency plan. *Computerworld.*

Smith, G. (2004, November 1). You can't outsource everything. *CIO Magazine.*

St. John, D. (2004). *Outsourcing pipelone.* Retrieved August 16, 2004, from www.outsourcingpipeline.com

Strigel, W. (2004). Outsourcing: What works. *Software Development.*

Sullivan, L. (2004, September 27). Wal-Mart's way. *Information Week.*

TechWeb. (2004). Retrieved from www.techweb.com

Wieggers, K. (2003). See you in court. *Software Development.*

Chapter XIII

Stakeholder Management

Always treat your employees exactly as you want them to treat your customers.

(Steven Covoy)

The identification and management of a project's stakeholders is vital to the complete success of a project. Well-planned and properly-executed projects often can still fail due to a lack of or inappropriate relationships between the project manager and various stakeholders. This chapter discusses matters related to the human side of project management, including stakeholder relations, communications, and project team management.

Stakeholder Identification and Analysis

The first step in good stakeholder management is the complete identification of all of the stakeholders. Cleland (1998) defines stakeholders as follows:

Stakeholders are people or groups that have, or believe they have, legitimate claims against the substantive aspects of the project. A stake is an interest or share or claim in a project; it can range from informal interest in the undertaking, at one extreme, to a legal claim of ownership at the other extreme.

Stakeholders are associated with both the performing organization and the benefiting organization; these are called internal stakeholders. The performing and benefiting organizations may or may not be part of the same company, and there may be a formal or informal contract situation. In addition, there are usually "external" stakeholders that are not part of these two groups. Traditionally, the key stakeholders have been individuals or other groups closely associated with either the benefiting or performing organizations. "However, long-run changes in the social, political, and economic environment of projects have meant that this is no longer necessarily the case for a number of reasons" (Winch, 2004). Today there may also be a number of key external stakeholders in terms of various social, political, or economic interests.

Internal stakeholders related to the *benefiting organization* might include:

- Project sponsor(s)
- Business owners or stockholders
- Customer line management
- Customer's users of the IT system
- Customer's IT group
- Customer's accounting group
- Customer's business units affected
- Customer's other employees
- Customer's customers
- Customer's contractors and vendors
- Customer's financiers

Internal stakeholders related to the *performing organization* might include:

- Project manager
- Business owners or stockholders
- Project team
- Performing organization's line management
- Performing organization's IT group
- Performing organization's accounting group
- Performing organization's other employees
- Performing organization's customers
- Performing organization's contractors and vendors
- Performing organization's financiers

External stakeholders may be concerned individuals, companies, or associations that can be termed *private* interests; they may be local, state, federal, or international government bodies that can be termed *public* interests (Winch, 2004). External private stakeholders might include concerned individuals, trade associations, environmental and conservationists associations, neighborhood association, and the like. External public stakeholders might include local governments, state governments, federal regulatory agencies, federal governments, or international agencies.

Once the stakeholders have been identified, then each must be analyzed carefully in order to determine the manner in which that stakeholder should be managed. Stakeholders that are more concerned about a project will have to be managed differently than those that are less concerned; similarly, stakeholders that are more powerful will have to be managed differently than those that are less powerful. Each stakeholder or group of stakeholders may have a different type of stake in the project including monetary, job security, position, influence, reputation, or convenience (time). The interests of all stakeholders in one group may not be the same, if the result of the successful completion of the project may alter the "balance of power" in that organization. For example, within the benefiting organization different stakeholders may be for, against, or neutral about the project and this may depend upon the way the final project manifests itself or the way it is implement in the benefiting organization. IT ERP projects, which involve a number of corporate business units, there is very much corporate change including work flow, policies and procedures, management structure, and so forth; for this reason different stakeholders within the same group (i.e., the benefiting organization) may have varying interest in the success of such a large project.

Figure 13.1 shows a power vs. concern graph that can be used to visually assign stakeholders into one of these four categories. Powerful and highly concerned stakeholders will have to have to be actively managed throughout the project; these are the people who will need their hands held. For each of these individuals or groups the project manager must ascertain:

Figure 13.1. Stakeholder classification

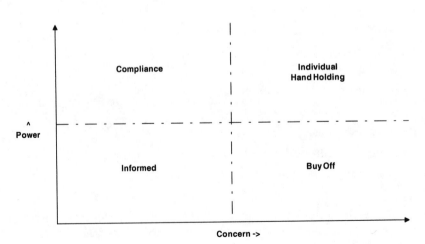

- What is the biggest thing this stakeholder has to gain if the project succeeds (fails)?
- What is the biggest thing this stakeholder has to lose if the project fails (succeeds)?

Next the project manager (or line management) must try to best align this person with the project and get early buy-in; and then check on this alignment during all phases of the project. Stakeholders that are powerful but not too concerned, usually have some standards or other manifestation of principle that they wish to be followed. An example here is regulatory agencies. This group of stakeholders is best managed by becoming very knowledgeable and clear on the principles and standards involved and then complying with same. Stakeholders that are not powerful but quite concerned need to be aligned with the project; this is the so-called buy-off group. This done first by finding out why they are so concerned, and then seeing if they can be aligned with the project initially; they do not need constant attention as does the powerful and very concerned group. Stakeholders that are not powerful and not too concerned simply need to be kept informed on a regular basis as a group.

In terms of power and influence over project affairs, there are four types of power in most organizations and communities of stakeholders:

- Power due to position (or rank)
- Power due to control over resources (like budget)
- Power due to unique expertise
- Power due to politics and/or charisma

Some authors define other types of power like physical power, which may have relevance on a sport team, but typically not in a project management environment. Other types of power defined by some are position subtypes of power as:

- *Reward:* Power based on being able to give an employee something he wants; does not necessarily mean money, may be a position/role on the team, or may be a positive evaluation supplied by the PM to a functional line manager
- *Referent:* Power bestowed from a higher point in the organization
- *Penalty:* Power based on being able to penalize someone (may be more than monetary)

A stakeholder may fall into more than one of these categories. Figure 13.2 shows one method to perform this stakeholder analysis including an analysis of power vs. concern and type of power. In this spreadsheet each stakeholder is listed and characterized by checking off columns.

After all the stakeholders have been identified and analyzed, a stakeholder action plan should be developed. This plan will explain how each stakeholder is to be managed and who (within the project team, line management, or project management office

Figure 13.2. Stakeholder analysis

Stakeholder Analysis																
	Internal		External		Stand			Power		Concern		Influence				
Stakeholder	Benefitor	Performer	Private	Public	For	Against	Neutral	High	Low	High	Low	Position	Resource	Political	Expert	

[Chapter XVI]) is responsible for carrying out each item in the action plan for that stakeholder. This stakeholder management plan can be a separate plan or be part of the communications plan, discussed later in this chapter. As part of the stakeholder management plan, potential claims by a stakeholder or other potential unfavorable actions should also be identified and included in the project risk management plan covered earlier in this book. As well as correlating with the communications plan and risk management plan, the stakeholder management plan should also map to the quality plan.

PMI's PMBOK does not specifically address the larger issue of general stakeholder management, but defines two knowledge areas directly concerned with stakeholder management: *communications management* and *human resource management.* Risk management has already been addressed in this book, and as stated earlier, stakeholder risk tolerances are a factor in determining an overall risk management plan.

Communication Management

Communications management involves managing the process of information flow to and from stakeholders. As discussed previously, there are many different stakeholders, each with differing roles, interests, priorities, and agendas. In addition there are many types of information some of which needs to go between different stakeholders at different times and frequencies, possibly using different mechanisms. *The project manager's role is not to try to control all these differing flows, but to influence project communications to the benefit of the project.* Remember that it is the role of the project team members to do their assigned duties and complete their assigned tasks; and it is the role of general management to define the project, support the project, and protect it from disruptive or unnecessary changes; however, the prime role of the PM is as the integrator and communicator for all project stakeholders. Thus the project manager serves as the focal point for project communication. The PM should try to influence communications to the extent that communications are following plan, but the PM cannot physically control communication. If there are N people involved, there will be $N*(N-1)/2$ possible communication channels; this is illustrated in Figure 13.3 for five people.

Figure 13.3. Communication channels

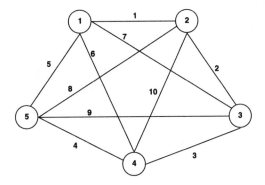

The PMI communication management processes are (PMI, 2000):

- Communications planning
- Information distribution
- Performance reporting (covered in Chapter XIV)
- Administrative closure (covered in Chapter XI)

Poor communication is a major cause of project problems and project team members may loose motivation or be caught up in rumors due to poor communication. Stakeholders also may become discouraged or angry with lack of proper communication. A typical project manager spends 90% of his or her time communicating (PMI, 2000). This includes:

- About 2 hours/day in meetings
- Over 1 hour per day in one-on-one coaching or discussion
- Much of the balance in reporting, both oral and written

Thus, PMs must be skilled in both oral and written communications. PMs communicate regularly with:

- Upper line management
- The project sponsor
- The project team
- Other PMs and related project teams
- Customers
- Other stakeholders

The direct purpose of all the PM communication is to keep all the stakeholders informed to the degree necessary as specified in the stakeholder analysis. However, the indirect purpose is to "take the pulse" of the stakeholders in regard to their opinion and concern over project direction, progress, risks, and other issues. This is illustrated in Figure 13.4.

In general, communications involves sending a message between a sender and a receiver over a particular medium in a mode with certain parameters (such as frequency). This is illustrated in Figure 13.5. Proper communications involves choosing the correct media, mode, and parameters for a given message to a given receiver.

The sender is responsible for making the message clear, unambiguous, and complete. The receiver is responsible for making sure that the message is received in its entirety, and that the message is completely understood. The message is encoded by the sender and decoded by the receiver. The encoding/decoding is done by each party based on their:

- Language (and dialect)
- Culture
- Units of measure (currency, size, weight, volume, time, etc.)
- Discipline
- Education and industry area
- Experience

Figure 13.4. PM and stakeholder communications

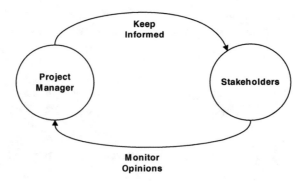

Figure 13.5. Communications

If there is significant mismatch between the sender and receiver in any of these areas *then the message may not be fully understood.* Earlier in this book we discussed the formal project management discipline and the formal software engineering discipline. However, much of project communication to stakeholders will involve individuals who are not familiar with formal project management or software engineering terms or acronyms. Terms like *critical path* should be replaced with phrases like *high-priority tasks.* Other common project management terms to rephrase to stakeholders may include *Gantt chart, earned value variances and indexes, dependency, slack, float, WBS,* etc.

The media (channel) may be:

- Spoken (voice/personal, phone, voice-mail, video conferencing)—one-on-one or group
- Written (paper, e-mail, fax, shared media)

and the mode may be:

- Listening or speaking
- Formal or informal
- Internal or external
- Vertical or peer-to-peer

Various types of written reports that are distributed also make up a significant portion of project communication; these would include:

- Status reports (see a later chapter for performance reporting)
- Assignments and direction
- General correspondence
- Topic specific memos
- Meeting notes
- Technical (designs, specifications, drawings, charts, test results, etc.)

Today many of these are transmitted via e-mail. However, spoken communication is still heavily relied upon for many stakeholders in many projects. A significant portion (about one half) of all spoken communication is effected via nonverbal modes such as physical mannerisms (body and face language) and paralingual (tone and pitch of one's voice). Effective listening involves watching the speaker for these nonverbal messages and using active listening and feedback. In active listening, the receiver confirms that he has received the message and asks a question to confirm that he understood the entire message. Feedback means that the sender requests acknowledgment from the receiver to confirm that he or she has indeed understood the entire message. *These communication techniques are very important when there is significant sender/receiver mismatch. For modern IT projects, there can be significant mismatch for global projects and/or for where any outsourcing is involved particularly, offshore outsourcing.*

Sender/receiver mismatch is one form of communication obstacles, and a list of such obstacles includes:

- Sender/receiver mismatch
- Distance (in space or time)
- Noise (channel is not clear or "cluttered")
- Hostility and other detrimental attitudes
- Lack of openness to hear ideas of others

A key task of the PM in is to work with his team and other stakeholders to specifically remove any such obstacles or to mitigate the impact of their presence. In this regard, the PM should:

- Avoid the aforementioned communication blockers/obstacles
- Have a proactive communications style
- Be a communications expeditor
- Make sure communications is following plan (discussed later in this chapter)
- Insure communications integrity through active listening and feedback
- Use a project war room (either physically or virtually)
- Make meetings effective (discussed later in this chapter)

For all communication, both written and spoken, a PM should keep documentation thereof. The PM has several reasons to maintain such *project documentation,* including the need to be able to reconstruct why certain decisions were made (including who said what)—"CYA"—and for historical value (lessons learned, settling disputes, etc.).

A *communications plan* involves determining the information reporting needs and other communication needs of stakeholders—*who, what, how,* and *when:*

- *Who* needs *what* type of information
        Content
        Format
- *How* is the information to be distribution
- *When*

Frequency (weekly, monthly, etc.)

Timing (specific day of week, or day of month)

The project communication plan should be formal written proactive plan that details the aforementioned aspects; that plan is used with or combined with the stakeholder analysis described at the start of this chapter. The communication plan should also cover

- Meetings (regular/special, when/where, how, notes, note-taker, etc.)
- Communication channels including phone numbers, e-mail addresses, and perhaps physical offices addresses (for all team members and stakeholders)
- Organizational structures and reporting relations
- Problem escalation procedures

Meetings represent a significant expense to a project, since the time of many expensive people are being consumed on indirect work activities. However some meetings are necessary to a project for team building, group decisions and group consensus, problem solving, and conflict resolution. In a PMI survey of PMs (PMI, 2000):

- Average meetings were six per week
- An average of 25% of meeting time was on nonproductive issues
- Causes of meeting time wastage: meeting not properly planned, inept leadership, undisciplined participants

A PM may have many different types of meetings with the project team or with other stakeholders; however, many PMs still try to manage via meetings, and many meetings are neither efficient nor an effective use of people's time. When meetings are used, only the people who need to be at a meeting should attend and only the necessary topics should be covered. Many project issues and much project communication (such as status) can be reported without having meetings. In this book, a dual gating process for project performance monitoring has been suggested. This approach not only provides for the exposure and analysis of both project completion and satisfaction success criteria, but minimizes the time of key individuals in meetings. This is illustrated in Figure 13.6, where upper management and the development team are relatively isolated from regular meetings.

A set of meeting guidelines such as the following should be included in the project communication plan:

- Set a meeting policy for regular and ad hoc meetings
- Have a meeting only when they are really necessary and consistent with the meeting policy

Figure 13.6. Dual stage gates and stakeholder involvement

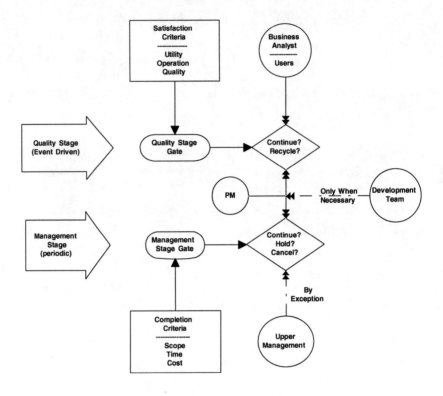

- Cancel any regularly scheduled meeting when there is little to discuss
- Establish a clear meeting purpose and prepare an agenda
- Check with team and possible other stakeholders on items for the agenda
- Carefully select participants; include everyone that should be there but be careful about inviting others
- Send participants a copy of the agenda in advance
- Prioritize agenda items in case of time overflow
- Follow agenda, encourage participation but control the flow of the meeting, include a team-building segment
- Take and file meeting notes
- Promptly distribute notes
- Identify and follow up on action items

There is software available to aid in the scheduling of meetings, including the display of all the participant's schedules to find open time/place slots. Today meetings may be virtual instead of physical, and there is much software available to facilitate virtual meetings both the synchronous and the asynchronous types.

Project communication may be spoken or written (paper or electronic), and it may be formal or informal. Generally, one of these four combinations is most appropriate for certain situations, and this may simply be part of an organization's culture or it may be made a formal part of the project communication plan.

Figure 13.7 is an example of such a formalization.

Also the communication may involve stakeholders at the same place or different places and the communication may be at the same time (synchronous) or at different times (asynchronous). This is illustrated in Figure 13.8.

Typical modern communication modes and media for each of these four cases would be

- *Same Place—Same Time:* Traditional meetings and in-person conversations
- *Different Place—Same Time:* Synchronous modes such as conference calls, video conference, instant messaging, groupware, and chat rooms

Figure 13.7. Appropriate type of communications

Method	When Appropriate
Formal Written	Project charter, project plans, performance reports, communications where "obstacles" are involved, discussions of complex problems
Formal Verbal	Project kick-off meting, presentations, speeches
Informal Written	Memos and e-mail
Informal Verbal	Conversations and meetings

Figure 13.8. Place and time of communications

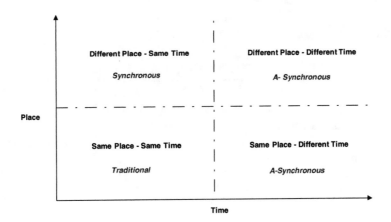

- *Same Place—Different Time:* Asynchronous local modes as rotating files, Post-it notes, e-mail, online forums
- *Different Place—Different Time:* Asynchronous distance modes as e-mail and on-line forums

The project communications plan should also specifies the details for these four cases. There are a number of software tools available to facilitate most of these communication tasks, places and times. These include:

- Office productivity suites (word processing, spreadsheet, and presentation software)
- Project management software (discussed later in this book)
- E-mail and instant messaging
- Internet and Intranet
- Virtual meetings, chat, forums, blogs, bulletin boards
- Groupware
- Imaging systems
- Design distribution and exchange (UML, CAD, etc.)
- Document routing and management systems
- Report generation software
- Standard formatting and info exchange software (XML, HTML, VRML, etc.)

Another aspect of the formal communications plan is definitive procedures for problem escalation. Without such defined procedures, the PM may be questioned in regard to the timeliness of bringing certain types of information to the attention of higher management. Those escalation procedures specify how much time each organizational component (project team member, project manager, line manager, etc.) should wait trying to contact someone else for problem solution and how much time to wait without resolution before escalating a problem to the next level.

Organizational Context

In examining stakeholder management for internal stakeholders, the organizational context of project management needs to be discussed; that is, how does a PM fit into the organization's overall management structure. The manner in which a PM manages and controls his or her project depends somewhat on this overall organization structure. In regard to the management of projects, there are several types and subtypes of organizational structures:

Figure 13.9. Problem escalation plan

Type of Problem	Project Team Member		Project Manager	
	Wait Time	Escalation Time	Wait Time	Escalation Time
...	...	...	...	...

- Functional
- "Project expeditor"
- "Project coordinator"
- Projectized
- Matrix
- Weak
- Strong
- Balanced

The functional organization is the traditional structure and the most common way to organize a company. Advantages of this structure are that their organization is well understood and has a rigid chain of command, each employee reports to only one manager, and it is easier to manage specialists. Figure 13.10 depicts this traditional functional organization.

The disadvantages of this traditional organization in regard to project management are that employees place more emphasis on their functional specialty than on the project and

Figure 13.10. Traditional functional organization

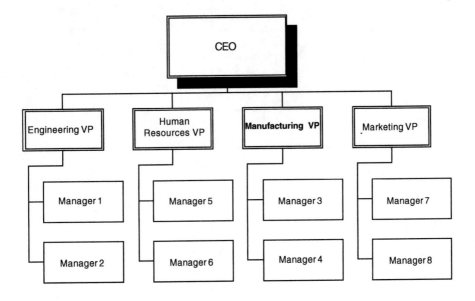

there is no explicit career path in project management. Here the PM role is weak (particularly if the project team is not all in one division/department), and the PM has to go to the functional manger to make and enforce decisions.

In functional organizations, sometimes there is a project expediter who typically reports to a functional manager (as a staff assistant) in the division/department that sponsors or is primarily affected by the project. This expediter has little power and typically only maintains the project schedule, status, and budget/costs; he or she cannot personally make or enforce decisions, and his or her main role is in the area of communications. Figure 13.11 illustrates the expediter role.

Instead of a project expediter, a functional organization sometimes uses project coordinators. The coordinator typically reports to someone high up in the organization, perhaps even to the CEO or in IT the CIO. Here the PM has more power than the project expeditor, including some power to make limited decisions (limited by scope, impact, costs, etc.). Figure 13.12 depicts this project coordinator.

At the opposite end of the extreme is the projectized organization. Here the project manager has full authority over project personnel. Advantages are that a PM has full control and it is efficient for project execution, employees have loyalty to the project, and project communication is direct and efficient. Disadvantages are that of a weak functional structure (may have lack of professionalism in disciplines), employees have no home when project is completed, and there may be a less efficient use of resources. Projectized

Figure 13.11. Project expediter

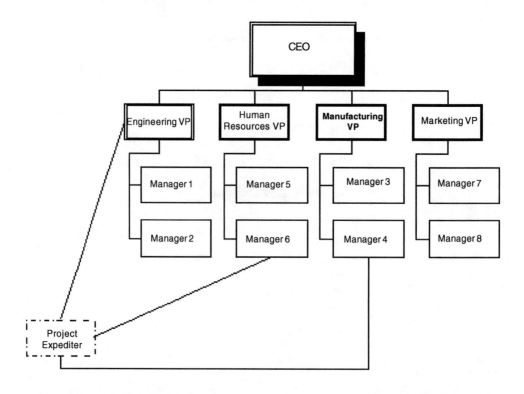

Figure 13.12. Project coordinator

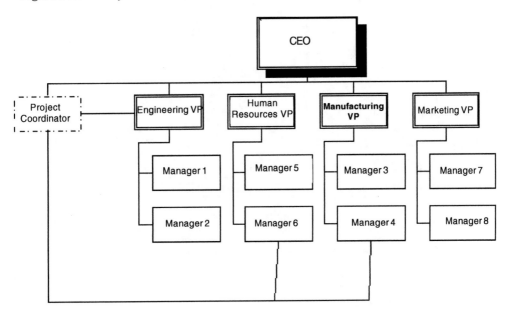

organizations are more common in professional services firms such as architectural and engineering companies. Figure 13.13 illustrates this type of organization.

Matrix organizations represent a compromise between functional and projectized organizations. Figure 13.14 shows the matrix organization. There are three subtypes of matrix organizations:

- *Strong:* Balance of power rests with project manager
- *Weak:* Balance of power rests with functional manager (here a project expeditor or coordinator my be common)
- *Balanced:* Power is balanced between functional and project manager

The commonly used term *tight matrix* has nothing to do with a matrix organization per se; it simply means colocating the project team members.

The *advantages* of a matrix organization are:

- The project objectives are very clear
- The PM has better control over resources
- More support from functional organizations
- Better utilization of human resources

Figure 13.13. Projectized organization

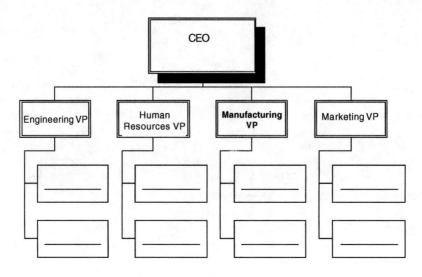

Figure 13.14. Matrix organization

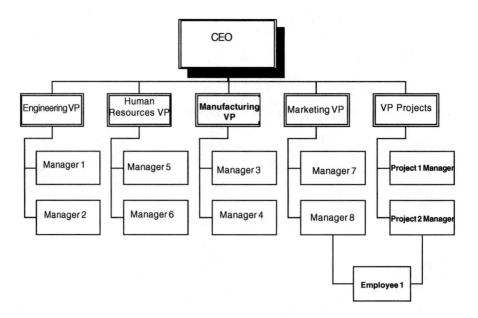

- Better coordination of project tasks
- Better horizontal and vertical information flow than functional
- Employees maintain a home

The *disadvantages* of the matrix organization are:

- Less cost effective because of extra administrative personnel
- More than one boss for project teams
- More complex to administer
- Possibly more and bigger resource allocation problems
- More detailed policies and procedures needed
- Functional managers may have different priorities than project managers
- Higher potential for duplication of effort and resulting conflict

Human Resource Management

Human resource management is the term used by PMI for a group of processes primarily concerned with the interpersonal interaction of internal stakeholders. In the PMBOK the specific processes are (PMI, 2000):

- Organizational planning
- Staff acquisition
- Team development

These processes involve methods for managing the human aspects of a project. Poor human resource management is often the cause of project failures. Common human resource (HR) project problems include:

- Upper management meddling
- Lack of upper management support
- Project estimated before appointment of PM (usually manifested in unrealistic time/ cost estimates)
- Project manager micro management
- Poor mix of project team members (too little or too much of certain skills, too little diversity, conflicting egos, immaturity, etc.)
- Lack of proper project staff motivation

A key part of proper HR management is to clarify and communicate the roles of different management components in an organization. These will vary somewhat depending on the organizational context. Generally, it is upper management's responsibility to approve a project business plan and charter, select and empower the PM, protect the project from adversarial stakeholders and other distractions, and approve the project schedule and cost plan (and significant changes thereto). It is the PMs responsibility to plan, estimate, and schedule a project. A PM should not be handed a project with the estimates and schedule already prepared; both the PM and project team need to buy-into these aspects of a project. It is the project team's responsibility to help plan (WBS, network diagram, estimates) the project and to carry out the work.

The PM has the main responsibility to assemble the project team and get the right mix of people for the project. The proper mix of people will include those who:

- Understand the project management process
- Understand the business justification for the project (business analysts)
- Understand the chosen software engineering methodology (software architects)
- Understand the details involved in constructing and delivering the product (system designers)
- Understand the customer and end users and their needs and wants (subject-matter experts)
- Understand the meaning of quality relative to this type of project and product
- Are specialists in regard to the technology that is to be embedded in the product or used on the project (technical experts)
- Can think outside the box and inject new ideas

If possible within the constraints of getting the correct skill mix from a technical perspective, it is usually helpful to get a mixture of people from differing perspectives, including:

- Left (analytical) brain versus right (intuitive) brain thinkers
- Adapters versus innovators
- Customer focused versus developer focused
- Insiders versus outsiders
- Shared (multiproject) versus dedicated (only this project)

"The riskier the project, the more diversity you need in the team. IT ends to attract similar types of people, and that's something you need to counteract." (Melymuka, 2004)

In an IT organization, the CIO and the HR department will typically work together to define and classify IT personnel into categories for the purposes of skill identification, experience levels, and salary ranges (for project cost estimation). This was discussed earlier in this book in regard to the development of a project's cost plan (budget). A PM needs to verify this classification and rate structure for use in his project. Typical IT categories may include:

- Project manager
- Subject matter expert
- Business analysis
- System architect
- Requirements analyst
- System analyst
- Programmer
- Technical writer
- Database analyst
- Webmaster
- Communications analyst
- Network administrator
- Testing specialist
- Security specialist
- Computer operator

Usually there are three or more expertise/experience levels within each of these categories. For each category and level there is usually a salary range. For project labor estimation purposes, the midpoint of these salary ranges is usually used. At one or more points in the project, specific employees are assigned to the project based upon availability and the necessary category type(s) for each WBS task. In assigning these specific human resources, the PM should consider a number of factors, including:

- Previous experience, including education and training (ability to do the job)
- Personal interests in and aptitude for the job
- Personal characteristics (e.g., do they work well in a team environment for this type of project)
- Availability within the time frames needed

To assist in this evaluation and selection process, the HR department or the IT department may maintain a skills-inventory database. In such a database, the skills for each employee are itemized along with the experience level (perhaps in months) for each skill either just for this company or for the employee's entire career. Some organizations maintain such a skill inventory database for not only employees but also for job applicants and contractors as well. An assessment matrix can be used where available personnel are mapped to needed job categories; this is illustrated in Figure 13.15, which shows months of experience in each category. This also helps identify any needed staff development, and it is important to define such training needs early so that they can be included in the schedule and cost plan.

A PM should assign all tasks and all team members without ambiguity or redundancy and in such a manner that follows the project WBS and detailed scope definition. One must be careful of the Halo effect (e.g., a great programmer will make a great system architect) when assigning staff. A formal HR plan can be documented to show the people that may be or will be a part of the project team. A sample simple HR plan form is shown in Figure 13.16.

There are several other types of forms and charts that are often used in this process:

- *Responsibility Assignment Matrix:* Relates tasks to people
- *Resource Histogram:* Shows resource utilization in time
- *Resource Gantt Chart:* Shows when staff is assigned

A responsibility assignment matrix is illustrated in Figure 13.17. The cells may show one or more types of information regarding the assignments:

- Primary versus Secondary (P = primary, S = secondary)
- % of time allocated to this task
- Role (P = participant, I = input required, R = review required, S = sign-off required, A = accountable)

Figure 13.18 illustrates a resource histogram which shows the hours scheduled for either a single resource or a single resource type by time period throughout the project.

Figure 13.19 illustrates a resource Gantt chart that shows the scheduled time periods for resources on the project. A resource Gantt chart can also be made for all resources on all projects; such a chart is used for resource allocation across projects and also resource leveling.

Figure 13.15. Skill assessment

Skill	Ed	Jane	Mary	Tom	Bill	Larry	Sue	Marge
Analyst	3		42			15		6
Sft. Designer	3		12			30	12	
Programmer				12		12		
Tech Writer		12			20			
Database						12	24	
UI Designer					12			6
Sys. Architect	3					6		
Tester		12			24			

Figure 13.16. Project HR plan

Project HR Plan

Project Code:_____   **Date:**_____

         Project Name:_____

         Befitting Organization:_____

         Performing Organization:_____

         Project Manager:_____

         HR Manager:_____

Human Resources:

Person	Code	Role/Resp	Burdened Rate	% Alloc to Proj	Training

1. _____
2. _____
3. _____
4. _____
5. _____
N. _____

Recruiting Needs:_____

_____

Team Building:_____

_____

Consulting:_____

_____

Contracting:_____

_____

Notes: _____

_____

Approvals

Benefiting Organization   **Performing Organization**

By:_____   **By:**_____

Date:_____   **Date:**_____

Figure 13.17. Resource assignment matrix

TASK	TEAM MEMBER			
	Jane	Tom	Bill	Mary
Task 1	P		S	
Task 2		P		
Task 3	S			P
Task 4			P	S

Figure 13.18. Resource utilization

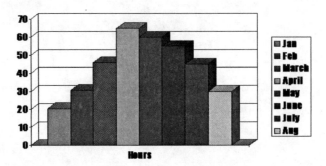

Figure 13.19. Resource Gantt chart

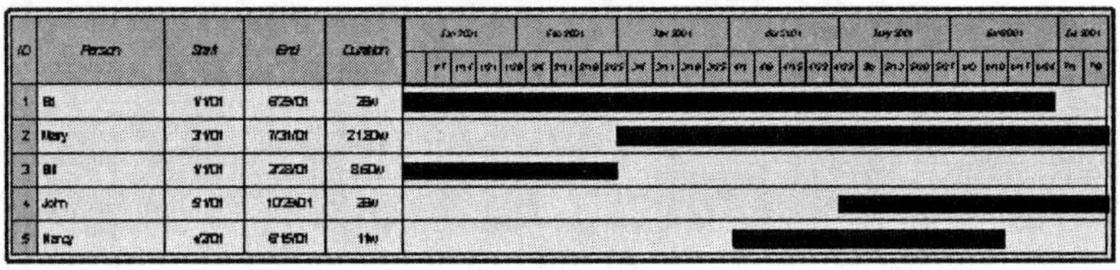

The Software Engineering Institute (SEI; www.sei.cmu.edu/cmm-p/) also has a "people" capability maturity model. Like their other maturity models, five levels of maturity are defined, and each of these levels has key processes defined:

1. *Initial.*
2. *Repeatable.* The key process areas at Level 2 focus on instilling basic discipline into workforce activities. They are:
   - Work environment
   - Communication
   - Staffing
   - Performance management
   - Training
   - Compensation
3. *Defined.* The key process areas at Level 3 address issues surrounding the identification of the organization's primary competencies and aligning its people management activities with them. They are:
   - Knowledge and skills analysis
   - Workforce planning

- Competency development
- Career development
- Competency-based practices
- Participatory culture

4. *Managed.* The key process areas at Level 4 focus on quantitatively managing organizational growth in people management capabilities and in establishing competency-based teams. They are:

- Mentoring
- Team building
- Team-based practices
- Organizational competency management
- Organizational performance alignment

5. *Optimizing.* The key process areas at Level 5 cover the issues that address continuous improvement of methods for developing competency, at both the organizational and the individual level. They are:

- Personal competency development
- Coaching
- Continuous workforce innovation

As discussed earlier in this book, security aspects should not be ignored in HR planning, and procedures such as background checks for all personnel (employees, contractors, consultants, etc.) involved with a project are becoming more appropriate. It is no longer sufficient simply to secure the perimeter physically and logically, but active security procedures need to be implemented for those objects already inside of the perimeter. Figure 13.20 shows the types of issues that should be addressed in a simple project security plan.

Managing the Project Team

In general, a manager *may* play many roles. There are interpersonal roles such as figurehead, leader, liaison, coach, motivator; informational roles including monitor, disseminator, spokesman, reporter; and decisional roles such as conflict resolver, entrepreneur, distance handler, resource allocator, negotiator, and facilitator. A project manager, however, *must* play most of these roles, as project management is a more comprehensive and perhaps more difficult type of management position. Like a line manager, a project manager must deal with direct reports and must motivate these individuals to do their best for the project, but like an upper manager, many and diverse stakeholders (as defined earlier) are involved, and each of these stakeholders have different interest in the success or failure of the project. In addition most projects will

Figure 13.20. Project security plan

```
                    Project Security Plan

Personnel (employees, vendors, contractors, users ...)
     Work History Verification
     Background/Criminal Check
     Credit History Check
     Security Training
     Security Clearance
Access Control
     Log On (User Name & PW)
     Access Privileges
     Encryption
     Access Logs
     Review of Access Logs
Backup
     Incremental
     Full
     Recovery Testing
Physical
     Buildings
     Work Areas
     Central IT Facilities (servers, hubs, routers, firewalls ...)
Software
     Code Security Walkthrough
     Trojan/Backdoor Scans
     Intrusion Prevention Software
     Code Randomization
     Intrusion Testing (Access, Session, Cookie, Buffer, XSS, Post/Get, ...)
     Change Security Review
```

bring about changes, which always introduces apprehensive and uncertainty into the job situation.

The key responsibilities (i.e., things that a project manager must possess or do) are:

- Be honest and ethical
- Motivate staff and team
- Understand deliverables and quality in regard to the deliverables
- Be sensitive to organizational values and politics
- Assign meaningful tasks for each employee
- Provide something "to look forward to" for each employee
- Shared goals (employee/supervisor & employee/organization)
- Delegate; generally, give direction, not directions (depends somewhat on performance, capabilities, maturity)
- Be a facilitator
- Be an example
- Be accessible and visible, then listen

- Look after the welfare of employees
- Be fair but firm
- Provide equal treatment for all employees

Conversely, an employee's responsibilities to his or her manager are:

- Honesty about your capabilities, desires, and opinions; about work status; about asking for help when you need it
- Cooperation/loyalty as team member, commitment to coworkers
- 100 % effort, commitment to work, team, and organization
- Keep superiors informed: *Remember, bosses hate surprises!*

A project manager must foster and encourage the above traits in his or her employees. Managers and supervisors are charged with activities like planning, budgeting, organizing, staff assignment, and control (taking corrective action). Leaders also assume activities such as projecting a vision, setting direction, inspiring teamwork, aligning employees and business units, motivating, and supporting. Project managers should be both.

Projects bring about change, thus it is important that a PM create and communicate a clear and important vision to his or her team. Thorns and Kerwin (2004) define *vision* as follows:

A vision is a cognitive image of an organization or project team that is positive enough to followers to provide motivation and elaborative enough to provide direction for planning and goal setting.

A vision and the goals derived from it should be challenging yet obtainable, and somewhat idealistic. PMs should show optimism about the project goals and have a positive attitude. Projecting the vision to the team and organization in a very positive manner is somewhat akin to being a visionary; being such a visionary is a key trait of an effective leader.

There are many theories of leadership; and leadership and management needs and styles vary somewhat by industry and discipline. For IT, leadership theories that deal with professional types of organizations and people are more applicable. The Situational Leadership Model (Hersey, 1977) is quite applicable for IT projects. It deals with the type of management style that may be most appropriate for different types of individuals depending upon their experience/capabilities versus their self motivation/initiative.

In this theory, management style is represented in two dimensions. The first dimension is directive (management) or task-oriented behavior, and the second dimension is supportive (leadership) or relationship-oriented behavior:

- *Directive (management):* Structure, Control, Supervision
- *Supportive (leadership):* Listen, Praise, Empower, Facilitate

This is illustrated in Figure 13.21. There are four quadrants representing four types of management style:

- *Directing:* High directive and low supportive
- *Coaching:* High directive and high supportive
- *Supporting:* High supportive and low directive
- *Delegating:* Low supportive and low directive

In addition to the four types of management styles there are five levels of employees:

- L0 - Low competence and low initiative
- L1 - Low competence and high initiative
- L2 - Some competence and low initiative
- L3 - High competence and some initiative
- L4 - High competence and high initiative

Competence in this instance means task-relevant knowledge, skills, and experience. *Initiative* means self-motivation and confidence. There is a natural evolutionary path for most professionals:

Figure 13.21. Management styles

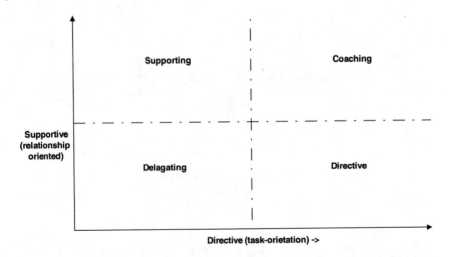

L1 -> L2

New employee is L1 (full of enthusiasm but with little job-specific knowledge). After a while, the employee realizes that there is a still a lot to learn therefore, his or her competence goes up while initiative goes down

L2 -> L3

Employee knows most things needed in job, and some initiative is restored

L3 -> L4

Employee fully knows job and thus has high initiative

For best results, managers needs to match their management style to the employee's level of development:

- L0 -> Reassign, transfer, or terminate
- L1 -> Direct
- L2 -> Coach
- L3-> Support
- L4 -> Delegate

Thus, for employees with low competence and low initiative, a project manager should avoid having any such people on the team. For employees with low competence and high initiative, a project manager should use a directing style. For employees with some competence and low initiative, a project manager should use a coaching style. For employees with high competence and some initiative, a project manager should use the supporting style. For employees with high competence and high initiative, a project manager should use the delegating style (stay out of their way).

The ability to delegation is often a problem for managers, particularly managers in professional occupations (like IT) and particularly for managers who have come up through the technical ranks. Most managers who do not delegate well are really afraid of losing control. These managers need to ask themselves, "What have I got to lose by delegation?" and then find ways to mitigate such potential losses. Such mitigation techniques include:

- Giving clear direction
- Monitor progress in a quantitative manner
- Building milestones into schedules
- Providing explanations and assistance if and when needed
- Monitoring team attitudes such as via quality stage gates

In contrast, they can ask themselves: "What have I got to gain?" and the answer to this question is typically a list of valuable items. Specific delegation techniques include:

- Delegate outcomes with the tasks
- Do not give team members ill-defined or unsolvable tasks
- Delegate only to people you trust (or should trust)
- Clearly point out to team members the consequences of this assignment to the organization and to them
- Delegate small tasks at first, the add more tasks as the first are handled well
- Have a reporting system so that you catch little problems before they become big problems (i.e., quality and management stage gates with earned value systems which are discussed later in this book)
- Ask the team member to develop the estimates and milestones (even if you may know what they should be, to obtain buy-in form that team member)
- Do not delegate tasks that should be automated
- Do not delegate tasks that only you can do

PMs sometimes have some degree of difficulty in getting people to perform and cooperate, particularly in a matrix-type setup. Organizational power types were discussed earlier, including position (and its subtypes: reward, penalty, referent), political, resource, and expert. In a functional or matrix organization, the PMs must rely on powers other than formal position power. The most effective forms of power for a PM are typically expert and reward; less effective is penalty and referent. Formal, reward, and penalty are powers derived mainly from position; expert power is earned. *True leadership is not based on position, but being able to motivate people in other ways. If you have to use formal power to tell your staff you are the leader, you're not!*

Motivation is an internal drive that initiates and sustains activity toward specific goals. An effective manager and leader must know how to motivate others, especially PMs with little formal power. An employee, even if fully capable, will not reach full (or perhaps even adequate) performance without motivation. Motivation may be derived from external sources (extrinsic) or from internal sources (intrinsic). Internal motivation is derived from the satisfaction of either doing or completing a task/activity. External motivation comes from a reward system based upon successful completion of a task/activity. Our hobbies and leisure activities generally involve internal motivation. Our employment activities generally involve external motivation, but for some there may also be much internal motivation (you really like your job).

Henry Gantt (1861-1919), who developed the Gantt chart, focused on motivational schemes, emphasizing rewards for good work (rather than penalties for poor work). He developed a number of such systems including incentive pay systems for groups and bonus systems for individuals. In management science, there are a number of motivation theories; the most applicable for professional work as IT are:

- Maslow's theory (hierarchy of needs)
- McGregor's theory (X and Y types)
- Herzberg's theory (hygiene and motivating agents)
- Expectancy theory
- Equity theory

In Maslow's theory, people are motivated based upon their level in a hierarchy of needs (from lowest to highest):

- *Physiological:* Air, water, food, shelter, clothing
- *Safety:* Security and freedom from harm
- *Social:* Love, approval, friends, association
- *Esteem:* Accomplishment, respect, attention, appreciation
- *Self-Actualization:* Self fulfillment, growth, learning

If one is satisfied with one level, then they will be motivated to get to the next level; and until satisfied with one level, they will not care about the next level

McGregor's theory state that all workers fall into one of two categories:

- *Theory X:* These workers need to be closely supervised; they are incapable, avoid responsibility, and avoid working whenever possible ["No" (X) people]
- *Theory Y:* These people are wiling to work without supervision and want to achieve ["Yes" people]

In my experience for IT projects:

- One third of people fall into category X
- One third of people fall into category Y
- One third of people's motivation can be significantly influenced by their management

Herzberg's theory defines poor hygiene factors that reduce motivation and good hygiene factors that foster motivation. To maintain motivation, poor hygiene factors need to meet adequate levels, but improving them further will not necessarily improve motivation. Adequate levels may be subjective, but are usually industry standard levels. These poor hygiene factors are:

- Working conditions
- Salary
- Personal life
- Relationships at work
- Security
- Status

The good hygiene factors or motivating agents involve the work itself for professional-type employees as:

- Responsibility
- Self-actualization
- Professional growth
- Recognition

Under expectancy theory, employees who believe their work efforts will lead to good performance and who expect to be rewarded for their accomplishments, remain productive as rewards meet their expectations. With equity theory, employees must believe that they are being treated in a similar manner to other employees; otherwise they will lose their motivation.

To adequately motivate IT project team members, I believe that a combination of methods that consider each of the major theories is best:

- Adequate (industry standard) working conditions, salary, benefits, security, and so forth
- Equity between employees
- Interesting and challenging assignments
- Delegation of responsibility
- Rewards (financial, position, office location, other perks) based upon performance
- Public recognition and praise (praise in public, criticize in private)
- Staff development (i.e., training)
- Other "team-building" methods

Team building is included in the list, and one of the responsibilities of the PM is to encourage and facilitate the involvement and contribution of all the stakeholders in the project and for each to feel a part of the team. Team building requires a deliberate and continuous effort on the part of the PM. There are many management theories concerning team building; a prominent one is the Tuckman model, which describes the phases of team development as Forming, Storming, Norming, and Performing (Tuckman, 1965). Tuckman's model explains that as the team forms and becomes more adapt at the tasks, relationships develop and solidify. The team leader also changes leadership style beginning with a directing style, moving through coaching, then supporting, and finally delegating, as was described earlier in this chapter. Whenever diverse people are brought together in a team, some time is necessary for them to evolve from a group of individuals into a team.

Figure 13.22 illustrates the differences between a group and a real team. Team-building activities facilitate and expedite team "forming and storming," and these activities should start very early and proceed throughout the entire project. Specific opportunities for team building include:

- Kick-off meeting
- Requirements review
- WBS specification
- Overall design review
- Prototype review
- Communication of status via stage gate meetings
- Staff development (project team training and end user training)
- Testing review

Tight organizations involving some colocation also foster team building such as a war room. This war room need not be physical, but may be a virtual meeting place via synchronous electronic communication.

Some conflict is unavoidable in any effort among many people (such as a project) due to the number and differing agendas and priorities of all the stakeholders. The limited authority of the PM and his need to compete for scarce resources (budgets and people) in the organization also leads to conflict. The classical view was that conflict is bad and that it happens in a dysfunctional group without good leadership. But the modern view is that conflict is inherent in teams and organizations and that conflict can be helpful to explore more solution alternatives. Another older view was that conflict could be resolved by separating the conflicting parties or by going up the management chain. But separation or upper management involvement is at best only a temporary solution. The

Figure 13.22. Groups vs. teams

Characteristics of a "Group"	Characteristics of a "Team"
Individual performers	Common goals
Responsibilities may drift	Task based structure
Mostly "organizational" meetings	Mostly progress or problem resolution meetings
Individual egos	Collective ego
Members have other more important duties	This is a major activity for each
Relative isolation	Much connection (either physically or electronic)

modern view is that conflict is best resolved through identification of the root causes and by problem solving discussions of the parties involved.

The main sources of conflict on a project in order of frequency are (PMI, 2000) as follows:

- Schedules
- Priorities
- Resources
- Technical opinions
- Administrative procedures
- Cost
- Personalities

Many people think that personality differences would be a major conflict source, and in some situations this may be still be true, but professional employees tend to put aside personality differences (or hide them) so that they can effectively negotiate their interests in terms of schedules, priorities, resources, and so forth. There are some management techniques that the PM can employ to avoid or at least minimize conflicts:

- Keep the team and other stakeholders informed:
  - Project goals and objectives
  - Schedule and cost
  - Assignments (task and times)
  - Changes (schedule, scope, assignments, etc.)
  - Other key project decisions
  - Assigning tasks fairly and clearly (who, what, when)
  - Design tasks to be relevant, interesting, doable yet challenging
  - Monitoring team attitudes such as via quality stage gates

The main techniques for formal conflict resolution are:

- *Compromising:* Identifying an acceptable solution that gives all the parties some degree of satisfaction
- *Withdrawal:* Postponing a solution decision until a later point in the project
- *Smoothing:* Focusing on the things the parties agree on and avoiding dealing with the other issues for the present
- *Forcing:* Mandating one proposed solution over the other
- *Structured Problem Solving:* Identifying root causes then solving the real problem

Withdrawal and smoothing are effective when a solution to the problem is not needed until later in the project—perhaps by then more information may be available, the issue may be less important, or the conflicting parties may have resolved it amongst themselves—but when a decision is needed immediately, many PMs and/or line managers result to forcing. However, forcing is not nearly as effective as structured problem solving in the long run. Smoothing is also more effective in the long term when structured problem solving cannot be used due to time, distance, or other constraints. In regard to conflict resolution and other decision making, there may be additional constraints imposed upon the PM in some organizations due to organizational structure, union agreements, quotas and regulations, and industry or government codes and standards.

Chapter Summary

In this chapter, the human aspects of project management were covered, including stakeholder management, project communications, and human-resource management. These plans are all highly interrelated, and also related to the project risk and security plans (which was also discussed in this chapter). According to Baker and Baker's (1998) 12 golden rules of project management:

1.   "Thou shalt gain consensus on project outcomes.

2.   Thou shalt build the best team you can.

3.   Thou shalt develop a comprehensive, viable plan and keep it up-to-date.

4.   Thou shalt determine how much stuff you really need to get things done.

5.   Thou shalt develop a realistic schedule.

6.   Thou shalt not try to do more than can be done.

7.   Thou shalt remember that people count.

8.   Thou shalt gain the formal and ongoing support of management and stakeholders.

9.   Thou shalt be willing to change.

10. Thou shalt keep people informed of what you're doing.

11. Thou shalt be willing to try new things.

12. Thou shalt be a leader as well as a manager."

References

Baker, S., & Baker, K. (1998). *The complete idiot's guide to project management*. Indianapolis, IN: Alpha Books.

Cleland, D. (1998). Stakeholder management. In J. Pinto (Ed.), *Project management handbook*. New York: Jossey-Bass.

Hersey, P., & Blanchard, K. (1977). *The management of organizational behavior*. Upper Saddle River, NJ: Prentice Hall.

Melymuka, K. (2004, April 12). How to pick a project team. *Computerworld*.

PMI. (2000). *The project management body of knowledge (PMBOK)*. Newton Square, PA. ISBN 1-880410-22-2.

Thorns, P., & Kerwin, J. (2004). Leadership of project teams. In P. Morris & J. Pinto (Eds.), *The Wiley guide to managing projects*. New York: Wiley.

Tuckman, B. (1965). Developmental sequence in small groups. *Psychological Bulletin, 63,* 384-399.

Winch, G. (2004). Managing project stakeholders. In P. Morris & J. Pinto (Eds.), *The Wiley guide to managing projects*. New York: Wiley.

Chapter XIV

Performance Reporting and Earned Value Analysis

Never mistake motion for action.

(Ernest Hemingway)

A PM must report on the project's performance to the upper management of the performing organization and perhaps also to the benefiting organization. Upper management usually realizes the complexity and rapid dynamics of IT projects, however, it still needs accurate projections of project completion time and cost so that interdependent business activities, including product release/migration can be planned. Traditional methods of progress-performance reporting are often inaccurate and misleading. Earned value analysis (EVA) has proven to be an extremely effective tool for project time and cost management providing good estimates of actual project completion cost and date. EVA is also is a good early indicator of project problem areas, so that appropriate corrective action can be initiated. The effective use of earned value in IT projects, however, is still low, particularly outside of the U.S. government and its contractors.

The application of EVA in IT projects is neither trivial nor straightforward because earned value requires careful planning and reporting in regard to work-packet specification, progress measurements, and actual cost determination. In addition, mechanisms to obtain all this information must be integrated into the organization's project management, software engineering methodology, and financial reporting systems. This chapter discusses and illustrates effective ways to integrate EVA into an organization's methodology and financial systems, and also presents specific techniques to deal with associated EVA complexities.

Traditional Performance Reporting

A PM needs to track and review progress and cost, but should not intervene directly unless there are problems. When there *are* problems, early intervention is more effective than delaying corrective actions; thus the PM needs methods and systems that not only accurately and efficiently track cost and progress but that also highlight problems and pinpoint the trouble spots. The problem is that traditional project progress reporting is neither accurate nor effective in the early identification of problems, nor in projecting cost or time to complete.

For illustrating traditional reporting problems and the merits of EVA, I will use a simple yet effective example from previously published works (Brandon 1998, 1999). An earlier chapter discussed the formation of the WBS for a project; and that formulation involves subdividing the work to be done into tasks, or work packets, which are organized into a logical pattern.

For this example, the WBS consists of Level 0 and Level 1, shown graphically in Figure 14.1 for Level 0, and for both levels in the list format of Figure 14.2. As discussed in an earlier chapter, the top level of the WBS is sometimes called Level 1, but in IT, the top level is usually numbered Level 0.

As discussed in an earlier chapter, in IT the work definition is usually based on the organization's software development methodology. Any type of methodology can be used (waterfall, overlapping waterfall, spiral, iterative, incremental, etc.), but this example uses use a classical waterfall methodology. Iterative and incremental methodologies can be more difficult to schedule and employ EVA because one does not know in advance how many increments or iterations may be necessary. However, a schedule and EVA cost plan can be set up for each iteration (at the beginning of that iteration). Alternatively, a "bounding box" methodology can be used. As was discussed earlier in the book, a time or cost boundary is established for the phase of the project being scheduled and costed.

Typically, each work packet is assigned to an organization at the upper WBS levels and to individuals at the bottom WBS levels. The organizational structure may also be

Figure 14.1. Example WBS (Level 0)

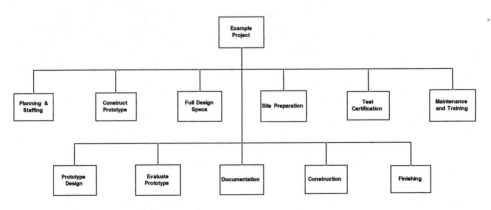

Figure 14.2. Example WBS

Level Zero	Level One
Planning & Staffing	
	Project Plan
	Resource Commitments
Prototype Design	
	Requirements
	Design
Construct Prototype	
	Detail Design
	Construction
Test/Evaluate Prototype	
	Test Plan Development
	Component Testing
	Full Testing
	Destructive Testing
	Test Documentation
Full Design Specs	
	External Specifications
	Internal Specifications
Documentation	
	Internal Specifications
	Required Documents
Site Preparation	
	Site Design
	Site Construction
Construction	
	Component Construction
	Component Assembly
Test/Certification	
	Test Plan Development
	Component Testing
	Full Testing
	Destructive Testing
	Test Documentation
Finishing	
	Component Finishing
	Assembly Finishing
Maintenance and Training	
	Maintenance Personnel
	Supervisory Personnel

represented in a hierarchically manner typically called an organizational breakdown structure (OBS). The amount and type of cost to complete each work packet is then estimated, and then those costs are rolled-up to the higher WBS levels. For IT projects, most packets involve only labor and the amount of work can be estimated by any of a number of techniques described earlier in the book. Resources to perform the work are identified either generically or specifically for each packet and may be coded by using a resource breakdown structure (RBS). Each packet also typically has one type of cost (labor, travel, materials, etc.), coded by an element of cost (EOC) breakdown or general ledger (GL) account number. If the full GL account number is used, reconciliation to the organization's accounting system may be easier.

Thus, each work packet is the intersection of these coding dimensions, and it has a detailed objective and work description plus a specification of WBS, OBS, RBS, EOC, estimated cost, and dependent tasks. "The work package usually has a short-time span schedule (40 to 100 hours), is limited to one performing department, and has defined completion criteria" (Kiewel, 1998). When these tasks are "rolled-up" the WBS hierarchically, the total cost plan is derived as shown in Figure 14.3 in spreadsheet form for the example project herein. This is also illustrated graphically in Figure 14.4.

In developing the cost plan using a bottom-up estimation method, each Level 0 WBS item would be further broken down into another spreadsheet that shows the estimated cost

Figure 14.3. Project cost plan in spreadsheet

Project Cost Plan	Ja	Fe	Ma	Ap	Ma	Jn	Jl	Au	Se	Oc	No	De	Total
Planning & Staffing	3	2											5
Prototype Design		3	3										6
Construct Prototype			8	8									16
Evaluate Prototype				5	10								15
Full Design Specs					5	6	3						14
Documentation							2	2	1	1	1	1	8
Site Preparation							8	3	3				14
Construction								20	50	50	20		140
Test/Certification										10	6	4	20
Finishing											8	4	12
Maintenance Training												4	4
Monthly Cost	3	5	11	13	15	16	28	54	61	27	13	8	254
Cumulative	3	8	19	32	47	63	91	145	206	233	246	254	

Figure 14.4. Project cost plan graph

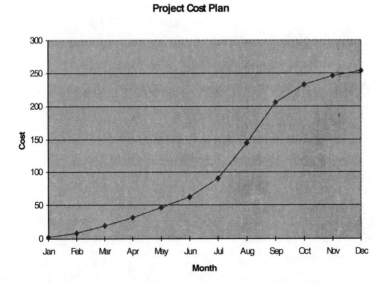

Project Cost Plan

Figure 14.5. Cost plan for prototype

Test/Evaluate Prototype										
	A	M	J	J	A	S	O	N	D	Plan
Test Screens	3									3
Test Reports	2									2
Test Processing		2								2
Audit Trail Verify		4								4
Destructive Testing		4								4
Monthly Plan	5	10	0	0	0	0	0	0	0	15

and schedule for associated the level one work packets, as shown in Figure 14.5 (for one of the level zero items).

This cost plan is sometimes called the *planned cost based on known work* and may include risk factors at the individual WBS work-packet level. The inclusion of added cost based upon risk factors at the WBS work-packet level (mainly estimation risk factors) and overall project risk was discussed in Chapter VIII. There may also be some unpriced additional (real or suspected) work added which brings the cost up to the expected work cost or the performance measurement baseline (PMB). The difference between the expected work cost and the planned cost based upon known work is called the "undistributed budget." The undistributed budget is for *known work* and sometimes used as a holding account until a formal contract change is made (and new WBS codes are added).

The project manager generally has responsibility to manage to the performance measurement baseline. In addition a management reserve may be added as a reserve for overall project risks, including unforeseen work that is still within the overall scope of the project. The performance measurement baseline plus the management reserve adds up

Figure 14.6. Cost breakdown in contracts

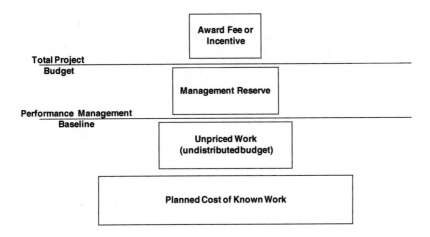

to the total project budget (or, for a contract situation, the negotiated cost). This is illustrated in Figure 14.6.

In contracting situations, the total contract price for a project will include a profit for the contractor. The performance measurement baseline normally excludes the profit for performance calculations (i.e., EVA) on both the part of the contractor and the buying organization in the case of cost-plus-fee contracts. In time and material contracts it is normally included, because it is typically built into the rate structure of the resources.

As the project progresses, actual costs are incurred by the effort expended in each work packet. Hopefully, these actual costs are measurable at least in total, as they may not be measurable for each work packet at the lower levels of the WBS (this is discussed later). However, the relative amount of things to be accomplished within the work packet that has actually been completed (percentage complete) can be estimated. The planned cost may change in time also (change orders), and thus work packets may need to be reestimated or new ones added or deleted. Figure 14.7 shows an example of a Microsoft Project entry screen for entering progress information. In Microsoft Project, cost information cannot be directly entered (without altering system defaults), but it is typically input via resource utilization, where resources have been given a particular rate. For tasks that span multiple progress reporting time periods, Microsoft Project generally assumes a linear distribution of both planned and actual costs across the task (although some front-loading or back-loading contouring patterns may be used).

Figure 14.8 shows an example of the Web-based FiveAndDime screen for entering progress information and cost data (a progress transaction). FiveAndDime has other screens for simplifying the labor entry process, illustrated later in this chapter.

There are several types of traditional performance reports. One type is status reports that describe the time and cost spent on each WBS item rolled up to the reporting level. The reporting level is typically Level 0 or Level 1. These may be displayed in a list format, or in a WBS tree diagram showing the person hours and/or dollars spent for each item. The progress report is a very popular report that describes what has been accomplished in terms of percentage complete by task. This information is typically shown superimposed

Figure 14.7. Task form in Microsoft Project

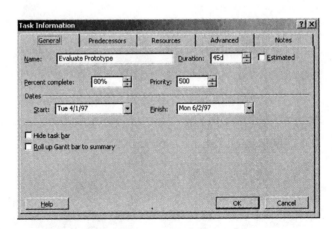

Figure 14.8. Progress transaction form

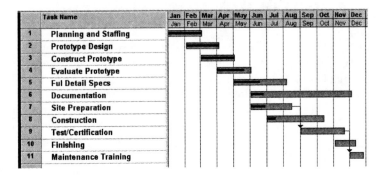

on the Gantt chart as percentage complete numbers inside of the bars or shading a portion of each bar in an amount proportionate to the percentage-complete value. An example of this is shown in Figure 14.9. There are also variance reports that compare actual values to planned values, usually in terms of cost either measured in currency or person-hours. This is usually reported for the entire project or at Level 0. Trend reports show metrics as a function of time, and common metrics to plot are planned costs, actual costs, or overall percentage complete. Figure 14.10 is an example of this for planned and actual cost in currency (dollars). Forecasting reports extrapolate trend curves.

For most organizations using traditional progress reporting, two types of displays are presented to management: progress data and cost data. Progress data are typically shown in a Gantt or similar type chart, as is shown in Figure 14.9 for the example project here.

Figure 14 .9. Gantt chart

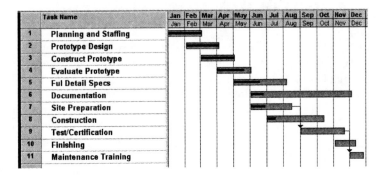

Figure 14.10. Planned and actual cost plan graph

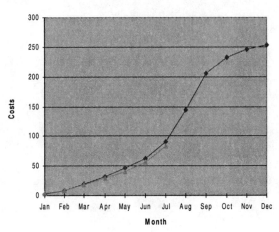

Cost data are typically reported as actual cost for the entire project versus planned cost, as is shown in Figure 14.10 for the example here. In that figure the planned cost curve is marked with the diamond symbols, and the actual cost curve is marked with the triangle symbols.

The problem with these usual methods is that they do not provide a clear quantitative picture of the true project status, nor do they provide a quantitative means for extrapolating project cost to complete or completion date. *For the example project here, consider the Gantt chart above (which also shows the task percentage complete as dark bars stripes inside the bars) and the actual cost versus budget graph. The project is not over budget (actual cost of $83,000 versus planned cost of $91,000), however it is hard to determine if it is on schedule or not. Actually this project is well behind schedule and is over-spent as the forthcoming earned value analysis will show.*

Earned Value Analysis

Earned value (EV) is basically the value (usually expressed in currency) of the work accomplished up to a point in time, *based upon the planned (or budgeted) value for that work.* The original U.S. government's term for earned value is *budgeted cost of work performed* (BCWP). EVA (or EVM—earned value management) is a progress-versus-plan–based metric to evaluate the true performance of a project in terms of both cost deviation and schedule deviation. It also provides a *quantitative* basis for estimating actual completion time and actual cost at completion; EVA can provide an early warning of project time and/or cost problems as early as 15% into the project (Fleming & Koppelman, 1998).

The EV concept has been around in several forms for many years, dating back to cost variance metrics defined in the 1950s. In the early 1960s, program evaluation review technique (PERT) was extended to include cost variances and the basic concept of earned value was adopted therein. PERT did not survive, but the basic earned value concept did. That concept was a key element in the 1967 U.S. Department of Defense (DoD) policy called "cost/schedule control systems criteria" (C/SCSC). Early implementations of C/SCSC met with numerous problems, the most common of which was overimplementation due to excessive checklists, data acquisition requirements and other paperwork, specialist acronyms, and overly complicated methods and tools. "Much of the criticism that has been levied on earned value in the past was due to an inflexible and dogmatic approach that was applied in the early days" (Webb, 2003). However, after several decades of refinement, C/SCSC is now very effective and the U.S. government has accumulated many years of statistical evidence supporting it. Also in the last decade, initiatives within DoD have been successful in removing excessive and ineffective components of the C/SCSC (Abba, 2000). The C/SCSC have now been successful, and have met the test of time for nearly 3 decades on major government projects (Abba, 2000).

EVA methods have migrated and evolved throughout the world and are now internationally recognized as an effective project management tool. However, these methods have not been widely applied in IT projects (Christensen & Ferens, 1995). Also, until recently EVA use was still minimal outside of the U.S. government and its contractors (Fleming & Koppelman, 1996). There are several reasons for this continued lack of use, including the overcomplication of some surrounding methodologies and procedures, the human factors involved in gathering the necessary input data, the careful planning and WBS setup required, and integrating of EVA effectively with other management information systems. Methods for overcoming these obstacles in general were discussed in the *Project Management Journal* (Brandon, 1998), and such effective methods for IT projects are discussed later in this chapter.

Earned value terminology was originally formalized in DoD standard 7000.2. The ANSI standard (ANSI/EIA-748-1998) on earned value management systems (EVMS) was approved in May of 1998. In 1999 the DoD adopted the ANSI EVMS Standard for use on defense acquisitions. Other governments and organizations have adopted similar standards for earned value such as the Canadian General Standards Board (CGSB 187.1-93 November 1993). These EVMS guidelines incorporate best business practices for EVA systems that have proven to provide solid benefits for enterprise planning and control. In EVA, the three key terms and definitions are:

- *BCWS:* Budgeted cost of work scheduled (the cumulative planned cost) as of a certain point in time
- *ACWP:* The cumulative actual cost of work done as of a certain point in time
- *BCWP:* This is the "earned value" and is determined from the product of the budgeted cost of each work packet times the percentage complete of each work packet as of a certain point in time

Figure 14.11. EV calculations in spreadsheet

	Earned Value—Through July										
	J	F	M	A	M	J	J	...	Plan	% C	EV
Planning & Staffing	3	2							5	100	5
Prototype Design		3	3						6	100	6
Construct Prototype			8	8					16	100	16
Evaluate Prototype				5	10				15	80	12
Full Design Specs					5	6	3		14	50	7
Documentation						2	2		8	12	0.96
Site Preparation						8	3		14	36	5.04
Construction							20		140	15	21
Test/Certification									20	0	0
Finishing									12	0	0
Maintenance Training									4	0	0
Monthly Plan	3	5	11	13	15	16	28	...	254		73
Cumulative	3	8	19	32	47	63	91	...			
Monthly Actual	4	4	10	11	12	15	27	0	83		
Cum. Actual	4	8	18	29	41	56	83				

For this example, Figure 14.11 shows the EVA calculation through July. Note that the calculation of EV does not involve actual costs, but is simply the product of the percentage complete and the planned cost.

Percentage complete is determined for each work packet and then EV is calculated for each packet. The total project earned value at a point in time is determined by a WBS rollup of the EV values. For example if a packet had an estimated total cost of $10,000, and if the things to be done in the packet were 70% complete (or 70% of the things were done), then the earned value would be $7,000. A WBS rollup example is shown in Figure 14.12, for the level one tasks corresponding to the Level 0 item of evaluate prototype.

Variances between the three values BCWS (planned cost), BCWP (earned value), and actual cost (ACWP) yield the earned value metrics. There are earned value metrics available for both cost and schedule variances. The cost metrics are:

- Cost Variance (Dollars) = BCWP - ACWP
- Cost Variance (%) = (BCWP - ACWP) * 100/BCWP

Figure 14.12. EV calculation for prototype activities

	Ap	Ma	...	Plan	% C	Value
Test Plan Devel.	3			3	100	3
Unit Testing	2			2	100	2
Full Testing		4		4	100	4
Destructive Testing		4		4	50	2
Test Documentation		2		2	50	1
Monthly Plan	5	10	0	15	80	12

- Cost Performance Index (CPI) = BCWP/ACWP
- Estimated Cost at Completion (EAC) = ACWP + (BAC - BCWP)/CPI
- Or in its simpler form, EAC = BAC/CPI

Where BAC is the budget at completion, ACWP is a sunk cost and (BAC - BCWP) is the estimated remaining work. The CPI is also called the cost efficiency factor; values less than 1 indicate that the project is costing more than planned, or that one is getting CPI of a dollar for each $1 spent. This is good prediction formula if one expects that future performance will be similar to past performance. There are several other (EAC) formulas, and the most appropriate depends upon project type, whether past performance is a good indicator of future performance, and when in the project the EAC is calculated (Christensen et al., 1995). The PMI PMBOK (PMI, 2000) provides this formula when past performance is not expected to be a good indicator of future performance:

$$EAC = BAC - (BCWP - ACWP),$$

which is the budget at completion adjusted for the cost variance. Here one is assuming that corrective action will be effective so that the poor performance of the past will not continue and future performance will follow the original plan.

The schedule metrics are:

- Schedule Variance (Dollars) = BCWP - BCWS
- Schedule Variance (Months) = (BCWP - BCWS)/(Planned Cost for Month)
- Schedule Variance (%) = (BCWP - BCWS) * 100/BCWS
- Schedule Performance Index (SPI) = BCWP/BCWS
- Estimated Time to Complete (ETTC) = ATE + ((OD - (ATE * SPI))/SPI
- Or in a simpler form, ETTC = OD/SPI

Where ATE is the actual calendar time already expended and OD is the original duration. The SPI is also called the schedule efficiency factor; values less than 1 indicate that the project is taking more time than planned. In the example project herein, the schedule variance is 0.67 months (behind schedule) and the cost variance is $10,000 (overspent). The estimated time to complete is 15 months instead of the 12 months planned, and the estimated cost to complete is $289,000 instead of $254,000. The calculation of these numbers for our example using the previous formulas is implemented in the spreadsheet of Figure 14.13.

Figure 14.14 shows a display from the Web-based FiveAndDime system for this same example showing EVA calculations (as well as percentage complete and cost data) using a "super-charged" Gantt chart format. The color in the Gantt chart bars is green for completed tasks, yellow for tasks in progress, and orange for tasks not yet started. The

Figure 14.13. EV variance calculations in spreadsheet

Schedule Variances	
Budgeted Cost of Work Scheduled (BCWS)	91
Budgeted Cost of Work Performed (BCWP, EV)	73
Schedule Variance (Dollars)	-18
Schedule Variance (Months)	-0.67
Schedule Efficiency Factor	0.8
Estimated Time to Complete (Months)	15
Cost Variances	
Actual cost of Work Performed (ACWP)	83
Budgeted Cost of Work Performed (BCWP, EV)	73
Cost Variance (Dollars)	-10
Cost Variance (Percent)	-3.9
Cost Efficiency Factor	0.88
Estimated Cost at Completion	289

Figure 14.14. EV display in Gantt table

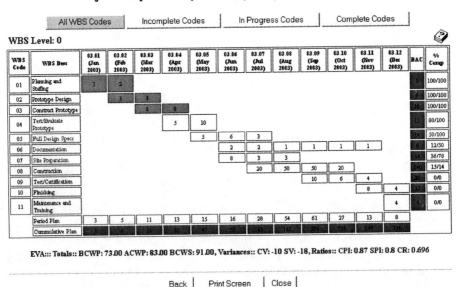

last column for percentage complete shows a ratio where the numerator is the rolled up percentage complete and the denominator is the percentage complete that should have been obtained as of the reporting date; the value of that ratio is actually the SPI for that task. WBS codes that have either the CPI or SPI below unity are displayed in red.

The EV can be projected onto the planned cost (BCWS) curve to graphically show deviations. This is illustrated in Figure 14.15, which shows the planned cost and actual

Figure 14.15. Graphical EV analysis

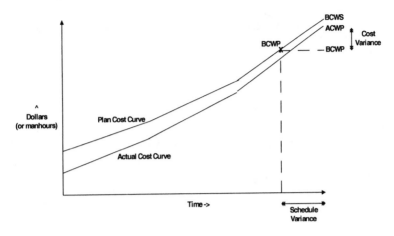

cost curves for a project analysis, for this example, through July. The schedule variance in time is also shown in that figure along the time axis.

There are other formulas that can be used for ETTC, and some may be better as a project draws closer to completion. In addition, there are EAC formulas that use both the CPI and SPI, and a popular one that is often called the "pessimistic" or "most likely" formula is (Webb, 2003):

$$EAC = ACWP + (BAC\text{-}BCWP)/(SPI * CPI)$$

If the SPI is more than 1, then this formula would be less appropriate. The critical ratio (CR) is the product of SPI times CPI; it is also called the cost-schedule index. The CR is the single most important overall metric for time and cost performance. Plotting CR (and also CPI and SPI) versus time is an excellent way to view overall project cost/time health over time and spot trends. Some project management software systems use a dashboard or traffic light indicator for project overall health, and the green-orange-red status color is a function of the project's CR.

The earned value metrics of CPI, SPI, CR, and EAC are very appropriate and useful in the great majority of projects. However ETTC is problematic and less reliable and should only be used as a very rough estimate (Webb, 2003). Whenever the overall project or any critical task activities go beyond their planned time, then the formula for ETTC goes negative. One adjustment is to modify the previous ETTC formula if the project is already past the original duration (OD):

$$ETTC = OD/SPI$$

However, a more detailed analysis would yield better results. In a more detail analysis, all incomplete tasks would be reestimated using one of the two ETTC formulas depending upon whether the original duration had been exceeded or not. Then a new critical path would be determined; then from that new critical path a new ETTC found.

EVA greatly facilitates management by exception. When there is a problem with a project as indicated by CPI and/or SPI less than unity, one can drill down in the earned value analysis to lower levels of the WBS. For example, if the overall project index(s) is below unity then one can view the Level 0 WBS codes that have their indexes below unity and then so on to the next level (Level 1 for our example). Some project management software supports this drill down capability and some software systems allow a PM to drill down interactively. Figure 14.16 is a screen shot from FiveAndDime showing a drill down from Level 0 to Level 1. This was accomplished by clicking on a particular WBS code (evaluate prototype) on the Level 0 display (Figure 14.14, where WBS codes with a CPI or SPI below unity are shown in red).

Effective Implementation of EVA

If earned value analysis is so useful, then why is not used more in industry and in particular for IT? There are several reasons for this. First, commercial awareness of earned value is still low; corporate training courses rarely discuss earned value, and there is still relatively little in commercial print on the subject (Brandon, 1999). Even recent comprehensive books on software development project management do not include earned value (Hallows, 1998; Yeates & Cadle, 1996). Second, the data acquisition required (for

Figure 14.16 EV drill down

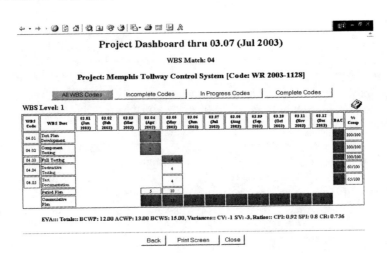

obtaining percentage complete and actual cost numbers), if implemented in a by-the-book method, may be too costly and time consuming. Third, earned value reporting has not been handled in a usable manner by most project management software. And last, there can be significant employee and contractor resistance problems when trying to put EVA into practice.

Timely and reasonably accurate progress reporting is necessary for EVA, but this data-acquisition process must be easy and inexpensive. Providing for easy and effective data acquisition requires that the methods used are nonintrusive yet provide for the necessary accuracy. Nonintrusive means that very little extra effort is required by project team members or managers to provide the input data for the analysis. The goal is to implement the necessary data acquisition as a by-product of existing corporate reporting or payroll ("time and attendance") procedures where possible. The key issues in the effective implementation of EVA are (Brandon, 1999):

- Setting appropriate work-packet size
- Progress reporting (defining and obtaining percentage complete information)
- Actual cost basis
- Level of effort tasks
- Human resource issues

If work packets are too small, then project team members will be required to acquire and report excessive data. If work packets are too big, then performance will not be measured frequently enough to allow effective corrective action. If project performance is to be measured monthly (the most common interval), then the work packets should be smaller than a month, such as a week or two. It is a best to tie the maximum size of work packets to the progress and effort data acquisition frequency, especially where employee labor is a significant cost item, as is the typical case with IT projects. In an earlier chapter, WBS packet size was discussed; a recap of the criteria for the packet size is:

- Are realistically and confidently estimable
- Cannot be (or should not be) logically subdivided
- Are to be assigned to one OBS/CBS code
- Can be completed relatively quickly (80 hours maximum rule of thumb; I prefers a maximum of 40 hours)
- Have a meaningful and measurable conclusion and deliverable
- Have enough "visibility" so that progress and cost can be determined
- Can be completed without interruption (i.e., need for more info)

As stated above, each work packet should be assigned to one organization which is responsible for the work to be completed. Additionally if possible, it is also best to have each work packet assigned to a single resource (RBS code), although this may not be possible in some IT organizations where techniques such as "pair programming" are used. Different types of work should not be lumped into a work package; for example design and coding should be in separate packages, particularly for estimation purposes. Earlier in this book, project calendars and time periods were discussed; time periods in a project calendars should correspond to the interval that is to be used for gathering project performance data, including hours expended and percentage complete estimates. It is important that a work packet not encompass many such periods; the optimal situation would be for a work packet to correspond to exactly one time period. For performance analysis, progress estimates (percentage complete) and cost data should be available at each time period for each work packet (incurred effort and cost during that period). Work packets that are highly interdependent should be combined (if such is possible without extending the time of that packet beyond a few time periods) to reduce overall work packet interdependencies for scheduling.

Progress Reporting

For EVA, percentage complete estimates must be provided for each work packet on a regular reporting basis. For most work packets, taking the time to calculate the percentage complete based on the amount of completed versus the amount of work remaining (or the number of things completed versus the number of things in the work packet) is too time consuming and an unnecessary burden on project team members. If the work packet size has been appropriately determined, then the packet percent estimates can be very rough without losing much accuracy on the overall project performance evaluation.

There are several methods that have been suggested for estimating project percentage complete that provide sufficient accuracy without much additional effort (Christiansen, 1995). The easiest percent completion method is the "all or nothing rule":

- Work on packet has not started   0%
- Packet is finished   100%

Another a very easy percentage complete scheme is the *halfling,* or 50/50 method:

- Work on packet has not started   0%
- Working on packet has started   50%
- Packet is finished   100%

Another common method is based upon the 80/20 rule (from the notion that 80% of the problems are due to 20% of the work items):

- Work on packet has not started   0%
- Working on packet has started   20%
- Packet is finished   100%

In contracting situations or other situations in which payments may be based upon percentage-complete progress reporting, the contractor can be expected to arrange his or her work to maximize payments. For example, in the 50/50 method, the contractor would start as many work packages as possible; in a 0/100 method, the contractor would break work packets down to a very low level to complete as many packets as possible (Anbari, 2003).

Another method is the weighted milestone, or interim milestone, method in which a percentage complete is allocated for each of several milestones. In most software development methodologies, there is a review, verification, and/or testing step involved in each phase of the methodology (requirements, design, coding, etc.). Common completion and/or monitoring methods include self-checking via unit testing, integration testing, team leader reviews, peer reviews, walkthroughs, or even Fagan inspections (Yeates & Cadle, 1996). Usually, by proper decomposition, that verification step can be subdivided and a portion placed in each work packet. For example, in the implementation or coding phase, the verification step could involve unit testing and/or peer code review (even in pure cleanroom approaches, programmers are going to do some unit testing). With that being the case, the percentage complete can be obtained by a standard interim milestone method where the milestones are:

- Not started   0%
- Started   50%
- Finished packet   75%
- Packet verified   100%

For coding packets, additional milestones can be introduced as:

- Not started   0%
- Started   25%
- Coding complete   75%
- Unit testing complete   90%
- Integration testing complete   100%

Rothman (2004) calls these interim milestones pebbles and prefers the pebbles to be of about a day or two duration. An example of *pebbles* from that reference for software development is:

- Verify design
- Check out code; implement changes
- Develop unit tests
- Successfully compile
- Review code with peer; check code back in
- Develop documentation
- Verification and validation

To be fully useful, any project management performance measurement system must be accepted by project team members and project managers. Thus it is very important that obtaining regular progress (percentage complete) and effort (labor hours) information be easily obtained. The effort required by team members to report their status must be insignificant relevant to the overall work being done. The easiest way to obtain percentage complete and effort statistics is to include such information with existing regular reporting. Some organizations may have timecards and/or progress reports that are completed regularly. The proper time interval for most software projects would be weekly or biweekly; any more frequently would be bothersome, and any less frequently would allow problems to grow before corrective action could be applied. The decomposition of overall work into work packets should be done so that most packets are completed in one or two reporting periods. Whether time cards or progress reports are used, the data obtained must include:

- Work packet ID
- Percentage complete
- Hours expended

If time cards are used, all of an individual's time (paid time) should be accounted for, including project objective work, project level of effort work, and nonproject time (including time off). By doing so, one system can perhaps be used for time and attendance, payroll, and EVA. Figure 14.17 shows an example of a very simple example of such a weekly timecard. Uncompensated overtime (i.e., extra unpaid time put in by

Figure 14.17. Time card

Employee ID:				
Week #:				
Project Code	WBS Code	Hours	% Complete	Notes
Total:				

professional employees) should not be included in EVA analysis, whether the EVA is based on currency or on person hours. If an organization wants to keep track of unpaid time, then separate codes need to be used that so that these numbers are not included in EVA analysis (or in payroll calculations). Modern software engineering methodologies discourage such uncompensated time, at least on a regular continuing basis. Some organizations keep an informal log of such unpaid time, and then provide some comp time to employees at the end of the project.

Ease of use and validity of user input are essential for project progress entry. Figure 14.18 shows a screen from the FiveAndDime system for the entry of progress. The resource ID can optionally be automatically obtained from the user's Web log-on. Look-up buttons are provided to allow the user to select resource ID, time period, and WBS code from the database via look-up windows. A look-up window is shown for selecting the WBS code, and if a partial WBS is first entered, then the look-up window will only display the WBS codes that begin with that text. All fields on the form are fully validated. The screen shows the default of five line items; however, when the window opens the user can specify any number of line items. FiveAndDime uses the open source MySQL database, and an organization can also build an SQL (or XML) interface directly into the system to automatically transfer progress information from its own time/payroll system.

Actual Cost Data

As described earlier, EVA uses a percentage complete for each work packet to calculate an earned value for each packet. This value requires knowledge of the planned cost and the percentage complete; it does not require knowledge of the actual cost. *Thus, EVA schedule variances can be calculated without any knowledge of actual costs.* For some projects, the determination of actual costs may not be practical in an accurate and/or timely manner. This may happen when much work is outsourced or when purchased components represent major parts of the system being built or integrated. It can also occur when there is no mechanism to gather costs at the project level; some organizations

Figure 14.18. Progress entry per resource

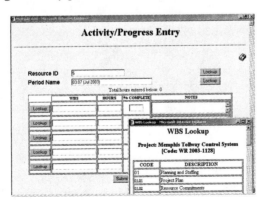

only code cost to general ledger accounts and have no "job/project costing" system. However, EVA can still be performed partially without any actual cost data including the SPI and estimated time to complete, as well as "drill down" to find problem spots in the WBS in regard to progress.

The total EV cost variances for the project only require knowledge of the total project actual cost not individual work packet actual costs. Thus the CPI and EAC can be determined; however, drilling down to find problem spots in the WBS in regard to cost overruns will not be possible. A major problem in many organizations is that actual costs, while coded to a project, are not subdivided further to the individual WBS codes.

Another problem in many organizations is that while actual costs may be captured at the project and even the WBS level, the close out time of the general ledger and/or job costing system is so slow that it could be many weeks after the end of the month before an actual cost breakdown is available. And while late is better than not at all, it may be too late to take corrective actions. Figure 14.19 illustrates the common method of obtaining actual

Figure 14.19. Actual cost from general ledger

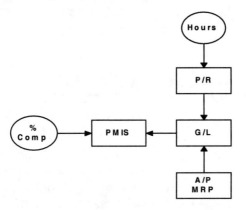

Figure 14.20. Actual cost from job control

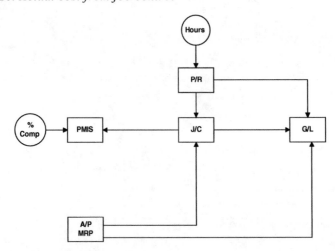

cost data from the organization's general ledger (GL) system into the project management system (PMIS). Usually the actual cost data gets into the GL form payroll (PR), from accounts payable (AP), and/or manufacturing/materials resource/requirements planning (MRP). There are so many major IT systems involved, one can see why there may be significant delays and also significant mispostings and other errors.

Figure 14.20 illustrates the common method of obtaining actual cost data from the organization's job-costing system (JC). The JC system, however, gets information from PR, GL, AP, and MRP. One can see why there may be significant delays, mispostings, and other errors.

Figure 14.21 illustrates a common hybrid method of obtaining actual cost data from the organization's IT systems where multiple systems feed actual cost information into the PMIS. This type of hybrid system is an attempt to get cost data into the PMIS faster; however, due to the complication thereof, there may be significant mispostings and other errors. This method may also suffer from the fact that there may be journal entry postings to affected accounts that are need to correct prior period errors (in AP, PR, or MRP), and this results in an out of balance condition between the GL and the PMIS.

In IT most of the cost is usually labor, and that being the case there are several ways that one can expedite the gathering of actual cost information. For IT projects, *one effective EVA method is to represent cost in terms of person hours instead of currency (Brandon, 1998)*. All of the EVA formulas still apply there is just a change to the dimension. This often provides sufficient accuracy for project control purposes, even where there is considerable variation between pay rates on the project team. Even nonlabor costs can be converted back into equivalent person hours using a standard average overall labor rate. This has another advantage for the PM, since it focuses his attention on the matters that he can control.

Another very effective EVA method for IT projects is to set up a feed forward cost reporting system instead of the "feedback" cost system coming from GL (Brandon,

Figure 14.21. Hybrid cost transfer

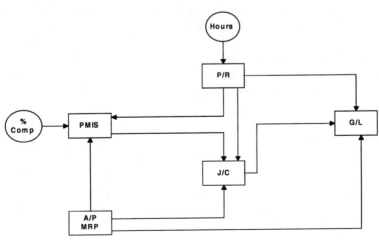

Figure 14.22. Feed forward cost transfer

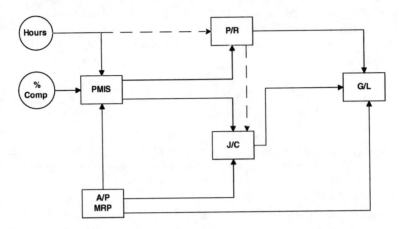

1998). This is illustrated in Figure 14.22, the hours worked are entered directly into the PMIS, and could also be sent to the PR system directly or indirectly.

With a feed-forward system, resource utilization is entered (as well as percentage complete), and the predicted cost is the resource utilized times the estimated resource rate. For labor, the resource utilization is in person hours. Using these two data items in each reporting period, earned value can be calculated in one of three manners:

- Expressing earned value in terms of person hours (or person days)
- Using the actual pay rate of project workers
- Using categories of skills and skill levels

As discussed in the first option, the entire work plan is expressed in terms of person hours instead of currency. This is the least accurate method, but the simplest.

In the second method, a table of burdened individual pay rates (pay rates multiplied by a factor, which includes all overhead, benefits, etc.) is maintained. This is the most accurate of the three methods, but requires more data to be stored and maintained. There may also be a confidentiality issue in using people's actual pay rates. When this method is used, a computer interface is typically set up between the PR/HR system (which is the system of record for the employee pay rates) and the PMIS.

The third method is fairly accurate yet simple; and it does not pose confidentiality problems. Categories are set up for skills (i.e., analysts, programmers, etc.) and for skill levels (i.e., programmer 1, programmer 2, etc.). For each category an average burdened rate is established (currency per person hour). Then each project worker is assigned one specific category. A spreadsheet or simple database program can be used for these tables also, and linked to the spreadsheet tables previously shown in the EVA; or the PMIS may be able to accommodate this type of information directly, as shown in the screen from FiveAndDime, in Figure 14.23.

Figure 14.23. Table of resources

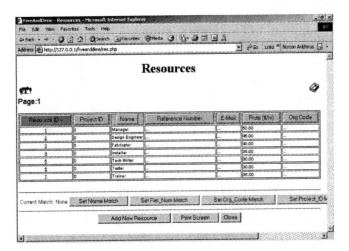

Other EVA Issues

Reporting earned value in many project scheduling software systems (PMIS) is usually not easy for several reasons. First, getting actual costs onto a project so that it can be used in the system's earned value mechanism usually means getting actual costs onto each task, and in many systems getting actual usage onto the resources for each task. Second, setting up an automatic interface between the corporate systems (or departmental databases) and a project management systems is not trivial and usually does not use a standard format such as XML. Third, using the earned value mechanism in these systems is typically not straightforward and simple (Brandon, 1998), and features such as "drill-down" are not available or available only in a batch (noninteractive) manner.

As stated earlier, to be fully successful any project management performance measurement system must be accepted by project team members and project managers. The system must be nonintrusive and *directed primarily towards measuring projects, not measuring individuals*. Because earned value analysis provides a level of insight deep into the project workings, it is likely to be viewed by some as a means of "employee (and/ or contractor) evaluation" instead of project performance evaluation. The best way to address this issue is to adopt earned value methodology along with some form of total quality management (TQM). If TQM (or a similar quality effort) is already in place, then earned value could be sealed within that overall envelope. Various quality programs were discussed in the chapter on quality management. Management must focus on the use of earned value for:

- Extrapolation of project cost to complete (EAC)
- Estimation of actual completion date (ETC)

- Identification of project trouble areas (so corrective action can be taken)
- Refinement of work packet estimation methods

and not on the use of earned value for individual evaluations (Brandon, 1998).

For IT projects, costs other than labor may be present and these may or may not be allocated to the project. Contractor and consultant costs are usually part of the WBS and RBS structures. Other direct costs, such as hardware, software, training, entertainment, and travel, may made be part of the WBS or just added to the cost plan developed via the WBS. Indirect, overhead or level of effort (LOE) types of cost may also be assigned to a project and become part of the project budget. These may be general and administrative (G&A), Internal operations and maintenance (I&O), allocations (space, utilities, consumables, communications, etc.), and nonproject time (general meetings, general training, etc.). In some organizations, some of these costs are included in the "burdened rates" for the labor categories. In some organizations these costs are given separate WBS codes. In projectized organizations, and even in traditional line management organizations, as more work becomes team- and project-based, it becomes desirable to associate these costs with projects. If given separate WBS codes, then their contribution to the cost plan is typically a linear, spread over the project life. This is easily handled by software systems in which costs are planned using a combination of time periods and WBS codes. For other software systems in which cost is estimated only at the WBS level for the entire project, handling these overhead costs and percentage complete progress information becomes difficult. One could also exclude these costs from the performance management baseline; however, in a contracted situation this may not be possible. Figure 14.24 shows an example of the input screen from FiveAndDime, where a WBS may be designated as an LOE code, and thus the percentage complete never needs to be input

Figure 14.24. Form to add WBS code (showing LOE and PB)

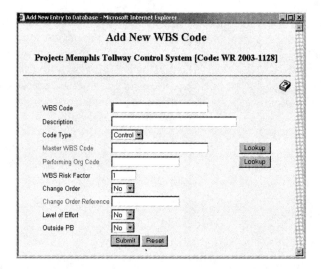

(the EV will equal the planned cost through the current period yielding no schedule variation). Also as seen in that same screen shot, a WBS may be designated as outside of the performance baseline (PB) in which case it will not be included in the EVA analysis. WBS codes may also be designated as baseline or change order, and EVA can be done with or without change orders.

As well as the web based FiveAndDime system, there are a number of other software products (both mainframe and client-server based) that were specifically made to handle earned value in a comprehensive manner including:

- C-Brat (www.cbratproject.com)
- PMOffice (www.systemcorp.com)
- Cobra (www.welcom.com)
- Microframe's MPM (www.businessengine.com)
- C/S Solutions's WinInsight (www.cs-solutions.com)
- DeckKer's Tracker (www.dtrakker.com)

EVA, Success Factors, and Stage Gates

Stage gates are the traditional way that project performance is monitored and controlled by upper management of both the benefiting and performing organizations. These stage gates may be event driven by project milestones or they may be periodic. The most common scenario for IT projects is periodic (i.e., monthly) using the traditional Gantt chart and budget-versus-actual cost data (as was discussed earlier in this chapter) plus whatever verification (product testing) and/or validation (user satisfaction) information is available at those times. Figure 14.25 illustrates this traditional stage gate approach.

The problem with this traditional approach is that considerable time (and cost) is expended at the stage gate review meetings, because the PM, users, line management of both the performing and benefiting organizations, and some project team members are

Figure 14.25. Traditional stage gate

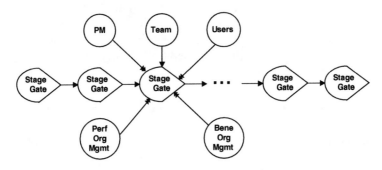

Figure 14.26. Management stage gate (using EVA)

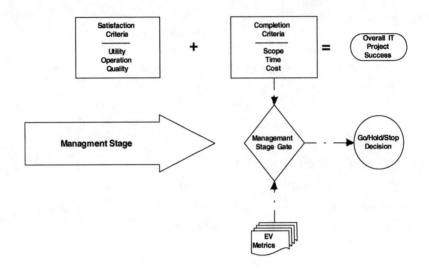

generally present. The project team members typically in attendance include the business analysts and, in some cases, even key designers and developers.

If the overall stage gate is divided into completion and satisfaction reviews, then both the frequency and number of participants can be reduced resulting in the consumption of less project time and cost. In earlier chapters, project completion and satisfaction success factors were discussed, and the notion of separating the gating process into these categories was presented. This dual gating process was illustrated in Figure 2.6 in Chapter II, where management stage gates are placed at regular time intervals (i.e., monthly or quarterly), and quality stage gates are placed at key delivery points for product manifestations (i.e., requirements documentation, use cases, paper prototypes, working prototypes, test results, etc.). There may be multiple quality stage gates within a management stage gate time interval, or vice versa.

EVA is used in the management stage gate not only to evaluate the completion factors, but the EAC is also used to reevaluate the chosen project benefit metric(s) as shown in Figure 14.26. The chosen benefit metrics might be any of those discussed earlier in the book such as IRR or scoring methods. The estimated completion date might also be used in recalculating benefit metrics, if calendar completion time is a key factor in the benefit analysis. It is important that these management reviews do not use sunk cost (how much has already been invested/spent) in determining whether a project should proceed or not; the only cost considered should be the estimated cost at completion versus the benefit. Keeping a badly performing project alive by sunk cost is a trap into which many organizations have fallen.

The dual gating approach not only provides for the exposure and analysis of both project completion and satisfaction criteria, but also minimizes the time of key individuals in meetings. This is illustrated in Figure 14.27, where upper management and the develop-

Figure 14.27. Dual stage gates and stakeholder involvement

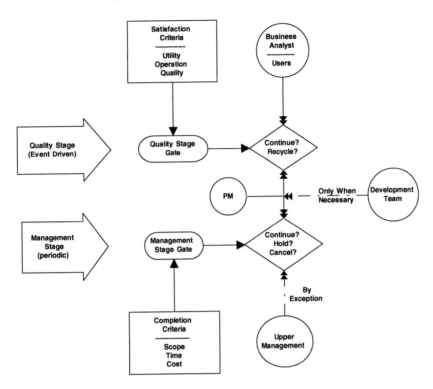

ment team are relatively isolated from regular meetings. The management stage gate reviews, while periodic, need to be held only if the EVA values are not good (CPI and/ or SPI below unity). In addition, upper management does not need to be involved in the quality stage gates at all, and neither does most of the project team; users, business analysts, and the PM may be the only personnel needed for these gate reviews.

Since earned value metrics are currency based, both schedule variance and cost variances can be rolled up along organizational lines for one project or even for multiple projects. In this way, the overall performance of organizational components can be evaluated. This is illustrated in Figure 14.28. A decision is made in regard to the management level for the organization, and the earned value metrics assigned to those organizational components are summed up. This is discussed further in Chapter XVI.

Chapter Summary

In this chapter earned value analysis has been discussed and illustrated in detail. EVA is often difficult to implement effectively and can have a number of problem areas.

Figure 14.28. EVA rollup by organizational component

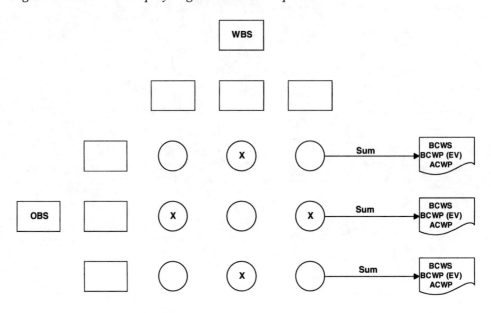

However, this chapter has identified the problem areas and their practical solutions. EVA is the only practical method to determine actual project status and develop reliable estimates for completion cost and time. EVA should be included in all IT projects of any significant size. EVA is one of the key metrics in the management-for-success philosophy that has been developed in this book via critical success factors and dual stage gates.

References

Abba, W. (2000). *Earned value management rediscovered.* Retrieved from http://www.acq.osd.mil/pm/newpolicy/misc/abba_art.html

Anbari, F. (2003, December). Earned value project management method and extensions. *Project Management Journal, 34*(4).

Brandon, D. (1998, June). Implementing earned value easily and effectively. *Project Management Journal, 29*(2).

Brandon, D. (1999). Implementing earned value easily and effectively. In J. Pinto (Ed.), *Essentials of Project Control* (pp. 113-124). Newton Square, PA: Project Management Institute Press.

Christensen, D., & Ferens, D. (1995). Using earned value for performance measurement on software projects. *Acquisition Review Quarterly*, Spring, 155-171

Christensen, D., et al. (1995). A review of estimate at completion research. *Journal of Cost Analysis,* Spring.

Fleming, Q., & Koppelman, J. (1996). *Earned value project management.* Project Management Institute.

Fleming, Q., & Koppelman, J. (1998). *Earned value project management.* A Powerful Tool for Software Projects. *CROSSTALK, The Journal of Defense Software Engineering,* July, 19-23

Hallows, J. (1998). *Information systems project management.* New York: Amacom.

Kiewel, B. (1998). *Measuring progress in software development.* PM Network, January, 29-32

Lewis, J. (1995). *Project planning, scheduling & control.* In Irwin.

Rothman, R. (2004, February 16). Using pebbles to track project state. *Computerworld.*

Webb, A. (2003). *Using earned value.* Burlington, VT: Gower.

Yeates, D., & Cadle, J. (1996). *Project management for information systems.* London: Pitman.

Chapter XV

Software Systems for Project Management

You miss 100% of the shots you don't take.

(Wayne Gretzky)

A vast amount of project management software is available today in a wide variety of capabilities, applicability, platform requirements, and prices. These software products significantly enhance the PM's job of managing a project in almost all aspects, including selection, planning, scheduling, execution, control, risk, and communications. PMs should therefore be aware of the types of tools available and the features and applicability of those tools. In this chapter, types of software products and some specific products are identified and discussed.

Spreadsheets

Spreadsheet programs are the most commonly used computer software programs for project management (and business in general). Spreadsheets are easy to learn, easy to use, inexpensive, generally available, and adaptable to most project management tasks. Consider the project planning and progress information shown in the spreadsheet of Figure 15.1; the last two columns are calculated columns. A graphical representation in the form of a classical Gantt chart can also be created from the spreadsheet data in the first three columns using the charting capability in most modern spreadsheet programs (such as Microsoft Excel). In addition, one can also use the columns for weeks completed and weeks remaining to draw a Gantt chart showing progress, as illustrated in Figure 15.2.

Figure 15.1. Project plan and progress

Project Plan and Progress - Week 30

Task	Start Week	Weeks	% Complete	Weeks Complete	Weeks Remaining
Planning & Staffing	0	8	100	8	0
Prototype Design	4	8	100	8	0
Construct Prototype	8	8	100	8	0
Test/Evaluate Prototype	13	8	80	6.4	1.6
Full Design Specs	17	12	50	6	6
Documentation	21	27	12	3.24	23.76
Site Preparation	21	14	36	5.04	8.96
Construction	25	18	15	2.7	15.3
Test/Certification	35	13	0	0	13
Finishing	43	9	0	0	9
Maintenance Training	48	4	0	0	4

Figure 15.2. Gantt chart

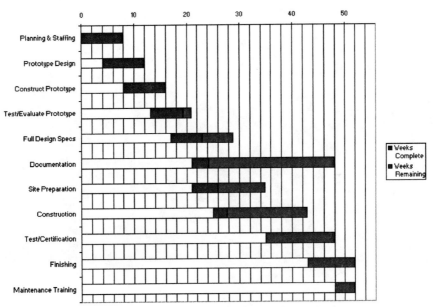

The Excel chart wizard was used to create Figure 15.2 with the columns for task, start week, weeks complete, and weeks remaining; the first part of each bar was made the same color as the chart background (the chart is shown in black and white here, but the completed and remaining parts of each bar are different in color). There are also spreadsheet templates available from a number of sources to facilitate Gantt-chart creation.

A cost-based Gantt chart is shown in Figure 15.3. The bars are represented as a series of cost numbers for each time period of each task. This provides for a nonlinear distribution of cost (and resources) across the time span for the task and allows one to quickly see at a glance both the time for a task and the cost distribution (cash flow).

Figure 15.3. Project cost plan spreadsheet

Project Cost Plan

	Ja	Fe	Ma	Ap	Ma	Jn	Jl	Au	Se	Oc	No	De	Total
Planning & Staffing	3	2											5
Prototype Design		3	3										6
Construct Prototype			8	8									16
Evaluate Prototype				5	10								15
Full Design Specs					5	6	3						14
Documentation						2	2	1	1	1	1		8
Site Preparation						8	3	3					14
Construction							20	50	50	20			140
Test/Certification									10	6	4		20
Finishing											8	4	12
Maintenance Training												4	4
Monthly Cost	3	5	11	13	15	16	28	54	61	27	13	8	254
Cumulative	3	8	19	32	47	63	91	145	206	233	246	254	

Figure 15.4. Project cost plan graph

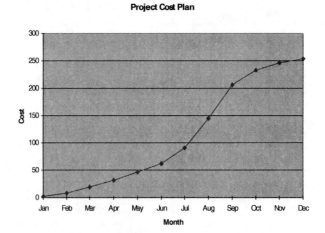

Figure 15.5. Project network diagram

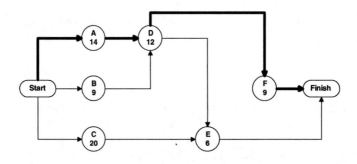

Figure 15.6. Project task information

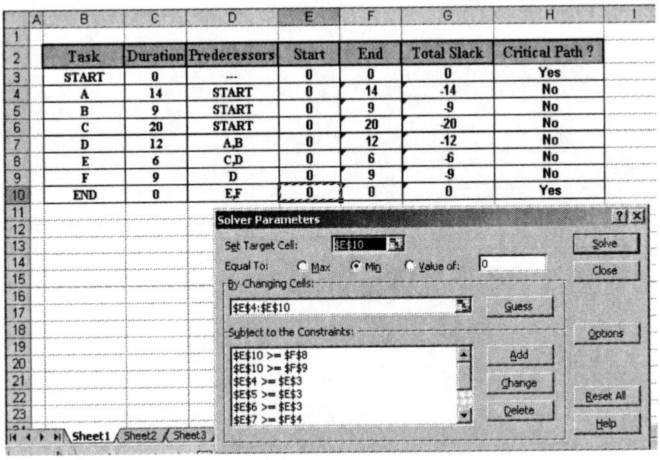

Task	Duration	Predecessors	Early Start Time	Late Finish Time	Total Slack	Free Slack	Critical Path ?
START	0	----	0	0	0	0	Yes
A	14	START	0	14	0	0	Yes
B	9	START	0	14	5	5	No
C	20	START	0	29	9	6	No
D	12	A,B	14	26	0	0	Yes
E	6	C,D	26	35	3	3	No
F	9	D	26	35	0	0	Yes
END	0	E,F	35	35	0	0	Yes

Using charting capabilities built directly into the spreadsheet products, one can use the project cost plan in Figure 15.3 to draw a cost plan graph as shown in Figure 15.4.

In an earlier chapter, the critical path model (CPM) was discussed including the determination of critical path, early/late start times, early/late finish times, and slack/float. Spreadsheet models can also be used to calculate these variables. Consider the CPM drawing in Figure 15.5: The heavy lines denote the critical path and task names and durations are shown inside the nodes.

Once the critical path is determined, a spreadsheet can be used to determine early and late start dates, early and late finish dates, and slacks. This is shown in Figure 15.6 using the network in Figure 15.5, with an example from Klastorin (2004).

Instead of first determining the critical path from inspection (or an algorithm like dynamic programming, used in most scheduling tools), sophisticated spreadsheet programs can

Figure 15.7. Spreadsheet determination of critical path

also be used to find the critical path via linear programming. This is illustrated in Figure 15.7 for the network in Figure 15.5. Using Microsoft Excel, in the solver dialog box, we have requested minimization of the start of the end task subject to constraints for the dependency relationships (i.e., the start time of a task must be greater than or equal to the finish time of its predecessors). Figure 15.7 shows the initial values in the spreadsheet; columns F, G, H are formulas, and column E has the starting values of the cells to be calculated by the LP solver. The formula for column F (task end time) is the start time plus the duration. The formula for column G (total slack or float) is:

(minimum of successor start times minus task end time) plus (task start time minus max of predecessor end times)

The formula column F (critical path) is "yes" if total slack is zero, otherwise "no."

Figure 15.8 shows the solution. Since the LP criteria was to minimize the end time, the solution started all critical path tasks at their earliest time; however, it also started all noncritical path tasks at the latest times. This can be seen because task E (not on critical path) is started at 29 instead of 26. To force the solution to start noncritical path task at their earliest start time we would minimize the sum of all task start times instead of just the "end" task.

LP solutions are no better in this simple case that regular algorithms in scheduling programs, but if there are other constraints such as cost, cash flow, late finish penalties, or early finish incentives, then a LP solution can handle these additional complexities whereas the standard scheduling programs cannot (Klastorin, 2004).

Throughout this book, spreadsheets have been already been used to illustrate the analysis and solution of problems in a number of project management knowledge areas; Figure 15.9 itemizes these spreadsheet models. There are many spreadsheet add-ons available to facilitate analysis in many knowledge areas. Although spreadsheets are very useful, they are less appropriate for large projects and should not be used for everything.

Figure 15.8. Spreadsheet determination of critical path (answers)

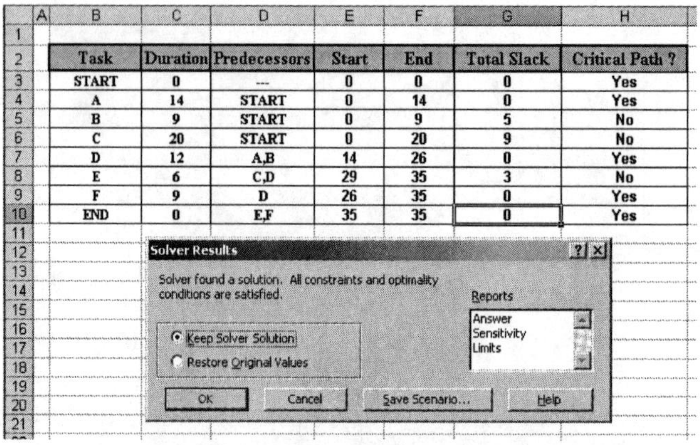

Task	Duration	Predecessors	Start	End	Total Slack	Critical Path ?
START	0	---	0	0	0	Yes
A	14	START	0	14	0	Yes
B	9	START	0	9	5	No
C	20	START	0	20	9	No
D	12	A,B	14	26	0	Yes
E	6	C,D	29	35	3	No
F	9	D	26	35	0	Yes
END	0	E,F	35	35	0	Yes

Figure 15.9. Spreadsheet models in this book

Spreadsheet Model	Chapter
Net Present Value	III
Internal Rate of Return	III
Decision Tree	III
Maximax/Minimax Selection	III
Requirements Specification	III
Organizational Assignment Matrix	VII
Generic Resource Table	VII
Function Point Analysis	VII
Cost Plan	VII, XIV, XV
Risk EMV	VIII
Risk Plan	VIII
Outsource Processes	XII
Outsource Country Analysis	XII
Stakeholder Analysis	XIII
Resource Assignment Matrix	XIII
Earned Value Analysis	XIV
Timesheet	XIV
Schedule & Gantt Chart	XV
Critical Path Analysis	XV
Project Portfolio Optimization	XVI
Project Scoring	XVI

General Project Management Software

There are many general-purpose project management software systems that handle project scheduling and progress reporting. Some of these systems may also include capabilities for some other aspects of project management, including risk. Many project management software systems also handle very specific aspects of project management, such as estimation, risk, change management, portfolio management, earned value, and so forth. Many such specific software programs have already been identified in chapters dealing with those specific aspects of project management.

In addition to features and capabilities, the general-purpose programs may be categorized based on several factors:

- Single or multiuser
- Single or multiproject
- Platform (PC/Mac, file services [redirection], mainframe, client-server, Web based)
- Server operating system (Windows, Unix, Linux, other)
- Data access (file system, ISAM, relational database, other)
- User interface (text, simple GUI, rich GUI, other)

- Import/Export (spreadsheet, XML, etc.)
- Sales/Support (proprietary, open source, shareware, freeware)

The most appropriate package would be a function of capabilities desired, size and complexity of projects, size and complexity of performing organization (number of projects), performance methods used (i.e., earned value or not), platform constraints, location and type of users, and budget constraints. Commonly used general packages include (in alphabetical order):

- @task (www.attask.com)
- Artemis (http://www.artemispm.com/)
- Autotask (www.autotask.com)
- BPSProject (www.bpsproject.com)
- Cooper (www.cooperproject.com)
- EasyProject (www.easyprojects.net)
- EPK-Suite (www.epkgroup.com)
- Microsoft Project & Project Server/Central (www.microsoft.com/project)
- Milestones Simplicity & Professional (www.kidsa.com)
- OpenPlan (www.welcom.com)
- Planview (www.planview.com)
- Primavera & TeamPlay (www.primavera.com/)
- Project KickStart (www.projectkickstart.com/)
- Projistics (www.projistics.com)
- PS Next (www.sciforma.com)
- TeamCenter (www.inovie.com)
- TurboProject (www.tekdeal.com)
- WebProject (www.wproj.com)
- Websystems' AceProject (www.aceproject.com)

The most appropriate software packages for modern IT projects would be Web based, would utilize a comprehensive relational database, are highly scalable, and have a modern GUI. Many of these packages do not have all these features. Some general purpose project management software systems are offered in the form of shareware; that is, one can try the system without charge and then pay a relatively modest fee to continue using the system; examples of shareware systems are MinuteMan, SmartWorks, PlanBee Pro, and QuickGantt.

Open Source Software

Organizations pay significant amounts for annual software license fees; the average Web retailer pays about $300,000 per year. It used to be that free open source software meant "buggy and without support"; the source code itself was the first line of support. However, many organizations are now taking a second look at open source.

There are open source *systems products* such as the Linux operating systems and the Apache Web server, and open source *application components*. The application components include database management systems, application servers, architectures, programming languages, integrated development environments, development tools, browsers, utilities, and various "middleware" components. Both of these types of components may be part of the environment for a project management overall software system. System software products like Linux and Apache are well established now, and their use for prime-time enterprise systems is well documented. For example, United Parcel Service (UPS), which rejected Linux 3 years ago, recently reevaluated this product and is now looking to move all of its RISC-based applications to Linux. Seventy percent of IT executives polled by *Information Week* say their companies now use Linux, up from 56% in 2003 (Greenemeir, 2004). Open source application components are now trying to make the same inroads as has the Open source system software.

The open source model of software distribution and usage is vastly different from commercial products. Open Source software is copyrighted but freely released; extensions and improvements are freely released also. There are a number of free license types, the most popular is the general public license (GNU). Open Source software is free to run, copy, distribute, modify, extend, and improve. Open source software may not have a single product provider. Open source may be developed by an individual, group, or organization and then extended by a "community" of cooperative groups of individuals, each of whom contributes parts of the product. Documentation, support, training, and consulting is generally not centrally available but provided by the community. Some products have sponsor organizations that become focal points for the coordination of official releases of the products and the documentation thereof; most documentation today is online. Sponsor organizations raise funds for their activities via sale of priority support, installation and integration services, other consulting, and/or related products. Sponsor organizations who are also the copyright holder may also release versions of the product under multiple open source–type contracts or under proprietary contracts.

Implementing an Open Source solution requires a different approach from the buyer's perspective. There is no salesperson, no license agreements to sign, and no serial numbers to record. Initial and ongoing license cost savings in using open source software can be huge. For example, the annual cost (per processor) for major vendor relational database management software (RDBMS) follows (Hall, 2003):

- Oracle Standard Edition: $15,000
- Oracle Enterprise Edition: $40,000
- IBM DB2 Workgroup: $7,500

- IBM DB2 Enterprise Edition: $25,000
- Microsoft SQL Server Standard Edition: $4,999
- Microsoft SQL Server Enterprise Edition: $19,999

"After the operating system, it (database management system) is the next significant layer in building an environment based entirely on open source" (Banerjee, 2001). An efficient and scalable relational database product is a key part of a modern general-purpose project management tool that can handle multiple projects. Most major open source products are comparable to their proprietary counterparts in basic features (as prescribed by relevant international standards bodies), and are also comparable in necessary business environment integrity in matters relating to security, backup, recovery, reliability, scalability (multiprocessor, etc.), clustering, replication, and so forth. Thus, a general feature-by-feature comparison of open source versus proprietary products would be meaningless, just as a feature-by-feature comparison of proprietary products is meaningless unless the comparison is with regard to the construction of a specific application for a specific platform.

The MySQL RDBMS is nearly free, depending upon any paid support purchased. In the past, the first line of support for open source products was the source code, but not anymore. For an organization to successfully and economically utilize open source software, it must assemble a coalition of providers for each open source product and use them to create the necessary support infrastructure. Some providers may be paid, such as for priority support (via e-mail, phone call centers, etc.), and others may be Web links to chat sites which link posted problems to proposed solutions. At first glance, it may seem risky not having a single provider responsible for the whole application, but in reality the overall risk is lessened. Major open source products have sponsors with various types of paid support plans, large communities of users who answer problem postings relatively quickly, and a large number of available knowledgeable individual contractors and potential employees. *CIO Magazine* lists (and then dispels) the main myths about open source software (Wheatly, 2004):

- The attraction is the price tag.
- The savings are not real.
- There's no support.
- It's a legal minefield.
- Open Source is not for mission critical applications.
- Open Source is not ready for the desktop.

The development of enterprise-class modern business applications (such as comprehensive project management systems) typically utilizes an application framework that is based upon a particular architecture. Application frameworks are a holistic set of specifications for the interaction and assembly of multiple reusable patterns. A pattern is the design of a core functional element, such as the MVC (model-view-controller) pattern found in many architectures such as J2EE (Java Two Enterprise Edition). Modern architectures may support one or more application servers, programming languages and integrated development environments (IDEs). The major architectures today are J2EE, Microsoft's .Net, and the Open Source LAMP (Linux, Apache, MySQL, PHP). The boundary between architecture, framework, and programming language is blurry and not the same in different architectures. Examples of modern proprietary application frameworks include IBM's Websphere, Macromedia's ColdFusion and Flex, Sun's I-Planet, and BEA's Weblogic.

Hard benchmarks between open source products and proprietary products are seldom published, and these benchmarks are very problem specific. However, *PC Magazine* performed a reasonably comprehensive benchmark using Java server pages (JSPs) and several RDBMSs; it also wrote the same benchmark using active server pages (ASP) in a .NET to include Microsoft SQLServer in the test (Dyck, 2003). The peak throughout results (in pages per second) for the products were:

- MySQL 4.0 (open source) – 608
- Oracle9i – 629
- Sybase ASE 12.5 – 476
- IBM DB2 Universal 7.2 – 494
- Microsoft SQLServer 2000 SP2 – 209

However, the acid test for open systems, both at the system and application levels, has to be Sabre's 4-year project to convert its massive airline reservations and related systems from proprietary mainframe-based system and application software to open systems software (Anthes, 2004). The Sabre systems process more transactions than the New York Stock Exchange—about 50 million transactions per day. Sabre is halfway finished its conversion and reengineering efforts for major applications, and has been successful in utilizing open source products as Linux, Common Object Request Broker, Lightweight Directory Access Protocol, MySQL, and Java. The open source MySQL database runs on a very large server farm of four-way HPrx5670 servers running Linux with about 100 GBs of information. Sabre CTO Craig Murphy stated that "we evaluated several database managers, and MySQL was really the winner from a performance standpoint, and it was certainly the lowest cost." Total cost of ownership is expected to be 40% less with anticipated savings of "tens of millions of dollars" (Babcock, 2004).

Some products are built using open source project management software (i.e., MYSQL), some can operated in an open source environment (i.e., Linux/Apache), and some are distributed completely in an open source manner. The FiveAndDime system utilizes open source software. Some fully open source project management systems are:

- dotProject (www.dotproject.net)
- Double Choco Latte (http://dcl.sourceforge.net)
- GForge (http://gforge.org)
- PHProjekt (www.phprojekt.com)

- ProjectOpen (www.project-open.com)
- Projectory (http://projectory/sourceforge.net)
- ToutDoux (www.gnu.org/software/toutdoux/en/index.html)
- WebCollab (http://webcollab.sourceforge.net)

The FiveAndDime System

Project management software systems are very complex applications. There are many entities involved (work breakdown structures, organization structures, personnel and other resources, time periods, both planned and actual costs, work schedules, etc.) and the database relationships between these entities is complex, including recursive relationships and many-to-many relationships. I have been involved in the design and development of several of these type systems using major RDBMSs such as Oracle, and these have been quite challenging applications to construct. The FiveAndDime system that is used to illustrate many of the concepts and methods in this book is an example of such a comprehensive system, Web based upon open source software. It system uses the MySQL database product and the PHP application server, and it will operate in an open source mode (Linux/Apache) or on proprietary platforms such as Microsoft Windows/IIS or a Unix operating systems. The general application framework for FiveAndDime is shown in Figure 15.10.

Figure 15.10. FiveAndDime application architecture

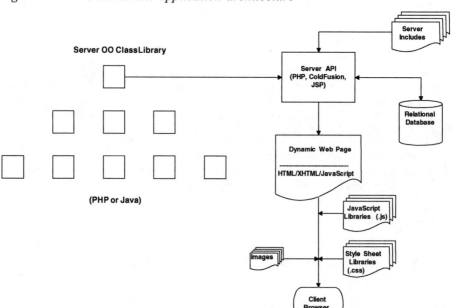

Figure 15.11. Earned value analysis superimposed on Gantt chart

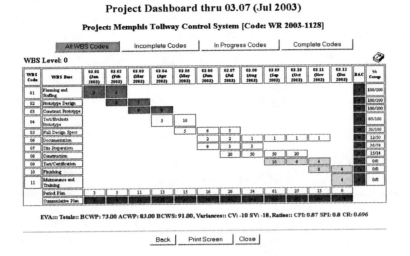

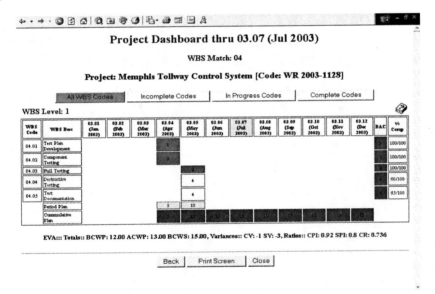

Figure 15.12. Earned value drill down

Figure 15.11 is a screen print from the FiveAndDime system of a rollup to the top level of a WBS showing progress (percentage complete), plan costs, actual costs, and earned value.

Figure 15.12 is another screen print from the system that shows the drill-down option. When one clicks on a top level WBS, code the system shows the subsidiary WBS codes (used to identify problem spots in a project). Note that the screen shots in the figure are black and white, but the actual screens are in color, to highlight WBS codes with cost and/or progress problems.

Chapter Summary

In this chapter, software for project management has been discussed. Spreadsheet models have been illustrated for a number of common project management tasks, software for specific project management functions have been identified, and general project management systems have been listed. open source software as it relates to project management was also discussed and illustrated. *However, these tools do not replace the need for a PM's complete understanding of the project management discipline, because "a fool with a tool is still a fool."*

References

Anthes, G. (2004, May 31). Sabre flies to Open Systems. *Computerworld.*

Babcock, C. (2004, March 29). Open Source, Part 2. *Information Week.*

Banerjee, P. (2001, September 18). Open to discussion. *Intelligent Enterprise.*

Dyck, T. (2003, March 26). SQL databases—Clash of the titans. *PC Magazine.*

Greenemeir, L. (2004, May 24). Going main stream. *Information Week.*

Klastorin, T. (2004). *Project management—Tools and trade-offs.* New York: Wiley.

Wheatly, M. (2004, March 1). The myths of open source. *CIO Magazine.*

Chapter XVI

Managing Multiple Projects

The best way to predict the future, is to invent it.

(Alan Kay)

Managing IT projects and being on an IT project team used to be simpler. PMs typically had one project to manage, and team members were on only one team. All the team members were located in close geographic proximity, and the work was all done at the workplace. Currently the project landscape has become much more complex, where everyone is concerned with multiple projects and teams may be spread out all over the world. The business needs of cutting costs and being quicker to market have increased the pressures on project teams and their managers.

According to the "Chaos Report" from the Standish Group (2004), unqualified IT project success only occurs in about one third of IT projects,. To improve this success rate, many associations (such as the IT Governance Institute) and companies are investigating broad IT governance issues. In regard to project management, these broad issues include such matters as project portfolio management, corporate-wide comprehensive standard project policies and procedures, and project knowledge management. As a vehicle for such consolidation and standardization and to deal with the complexities of project teams, companies have started to establish a Project management office (PMO). The PMO, its key current functions, and the future role of the PMO in global projects, project management maturity, Web portals, and strategic planning are discussed further in this chapter.

The Project Management Office

The *program office* has been a common organizational construct in governments and companies for decades. A *program* is a group of projects managed in a coordinated way to obtain benefits not available from managing them individually (PMI, 2000). Program offices typically have some operational responsibility as well. Within a program office, the projects are all related in some way, typically advancing the goals of the overall program. For example, in the United States, a government agency would have program offices devoted to particular specific efforts generally funded by a specific source.

However, the *project management office* is an umbrella organization for all the projects in an organization and does not have any operational responsibility. The organization in question may be the entire corporation or one division, such as the IT division. In 2003, about two thirds of organizations with IT departments had PMOs, either inside or outside of the IT department (Hoffman, 2003). PMOs are sometimes called "project management support offices" (Powell & Young, 2004), and they are usually set up in one of two manners: with administrative authority or with a consultancy role. There may, however, be PMOs that have combinations of these basic roles. One definition of a PMO is that "a project office is a corporate management organization that evaluates, measures, and essentially enforces the performance and interaction of the implementation of IT project processes across a company's business units" (Elkins, 2003). Whether a PMO is an administrative function or purely a consulting function, a common goal of the PMO is to foster the *discipline of project management* within the organization. As state in the *PM Network*: "The project office's long-term vision is to transform project management knowledge throughout the organization so that it becomes part of the culture" (Block, 1999). According to Computerworld the roles of the PMO are as follows (Elkins, 2003):

*   Eliminate project redundancies (across different departments or even divisions)
*   Standardize the delivery process
*   Access project ROI (both upon proposal and after project completion)
*   Avoid the "latest and greatest" syndrome

CIO Magazine also itemized the roles for a PMO (Santosus, 2003):

*   Project support: project management guidance
*   Project management process/methodology
*   Provide training
*   Provide a "home" for project managers
*   Provide internal consulting and mentoring
*   Project management software tools (evaluate, select, configure, maintain)
*   Project portfolio management

In addition to the lists provided by leading IT publications, other (and more specific) roles often given to or assumed by PMO's include:

- Making sure projects are in line with the organization's strategy and goals
- Aiding in the project selection process
- Helping develop a project WBS, schedule, and cost plan
- Helping with software engineering methodologies, standards, and reuse
- Doing or checking estimation at both the task level and at the project deliverable level
- Doing or checking the risk analysis
- Developing detail policies and procedures
- Developing detail templates, forms, spreadsheets, and so forth.
- Reviewing all project plans (communications, risk, human resource, procurement, etc.)
- Coordinating the use (or acquisition) of scarce resources (including key personnel)
- Performing EVA and other performance analysis on projects
- Checking verification and validation efforts
- Being involved with project change control boards
- Performing or checking stage gate analysis
- Keeping project managers focused on priorities
- Integrating performance information for all projects as a part of executive level reporting
- Coordination of interacting or dependent projects in terms of business issues, technical issues, and corporate politics
- Coordination of diverse projects such as global efforts involving different time zones, currencies, measures, languages, cultures, and so forth
- Troubleshooting and proposing remedies for projects that run into schedule, cost or other difficulties
- Managing common key stakeholders
- Serve as a repository for project lessons learned
- Facilitating effective and consistent use of PM tools
- Making sure projects (and contracts) are properly closed out
- Being an advocate for project managers
- Guiding the organization in the improvement of PM (PM maturity)
- Helping project managers in their career development

PMOs established within the IT division often encompass more than just the project management discipline and may also include the software engineering discipline. For example, software engineering and architectural services which in the past may have been centralized in a chief technology officer (CTO) may be migrated into an IT PMO. PMOs may also include IT integration expertise and services that are often consolidated in an integration competency center (ICC).

In theory, the successful execution of all these roles will result in improved organizational performance, including reduced overall project costs, reduced lead time in implementing solutions, increased quality of delivered products, increased overall business benefit of project implementations, reduced risks of carrying out projects, and ability of the organization to handle bigger and more complex projects. The Sarbanes-Oxley Act (SOX)[1] now requires organizations to disclose large investments, including large projects; PMOs can facilitate compliance with this act.

A PMO requires extra overhead costs, and the benefits of the PMO must exceed these overhead costs. *CIO Magazine* reported that about one half of the companies it surveyed with PMOs indicated overall success, 16% saw no improvement, and 22% did not know yet (Santosus, 2003). However, *Computerworld* reported that 16% to 33% of organizations (depending upon industry) feel that their PMO is ineffective, and only 12% to 19% feel that their PMO is very effective (Hoffman, 2003). It is still often felt that PMOs spend too much time compiling reports for upper management and too little time ensuring that projects are running smoothly (Hoffman, 2003). Some "secrets" for PMOs to get off to a quick successful start and still follow their long-term vision were listed in *PM Network* (Block, 1999):

- Rein in runaway projects
- Assist project startups
- Establish risk management
- Establish portfolio management
- Conduct reviews and audits
- Organize and manage the resource pool
- Identify and develop potential PMs
- Establish and enforce a project management process

The last item in the above list is of paramount importance, and earlier in this book the concepts of critical success criteria and the dual stage gate review process were developed. Completion criteria are monitored by management stage gates primarily using earned value analysis (EVA), and satisfaction criteria are monitored by quality stage gates primarily via stakeholder opinions of preliminary product manifestations (risk and financial metric status are also part of these stage gate reviews). This process is illustrated again in Figure 16.1.

How to measure the success of the PMO can be a difficult issue, and different organizations have different approaches. Some look at the cumulative success rates of the projects and see if the PMO is responsible for improving that overall rate (for projects that produce products that are actually put into use). Some look only at the improvement of estimated time and cost versus actual time and cost for the projects. Some base PMO success on the opinion of stakeholders for all of the projects. Project closeout was also discussed in an earlier chapter and that closeout would go through a final stage gate review with a form such as that in Figure 16.2. The metrics shown in that closeout form could be aggregated for all projects and used to clearly quantify the success of the PMO.

As mentioned earlier, there are two basic ways that PMOs may be set up within an organization. The first way is without any administrative authority, where the PMO staff act as consultants, mentors, and trainers. Here the PMO may have many of the same roles as the authoritative PMO such as developing standard PM policies, procedures, forms, templates, and so forth, but it has no direct authority to enforce any of its suggestions. In this role the PMO observes and reports on what is going on and may or may not try to influence it, but has no direct authority to change anything. On the other hand, the authoritative PMO can enforce its policies and procedures, and often the project managers report to the PMO directly. For some IT divisions the PMO office is simply a staff position or positions to the CIO or CTO, and its authority comes through the CIO. In either case, the PMO should be kept separate from project teams so it can maintain its objectivity. *CIO Magazine* observed that the creation of an authoritative PMO which has the power to approve or kill projects and the power to audit projects for strict compliance with policies and procedures may be too bureaucratic and not work well in many organizations (Santosus, 2003). Some PMs resent PMO staff and consider them as paper shufflers or know-it-alls. In today's knowledge-worker–based world, a PMO with primarily a consultancy role may be a better fit in most IT organizations. Thus, when a project is in trouble, and if its PM did not follow the recommended PMO policies and procedures, then that PM would have "a lot of explaining to do" to the CIO.

The nature of the people that staff a PMO typically include project management specialists, subject matter experts, and project analysts. The PM specialists have gained their PM expertise through specialized training (such as through PMI certified training organizations) and/or years of experience. Subject matter experts are usually IT experts from a software engineering perspective and/or expertise in the specific type of IT applications involved. The project analysts are experienced in working with project information and specific tools. PMO staff members are usually well versed in both the business and technical aspects of IT projects, and it is not uncommon for some PMO staff to be outside consultants. The process of creating a PMO should be carried out like any project, and a part of that process is the evaluation of the effectiveness of the PMO. This is illustrated in Figure 16.3. That figure also indicates the main concepts that an IT PMO must develop, evaluate, and update including the organizational structure of the PMO, the roles and responsibilities of its staff, the office infrastructure, the PM methodology and software engineering methodology, the communications, and the tools and systems. For a PMO to be successful, it may take several years. *CIO Magazine* reported that 37% of PMOs were successful within 1 year, but that the success rate went rose to 65% for PMOs over 4 years old.

PM Solutions (www.pmsolutions.com) has identified the top 10 critical success factors for a PMO:

Figure 16.1. Dual stage gates

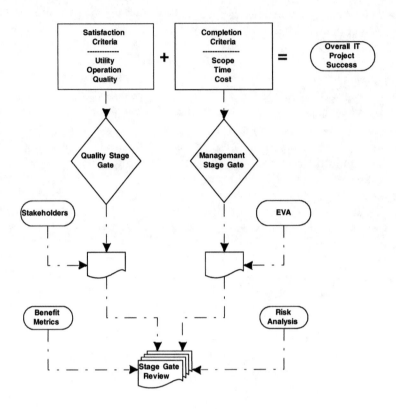

- The PMO has senior executive-level support.
- A superior process for selecting project managers and teams has been established.
- Project teams include participants from multiple business functions and disciplines.
- A high standard of truthfulness and integrity exists within the PMO.
- The PMO serves as an ambassador, communicating with all internal and external stakeholders.
- Training of project managers is competency-based (rather than purely academic).
- Project management methodologies, tools and templates are standardized.
- A useful knowledge library of best practices is maintained as part of the PMO.
- The PMO is involved in all projects from start to finish.
- The organization's project portfolio is managed by the PMO.

Figure 16.2. Final stage gate review form

An organization's project portfolio is the set of projects currently underway as well as projects that have been proposed. IT management has to be concerned not only with doing projects correctly but also that the correct projects are being done. Projects are normally prioritized based on the three R's: reward, risk, and resources. IT projects generally fall into several categories: mandatory, sustaining, and strategic. Mandatory projects are those that have to be done to remain in compliance with regulations of governing bodies or perhaps due to other legal or security issues. Sustaining projects are those that maintain the integrity of the IT infrastructure. Strategic projects are those which promise to improve the competitive position of the organization. IT portfolio management is the process of assessing the portfolio of projects to make sure that priority is given to the projects that are expected to add the greatest value to the organization

Portfolio Management

An organization's project portfolio is the set of projects currently underway as well as projects that have been proposed. IT management has to be concerned not only with doing projects correctly but also that the correct projects are being done. Projects are normally prioritized based on the three R's: reward, risk, and resources. IT projects generally fall into several categories: mandatory, sustaining, and strategic. Mandatory projects are those that have to be done to remain in compliance with regulations of governing bodies or perhaps due to other legal or security issues. Sustaining projects are those that maintain the integrity of the IT infrastructure. Strategic projects are those which promise to improve the competitive position of the organization. IT portfolio management is the process of assessing the portfolio of projects to make sure that priority is given to the projects that are expected to add the greatest value to the organization within acceptable levels of risk. Projects that duplicate effort, are too risky, or produce smaller benefits are not done, canceled, or placed on hold. Unfortunately 75% of companies do not do formal project portfolio management; most CIOs "steer project funding with little thought for the entire investment picture" (Stone, 2004). "Often the only hard information an organization can collect about its projects is how much they're spending—which is like trying to steer an airplane by looking at the fuel gauge" (Wayne, 2004). CIO Magazine lists the benefits to an organization via project portfolio management (Stone, 2004):

- Fairer decisions about funding (not just the political muscle of the sponsor)
- Optimal mix of risk and reward
- Better communication between IS and business leaders due to a common financial model
- Greater understanding and cooperation over funding allocation
- Greater business accountability for investment decisions
- Strengthened alignment between IS and business
- More efficient use of resources
- Fewer project and effort overlaps

Figure 16.3. PMO processes

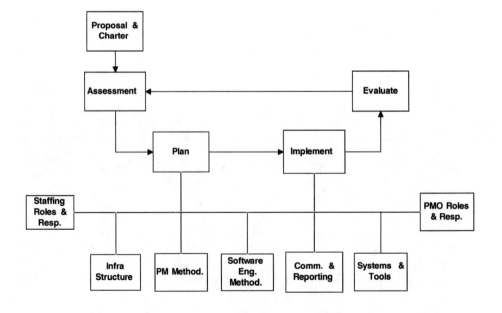

PortfolioStep lists the value of PMO portfolio management as (PortfolioStep, 2004):

- Improved resource allocation
- Improved scrutiny of work
- More openness of the authorization process
- Less ambiguity in work authorization
- Improved alignment of work (IT versus business units)
- Improved balance of work (type of work and risks involved)
- Changed focus from cost to investment
- Increased collaboration
- Enhanced communication
- Increased focus on when to "sell" (bail out)

A serendipitous beauty of project portfolio management is that it's actually impossible to do it without being aligned with the business, because creating a portfolio requires close collaboration with the business. It will elevate the CIO in other executives' eyes because he (finally) will be speaking in their native tongue (Berinato, 2004).

A portfolio must be "balanced" to make sure that potential rewards are weighed against risk levels. One might undertake a few very risky projects if the rewards are quite high, but one would not engage in many very risky projects. The process is similar to maximizing the returns from a portfolio of investments subject to risk constraints. In addition to maximizing returns and minimizing risks, the optimization of the project portfolio also needs to consider the availability and allocation of key resources and the time phasing of resource usage. Consider Figure 16.4, which shows several projects in a graph of risk versus reward.

Projects in quadrant A are no-brainers and are always to be done if resources permit. Projects in quadrant D are to be avoided, unless they are "must do" because of some compliance issue. Projects in quadrants B and C would be balanced off against each other to match the risk tolerance of the stakeholders. Some software systems might show the projects with different size circles, so that the absolute size of the projects was part of the above visualization. Suppose the estimated annual cost (in thousands of dollars) for the eight projects in that figure were as shown in the following list:

- P1 – 350
- P2 – 150
- P3 – 350
- P4 – 250
- P5 – 200

- P6 – 300
- P7 – 150
- P8 – 150

If our total annual budget for the period was $1,000,000, we would likely choose P1 and P2 because they are in quadrant A, then chose P3 and P7 to balance high-risk and low-risk projects. The total of these four project budgets is $1,000,000.

Spreadsheet models in conjunction with integer linear programming (LP) can also be used to find the optimal mix of projects. Consider the eight projects shown in Figure 16.5. For each project the internal rate of return (IRR), cost, and risk factor has been tabulated. The risk factor translates to a money amount of contingency (factor times cost) that is estimated for each project.

Figure 16.6 shows the spreadsheet after calculated columns have been added to determine the total investment (investment % times cost), total return (cost times IRR), and dollars at risk (cost times risk factor). The LP solution involves maximizing the return with constraints such that the dollars invested does not exceed the budget ($3,000 in this example), such that the dollars at risk does not exceed the total contingency (20% in this example, $600), and that the investment % are between zero and 1 and also must be integers (i.e., zero for not doing a project and 1 for doing a project):

Max: Return = X_i * IRR_i * $Cost_i$

Subject to:

X_i * $Cost_i$ <= Budget

X_i * $Cost_i$ * $Risk_i$ < = Contingency (Overall Risk Factor * Budget)

$0 <= X_i <= 1$ and X_i is integer

These formulae are also shown in Figure 16.6 in the Excel Solver window.

Figure 16.7 shows the solution; again, the 1s in the investment % column indicate the chosen projects. Projects 1,2,6,7, and 8 would be done with our budget of $3,000 and overall risk factor of 20%.

A number of financial benefit metrics were discussed and detailed in Chapter III. In addition to (or instead of) risk versus reward or one of these financial benefit metrics, projects can be scored and ranked using "holistic" techniques that include both quantitative and qualitative metrics. Most of these methods define a list of metrics with a corporate weighting assigned to each metric. A score, such as a value between 1 and 10 (not all methods use a linear scale), is then given to each metric. The definition of each metric is usually worded so that a high score is good and a low score is bad. As part of the definition of each metric, examples of the meaning of high and low scores should be specified. For example, in considering technical feasibility, a score of 10 may mean that "this type of project has been done in this organization successfully in the recent past"; a score of 5 may mean that "this type of project has been done in similar types of organizations with success"; and a score of 1 may mean that "we have not seen it done successfully anywhere yet." Statistically it is best if the metrics do not interact too much, but in reality many metrics are going to indirectly affect other metrics. Figure 16.8 is an example of such project scoring.

After projects are scored, they are ranked by the score and a cut-off line is drawn when the sum of project budgets (for the period in question, such as the fiscal year) matches the period budget limit; a limit point on resources could also be used. Many organizations have some type of project review board made up of executive members from both IT and business units. This board periodically reviews both the scoring and ranking process as well as other issues that may be involved with the selection and cancellation of projects.

CIO Magazine discusses the process of building a portfolio and breaks it down into five levels (Berinato, 2004):

1. Put all projects into one database; include such information as name, description, purpose, estimated time and costs, benefit metric (i.e., ROI or IRR), and key resources. This step alone will let IT management see the whole project landscape and allow pruning of duplicated efforts.

2. Prioritize the projects based on either the reward/risk or a scoring/ranking method.

3. Divide projects into two (mandatory versus discretional) or three budgets (mandatory, infrastructure, or strategic) based on the type of investment.

4. Automate the repository – reexamine key parameters regularly.

5. Apply modern portfolio theory (i.e., Markowitz methods).

Figure 16.4. Project risk vs.reward

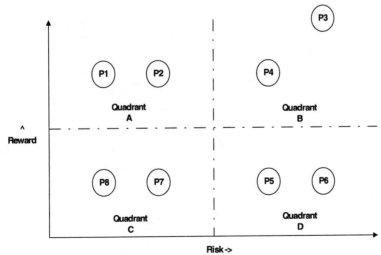

For large organizations, step 1 may be a bit overly ambitious to do for all projects, and the old 80/20 rule should be applied at first; concentrate on the 20% that make up the dollar bulk of your projects. For step 3, an organization has to decide how much of its total budget to place in each of the two or three investment categories, such as 60% into infrastructure and 40% into strategic projects once the funding for mandatory projects is set aside. The last step requires a lot of data and discipline and many argue that it is not worth the cost of the effort. *On this point* CIO Magazine *presents a quote from Douglas Hubbard: "The cancellation rate of IT projects exceeds the default rate on the worst junk bonds; and the worst junk bonds have a lot [of formal portfolio management] applied to them" (Berinato, 2004).*

Tools for project portfolio management range from simple spreadsheets to complex software utilizing the very detailed math and economics of Markowitz modern portfolio theory. Spreadsheets and simple databases are good starting points. A number of specialized software products for portfolio management are available and evolving, including those based on simulation techniques (i.e., Monte Carlo) such as Crystal Ball Pro. Other notable products are PlanView (www.planview.com), ProSight's Portfolios (www.prosight.com), Artemis International Solutions' PortfolioDirector (www.artemisintl.com), Niku's Clarity (www.niku.com), Pacific Edge's Portfolio Edge (www.pacificedge.com), SystemCorp's PMOffice (www.systemcorp.com), ChangePoint's ChangePoint 8 (www.changepoint.com), Deltek Systems' Project Planner (www.sema4.com), and SystemCorp's PMOffice (www.systemcorp.com). Many of these products combine portfolio management with other PMO functions discussed later in this chapter including knowledge management and performance report consolidation with dashboards. Most of the IT portfolio software products do not include risk assessment or life-cycle cost of IT assets (Hoffman, 2004).

However, WiseTechnology suggests that "before you're ready to go shopping for software to help you manage your project portfolio, you need to be sure that your organization is ready for portfolio management" (Glick, 2004). There are many models for "project management maturity," but none of them puts portfolio management at the basic levels. Without basic sound project management skills and processes, any amount of expensive portfolio management software will not help much.

Figure 16.5. Project risk/reward

B	C	D	E
Project	IRR	Risk Factor	Cost ($)
1	0.35	0.15	200
2	0.25	0.05	500
3	0.3	0.5	700
4	0.15	0.3	300
5	0.28	0.25	400
6	0.25	0.3	900
7	0.2	0.2	600
8	0.3	0.1	800

Figure 16.6. Project risk/reward spreadsheet

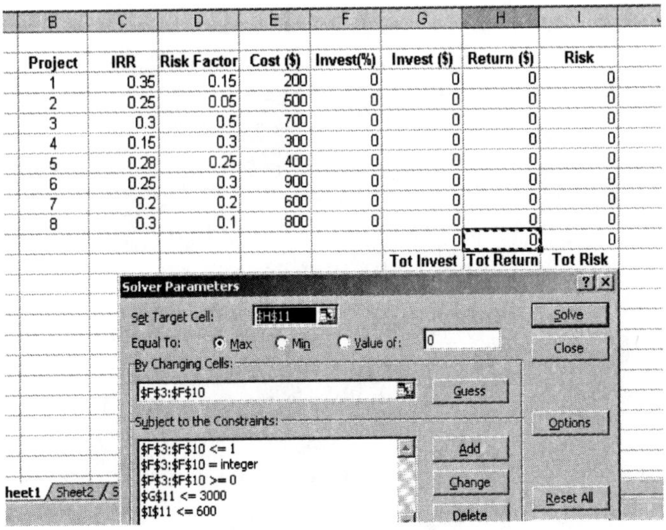

Project	IRR	Risk Factor	Cost ($)	Invest(%)	Invest ($)	Return ($)	Risk
1	0.35	0.15	200	0	0	0	0
2	0.25	0.05	500	0	0	0	0
3	0.3	0.5	700	0	0	0	0
4	0.15	0.3	300	0	0	0	0
5	0.28	0.25	400	0	0	0	0
6	0.25	0.3	900	0	0	0	0
7	0.2	0.2	600	0	0	0	0
8	0.3	0.1	800	0	0	0	0
					0	0	0
					Tot Invest	Tot Return	Tot Risk

Solver Parameters

Set Target Cell: $H$11

Equal To: ⦿ Max ◯ Min ◯ Value of: 0

By Changing Cells:
$F$3:$F$10

Subject to the Constraints:
$F$3:$F$10 <= 1
$F$3:$F$10 = integer
$F$3:$F$10 >= 0
$G$11 <= 3000
$I$11 <= 600

Solve Close Guess Options Add Change Reset All Delete

heet1 / Sheet2 / S

Mark Jeffery, of the Kellogg School of Management at Northwestern University, has developed a formal IT Portfolio Management Maturity Model (Melymuka, 2004a):

Level 1—"ad hoc":

Random projects

Uncoordinated decisions

Level 2—"defined":

Standard methods for evaluating and prioritizing project proposals

Central project management office

Central budget oversight

Central database of projects, with rough estimates of costs and benefits

Basic understanding of financial metrics used to make investment decisions

No consistent organization wide compliance

No links into budgeting cycles

No assessment of results or feedback into decision making

Level 3—"managed":

Links to budgetary cycle

Financial metrics such as ROI and net present value consistently calculated and used in annual reviews with business leaders

Figure 16.7. Project risk/reward spreadsheet (answers)

B	C	D	E	F	G	H	I
Project	IRR	Risk Factor	Cost ($)	Invest(%)	Invest ($)	Return ($)	Risk
1	0.35	0.15	200	1	200	70	30
2	0.25	0.05	500	1	500	125	25
3	0.3	0.5	700	0	0	0	0
4	0.15	0.3	300	0	0	0	0
5	0.28	0.25	400	0	0	0	0
6	0.25	0.3	900	1	900	225	270
7	0.2	0.2	600	1	600	120	120
8	0.3	0.1	800	1	800	240	80
					3000	780	525
					Tot Invest	Tot Return	Tot Risk

Level 4—"synchronized":

    Professional project management processes

    Use of evolving metrics to measure project value through its life cycle

    Frequent reviews to realign projects and weed out underperformers

    Assessment of both project and portfolio risks

    Assessment of future opportunities the project enables

    Disciplined feedback from business

    Results feed decision making

Figure 16.8. Project scoring

Project Scoring

	Factor	Weight	Project 1	...	Project N
1	Consistency with Mission (1 = low, 10 = high consistency)	9			
2	Technical Feasibility (1 = low, 10 = high)	7			
3	Operational Feasibility (1 = low, 10 = high)	7			
4	Economic Feasibility (1 = low, 10 = high)	7			
5	External Risk (1 = high, 10 = negligible)	6			
6	Internal Risk (1 = high, 10 = negligible)	6			
7	Risk of Not Doing this Project (1 = high, 10 = low)	5			
8	Internal Rate of Return (1 = low, 10 = high)	6			
9	Capital Investment (1 = very significant, 10 = little)	4			
10	Payback Period (1 = long, 10 = short)	4			
11	Degree of Contracting/Outsourcing (1 = much, 10 = little)	4			
12	Development Time (1 = long, 10 = short)	4			
13	Geographical Dispersion of Team (1 = much, 10 = little)	3			
14	Impact on Customer Base (1 = little, 10 = much)	5			
15	Impact on Organization (1 = little, 10 = much)	4			
16	Socio-Political Impact (1 = little, 10 = much)	3			
17	Legal and Ethical Issues (1 = many, 10 = none)	5			
18	Environmental & Safety Issues (1 = many, 10 = little)	3			
19	Increase in Org. Knowledge (1 = little, 10 = much)	4			
20	Increase in Org. Competitiveness (1 = little, 10 = much)	4			
	Totals:	100	0	0	0

In his survey of 130 Fortune 1,000 IT groups he found the following distribution:

- Level 1—4.5%
- Level 2—24.5%
- Level 3—54%
- Level 4—17%

Knowledge Management

Another key function of a modern project management office is to be the focal point for corporate knowledge management or at least of knowledge management with respect to projects and project management. Information is data endowed with relevance and purpose, but knowledge is distinct from information and provides a higher level of meaning. The ability to act is an integral part of being knowledgeable. Having knowledge implies that it can be exercised to solve a problem, whereas having information does not. Knowledge management (KM) is a process that helps organizations identify, select, organize, and transfer important knowledge and expertise that are part of the organization's memory.

Figure 16.9. Organizational value

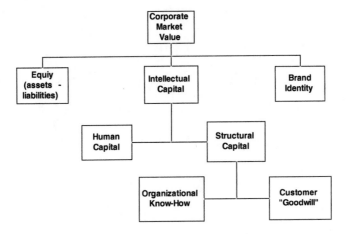

The PMO fosters knowledge management by sponsoring and/or undertaking initiatives to:

- Identifying knowledge
- Share knowledge in a formal manner
- Leverage the value of knowledge through reuse

Knowledge management promotes organizational learning and is used to help solve problems. Knowledge is a main ingredient in the value of a modern organization. Figure 16.9 shows a breakdown of an organization's value.

Historically, the main value was a business's equity, and the three factors thereof—land, labor, and capital—were the key to economic success. Today, knowledge is the fourth factor and is becoming the most important factor in many industries. From the industrial revolution until about 1980, the business landscape was mainly product driven. From about 1980 until 2000, most business was primarily market driven. Today, business is becoming knowledge driven; customers need an additional reason to buy, and a company's knowledge about how best to use/deploy the product or service is becoming of paramount importance. Thus, intellectual capital, which is made up of human capital and structural capital, is becoming the driver of business valuation. Information and knowledge have become the fields in which businesses compete. Ultimately, an organization's only sustainable competitive advantage lies in how its employees apply knowledge to business problems.

Figure 16.10. Knowledge management system

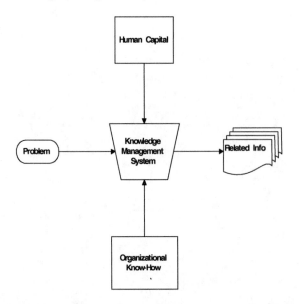

There are two kinds of knowledge: explicit and tacit. Explicit knowledge is easily collected, organized, and communicated. *Tacit knowledge* is "knowing more than one can tell," such as how to ride a bicycle; it is personal, context specific, and very hard to formalize and communicate. Human capital embodies tacit knowledge whereas structural capital is mostly explicit knowledge. Modern knowledge management systems can contain and make available both types of knowledge, as is illustrated in Figure 16.10. Explicit knowledge matches *problems with solutions* in the form of facts (including historical data), procedures, best practices, recipes, standards, and the like. Tacit knowledge matches *problems with people* who have encountered or solved such problems in the past; this approach builds social environments to facilitate the sharing of such understanding.

A functioning knowledge system follows six steps to develop an effective knowledge base:

- Create knowledge
- Capture knowledge
- Refine knowledge
- Store knowledge
- Manage knowledge
- Disseminate knowledge

A state-of-the-art dissemination process makes knowledge visible through maps, directories (yellow pages), hypertext linkage, and search techniques.

For knowledge management to be effective in a company, however, organizational culture must change; employees must be willing to contribute knowledge and use knowledge. Thus there must be strongly committed top leadership, clearly expressed and communicated goals, and end users involved in the implementation process. A direct or indirect reward structure for contributing and using knowledge should also be included.

Lessons Learned

Lessons learned (LL) is the most common form of project knowledge management. As was discussed earlier in this book, a key part of the closeout of each project is a formal post-mortem meeting. This should be conducted preferably by the PMO. In such as meeting the discussion would involve general evaluating questions such as:

- Was the business justification realized (or does it appear that it will be realized); if not, why not?
- What risks events occurred and how they were handled?

- What risks events did not occur, and perhaps why not?
- What in general should be done differently on the next such project?

The discussion would also involve process-specific questions, such as:

- What methods, tools, techniques, resources worked well?
- What methods, tools, techniques, resources did not worked well?
- What artifacts and components can be reused?

Each PMI project management process group (scope, time, cost, risk, quality, etc.) as well as each project deliverable, should be revisited in regard to these questions.

There are a number of formal management techniques that can be used for the LL process. Two commonly used techniques are structured walkthroughs and the external, internal, self-assessment (EISA) approach used in ISO, TQM, and CMM appraisals. In a structured walkthrough, the project team selects the participants and agenda and runs the meeting. No upper management personnel attend these meetings, so team members are not hesitant to be open and honest (Yourdon, 1988). In the EISA approach, an internal self-appraisal is followed up first by an appraisal using independent auditors from the same organization, then by an appraisal using external auditors (Wilson, 1995).

The intent of LL is not only to capture problems and related events, but to initiate solutions for use in future projects. This may involve formal processes (such as fishbone diagrams) to identify "root causes," as was covered earlier in the book. This LL process is a leading indicator of the maturity of an organization with respect to project management. Ewusi-Mensah (2003) systematically analyzed software development failures. *He*

Figure 16.11. NASA lessons learned Web site

found it most distressing that companies continue to make the same mistakes over and over again on projects. Most of these companies did some type of post-mortem analysis, including lessons learned, but most either did not keep those records or make any use of that archived information.

Like any information knowledge repository, a formal LL information system gathers information, stores it, organizes and indexes it, makes it available, and monitors the usage thereof. The major uses of lessons learned knowledge is:

- Changing organization policies, procedures, methodologies, techniques, and tools
- Improving cost and time estimation methods and parametric data
- Improving risk assessment methods and parametric data
- Correlating problems with solutions (and/or those who may how to solve such problems)

Figure 16.11 shows the gateway screen for the NASA LL system.

NASA's described their LL information system as follows (Smith, 2004):

The NASA LLIS is an on-line, automated database system designed to collect and make available for use the NASA lessons learned from over forty years in the aeronautics and space business. The LLIS enables the knowledge gained from past experience to be applied to current and future projects. Its intent is to avoid the repetition of past failures and mishaps, as well as the ability to share observations and best practices. Through this resource, NASA seeks to facilitate the early incorporation of safety, reliability,

Figure 16.12. NASA lessons learned search

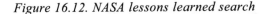
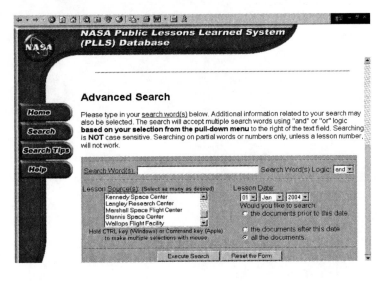

maintainability, and quality into the design of flight and ground support hardware, software, facilities, and procedures.

Figure 16.12 shows the search screen for the NASA LL Web-based system, which searches for keywords within date range for all or a particular space center.

Today, large, effective LL systems can be built using modern data warehouse information technology. A central fact table is constructed and a star topology (related tables) is typically used, as illustrated in Figure 16.13. Relational database technology and/or multidimensional technology (online analytical processing, or OLAP) can be incorporated. Using this approach, topics and/or problems are easily related to solutions and/or people.

Project management lessons learned type of information is not only obtained at the corporate level but also at the trade organization level. A number of IT project management organizations from time to time publish general lessons learned across their industry area, such as the project management organizations (e.g., PMI), software engineering organizations (e.g., IEEE or SEI), and trade publications. For example, InfoWorld's 2004 top 20 IT mistakes were (Dickerson, 2004)

- Botching your outsourcing strategy
- Dismissing open source or bowing to it
- Offshoring with blinders on
- Discounting internal security threats
- Failing to secure a fluid perimeter
- Ignoring security for handhelds

Figure 16.13. Lessons learned as OLAP system

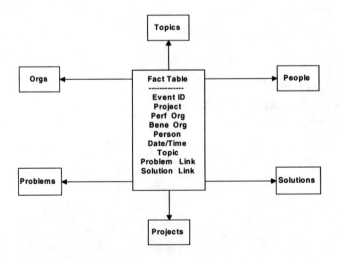

- Promoting the wrong people
- Mishandling change management
- Mismanaging software development
- Letting engineers do their own QA
- Developing web applications for IE only
- Relying on a single network performance indicator
- Throwing bandwidth at a problem
- Permitting weak passwords
- Never sweating the small stuff
- Clinging to prior solutions
- Falling behind on emerging technologies
- Underestimating PHP
- Violating the kiss principle
- Being a slave to vendor marketing strategies

Most of these issues have been discussed in prior chapters of this book as they relate to IT project management.

Figure 16.14. Forms and templates in this book

Process Group	Forms/Templates	Chapter
Initiation	Project Proposal	3
	Project Business Plan	3
Planning	Project Charter	6
	Overall Project Plan	6
	Methodology & SE	5
	Software Management Plan	6
	Communications Plan	6, 13
	Requirements Document	6
	Security Plan	6, 13
	WBS	7
	Schedule	7
	HR Plan	7, 13
	Cost Plan	7
	Procurement Plan	12
	Risk Plan	8
	Quality Plan & Standards	10
	Change Control Plan	11
Exec & Control	Management Stage Gate	3, 9, 11, 14, 15
	Quality Stage Gate	9, 10
	Status Report	9
	Change Order	11
Closing	Project Close Out	11
	Final Stage Gate	11, 16
	Lessons Learned	11, 16

Standard Forms and Templates

Another key function of a modern project management office is to develop standard polices and procedures relevant to the initiation, approval, management, and closeout of projects. A closely related responsibility is the creation and distribution of standard forms and templates based on those procedures. Policies, procedures, forms, and templates may be paper based, but in a modern organization these will all be in an electronic format, and some may be embedded in project management software tools, as was discussed in Chapter XV. Figure 16.14 is a recap of sample forms and templates that have been illustrated in this book. This recap can also be used as a checklist for an IT project life cycle.

Global Projects

Ever since the end of the Cold War, the world has been rushing toward international convergence of capital markets, business regulation, trade policies, and the like. More than 95% of world population lives outside of the United States, and for most countries the majority of their potential market for goods and services is outside of their borders. In addition, more than 60% of the world's *online* population resides outside of the United States, with the average Web site getting 30% of its hits from foreign surfers (Brandon, 2002). Business needs today are forcing organizations to manage projects outside of their home countries and often in multiple countries. In the last decade, domestic profits of U.S. companies increased about 20% while profits of their foreign subsidiaries increased almost 200%. Because the PMO is the corporate focal point for managing multiple projects, it makes sense for the modern PMO to coordinate foreign and multicountry projects.

Obviously, the spoken language is a major issue for managing projects on a global scale. English is the native language to only 8% of the world, and more than 70% of the 1 billion Web users around the world are non-English speakers. Most users in foreign countries prefer document content in their own language; it was found that visitors spend twice as long and are three times more likely to buy from a Web site presented in their native language (Brandon, 2002). Multiple languages are used in many areas. Belgium uses both French and Dutch. In Switzerland, German, French, and Italian are used. One has also to take into account differing dialects across various countries speaking the same language. One cannot use "classic German" in Germany, Austria, or Belgium because all those countries speak a different form of German. The combination of language and dialect is called a "locale," and the ISO has established a coding system for such locales.

Language, however, is just one of the many difficult issues in managing projects on a global scale. Other problem areas include cultural diversity, political, legal, logistic, regulatory, monetary, measures, standards, technical, and geographical. For example, an organization's contract may stipulate that it get paid in dollars, but the expenses may be incurred in foreign countries under a different currency; thus, the actual costs may vary

Figure 16.15. Project global issues by success factor

Global Issues by Success Factor

Success Criteria	Global Issues
Completion Factors	
Project Management	
Schedule (Time)	Foreign holidays, vacations, time zones
Cost	Foreign currency; multiple currencies, conversion costs
	Exchange rate fluctuations
	Need for foreign "on-site" manager
	Travel expense
	Long distance voice costs
	Tax issues (VAT, duties, import/export, etc.)
	Additional legal costs for contracts
Progress	Delays in getting progress info
Stakeholders/Communication	Language/culture communication difficulties
	24 hour communication needs (time zones)
	Email, network, internet outages
	Need virtual "war room"; can't use collocation
	Foreign labor laws
	Knowledge retention
	Employee performance evaluation difficulties
Risk	More risk factors and mitigation plans
	Political uncertainties
	Legal uncertainties & different judicial systems
Methodology	Cultural differences
Commitment to Perform	Authority overlaps and gaps
Ability to Perform	Cultural differences including work ethics
Verification	Differing quality standards
Technology	Differing units of measure (English vs Metric)
Satisfaction Factors	
Business Justification	Offshore outsourcing issues
Validation	Distance/Time factors complicate customer involvement
Workflow & Content	Developing/maintaining content for multiple locales
Standards	Differing national standards & conventions
	Compromise of certifications (CMM, ISO, etc.)
Maintainability & Support	24 hour support requirements
	Version control for multiple locales
Adaptability	Differing OO implementation languages/methods
Trust/Security	Political differences
	Difficulty of background checks
	Information privacy

Figure 16.16. Multiple project dashboard

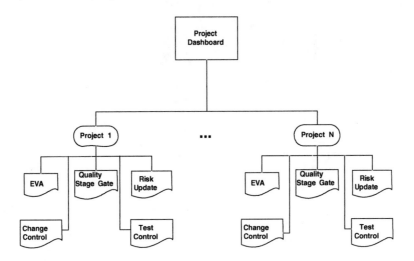

widely with the exchange rate. To effectively identify and thus manage all these global issues, one can relate such issues to the project's critical success factors; this type of analysis is shown in Figure 16.15.

The PMO Portal

In a move to reduce the overhead costs of the PMO yet still obtain many benefits thereof, some organizations are starting to develop *virtual PMOs*, or a *PMO portal*. With a virtual PMO, many of the functions of that office are provided online to project managers, project team members, and line management. Thus, the expertise of the PMO staff is leveraged to provide support to more people in more locations even on a global scale. Today's model for the virtual PMO is a Web-based system with central information repositories. For example, one component of the virtual PMO is typically a project dashboard, as is illustrated in Figure 16.16.

The dashboard provides current status information on all projects that may include earned value ratios, risk status, change control status, defect introduction and correction status, and quality stage gate stakeholder input. Because earned values are quantitative numbers expressed in currency (i.e., dollars) for both cost and schedule deviations, these

Figure 16.17. Project dashboard indicators

Vital Sign	Variance	Points
Schedule Delay	< 10%	0
	10% to 20%	1
	> 20%	2
Milestone Delay	< 10%	0
	10% to 20%	1
	> 20%	2
Deliverable Delay	< 10%	0
	10% to 20%	2
	> 20%	4
Unresolved issues	No issues	0
	< deliverables	1
	> deliverables	2
Cost Over Budget	< 10%	0
	10% to 20%	1
	> 20%	2
Resource Shortage	< 10%	0
	10% to 15%	2
	> 15%	4
High Probability, High Impact Risk Events	1 – 3 risks	1
	4 - 5 risks	3
	6 – 7 risks	5
Disposition of Team	Good	0
	Fair	2
	Poor	4
Sponsor's Commitment	Good	0
	Fair	3
	Poor	6

Figure 16.18. Instrument gauge analogy of project dashboard

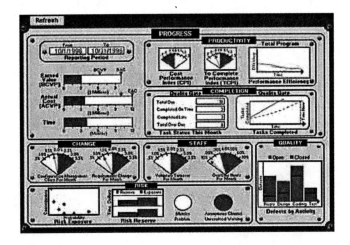

Figure 16.19. PMO portal

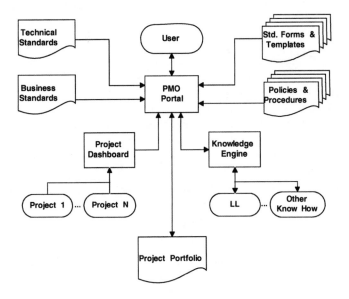

numbers can be rolled up along an OBS for example, to give a picture of how all projects are performing in an organization. Some dashboards use vital signs based upon a point system. An example from *Computerworld* is shown in Figure 16.17 (Melymuka, 2004b). If the total number of points is below 9, then the project is considered *healthy*; 9 to 15 is rated as *caution*, and over 16 is rated as *danger*. The recommended approach herein is to make vital signs correlate with project critical success factors (using the metrics for each success factor as was discussed earlier in this book).

Some organizations use software tools that show the dashboard concept visually, with gauges and charts. One example of this is the Project Control Panel developed as an Excel add-on by the Software Program Managers Network (www.spmn.com/pcpanel.html) as illustrated in Figure 16.18. While the dashboard concept is quite useful for keeping upper management informed, a physical dashboard analogy may only appeal to pilots; most PMs likely prefer information displayed in a more common format such as tables, spreadsheets, and Gantt charts.

Figure 16.19 illustrates the conceptual organization of a comprehensive virtual PMO portal. The user of the system can view or download policies and procedures as well as standard forms and templates. The project portfolio can be viewed or even updated if the user has the authority to do so. A knowledge engine provides the user with solutions to problems from the lessons learned, puts the user in touch with people who have dealt with that problem previously, and provides training information via documents, slide shows, or videos. Chat rooms, bulletin boards, blogs, and wikis can be added to this virtual PMO so that physical meetings of various "boards" can be replaced with virtual meetings; for example, the project approval board, the change control board, or the stage gate board could go virtual. Intelligent software agents can also be added to the virtual PMO; these agents watch all the information available in the system and report exceptions and trends to upper management.

Project Management Maturity

Just as the SEI develops maturity models for software engineering, a number of project management organizations have been developing project management maturity models. The purpose of these models, just like the SEI models, is twofold:

- **Internally:** Companies access their maturity to find ways to improve
- **Externally:** Companies use their maturity rating to sell their project management services and other services that utilize project management (such as building things like IT systems)

PMI has been working on such a model for a number of years and has just recently introduced the organizational project maturity (OPM3). More than 30 other earlier maturity models were part of the research that PMI did for its model using over 800 volunteers (Cooke-Davies, 2004). The PMI model defines three domains to project management (portfolio management, program management, and project management) and four levels (stages) of maturity for each (standardize, measure, control, and continuously improve). Within each domain there are the five PMI process groups (initiating, planning, executing, control, and closing). Process within the process groups are described in terms of five entities: best practices, capabilities, outcomes, key performance indicators (KPI), and pathways. A practice is a component of a process or process group. A combination of certain capabilities result in a particular best practice through a defined pathway, and the outcomes signify the attainment of a capability via KPI metrics. There are one or more outcomes and corresponding KPIs for each capability.

The office of government commerce (OGC) in the United Kingdom has also released a comprehensive maturity model called project management maturity model (PMMM). Like the SEI CMM, PMMM defines five levels of maturity (Initial, Repeatable, Defined, Managed, and Optimized) with specific processes at each level. Like CMM, maturity is typically assessed by questionnaires that determine if those key processes are being carried out. PMMM is considerably less complex that OPM3 and may be more appropriate for many companies. However, PMMM does not include program or portfolio management.

The responsibility for project management maturity in an organization is typically logically housed with the PMO. Thus the PMO would determine the organization's initial maturity, take steps to raise the maturity level, and re-access the maturity as needed. Our model for IT project management maturity (at the single-project level) has been developed throughout this book and is summarized again in Figure 16.20. This model is a combination of best software engineering and project management principles and practices, and the project management practices and metrics thereof are based on identified critical IT project success factors.

Figure 16.20. IT project management maturity

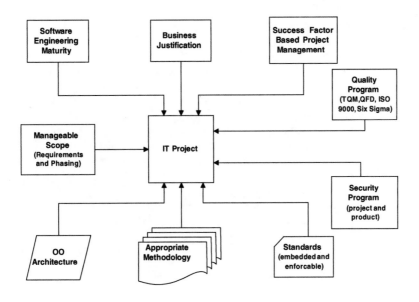

Project Management and Strategic Planning

EVA and other stage gate methods provide management key information to take corrective action primarily at the operational level for a particular project. When EVA metrics from all projects in a program are rolled-up and combined, then management has a greater visibility to examine issues across multiple projects and take actions some of which may be tactical as well as operational. Many project management techniques are often criticized as being too short-sighted and limited to control tactics that may not be in the best interest of the long-term success of an organization (Brandon, 2004). Certainly we understand (and most of us have seen cases) where employees are pushed too hard for success on one project only to become demoralized for performance on future projects.

One of the main responsibilities of a PMO is to implement an overall corporate project management strategy. Implementing such strategy involves the development and/or adoption of some type of strategic foundation upon which to translate corporate vision and goals into winning strategies with effective tactics. Long-term winning strategies must address both the quality and satisfaction dimensions as well as the financial and temporal dimensions (Brandon, 2004).

A number of strategic foundations have been used by organizations in the past, but the modern balanced scorecard (BSC) approach seems most successful and relevant in today's global and fast-paced economic setting. The BSC is a modern approach to strategic management that was originally proposed in 1992 by Robert Kaplan and David Norton (Kaplan & Norton, 1992). They recognized the shortcomings of traditional management approaches which have an overemphasis on metrics that are strictly financial based and looking for the most part at the results of past actions and plans. This rear-facing approach is becoming obsolete in today's fast moving, global, and technology-based economy. The balanced scorecard approach provides definitive procedures

Figure 16.21. Intangible assets

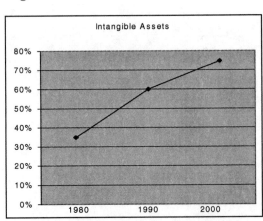

as to what companies should measure in order to balance that traditional prime focus on solely a financial perspective.

While the processes of modern business have changed dramatically over the past several decades (especially with the growth of the Internet), the methods of performance measurement have stayed much the same. Past measurement methods are well suited to asset-based, slow changing manufacturing organizations. But past-performance measurement systems are no longer as relevant to capture the value creating mechanisms of today's modern business organizations (Kaplan & Norton, 1996). Today, intangible assets such as employee knowledge, customer base and relations, supplier base and relations, and access to innovation are the key to creating value; Figure 16.21 shows this shift for U.S. companies. When financial statements (profit/loss, balance sheet, cash flow), Gantt charts, or even EVA analysis are reviewed, the results of those reports reflect actions and decisions that occurred in the past. Some of the past actions and decisions that determine an organizations present financial state may have taken place a month ago, a year ago, or a decade ago (Brandon, 2004).

The balanced scorecard does not ignore financial matters but changes the perspective from a reactive to a proactive involvement. The balanced scorecard approach takes a look at the key management actions (including metrics) that will most likely affect a company's future financial state; these are termed *leading indicators* (Eickelmann, 2003). The balanced scorecard is a management system, not only a system of metrics. Using BSC, organizations first clarify and quantify their vision and strategy and then turn them into actions. BSC provides feedback around both the internal business processes and external outcomes to continuously improve overall performance. When appropriately implemented, a BSC approach transforms strategic planning from an academic exercise into the primary control mechanism of an organization (Averson, 2002; Niven, 2002).

In the language of the founders of BSC:

The balanced scorecard retains traditional financial measures. But financial measures tell the story of past events, an adequate story for industrial age companies for which investments in long-term capabilities and customer relationships were not critical for success. These financial measures are inadequate, however, for guiding and evaluating the journey that information age companies must make to create future value through investment in customers, suppliers, employees. (Kaplan & Norton, 1996)

BCS has been successfully implemented in thousands of organizations around the world, both for profit and nonprofit; success ratios (success in the last major change effort) are reported as (Averson, 2002)

- Non-measurement Managed organizations (55%)
- Measurement Managed Organizations (97%)

Figure 16.22. BSC perspectives

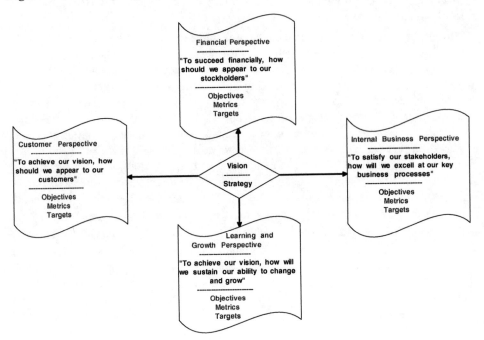

The BSC approach defines four perspectives from which an organization is viewed. Metrics are developed then data is collected and analyzed relative to each of these perspectives. This is illustrated in Figure 16.22 (Brandon, 2004).

The first perspective is the learning and growth perspective. It involves the investment in human capital through activities like positive feedback, motivational techniques, setting up mentors, communications facilitation, employee training, and the development of a company-cultural and code of ethics. Chapter XIII discussed many of these issues from an operational perspective. In the current climate of rapid technological change, it is becoming necessary for knowledge workers to be in a continuous learning mode. Organizations often find themselves unable to hire new technical workers and at the same time allow a decline in training of existing employees. This is a leading indicator of "brain drain" that will ultimately kill an organization. Metrics can be put into place to guide managers in focusing personnel development funds where they can help the most. This perspective is the foundation for long-term success of an organization. From a project team perspective, short-term learning and growth perspectives are already included in the metrics for our quality stage gates. However, for long-term success, long-term actions and metrics need to be established.

The next perspective is the business (or internal) process perspective. This perspective relates to the internal business processes. Metrics based on this perspective allow the managers to know how well their business is running, and whether its products and services conform to customer-stated requirements and unstated expectations. These metrics have to be carefully designed by those who know these processes best. There

Figure 16.23. BSC perspectives cause and effect

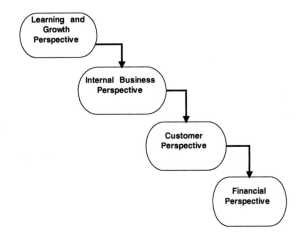

are two kinds of business processes in an organization's value chain. Primary (mission-oriented processes) are the special functions of an organization often used for competitive advantage, and support processes (i.e., accounting, legal, procurement, HR, etc.) which are more repetitive in nature, and hence easier to measure and benchmark using classical metrics. From a project perspective, business process metrics are included in the metrics for both our management and quality stage gates.

The next perspective is the customer perspective. Recent management philosophy and IT products as customer relations management systems (CRMs) and sales force automation systems (SFAs) have shown an increasing realization of the importance of customer focus and customer satisfaction in any business. If customers are not satisfied, they will eventually find other suppliers that will meet their needs. Poor performance from this perspective is thus a leading indicator of future decline, even though the current financial picture may look good. From a project perspective, customer relations are included in the metrics for our quality stage gates.

The last perspective is the financial perspective. Kaplan and Norton do not disregard the traditional need for financial data. Timely and accurate funding data will always be important. Their point is that the current emphasis on financials leads to the unbalanced situation with regard to other perspectives. There is also a need to include additional financial-related data, such as risk assessment and cost-benefit data, in this category. Again, from a PM perspective, financial data is a key metric of our management stage gate, including EVA and risk analysis.

Figure 16.23 shows the perspectives in a waterfall, long-term, strategic cause-and-effect scenario. Motivation, skills, and satisfaction of employees are the foundation for all improvements. Motivated, skilled and empowered employees will improve the ways they work and also improve the work processes. Improved work processes will lead to improved products/services, which will mean increased customer satisfaction. Increased

Figure 16.24. PMO BSC metrics

Perspective	Activities	Metrics
Learning & Growth	Effective Communications	Communication Problems
	Management Team Building & Motivation	PM and Employee Feedback
	Project Manager Development	Training Funding
	Motivation	PM Incentive Packages
	PM Forum	Sharing of "Lessons Learned"
		Use of "Lessons Learned"
Customer	Customer Relations	Customer Satisfaction
	Customer Involvement	Customer Feedback (about PM, and line management)
Internal	Planning	Rollup of EVA Time
	Process Standardization	Standard Forms & Procedures
	PM Support (from line management)	PM Feedback
Financial	Use of Resources	Rollup of EVA Cost
	Contracting/Procurement	Procurement Problems

customer satisfaction will in turn lead to long-term improved financial performance (Brandon, 2004).

In the early industrial revolution in order to shield the customer from receiving poor-quality products, aggressive efforts were focused on inspection and testing at the end of the production line. The problem with this approach, as pointed out by Deming (as cited in Walton, 1991), is that the true causes of defects could never be identified, and there would always be inefficiencies due to the rejection of defects. What Deming saw was that variation is created at every step in a production process, and the causes of variation need to be identified and fixed. Deming emphasized that all business processes should be part of a system with feedback loops. The feedback data should be examined by managers to determine the causes of variation, and then attention could be focused on fixing those particular problems. These aspects of quality management were discussed in detail earlier in this book. BSC emphasizes *feedback control from each of the four perspectives in each major business process*; that is, each perspective for each key process should have objectives, metrics, and targets for proper feedback control.

The successful concepts of BSC can be integrated into the project management context. Considering a project as a key business project, one needs to establish metrics for each of the four perspectives at the individual project level and also at the PMO level. BSC performance metrics at the project level have already been included in our dual stage gate methodology and comprehensively discussed earlier in the book. For example, EVA would be a key metric for the project level BSC financial perspective. Success factors from the completion perspective are used in the BSC internal perspectives, and success factors from the satisfaction perspective are used in the BSC customer perspective.

An BSC scorecard defines the key activities for each perspective and the metrics that are going to be used to monitor the performance of that activity. One possible very simple score card at the PMO level is shown in Figure 16.24 (Brandon, 2004). For example, at the BSC customer perspective, we would measure not only the customer's satisfaction with our projects, but how involved our project team, project manager, and line management was with customer personnel. *Thus, using the combined principles of dual critical success factor-based stage gates, and BSC, a PMO office can more effectively manage all project work across an organization from a strategic perspective.*

References

Averson, P. (2002). *The Balanced Scorecard Institute.* Retrieved from www.balancedscorecard.org

Berinato, S. (2004, October 16). Do the math. *CIO Magazine.*

Block, T. (1999, April). The seven secrets of a successful project office. *PM Network.*

Brandon, D. (2002). Issues in the globalization of electronic commerce. In V. K. Murthy & N. Shi (Eds.), *Architectural issues of Web-enabled electronic business.* Hershey, PA: Idea Group Publishing.

Brandon, D. (2004). Project performance measurement. In P. Morris & J. Pinto (Eds.), *The Wiley guide to managing projects.* New York: Wiley.

Cooke-Davies, T. (2004). Project management maturity models. In P. Morris & J. Pinto (Eds.), *The Wiley guide to managing projects.* New York: Wiley

Dickerson, C. (2004, November 22). The top 20 IT mistakes. *InfoWorld.*

Eickelmann, N. (2003). Achieving organizational IT goals through integrating the balanced scorecard and software measurement frameworks. In *Technologies and methodologies for evaluating information technology in business.* Hershey, PA: IRM Press.

Elkins, W. (2003, February 17). Maximize ROI with a project office. *Computerworld.*

Ewusi-Memsah, K. (2003). *Software development failures.* Cambridge, MA: MIT Press.

Glick, B. (2004). *Steering a project takes more than expensive software.* Retrieved October 16, 2005, from www.wisetechnology.com

Hoffman, T. (2003, July). Value of project management offices questioned. *Computerworld.*

Hoffman, T. (2004, February 10). Balancing the IT portfolio. *Computerworld.*

Kaplan, R., & Norton, D. (1992, January). The balanced scorecard—Measures that drive performance. *Harvard Business Review*

Kaplan, R., & Norton, D. (1993, September). Putting the balanced scorecard to work. *Harvard Business Review.*

Kaplan, R., & Norton, D. (1996). *The balanced scorecard.* Cambridge, MA: Harvard Business School Press.

Melymuka, K. (2004a, May 3). Harrah's betting on IT value. *Computerworld.*

Melymuka, K. (2004b, September 27). How to kill an IT project. *Computerworld.*

Niven, P. (2002). *Balanced scorecard—Step by step.* New York: Wiley.

PMI. (2000). *The project management body of knowledge (PMBOK).* Newton Square, PA. ISBN 1-880410-22-2.

PortfolioStep. (2004). *The value of portfolio management.* Retrieved from http://www.porfoloistep.com

Powell, M., & Young, J. (2004). The project management support office. In P. Morris & J. Pinto (Eds.), *The Wiley guide to managing projects.* New York: Wiley.

Santosus, M. (2003, July 1). Office discipline: Why you need a project management office. *CIO Magazine.*

Smith, E. (2004). *Welcome to the NASA lessons learned information system.* Retrieved from http://llis.nasa.gov

Standish Group. (2004). *Chaos chronicles.* Retrieved from www.standisgroup.com

Stone, P. (2004, October 16). The case for portfolio management. *CIO Magazine.*

U.S. Department of Commerce. (1999). *Guide to balanced scorecard performance management methodology.* Retrieved from http://oamweb.osec.doc.gov/bsc/guide.htm

Walton, M. (1991). *Deming management at work.* New York: Perigee.

Wayne, R. (2004). Conscious choices. *Software Development,* January.

Wilson, P., & Pearson, R. (1995). *Performance-based assessments: External, internal, and self assessment tools for total quality management.* Englewood Cliffs, NJ; American Society for Quality Control Press.

Yourdon, E. (1988). *Structured walkthroughs.* Prentice Hall.

Endnote

[1]   The Sarbanes-Oxley Act was signed into U.S. law on July 30, 2002, and introduced highly significant legislative changes to financial practice and corporate governance regulation. It introduced stringent new rules with the stated objective: "to protect investors by improving the accuracy and reliability of corporate disclosures made pursuant to the securities laws."

Glossary and Acronyms

Acceptance: Accept a risk (take no preventive action).

Activity Code: A WBS code to which budgeted costs and actual costs are assigned.

Activity-on-Arrow (AOA): A network diagramming technique in which activities are represented by arrows and the nodes represent the coordination of activities in regard to the sequencing of the work (same as ADM).

Activity-on-Node (AON): A network diagramming technique in which activities are represented by nodes and the lines represent dependencies (same as PDM).

Actual Cost: The costs that are to be incurred and are to be charged to the project.

Actual Cost of Work Performed (ACWP): The costs that have already been incurred and are charged to the project as of a point in time.

Alpha Testing: Prerelease testing in which a small friendly sampling of the targeted customer base tries out the product.

AP: Agile Programming or Accounts Payable.

Application Frameworks: A holistic set of software specifications for the interaction and assembly of multiple reusable patterns.

Apportioned Effort (AE): In earned value analysis, a method of distributing value to activities whose progress is governed by another activity.

AR: Accounts Receivable.

Arrow Diagramming Method (ADM): A network diagramming technique in which activities are represented by arrows and the nodes represent the coordination of activities in regard to the sequencing of the work.

As-Built Documentation: Text and diagrams that describe the system as it was actually built.

Authorized Unpriced Work (AUW): Work that has been authorized, but for which a budget has not set.

Authorized Work (AW): Work that has been planned, priced, and for which authority has been received to commence.

Avoidance: Eliminate the cause of a risk event or reduce the EMV via reducing risk probability.

Backward Pass: Calculating the latest start dates moving from the finish date of a project to the left along a network.

Balanced Matrix: A matrix type of organizational structure functional managers and project managers have the same priority.

Balanced Score Card (BSC): A modern method for strategic planning.

Bar Chart: A depiction of project task and schedule data that uses horizontal bars on a time scale to represent activity. The most common form of such is the Gantt chart.

Baseline Schedule: A copy of the project schedule when the project starts before change orders; the original plan.

Benefiting Organization: The organization benefiting from the work of the project.

Beta Testing: Prerelease testing in which a significant sampling of the targeted customer base tries out the product.

Bid Documents: A set of documents issued for purposes of soliciting bids in the course of the procurement process.

Black Box: A process done without knowledge of the inner workings of the subject of the work, as in Black Box Testing.

Budget at Completion (BAC): The total budget for a project.

Budgeted Cost of Work Performed (BCWP): A measure of the value of work performed so far based upon the initial estimated cost for said work as of a point in time (same as "earned value").

Budgeted Cost of Work Scheduled (BCWS): The planned cost for project work as of a point in time.

Bug: A malfunction in a hardware or software product.

Burden: The difference between the full cost of a resource (i.e., a person) and the amount paid to that resource. For a person, it would include employer taxes (FICA, MEDI, FUTA, SUTA), workmen's compensation, benefits, and so on.

Business Risk: An uncertain situation that could result in a gain or a loss.

CBS: Contractor Breakdown Structure.

CBSE: Component-Based Software Engineering.

CFO: Chief Financial Officer.

Change Control: The process of managing changes to the project's baselines to determine which changes to include and which not to include.

Change Control Board (CCB): A formal group of stakeholders responsible for approving or rejecting changes to the project baselines.

Change Management: A formal process for managing changes to the project.

Change Management Plan: The formal plan for managing changes to the project.

Change Order: A request to the performing organization to modify a requirement or deliverable.

CIO: Chief Information Officer.

CKO: Chief Knowledge Officer.

CMM: Capability Maturity Model.

COCOMO: Constructive Cost Model.

Communication Plan: A formal plan for how, when, where, and what information will be exchanged amongst project stakeholders.

Configuration Management: Managing changes to a hardware/software configuration in a holistic and cohesive manner so that performance and integrity is not compromised.

Conflict Resolution: The process of seeking resolution to conflicts amongst project stakeholders.

Contingency: Money or amounts of time may be set aside to be used in the event of risks occurring during the project.

Contract: A legally binding agreement between competent parties to acquire legal goods or services in trade for some form of compensation.

Contract Administration: Managing a relationship with a vendor including all necessary documents and deliverables.

Contract Closeout: Processes and activities which assure that the contractor has fulfilled all contractual obligations and has released all claims in regard to the work performed.

Contract Price: The amount payable by the customer under the terms of the contract for work done and deliverables received.

Contract Target Cost (CTC): The sum of authorized and priced work excluding unpriced work.

Contractor: The party who performs work on behalf of another based on a legally binding contract.

Control Code: In our notation, a WBS code which has subsidiary activity codes. Costs, both planned and actual, are posted to the activity accounts and rolled-up to control accounts. (In C/SCSC, a cost account.)

CORBA: Commonobject request broker architecture.

Cost Account: In the United States C/SCSC, a budget account associated with a WBS element, at which lower level tasks are gathered for management purposes (and assigned to one organizational element). (Also called control code in ANSI and DoD EVA.)

Cost Benefit Analysis: The ratio of a endeavor's estimated cost to its anticipated benefit.

Cost Performance Index (CPI): The cost efficiency factor representing the relationship between the actual costs incurred and the planned value of the work performed (earned value)—BCWP/ACWP.

Cost/Schedule Control System Criteria (C/SCSC): A reporting and control system devised by the U.S. Department of Defense for its contractors to use to minimize and anticipate cost overruns.

COTS: Commercial Off the Shelf Software.

CPAF: Cost Plus Award Fee.

CPFF: Cost Plus Fixed Fee.

CPIF: Cost Plus Incentive Fee.

CPM (Critical Path Model): A network diagram using a single time estimate per task to determine the longest sequence(s) of connected (dependent) tasks.

Crashing: Decrease the duration of a task(s) or activity typically by increasing the expenditure of resources or moving resources to critical path tasks.

Critical Path: The set of inter-dependent tasks that must finish on time for the entire project to finish on schedule.

Critical Success Criteria (CSC): The principles or standards by which the success of a project will be judged.

Critical Success Factors (CSF): Any circumstance, fact, or influence which contributes to a critical success criteria; measurable factors that are most important to a project's success criteria.

CSD: Cleanroom Software Development.

CTO: Chief Technical Officer.

Decision Tree: A graphical representation of a decision process with alternatives.

Deflection: Assign (transfer) a risk to another party.

Deliverable: A specific tangible product or observable event that is to be produced by a project. Examples include such things as an item of hardware, document, a software product, a process definition, a training session, etc. Deliverables are usually nouns, as opposed to tasks which are verbs.

Delphi Technique: A process where a consensus is reached facilitated by experts; for projects it is often used as an estimating technique.

Dependency: A relation between task, such that one cannot either start (or finish) until another either finishes (or starts).

Design Review: A formal review of the design of a product in regard to the project requirements and other standards or constraints.

Direct Costs: Costs that are directly the result of the activity associated with a project task.

Discounted Cash Flow (DCF): Calculation of the present value of a projected cash flow (income minus expense) based on some an interest rate and compounding period.

Drill Down: The opposite of "roll-up" or summarization; digging deeper into a structure (such as the WBS) to get more detail information.

Dummy Activity: An activity of zero duration used to show a dependency relationship in the arrow diagramming method.

Duration: The length of calendar time needed to complete an activity. Original duration is the original planned completion time of a task, remaining duration is the time left to complete the task.

Early Finish: The earliest date on which a task can finish. It is based on the task's early start which may depend on the finish of predecessor activities and the activity's effort requirements.

Early Start: The earliest date on which a task can begin. It is dependent on when all predecessor tasks finish.

Earned Value (EV): The planned cost for project work completed as of a point in time; a measure of the value of work performed so far based upon the initial estimated cost for said work (same as "budgeted cost of work performed").

Effort: The amount of labor units necessary to complete a task, usually expressed in person-hours.

Engineering Change Notice (ECN): The formal release of a software design change.

Enterprise Resource Planning (ERP): Integrated software and procedures for an organization to operate and automate its key business processes; typically relies on a central relational database management system.

EOC: Element of Cost.

Estimate at Completion (EAC): Estimated total cost of project work when the project is finally completed.

Estimate to Complete (ETC): The estimated money required to completed the work of the project.

EVA: Earned Value Analysis (also EVMS).

Executive Sponsor: The executive typically responsible for the project purpose and direction; may have sponsored the project or had the initial idea for the project (also called "project sponsor" or "champion").

Expected Monetary Value: The product of an event's probability of occurrence and the monetary gain or loss that will result.

Factor: A circumstance, fact, or influence which contributes to a result or has an effect on a result.

Fast Tracking: Compressing a project schedule by doing some tasks in parallel that would normally be done in sequence; starting a task before its predecessor task(s) have completed.

FFP: Firm Fixed Price.

Float: The difference between the time available for performing a task and the time required to complete it.

Forward Pass: Calculating the earliest start dates moving from the start date of a project to the right along a network.

FPIF: Fixed Price Incentive Fee.

Free Float: The maximum amount by which a task can be delayed beyond its early dates without delaying any successor task beyond its early dates.

Free Slack: The amount of time a task can slip without delaying another task.

Function Point (FP): Individual high level software components such as screens and reports that are classified by degrees of complexity.

Function Point Analysis (FPA): A software development estimating technique that was is characterized by breaking software deliverables into function points.

Gantt Chart: A chart using horizontal time lines that illustrates tasks in a project.

GL: General Ledger.

Goal Seek: Back solving a model by allowing certain variables to change to optimize some criteria.

Groupware: Software which facilitates groups of people working together to collaborate in decision processes or other work efforts.

GUI: Graphical User Interface.

Hammock: A summary activity that encompasses several tasks; it does not change or schedule dates for the tasks that are encompassed.

Headcount: Total hours expended divided by the average hours worked per employee per week.

Human Resource Management: The processes, functions, policies, and procedures involved with the management of people and their needs.

Impact: An assessment of the adverse effect (usually in money) of a risk event.

Incentive Contract: A contractual arrangement where the contractor is rewarded with a higher fee if performance (time, cost, quality) is above contract specified level.

Indirect Costs: The costs for common resources or expenses that are not associated with any one task.

Insurable Risk: A particular type of risk which can only involve a loss (not a gain) which is often covered by an insurance policy.

Internal Rate of Return (IRR): The value of the interest rate that causes the net present value of future cash flows (income minus expense) to be zero.

Invitation for Bid (IFB): A formal request to a vendor for one price for total job, perhaps with a breakdown or with rates for specific extras.

JAD: Joint Application Development.

Key Performance Indicators (KPI): Those management indicators that are determined to reflect most directly on the key objectives of the project.

Kick Off Meeting: The first official stakeholder meeting for a project.

KISS: Keep It Simple, Stupid.

KLOC: Thousands of lines of code.

Knowledge Management: The formal management of information and knowledge as an asset; includes information acquisition, maintenance, access, and distribution.

Lag: The amount of time after one task is finished before the next task can be started.

LAMP: An open source architecture for the development of software (Linux-Apache-MySQL-PHP).

Late Finish: The latest time a task may be completed without delaying the entire project.

Late Start: The latest time a task may start without delaying the entire project.

Lead: The minimum time between the start of one task and the start of an overlapping task.

Lessons Learned: The stakeholders' learning from the project; usually documented during closeout.

Letter of Intent: A non-legally binding letter issued to a contractor to confirm the award of a contract pending the signing of a formal contract.

Level of Effort (LOE): A task of a general nature that has a uniform rate of effort over all or a portion of the project.

Lifecycle: A group of work phases which determines the formal methodology for building and maintaining something

Liquidated Damages: A contractual arrangement that provides for a final non-negotiable settlement for a loss due to some aspect of non-performance on a contract other than cost such as time or quality.

LOC: Line of Code.

M&A: Management and Administration.

Managerial Reserves: The reserve accounts for various contingencies (such as risk) of a project.

Matrix Management: A cooperative organizational approach in which both project managers and line managers cooperate in regard to resource management.

Maturity Model: A framework used as a basis for determining the degree of maturity of an organization with regard to a particular discipline or part thereof.

Mean: A measure of central tendency that divides the area under a probability curve into two equal parts.

Methodology: An organized system of "know-how."

Milestone: A major event in a project's schedule that is easily identifiable by such things as the completion of a significant deliverable, the occurrence of an event, and so on.

Mitigation: Reducing risk EMV via reducing the impact of the risk event.

Monte Carlo Method: A statistical method involving the generation of random numbers within a prescribed range to represent the value of a factor in a project.

Most Likely Time: The most realistic time estimate for completing a task under normal conditions.

MOU: Memo of Understanding.

MRP: Manufacturing (material) Resource (requirements) Planning.

MVC: Model View Controller (a design pattern for user interface construction).

Net Present Value (NPV): The difference between the discounted (based on a fixed interest and compounding period) present value of benefits (income) and the discounted present value of expense (costs).

Network Diagram: A schematic drawing of the logical relationship of the tasks in a project.

Nonconformance: The failure of a product (or component thereof) to conform to specified requirements for any quality attribute.

Noncritical Activity: A task which is not on the critical path.

O&M: Operations and Maintenance.

OBS: Organizational Breakdown Structure.

OO: Object Oriented.

Open End: An activity other than project start or finish that does not have both a predecessor task and a successor task (to be avoided in good scheduling).

Optimistic Estimate: The minimum reasonable time in which a task might be completed.

Organizational Breakdown Structure (OBS): A hierarchical structure of organization components.

Original Duration (OD): The original planned time for a project or task.

Outsourcing: The procurement of goods or services from outside of one's own overall organization.

Parametric Estimating: An estimating technique that uses a mathematical relationship between relevant variables. The constants in these relationships are derived from historical data.

Parent Task: A task within the work breakdown structure that encompasses one or more subordinate child tasks.

Pareto Diagram: A histogram of relevant, ordered by frequency of occurrence.

PBS: Part Breakdown Structure.

Percent Complete (PC): A ratio comparing the part of a task complete to the total effort of the task.

Performance Indexes: Project planning and status indicators that measure variances in regard to key metrics.

Performance Measurement Baseline (PMB): The portion of the total project budget for which the project manager is responsible and against which performance is to be measured.

Performing Organization: The organization doing (or primarily responsible for) the project work.

PERT Analysis: A process by which a probable outcome (i.e., a task effort estimate) is based on three specific estimates: best case, most likely, and worst case.

PERT Chart: A network diagram that shows all tasks and task dependencies.

Pessimistic Estimate: The maximum reasonable time to complete a task should all things go poorly (does not include the occurrence of unforeseen risks).

Phase: A major period in the life of a project.

Planned Cost: Costs set when the project work starts and he current schedule becomes the baseline.

PMBOK: The Project Management Institute's Project Management Body of Knowledge publication.

Portfolio Management: The management of a number of projects (that do not share a common objective) in regard to the selection of which projects to initiate.

Precedence: A task has precedence over another task, if the first must be completed before the second task starts.

Precedence Diagram Method (PDM): A method of drawing a network diagram using nodes to represent the activities and lines to show dependencies.

Predecessor Task: A task that must start or finish before another task can start or finish.

Present Value: The calculation in current dollars of a regular stream of future payments or income using a specific interest rater and compounding period.

Prime Contractor: The contractor with overall responsibility for delivery a project or a contract in general; the prime contract will coordinate and oversee the work of subcontractors.

Probability: The likelihood of occurrence.

Procurement: The establishing contractual relationships to obtain goods or services.

Production Rate: An older term for SPI.

Productivity: The rate of output creation per unit of time.

Program: A set of projects with a common goal managed collectively.

Program Evaluation and Review Technique (PERT): A project management technique for estimating how much time is needed to complete the work. Each task is assigned a best, worst, and most likely completion time estimate. These estimates are used to determine the mean completion time via a Beta distribution.

Program Management: The management of a set of projects with a common goal which may also include operational aspects.

Project Charter: A document that describes a project in terms of its overall scope, schedule, dependencies, assumptions and resources. It is the official "go-ahead" document for the project and establishes a clear overall level of understanding between the sponsor, upper management, and the rest of the project team.

Project Management (from Wikipedia): "The ensemble of activities (such as tasks) concerned with successfully achieving a set of goals. This includes planning, scheduling and maintaining progress of the activities that comprise the project. Reduced to its simplest project management is the discipline of maintaining the risk of failure at as low a value as necessary over the lifetime of the project. Risk of failure arises primarily from the presence of uncertainty at all stages of a project. An alternate point of view is that project management is the discipline of defining and achieving targets while optimizing the use of resources (time, money, people, space, etc)."

Project Management Information System (PMIS): A system for gathering, processing, and reporting project related information; usually the system involves (or is) a software package(s).

Project Management Office (PMO): A group of technical and business personnel who oversee and/or foster professional project management practices within an organization.

Project Management Professional ("PMP"): The highest level of professional certification by the Project Management Institute.

Project Manager (PM) (from Wikipedia): Project management is the province and responsibility of an individual project manager. This individual seldom participates directly in the activities that produce the end result, but rather strives to maintain the progress and productive mutual interaction of various parties in such a way that overall risk of failure is reduced."

Project Sponsor: The executive typically responsible for the project purpose and direction; may have sponsored the project or had the initial idea for the project (also called executive sponsor or champion).

Projectized Organization: Any organizational structure in which the project manager has full authority over the personnel assigned to a project.

Prototype: A model encompassing some but not all features of the desired product.

QFD: Quality Function Deployment.

Quality: Conformance to requirements, specifications, and standards and fitness for use in a defined environment for specific purposes.

Quality Assurance (QA): Actions, policies, and procedures necessary to provide adequate confidence that a product or service will satisfy given requirements for quality.

Quality Control (QC): The process of monitoring specific quality tests to determine if they comply with relevant quality standards.

Quality Management: Those portions of the overall project management processes that determines and implements the quality policy.

Request for Proposal (RFP): A formal invitation containing a scope of work which requests a formal response from a vendor indicating how a job will be done and often who (generically or specifically) will be doing the work.

Request for Quotation (RFQ): A formal invitation to submit a price or rates for goods and/or services as described in the requesting document.

Requirements: A formalized set of measurable customer/user wants and needs.

Reserve: Money or time set aside in the total project budget for risks and other unknowns.

Resource: Items necessary to complete project work including money, people, equipment, and so on.

Resource Breakdown Structure (RBS): A coding structure to identify resources to be used on a project(s).

Resource Leveling: A form of network and schedule analysis in which resource requirements are spread evenly across time periods (and possibly projects) for one or more resources.

Responsibility Assignment Matrix (RAM): A table correlating resources (either generically or specifically) to tasks; may also be used to correlate organizational responsibility to tasks or groups of tasks.

Return on Investment (ROI): The financial return in terms of an interest rate for a given monetary investment.

Risk: The possibility of an undesirable outcome.

Risk Analysis: An examination of risk areas to assess the impact and likelihood of a risk event (also risk assessment).

Risk Avoidance: Eliminate the cause of a risk event or reduce the EMV via reducing risk probability.

Risk Deflection: Transferring all or part of a risk to another party, usually by some form of insurance.

Risk Identification: The process of identifying all possible risk events which may happen during a project.

Risk Response: The planned or actual action in response to a risk event.

RMI: Remote Method Invocation.

ROM: Rough Order of Magnitude (estimate).

RUP: Rational Unified Process.

Schedule: A calendar based sequence of tasks representing the order and time at which work will be done.

Schedule Performance Index (SPI): The ratio of the value of the work performed (earned value) to work planned (BCWP/BCWS).

Schedule Variance (SV): A difference between the scheduled completion date of a task(s) and the actual completion date of that task(s); in EVA: BCWP minus BCWS.

Scope: A description of the project work to be performed in terms of the desired results and deliverables.

Scope Creep: A progressive increase in scope as the project continues.

Scope Definition: Breaking down a deliverable in to smaller more manageable parts to allow improved estimation, assignment, and control.

Scope Management: The parts of the overall management processes that deal with controlling the work definition.

Scope of Work (SOW): A formal description of the work involved in the production and delivery of the goods or services and/or a description of the goods or services themselves that are part of a job or project.

SDLC: Software Development Lifecycle.

Single Source: There is a preferred seller for good and/or services to be procured.

Slack Time: The amount of time a task can be delayed before it affects another task's dates or the project completion date.

SOA: Service Oriented Architecture.

SOAP: Simple Object Access Protocol.

Sole Source: There is only one qualified supplier for goods and/or services to be procured.

Sponsor: A person who initiates, finances, has a controlling interest, or champions a project; the sponsor is normally a person in upper management.

Stage Gate: A point in time of a project at which progress and other factors will be reviewed for the purpose of deciding whether the project will continue or not.

Stakeholder: One who has a stake or interest in the outcome of the project.

Standard Deviation: A measure of the dispersion of data points around a mean of a probability distribution.

Statement of Work (SOW): A formal description of the work involved in the production and delivery of the goods or services and/or a description of the goods or services themselves that are part of a job or project.

Status Report: A report produced by the project team on a regular basis showing progress and cost versus plan

Success Criteria: The principles or standards by which the success of a project will be judged.

Success Factors: Any circumstance, fact, or influence which contributes to a critical success criteria; measurable factors that are most important to a project's success criteria.

Successor Task: A task that cannot begin until another task has started or finished.

Sunk Costs: Costs which have already been incurred, and cannot be reversed even if the project was canceled.

SWAG: Systematic (scientific) Wild Ass Guess

SWOT Analysis: A business or technical analysis of an organization's strengths, weaknesses, opportunities, and threats.

Task: An individual unit of effort which refers to the work that will be assigned to individuals to produce the project's deliverables. Typically tasks are verbs, and deliverables are nouns.

TCO: Total Cost of Ownership.

Test Plan: A description of the tests needed to satisfy requirements and standards for the proper completion of a project.

Time Box: An amount of calendar time allocated for the completion of a project or phase of a project.

Total Float (TF): The amount of time by which a task can be delayed without delaying the project planned completion date.

Total Quality Management (TQM): A quality program to encourage guide employees to strive for high quality in all aspects of their work.

Total Slack: The amount of time a task can be delayed without affecting the project planned completion date.

UDDI: Universal Description Discovery and Integration.

UML: Unified Modeling Language.

Uncertainty: Lack of knowledge of future events.

Undistributed Budget (UB): Budget for work to be done on a project that is within the project's scope but has not been specifically identified yet.

Validation: The process of guaranteeing that the customer/user is satisfied with the product.

Variable Cost: A cost that changes with the amount of product produced or the effort expended.

Variance: Deviation from a plan, or a measure of uncertainty or dispersion.

Verification: The process of guaranteeing that the work processes and products comply with specifications.

Version: A time sequenced variant of some artifact or product manifestation.

Version Control: The process of controlling changes, additions, and deletions to product manifestations as a development process moves from one version of a product to the next.

Walk-Through: The physical or logical comprehensive examination of the quality of a work product (such as a design or program unit) in regard to quality metrics and standards; in IT, the walk-through is usually performed by peers.

W3C: World Wide Web Consortium.

White Box: A process done with detail knowledge of the inner workings of the subject of the work, as in White Box Testing.

WIMP (Wheels in Motion Person): Someone who confuses activity with progress.

Work Breakdown Structure (WBS): A deliverable oriented grouping of project elements that organizes and defines the total work scope of the project.

Work Package (WP): A unit within a work breakdown structure at the lowest level of a branch, not necessarily at the lowest level of the whole WBS.

WSDL: Web Services Description Language.

Workaround: An unplanned alternative solution to a problem that has arisen.

XF: Expected Finish.

XP: Extreme Programming.

About the Author

In a speech in Cape Town, South Africa, in June of 1966, Robert F. Kennedy said, "May you live in interesting times." He said the phrase was of Chinese origin, although even the Chinese are not sure about this, but it certainly applies to we who have become deeply involved with information technology (IT). This book's author, **Dan Brandon**, took his first computer course in college in 1966 and has been fascinated by IT ever since.

As Brandon began his career, IT was also just starting. The disciplines of computer science, software engineering, and IT project management were formulated and solidified during his working years. He has designed and developed software for every generation of software (assembly through object oriented), and almost every generation of IT architecture and hardware (mainframe, mini, PC, client-server, Web). He has also programmed in most major computer languages, including ALGOL, FORTRAN, Pascal, Ada, COBOL, Basic, C, C++, Java, and in modern Web-based languages such as PHP to develop applications in a wide variety of areas encompassing the business, engineering, and scientific fields.

As his career moved him from programmer to designer to manager, he was always involved with the application of new computer technology and concepts to the solution of application problems. The effective management of all the resources and stakeholders involved with building, integrating, and deploying IT applications has always represented a major interest and challenge to him. Along the way he managed to fit in some schooling, earning a BS (Case Western Reserve University), MS, and PhD in engineering (University of Connecticut); his PhD specialization was in computer methods.

Before returning to the university environment, Dr. Brandon accumulated more than 30 years of commercial experience in both the IT technical and management arenas. He was a senior engineer at Mobil Research, a manager of application development for Control Data Corporation, an MIS manager for several companies, and director of information services at the NASA Stennis Space Center.

He is currently a professor of information technology management (ITM) and chairperson of that department at Christian Brothers University (CBU) in Memphis, Tennessee. CBU is a part of the De La Salle Christian Brothers global educational organization, with more than 1,000 schools in more than 80 countries. Dr. Brandon's research interests include both the management and technical side of IT. At CBU he teaches undergraduate and graduate courses in IT, including information systems management, project management, software engineering, database design, decision support systems, Internet systems, and programming.

He has been published in a number of books, journals, and conference proceedings including *The Project Management Journal, The Wiley Guide to Managing Projects, Essentials of Project Control, Encyclopedia of Information Technology, Journal of Computing Sciences in Colleges, Successful Software Reengineering, Technologies & Methodologies for Evaluating Information Technology in Business, Issues and Trends of Information Technology Management in Contemporary Organizations, Architectural Issues of Web-Enabled Electronic Business, Managing Information Technology Resources in Organizations in the Next Millennium,* and *Managing Information Technology in a Global Economy.*

He is a member of the Society of Information Management (SIM), the Information Resource Management Association (IRMA), and the Project Management Institute (PMI). He also holds the PMP (Project Management Professional) Certification which is the highest certification granted from PMI. He continues to do consulting with a number of companies, both locally and internationally. Currently he is involved in the design and development of comprehensive open source software systems for project management and other business applications.

Index

ROI 43
rollup 318

S

sampling 217
Sarbanes-Oxley Act (SOX) 110, 354
satisfaction criteria 19
scalability 72, 191, 192, 217
schedule 22
schedule compression 146
schedule control 185
schedule performance index (SPI) 187
schedule variances 327
scope 13
scope change control 106
scope change control 185
scope creep 178, 188
scope definition 106
scope definition 121
scope initiation 106
scope management 52, 106
scope planning 106
scope verification 106
scope verification 55
scoring and ranking methods 43
screening criteria 255
screens 129
secure 203
security holes 193
security risks 272
selective outsourcing 259
service level agreement (SLA) 208
Service Oriented Architectures 79
shareware 343
short list 255
silver bullet 176
SIMULA 83
single-phase 113
single-source procurement 254
Six Sigma 225
skill mix 292
slack 146
smalltalk 84
smoothing 306
SOA 79

(Simple Object Access Protocol
    (SOAP) 79
software acquisition 79
software acquisition 249
software architects 292
software capability maturity model 89
software development life cycle (SDLC)
    58
software development standards 227
software engineering 59
software engineering 22
software engineering body of knowledge
    (SWEBOK) 92
Software Engineering Institute (SEI)
    22, 88
software reuse 85
sole source procurement 254
solicitation 248
solicitation planning 248
solver 36
source selection 248
structured query language (SQL) 71
staff acquisition 291
stakeholder action plan 277
stakeholder identification 274
stakeholder management 274
stakeholders 6
standard calendars 154
standard deviation 143
standard forms 371
standards 23
standards manuals 229
star topology 369
stated requirements 191
statement of work 11
statement of work (SOW) 110, 250
static testing 220
status reports 281
storming 304
storyboards 73
strategic alliances 264
strategic level 29
structural capital 366
structured interviews 110
structured problem solving 306
structured walkthroughs 367

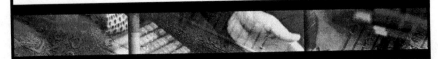